MW01259835

Sex and Citizenship in Antebellum America

Gender and American Culture

NANCY ISENBERG

Sex and Citizenship in Antebellum America

THE UNIVERSITY OF NORTH CAROLINA PRESS

CHAPEL HILL AND LONDON

© 1998 The University of North Carolina Press
All rights reserved
Designed by April Leidig-Higgins
Set in Galliard by Tseng Information Systems, Inc.
Manufactured in the United States of America

Library of Congress Cataloging-in-Publication Data
Isenberg, Nancy   Sex and citizenship in antebellum America /
by Nancy Isenberg.   p. cm. — (Gender and American culture)
Includes bibliographical references and index.
ISBN 0-8078-2442-9 (cloth : alk. paper).
— IBSN 0-8078-4746-1 (pbk. : alk. paper)
1. Women — Suffrage — United States — History.
2. Women's rights — United States — History.
3. Feminism — United States — History. I. Title.
HQ1236.5.U6I83   1999 98-13349
305.42'0973 — dc21   CIP

Frontispiece: Ye May Session of ye Woman's Rights Convention — Ye Orator of ye Day Denouncing ye Lords of Creation.

02 01 00 99 98 5 4 3 2 1

To my mother, Jeannie MacDougall Isenberg,
and the memory of my father, Paul Isenberg

Contents

Acknowledgments

In graduate school I discovered early that modern historians had paid scant attention to women's rights conventions other than the famous 1848 gathering in Seneca Falls. At the Schlesinger Library of Radcliffe College, I read the proceedings of the 1850 convention held in Worcester, Massachusetts, and was impressed by the intellectual sophistication of the arguments presented. Knowing that my adviser, Gerda Lerner, had long felt that Ohio in general, and the Salem convention in particular, had been unjustifiably placed in a position subordinate to activism in New York, I resolved to do a more thorough investigation of the antebellum women's rights movement. Throughout this period Gerda's example, her determination and inventiveness, invigorated my work. Committed to creating a feminist environment in the history department, she established and supported the Women's History Program at the University of Wisconsin. Also at Wisconsin, I benefited from my studies with Paul Boyer and Charles Cohen, scholars who shared my intellectual commitment to the field of American religious history. Linda Gordon and Elaine Marks reaffirmed the importance of feminist politics and theory. Hendrik Hartog read the dissertation and the manuscript and added invaluable suggestions.

Since then, I have been impelled to reconceptualize feminist theory for the nineteenth century by examining the ways in which church, state, and family all contributed to the notion of citizenship. The Commonwealth Center at the College of William and Mary, which provided a two-year postdoctoral fellowship, allowed me time to pursue my growing interest in political theory. While in Williamsburg, I profited from my association with Thad Tate, Chandos Brown, Richard John, and the fellows and staff at the Institute of Early American History and Culture, especially Saul Cornell. Also in Williamsburg, Kathy Brown and Ted Pearson, good friends since Wisconsin days, remained always supportive. Attending a summer institute sponsored by the National Endowment for the Humanities, I met Liz Faue, now my valued friend, who has provided a necessary balance of humor and cynicism as I worked on the book. Ellen DuBois, Nancy Hewitt, Linda Kerber, Kathryn Sklar, and Deborah Van Brockhoven read portions of the manuscript and offered useful insights. I am especially grateful to Jan Lewis's judicious and extremely helpful advice in strengthening the final version of the book.

I want to acknowledge the following institutions for funding my research: the American Antiquarian Society and its director, John Hench, for the Frances L. Hiatt Fellowship; the Library Company of Philadelphia and its librarian, John C. Van Horne, its associate librarian, James Green, and its chief of reference, Phillip Lapsansky, and the Historical Society of Pennsylvania for the summer research grant; the Wisconsin State Historical Society for the Alice E. Smith Fellowship; the Woodrow Wilson National Fellowship Foundation for the Charlotte W. Newcombe Doctoral Dissertation Fellowship; and the Institute for Research on Women, Rutgers University, for the appointment as a visiting scholar. I owe a special debt of gratitude to Ann Gordon, editor of the Papers of Elizabeth Cady Stanton and Susan B. Anthony, who provided access to materials and directed my attention to crucial sources, when the project was located at the University of Massachusetts.

At the University of North Carolina Press, I am particularly thankful to Lewis Bateman for his generosity and confidence in my work. My sister Susan deserves my deepest respect; she is a pillar of support, and she has never failed me. Earl Mulderink has seen this manuscript from its very conception, and at various stages he scrupulously read chapters and made suggestions that contributed immeasurably to the final product. Andrew Burstein read each page with care, adding sensible suggestions that undoubtedly have made this a better book. His enthusiasm, counsel, and intellectual affinity are irreplaceable.

Portions of Chapters 2 and 4 were previously published in " 'Pillars in the Same Temple and Priests of the Same Worship': Woman's Rights and the Politics of Church and State in Antebellum America," *Journal of American History* 85, no. 1 (June 1988): 98–128.

Introduction

Then, again, men say, "She is so different from man, that God did not mean
she should vote." Is she?—then I do not know how to vote for her. (Applause.)
One of two things is true. She is either exactly like man,—*exactly* like him,
teetotally like him,—and if she is, then a ballot-box based upon
brains belongs to her as well as him: or she is different,
and then I do not know how to vote for her.
—Wendell Phillips, National Woman's Rights Convention, 1860

In the year of Abraham Lincoln's election, the year the Constitution was to
face its most strenuous test, antislavery activist and women's rights supporter
Wendell Phillips insisted that it was impossible for any man to know how
to vote for—that is, on behalf of—a woman. He was speaking to an audience numbering in the hundreds, an audience concerned with a profoundly
American yet dramatically uncertain concept: equality.[1]

Americans during Phillips's lifetime had a curious love-hate relationship
with the principle and practice of equality. They eulogized the Declaration
of Independence, granting it sacred status as national scripture, crediting the
revolutionary text with having elevated equality into a "self-evident truth."
But equality, then as now, was not unambiguous; it has always meant different things to different people. In antebellum America it could apply to
certain legal rights, or to birthright citizenship (the national entitlement of
native-born Americans derived in part from the divine right not to be born
subject to the rule of another), or to the broad meaning of due process and
equal standing in the court system (protection against "artificial distinction,"
"exclusive privileges," and grossly unfair treatment). It is just as clear that the

idea of equality coexisted with conditions sanctioned by civil law that upheld unequal stations: equal rights were routinely denied to slaves, children, and the so-called dangerous classes of free blacks, paupers, resident aliens (particularly non-Caucasian or Catholic foreigners), criminals, and those considered insane.[2]

The largest portion of the population in antebellum America, freeborn women, introduced another serious problem for those trying to make sense of equality. As early feminist[3] writer and organizer Paulina Wright Davis remarked in 1852, women represented an "enigma." Freeborn and thus logically entitled to their privileges and rights as "birthright" members of the United States, women nevertheless constituted a politically and legally "disabled caste." The enigma, then, was this: freeborn women had the appearance of citizenship but lacked the basic rights to be real citizens. Equality remained a concept that somehow did not apply to women. Defenders of this enigmatic status for women disliked and ridiculed the idea of "woman's rights," assuming that, at best, women were to be accorded select privileges—the informal and personal guarantees they gained through men, especially male relatives, who served as their "charmed representatives" in the courts, the halls of Congress, indeed in all public affairs.

Equality was a difficult concept because it was premised on a false dichotomy. Women had to act exactly like men to secure equal rights, and yet they were supposedly so different that they had to be treated as a special sexual caste. Phillips, for one, recognized the potency of this defensive ideology, but he proceeded to expose its flawed constitutional logic with a subtle, sardonic touch. Differences between the sexes rested, he noted at the 1860 women's rights convention, on the mistaken belief that men and women were "so different" that they could not be considered coequal citizens. If this were true, then women stood outside constitutional guarantees and claims to natural and inalienable rights, those attributes of citizenship most critical to the American legal and political tradition. Did women acquire their special status from some other source (and here Phillips mockingly suggested divine authority), or did they share a common identity with men as human beings endowed with a comparable capacity for reasoned judgment? He asked, Did God ordain woman's eternal differences from man to be permanent, unchanging, and beyond the rule of law? Or did nature (human nature as the source of natural rights) grant women the same potential for use of their brains, to make reasonable decisions, and to fulfill the requisite requirement for the vote?

As much as he credited women and men with an equal potential to vote responsibly, Phillips did not really wish to pursue this argument. He aimed instead to demonstrate a false dichotomy. The argument over sexual difference versus natural parity was, to him, purely rhetorical, an artificial construction that had emerged from a public discourse about rights. The terms of this dynamic discourse were far broader than most historians have acknowledged, drawing on religious, legal, and political practices as well as key notions of publicity and representation that, taken together, defined antebellum political culture.

Here, then, is what Wendell Phillips did to reconfigure the terms of debate. He was not claiming merely that women were equal and not different from men. He was advocating that women required the vote on the constitutional grounds that *democracy* protected the idea of equal representation. Indeed, Phillips reasoned, if women were different, then they deserved an equal right to have their views receive a fair hearing, since men could not represent their interests. And if women were "teetotally" the same as men, or at least similar in their mental capabilities, then they deserved equal access to the political process through the franchise. Equal protection (the constitutional guarantee of freedom from harm, invasion, and divestment of rights) combined with the right of self-representation (the essence of the phrase "consent of the governed," which defined "the people") carried more constitutional validity for Phillips than the tired, if not tyrannical, rhetoric of sexual difference.

This book examines the many ways in which women's rights advocates encountered antebellum political culture. It shows how early feminists defined themselves as public critics. What united antebellum activists into a social and political movement was their shared community of discourse. And so this work emphasizes throughout its understanding of the intellectual and linguistic meaning of "woman's rights," unabashedly arguing that supporters of the movement developed a coherent feminist critique. The orientation of antebellum feminists was premised on a sophisticated theoretical model that could explain citizenship, the public sphere, and the constitutional limitations that had evolved in the nineteenth century that curtailed women's rights to due process, redress, self-protection, and civil liberty, and rights within the home, church, and state. To conflate women's rights with liberal individualism or focus solely on the effort to achieve the vote ignores how feminists constantly engaged in a contest over rights; they entered political struggles over legal ideas and cultural beliefs peculiar to the antebellum period. This study shows, too, that the restriction of women to the home, known as "woman's sphere," was not the only ideological framework defining women's "proper" role in society. Inherited arguments—religious, political, and legal—already existed that were used by opponents of women's rights to justify women's difference and their subordinate status. Antebellum feminists were neither a disgruntled minority nor defenders of woman's sphere. Their preeminent value to society was as a "critical public" that exposed gendered assumptions.[4]

Throughout the nineteenth century, citizenship was complicated by competing and contradictory definitions of political identity. One civic ideal celebrated active participation, measured not only by the vote but by jury and militia service, while another, more legalistic understanding defined citizenship as a passive inheritance of "birthright" entitlements. The legal capacity to act as an independent citizen (to own property, make contracts, and exercise self-representation before one's peers in court) was held up against the right of consent, a right based on a "fictive" membership in the original social contract—on being one of the sovereign people. Each of the guidelines Americans used to declare rights engendered the idealized citizen in decidedly masculine terms. Female activists and male supporters of women's rights keenly understood that the citizen of the republic, whether "common man," "citizen-soldier," or "partyman," was presumed to be above feminine weakness, to be a civic person capable of self-mastery, independent judgment, manly honor and virtue, and freedom from dependence.

The first major question of my study, then, is: How did feminists frame their understanding of rights within antebellum theories of representation? By putting the focus on rights, I place the issues of suffrage and citizenship in a much broader cultural terrain, the intersection of law and society. Changes in American jurisprudence and radical reforms of the common-law tradition contributed to debates over women's legal standing and civil liberties. In an era when many were promoting constitutional revision and when individual states called conventions to redraft their original compacts, antebellum activists recognized that public "woman's rights" conventions offered a more important avenue for political transformation than an entrenched party organization. It was impossible to conceive of women as full and enfranchised citizens without first changing the rules, beliefs, and biases derived from republicanism. Thus, the women's movement refracted a range of crucial issues in reassessing the meaning of the term "rights-bearer" in American legal thought and practice.

My second question is: How did this struggle over rights incorporate several distinct but overlapping legal and political debates that characterized the antebellum period? Examined independently, the church, the state, and the family were complementary arenas in defining rights. In highlighting civic duty, discipline, and religious liberty, Sabbatarianism opened a crucial discourse for delineating church-state relations and reviewing the moral and gendered fabric of society. Almost all the supporters of antebellum feminism ventured into church politics, joining dissident churches and calling for a new kind of religious forum that recognized women's coequal representation. At the same time, masculine political authority, or the power of the state to exercise brute force, emerged as a recurrent controversy in protests waged against fugitive slave laws, capital punishment, prostitution, and the Mexican War. Feminists drew several lessons from these pressing political campaigns as well. They saw that the meaning of treason, divestment, and the relegation of women to a "civilly dead" status still informed the ways in which their legal and political rights were circumscribed. Fugitive slave laws demonstrated the similarity between common-law definitions of runaway slaves and wives: their shared loss of personal liberty. Prostitution, cases of seduction, and the death penalty all underscored the sexual double standard in the law, reinforced by women's exclusion from juries and from the "field of honor," both of which defined the domain of state-sanctioned vengeance through execution. Finally, sexual politics entered into racial conquest through the doctrine of manifest destiny used in support of the Mexican War. By defining Mexican women as "trophies of war," and yankee soldiers as "valiant knights," the rhetoric of military conquest reinforced the image of women as "ciphers" (weak, dependent, and without civic agency) and white men as citizen-soldiers, strong, independent, and worthy of the vote, who demonstrated their right to rule through the natural and manly capacity to dominate the land and master all its resources.

The politics of the family raised a related but different set of constitutional issues. Temperance and health reform advocates exposed the dangers of domestic violence, sexual abuse, and the complicated common-law legacy for denying wives the right of redress for private wrongs. Labor protests over the modern wage contract made plain the intimate connection between the sexual economy of the household and the market. Feminists likened wives to "upper-servants" and exploited workers, exposing how the common law defined married women as debtors or indentured servants. Married women's property rights and land reform revealed the common-law roots that linked inheritance practices—rules of paternity—to child custody laws.

By examining activists' "rights consciousness" or "rights discourse," I have placed the language of women's rights within the much larger context of the meaning of citizenship, the public sphere, representation, and consent and dissent. Suffrage was not a self-evident truth, but a complicated political goal infused with political and cultural ramifications of legal standing, civic personality, consent of the governed, and the legacy of imposed statuses derived from inherited political identities. That women did not receive the right to vote until 1920 reflects the layers of ideological uncertainty that persisted throughout the nineteenth century and that successfully rationalized women's exclusion from the ranks of full citizenship as a legitimate political practice even in a democracy.[5]

Chapter 1 focuses on how the story of the origins of the movement has been told. Although there was more than one story, historians have tended to reduce the beginning of the movement to a single account of the quest for suffrage. Undue attention has been given to the 1848 Seneca Falls convention, ignoring other conventions and activists outside New York and holding up Elizabeth Cady Stanton exclusively as the dominant strategist of the early movement. In discussing citizenship, Chapter 2 compares the first conventions held in New York, Ohio, and Massachusetts, addressing how activists collectively developed critiques of consent, national citizenship, and equal protection. In both chapters I offer evidence that the process of developing a rights discourse went well beyond a liberal faith in individualism or abstract rights.

Chapter 3 pursues the dilemma of women's relationship to the public sphere. It employs the theories of Hannah Arendt and Jürgen Habermas to frame a new debate about rights and publicity. Rather than embrace the simple division of male (public) and female (private) spheres, I propose that the public sphere inherited a complicated framework of assumptions and practices from eighteenth-century republicanism and the Enlightenment that contributed to the gendered construction of nineteenth-century democracy. Publicity had several different meanings: it connoted public opinion, public appearance, and the question of whether any individual had the political legitimacy to assume a public persona or to act in an official capacity as a public representative. Furthermore, the category of "woman" or "female nature" was fractured by class and caste differences, which measured men and women in terms of normative assumptions about physical appearance and public speaking as well as women's exposure to and concealment from the public eyes of men. In searching for a stable past, historians have simplified the gendered complexity of publicity, a category fraught with contested meanings.[6]

Chapter 4 addresses another critical problem in the literature on women's rights, namely, its relationship to religion. Some scholars have viewed antebellum activists in the process of secularizing religious beliefs, implying that when moral reform was politicized, it had to be secularized. Other scholars who emphasize the political underpinnings of religion often exclude women, or separate women's contribution because it is seen as less concerned with politics, inherently more parochial, or focused on family-related issues. In fact, religion in the nineteenth century violated these neat boundaries and challenged concepts normally conceived of as secular, such as public opinion, representation, and equality. The church was not a neutral social or moral space; it could and did function politically. Early women's rights advocates defined themselves as dissidents, developing a critical perspective of religious castes (particularly men's control of church offices such as the clergy and elders) and church creeds (inherited law that prescribed blind obedience to customs that inhibited religious liberty).[7]

I also reexamine the commonly held view that women's rights emerged principally from the antislavery movement. In his influential study on the origins of women's rights, *The Beginnings of Sisterhood: The American Women's Rights Movement, 1800–1850*, Keith Melder described a series of stages, beginning with educational reform, benevolence, and then abolition, which culminated in the campaign for women's rights. But there was not, in fact, a neat sequence of stages. Chapter 5 reframes this interpretation by exploring the decade of the 1840s and looking at the range of critical political issues that captured the attention of activists in the later women's movement. Rights arguments were surely not restricted to antislavery, and as Debra Gold Hansen concluded in her recent work on female abolitionists, *Strained Sisterhood: Gender and Class in the Boston Female Anti-Slavery Society*, not all women active in this reform decided to join the campaign for women's rights. The social histories of Nancy Hewitt on Rochester and Judith Wellman on Seneca Falls both point to the distinctive political and religious influences that forged the early women's rights coalitions. With the appearance of Hewitt's *Women's Activism and Social Change: Rochester, New York, 1822–1872* in 1984 and Wellman's article "The Seneca Falls Women's Rights Convention: A Study in Social Networks," in *The Journal of Women's History* in 1991, the linear progression from benevolence to antislavery no longer seemed viable, given that activists simultaneously engaged in a wide range of political campaigns.[8]

Still, certain political campaigns of the 1840s have not been fully explored. Forgotten political and legal issues include the campaigns against capital punishment and against seduction and prostitution, and the growing opposition to manifest destiny found in protests against the Mexican War. Moreover, that strain of antislavery agitation which had the greatest impact on women's rights activists was the debate over fugitive slave laws. This was, in part, because the theory behind the divestment of fugitive slaves paralleled women's status under the common law. When women's rights activists discussed slavery during their conventions, the plight of the fugitive slave captured their particular attention.

Chapter 6 builds on this perspective and the work of scholars such as Norma Basch, Jeanne Boydston, Elizabeth Clark, Peggy Rabkin, and Amy

Dru Stanley, who collectively have recognized that women's sphere in the home did not remain isolated from the economic and legal changes occurring during the nineteenth century. Women's rights advocates did offer a compelling series of critiques of marriage law, focusing mainly on the fiction of marriage as a union of "one flesh." The husband's sexual rights, his right to his wife's wages, and his custody rights all reinforced a sexual economy of rights. Influenced by the legal and political discourses developed by temperance, labor, health, and land reformers—all popular campaigns in the antebellum period—women's rights advocates looked at marriage, the household economy, and property rights in children from a critical perspective. Law and society were not divided into two domains, and neither were the rights of husbands and wives disjoined, for the intrusive qualities of the law continually interacted with the private domain of the family. The home was never an autonomous or distinct culture.[9]

This study hopes to change how scholars understand the origins of the women's rights movement in America. Because the antebellum campaign for women's rights palpably influenced the later suffrage movement, we must reconsider how gender informed American constitutionalism. The suffrage issue must no longer be isolated and privileged above all others. Political or legal rights were not narrowly defined but were thoroughly intertwined with ideas about religion and the family. Within this context, the critiques offered by early feminists exposed contradictions in the democracy's idealized self-image and disparities in the constitutional principles of protection and due process. The genius of the antebellum women's rights movement lay in these critiques and in linking rights to all the personal and political issues that affected women in the family, the church, and the state.

Equality and difference alone could not circumscribe the many issues and theoretical debates that antebellum activists contemplated. This was why they coined the term "co-equality." Both sexes were deemed to possess equivalent capacities at birth (and, in a biblical sense, at creation). Activists saw men and women as "co-equals," simultaneously the same and different. If we understand coequality as a democratic ideal, then the early women's rights movement emerges as much more than a political campaign for suffrage. Indeed, the concept of co-equality must be acknowledged as the cornerstone of American feminist theory.

Sex and Citizenship in Antebellum America

1

Firstborn Feminism

As an autobiography is more interesting than a sketch by another, so is history
written by its actors, as in both cases we get nearer the soul of the subject.
—Preface, *History of Woman Suffrage*, vol. 1 (1881)

In May, 1881, the first volume of our History appeared; it was an octavo,
containing 871 pages, with good paper, good print, handsome engravings, and
nicely bound. I welcomed it with the same feeling of love and tenderness
as I did my firstborn.
—Elizabeth Cady Stanton, *Eighty Years and More* (1898)

Within two years after the first women's rights convention in 1848, Elizabeth
Cady Stanton had already begun writing a history of woman suffrage. Her
account, revised and expanded several times, reappeared in various forms
during Stanton's life, most notably in the *History of Woman Suffrage*.[1] When
the first volume appeared in 1881, William Henry Channing praised the narrative as a "wonderfully rich book, which reads like a 'romance of history.'"
Channing saw the *History* to be based on "substantial facts," a text capable of
countering charges that the movement sprang from "visionaries . . . chasing
cloud-castles of theory."[2] The editors agreed and measured the value of the
narrative by its persuasive "arsenal of facts" as well as its emotional appeal to
readers.[3] Whether read as positive history (based on facts, documents, and
the weight of evidence) or as romantic drama (based on story, characters, and

subjective impressions), Stanton's master narrative was more than a compendium of useful information. This "firstborn" child, this historical interpretation she so tenderly embraced, marked the author-activist's self-conscious delineation of the "origins" of the suffrage movement.

To date, the *History* retains a privileged place in the historical canon as a rich and eclectic selection of primary sources. Despite the difficulties posed by the length and organization of the work, few scholars seriously consider how its internal logic might influence contemporary interpretations of the movement.[4] Certain interpretative codes and traditions inform the picture of reality presented in the *History*. Instead of simply offering a documentary, the *History* explains the origins of things, providing an allegorical interpretation of the past.[5] Possible gaps in the "arsenal of facts" therefore reflect more than careless oversight or the inability of the editors to write an impartial history.[6] The process of creating a total historical account means that some of the cultural imperatives that defined the movement have been lost or masked, because all stories and myths of origins create the illusion of completeness.

Contemporary scholars, especially those publishing from the 1950s until the 1970s, for the most part inherited the story of origins from the *History*. The decisive event leading to the Seneca Falls convention was the London World Anti-Slavery Convention held in 1840. Although the American Anti-Slavery Society sent a delegation of women to be seated at the convention, their efforts to secure formal recognition were rebuffed. The members of the convention ruled that only men would speak, relegating the women to the gallery. Lucretia Mott was one of the excluded delegates, and Elizabeth Cady Stanton attended because she accompanied her husband, Theodore Stanton, to the convention.[7]

As Keith Melder wrote in his 1977 study, *The Beginnings of Sisterhood*, the 1840 London antislavery convention occupied a special place in the history of the suffrage movement.[8] The mythic lore of the World Anti-Slavery Convention rested on the fateful meeting of Mott and Stanton. In *Century of Struggle*, published eighteen years before Melder's account, Eleanor Flexner contended that through the chance acquaintance of Stanton and Mott at the London gathering the "seed" of the Seneca Falls convention was "actually planted."[9] Stanton gave this meeting particular significance. In the *History*, which reprinted her lengthy eulogy to Mott, she described her initial encounter with Mott as "an entire new revelation of womanhood."[10] In an interview with Mary Clemmer for a brief biography of Mott, and in the *History*, Stanton further claimed that "when I first heard from the lips of Lucretia Mott that I had the same right to think for myself that Luther, Calvin, and John Knox had, I felt at once a new-born sense of dignity and freedom."[11] Clemmer shared Stanton's sentiments; she pictured Mott as a prophet and oracle, and she added another allegorical dimension to her religious portrait. More than a message or medium, Mott represented for Clemmer the "mother of Israel" and chosen matriarch of the suffrage movement. Stanton extended her use of biblical allusions for Mott to Christ himself, noting that she felt "unworthy to touch the hem of her garment" when they met in 1840.[12]

Stanton conveyed more than respect for the "saintly Quaker," because she transformed Mott from a historical actor into a prophetic sign. More importantly, Stanton infused her reminiscence of their meeting with the language of a conversion experience. Granted the status of a visionary and divine messenger, Mott led Stanton to discover a "new-born sense of dignity and freedom." This allusion reappeared in the contemporary scholarship. Flexner described Mott as an almost ethereal presence endowed with "a gentle manner, luminous countenance, and soft voice." By changing the "beloved" saint from prophet to mentor, Flexner reinterpreted Mott's influence as "helping to free the gifted and eager mind" of Stanton, her younger disciple.[13] Through her efforts to mask the religious implications of Stanton's account, Flexner nevertheless concealed its political and figurative message. By depicting Mott as the high priestess and herself as the first disciple, Stanton legitimatized the delegation of authority from one generation to the next. Stanton also carefully distinguished Mott from herself as a historical and political agent. Although they both shared the capacity for political action, Mott's role was to initiate the movement, while Stanton inherited the mantle of leadership. Like Peter, the chosen apostle of Christ, Stanton positioned herself in her master narrative as the heir and founder of the suffrage campaign.

Stanton's story raises a series of important questions about the relationship between history and feminism. Was her religious vocabulary atypical among women's rights activists? What were the origins of the theory that linked religious and political representation, especially as a strategy for incorporating women into the social compact? Did Stanton's account include all the "facts," or did her focus on the 1840 meeting displace other plausible explanations for the beginning of the movement? And what does a story of "origins" have to do with feminist theory in general?

Few scholars have questioned the historical accuracy of Stanton's account, and most have endorsed the central tenet that the Seneca Falls convention signaled the origin of the movement. Held in a town in west-central New York State where Stanton had moved in 1847, the convention is portrayed primarily as Stanton's political debut, since she is given most of the credit for organizing the event. Even the most recent work on the convention, such as Judith Wellman's examination of the different coalitions brought together at

Seneca Falls, still positions Stanton as the most strategically important organizer of this historic event.[14] The Declaration of Sentiments, which Stanton
drafted at a table resembling the desk at which Thomas Jefferson wrote the
Declaration of Independence, was enshrined (by twentieth-century suffrag-
ists and, later, in Flexner's work) as the founding treatise of the movement.[15]
Stanton added to this narrative tradition by highlighting the inevitable and
foreordained nature of the first convention. It was destiny that Mott and
Stanton should meet again in 1848. Recollecting their reunion almost eight
years after their meeting at the World Anti-Slavery Convention, Stanton
wrote in her autobiography that they decided "then and there, to call a
'Woman's Rights Convention.'" Subsequently the Seneca Falls convention,
Stanton believed, "set the ball in motion," triggering conventions in other
cities, towns and states.[16] A seed planted in 1840 had by 1848 flowered into
the national woman suffrage movement.

Historians have recognized the discrepancies between Stanton's version
and competing accounts of the events leading to the Seneca Falls convention.
Keith Melder acknowledged that Mott had a different recollection of their
encounter at the London convention and that she met Stanton again in 1847
in Boston.[17] Yet despite this qualification, Melder followed Stanton's master
narrative when writing his historical account. Other scholars, such as Flexner,
have elevated Stanton into the "leading intellectual force" behind the movement.[18] Anne and Andrew Scott agreed, arguing that Stanton's decision to
model the Declaration of Sentiments on the Declaration of Independence led
to the invaluable insight that women should have an "'inalienable right to
the elective franchise.'"[19] In *Feminism and Suffrage* Ellen DuBois granted the
Declaration of Sentiments an unparalleled if not prophetic status, claiming
that this one text "anticipated every demand of nineteenth-century feminism."[20] Suffrage, the "one great leading idea [that] was a suggestion of her
brain," as Theodore Tilton asserted in 1869, became another credit to Stanton's singular achievement and historic immortality.[21] Similarly, but for more
pragmatic reasons (suffrage as the most logical pursuit for obtaining political
rights in a democracy), DuBois asserted as well that suffrage quickly rose to a
"preeminent position" after the Seneca Falls convention as "the cornerstone
of the women's rights program."[22] By the late 1970s the Seneca Falls convention, Stanton, and suffrage had been fashioned into a coherent and complete
explanation, as if other activists, conventions, and principles were less crucial
for explaining the origins of the women's rights campaign.

Interestingly enough, as she developed her own history of the movement,
DuBois lessened the significance of the 1840 London meeting between Mott
and Stanton. Instead she argued that Stanton and Susan B. Anthony were

the leading activists after the Civil War and that their "friendship," which began in 1851, was the most "enduring and productive" alliance of the movement. Why did Mott and the 1840 meeting fade from DuBois's view? This occurred, in part, to privilege Mott's alternative mythic role as the voice of caution rather than inspiration, a role that DuBois emphasized by quoting Sarah Pugh's words of 1871 in the last line of her study: "Only twenty years ago even L. Mott doubted the wisdom of Elizabeth Cady Stanton claiming the ballot for women; now thousands follow her lead." Throughout her study DuBois contended that the radical edge of feminism truly came of age when the movement severed its ties from antislavery and religious reform. Like a child, the nascent movement had to separate and distinguish itself from all parental influence. A leading antebellum figure in the crusade for the abolition of slavery, a distinguished Quaker minister, and the matriarch of the movement, Mott had to be superseded in order to announce a new beginning for American feminism in the postbellum decade.[23]

DuBois's rejection of Mott and antebellum feminism is hardly a satisfactory solution for explaining the early movement. The choice of either accepting or altering Stanton's story is a problem that nineteenth-century activists confronted as well. Perhaps the most important challenger was Paulina Wright Davis, who wrote her own history for a suffrage celebration in 1870. By claiming that the 1850 Worcester convention had initiated the national movement, Davis provoked a small controversy, leading one younger suffragist to question her historical facts in the *Woman's Journal* that year.[24] But Davis was not alone in her belief that the Worcester gathering, as a national convention, represented a turning point in the early campaign. Channing and, more recently, Melder concurred with her conclusion, and both dated the real "birth" of the "independent" movement as 1850, acknowledging the Worcester meeting as an important development in its own right.[25] Davis's story was different for another reason, as she situated the origin of the movement in agitation for reform in 1831. In that year, she wrote, "a new spirit broke out in the churches," and "women spoke and prayed as they were moved by the spirit." Davis also revealed that the idea of holding a convention circulated among a wider circle of activists in 1847, a fact missing from Stanton's account.[26] The evidence makes clear that Davis, Mott, and other activists organized a series of "public meetings" for women in Philadelphia from 1846 until 1849.

Thus, Davis and Channing were suggesting that other reformers, alliances, and issues contributed to the organization of the early conventions. In doing so, both pointed to the glaring problem of the eight-year gap in Stanton's chronology between the 1840 London meeting and the 1848 Seneca Falls convention. The significance of dates did not escape either Stanton or Davis. At the 1870 celebration Mott and Stanton gave their approval to Davis's "history" of the antebellum movement, and Stanton remarked that "the movement in England, as in America, may be dated from the first National Convention, held at Worcester, Mass., October, 1850."[27] When Stanton drafted the version for the 1881 *History*, the sequence of events changed. She wrote that the "movement for woman's suffrage, in both England and America, may be dated from this [1840] Anti-Slavery Convention."[28]

This study is a history of the women's rights movement prior to the Civil War. It is a history of feminism and its incisive engagement with antebellum political culture. My approach begins with the assumption that although suffrage became the major plank of the late nineteenth-century campaign, antebellum activists had not only conceived of women's rights in broader terms, but they also developed a rich theoretical tradition that contributed in significant ways to a national discourse on constitutional practices in a democracy. Feminist theories of representation had their beginning not in the idea of suffrage alone but in disputes surrounding changes in the polity of the church and the family. This approach exposes inherent problems in previous attempts to explain the origin of the movement as a single event involving a few leaders and centering only on the issue of suffrage. Indeed, the broader cultural meanings of representation and constitutionalism must be examined as part of a complicated relationship between gender and the political order that characterized the antebellum period.

A political history of feminism may seem conventional. Enfranchisement has always been considered the preeminent concern of the women's rights movement. Suffrage has been treated as a simple, even self-evident term by most scholars, who have asserted its importance without defining exactly what it means within a broader ideological framework. Interest in this subject has been revived by the scholarly work on republicanism and its usefulness for explaining nineteenth-century political culture. Although republicanism has a chameleon-like quality, which makes it vulnerable to broad and ambiguous definitions, most antebellum reformers, lawyers, and legislators followed the lead of legal commentator James Kent in identifying republican governments with the right of protection. Common law and the federal constitution recognized this right as the fundamental agreement between the state and its citizenry. While the federal government promised to "guarantee to every state in this union a Republican form of government, and [to] protect them against invasion," every state promised to guarantee to individual citizens the protection afforded by law. Drawn from social contract theory, the right of protection laid out specific terms: in return for allegiance, the state was obligated to protect the "life, liberty, and property" of its citizens.[29]

Republicanism influenced the meaning of political status, as allegiance implied the ability of citizens to bear arms and, if necessary, risk their lives for the state.[30] Risk and sacrifice continued to define citizenship throughout the antebellum period, although it assumed two new forms in the requirements for suffrage: militia service and taxation. Granting the ballot to "every man who fights and pays," in the words of Thomas Jefferson, provided a republican theory for universal white male enfranchisement.[31] Physical risk and economic sacrifice implied that citizens had a substantial stake in society, whether it took the form of capital (property or taxes) or physical sacrifice (subjection to violence or death).

The "allegiance/protection" equation was derived from English common law. In explaining the theory of the social compact, Sir William Blackstone wrote in his influential *Commentaries on the Laws of England* that "the whole should protect all its parts, and that every part should pay obedience to the will of the whole."[32] Identifying who actually constituted the whole and the parts became the linchpin of antebellum struggles over representation. Although single women paid taxes and had a stake in society, their contributions were dismissed as rare exceptions to the common-law rule of women's legal and economic dependence.[33] Married women, who were used as the standard for all women in legal and political rationales for women's disenfranchisement, did not own property or control their wages in their own right.[34] Under the terms of coverture, the common-law rule that placed the wife under the "wing, protection and cover" of the husband, marriage for women implied not only economic dependence but civil death. According to Blackstone, "the very being, or legal existence of woman is suspended during the marriage."[35] As Hannah Arendt contended, "civil dis-appearance" was simply another word for civil death, since life itself was defined by participation in the "polis."[36] Denied full legal and political standing, women retained the status of subjects, not citizens, and they were permitted to exercise only a few privileges, such as the right of petition.

The discourse of republicanism posed many difficulties for women attempting to redefine female citizenship into an active and public role. Such difficulties became apparent when women and free blacks assumed center stage in the debates over suffrage in the antebellum state constitutional conventions.[37] Repeatedly, delegates at the constitutional conventions claimed that women and free blacks lacked the independence of character and judgment necessary for voting. In theory, a republican form of government required a uniform population of citizens who shared an active public life. Following the election of Andrew Jackson as president in 1828, the "age of the common man" created the illusion of a homogeneous electorate. In contrast, women and free blacks represented two distinct and disabled castes, both viewed as potentially dangerous factions capable of undermining the family or the nation-state.[38]

In the antebellum period, important constitutional distinctions were drawn between basic legal entitlements and political "privileges" such as the vote. Free blacks, however, were not only disenfranchised; they were excluded from other areas of public service as well. "Blacks might be accounted free men and pay taxes," one delegate to the 1837 Pennsylvania state constitutional convention insisted, "but they had never been permitted to serve on juries or in the militia."[39] That same argument was applied to women.[40] Despite the promise of broad-based entitlements, the "common man" served as a false universal, concealing the ways masculinity and race defined citizenship.[41]

Theories of representation therefore retained the republican feature of distinguishing between ranks and orders, but new boundaries were drawn across the democratic population. Instead of class-based distinctions centered on property ownership, the new political order required citizens who exercised the capacities for self-ownership and self-mastery.[42] Certain public "virtues" were used to justify suffrage qualifications. These included autonomy, which implied freedom of movement, economic independence, and the ability to circulate freely in civil society, and accountability, which implied the ability to defend one's actions and words before the scrutiny of the public. Not surprisingly, both women and free blacks came to symbolize the absence of these political virtues. Thus, the tyranny of the majority gained new meaning as race and gender visibly distinguished the white male citizenry from its lesser parts.

Women's historians have not addressed fully how these political changes influenced the separation of male and female spheres. Republicanism has proven useful to studies about women in the eighteenth and early nineteenth century, as evidenced by the work of Linda Kerber, Jan Lewis, and Rosemarie Zagarri, but less effort has been made to apply its theories of citizenship to representative democracy as it unfolded in the Jacksonian era.[43] Generally the antebellum period has been defined by a division between the public and the private, a split rooted in the rise of industrialization rather than changes in the American polity. Much of the scholarship in the past two decades has focused on women's activities within the family or the "domestic sphere," or it has extended this framework by examining the domestication of the political or public domain. By creating a model of a distinct female culture, historians have paid less attention to the gender dynamics of the public sphere. Too often, scholars have assumed that the private domain was, in Kerber's words, the only "locus for the battle of the sexes."[44] Similarly, feminism has been portrayed as a cultural ideology that emerged within the context of this separate female world. Here women developed a "consciousness" and "common identity of womanhood" that propelled them to understand the collective problems of their sex.[45] Yet separation in and of itself does not adequately explain all the gendered nuances of the public sphere. Nor can it be assumed that the public and private are necessarily defined as distinct and opposing realms at all times. Feminism and the gendered construction of the public sphere need to be studied for their inherently political and legal nature.

Among American historians, the attempt to recover the political meaning of the public sphere has been less successful than similar scholarship on European societies. Mary Ryan rather quickly dismissed the usefulness of modern theories of the public sphere, claiming that neither Jürgen Habermas nor Hannah Arendt offer much guidance to historians of nineteenth-century America.[46] But scholars such as Joan Landes have demonstrated how valuable this theory can be to explain the role of gender in defining the "Public" during the French Revolution.[47] No doubt the political theory of Arendt and Habermas would require some modification if it is to be applied to the cultural conditions of antebellum America. Most theoretical interpretations of the public sphere have excluded religion from their discussions of publicity. Arendt and Habermas both have separated religion from the public sphere, and they both have equated religion with the "social" or the "private" realm. Yet recent studies of democracy and antebellum politics have demonstrated that the church shaped how Americans understood the public sphere.[48] Other scholars have noted that Immanuel Kant and Alexis de Tocqueville used religion to define publicity and public opinion.[49] New forms of communication and public institutions emerged from tensions between the church and the state, thereby raising crucial issues about the shifting, if not overlapping, boundaries between publicity and privacy, political action and moral reform, and religious belief and public opinion.

Rights and social contract theory similarly have been portrayed as divorced from religious reasoning. Political scholar John Dunn has astutely observed, however, that at least in John Locke's *Two Treatises of Government*, considered a major influence on American constitutional thought, the "state of nature" derives its central tenets from theological rather than purely political arguments.[50] For Locke, the state of nature represented the first building block in the establishment of all human government. The state of nature is the imagined theoretical model of how civilized society came into being—

the primordial component of the first social contract. In Locke's first treatise, he defined a civil government based on natural rights. In doing so, he dismantled Sir Robert Filmer's *Patriarchia*, the classic defense of the divine right of kings. Locke's theory of the origins of government was an exercise in biblical exegesis, making the state of nature an extended allegory for the creation story.

When rights are explored in the context of antebellum politics, such religious complexities and associations have been lost. The same pattern holds true for studies of woman suffrage that reduce the campaign to a purely secular movement distinct from religion, church politics, and biblical interpretation of any kind.[51] On the other hand, when religion is treated as a factor in women's political activism, scholars have subsumed religion under moral reform. The religious content of moral reform is downplayed, and women's involvement generally is categorized as a gender-specific contribution that only adds feminine influence or domestic concerns to the public sphere.[52] Neither the secular paradigm of politics nor the feminized and domesticated framework has captured accurately the political transformation wrought by disestablishment or democracy. Consequently, in the field of American history, either women have been neglected in traditional studies that focus on elections, the party system, and presidents—and that discount feminized politics—or women have been distorted to fit secular and masculine models of political engagement. Separate spheres has resulted in separate histories, with women dominating the moral domain, men the political, and feminists have been forced to fall within either the feminine sphere of moral reform or the masculine realm of partisan politics.

The connections between biblical exegesis and political theory can illuminate our understanding of women's rights. By employing the creation story to define the state of nature, John Locke introduced the essential paradigm of sexual difference into liberal contract theory. Political theorist Carole Pateman argues that Locke's critique of Filmer did not dismantle patriarchy but simply gave it a new fraternal formulation. While Locke divested the "father" of his divine rights, he simultaneously invested the sons with the powers of "civil mastery."[53] The social compact represented an agreement between the sons, who figuratively inherited all the powers of the father, including his marital authority as husband. Civil mastery, like self-mastery, was defined as a masculine prerogative rooted in divine and political authority.

As a complex metaphor, the creation story details several overlapping allusions to explain marital and religious relationships. From the seventeenth through the nineteenth centuries, ministers and politicians used the creation story as their major proof text for defining the polity of the family.[54] The marriage covenant likewise bore certain similarities to republican political theory. Through her vows of allegiance and sexual fidelity, the wife gained protection from her husband—the same formula of exchanging rights for duties used to define citizenship. Additionally, the husband was the "head" of the family, and since the head rules the body, the husband had the same authority to supervise his family members as political leaders had over their subjects. The marriage covenant also defined the husband and wife as "one flesh," which made the wife the figurative body and the husband the figurative head of the family.[55] Under the care and supervision of her husband, the wife was "made useful," and her labors became part of the husband's marital and property rights. One biblical passage, then, represented the major political text for defining women's subordinate status in the state and family.

The political weight given to creation explains why stories of origin were important for the early women's rights movement. By portraying Mott as the gifted prophet, Stanton alluded to the theme of matriarchy as a counterpoint to the dominant patriarchal myths. Of course, Stanton's strategy had its root in the antebellum period and the language used by activists to redefine the state of nature. Channing aptly summarized this view with his appeal for a "new day of 'woman and man made one in co-sovereignty,'" a direct reference to his own biblical exegesis of the creation story.[56] Coequality or cosovereignty signified the way in which antebellum feminists had revised the creation story. They claimed it was the first biblical account ("God created man, male and female" [Genesis 1:27]) that laid the foundation for sexual equality. Simultaneous creation of the sexes made men and women equals in the eyes of God as morally accountable beings. Cosovereignty further implied that men and women shared in the dominion over the earth. Male political leadership, whether in civil society or the family, was not ordained by God or nature.

But Channing's usage had an additional meaning, captured in his equally powerful call for the day of "Woman's Peerage with Man."[57] Creation not only established equal rights in an abstract sense, but it also functioned as an allegory for equal standing before the public. Channing emphasized publicity as a fundamental feature of the antebellum campaign, describing the commanding "presence" and "thrilling" oratory of the "heroic Christian antislavery" women.[58] Risk-taking remained a key component of appearing in the public sphere, because risk required the courage to expose oneself before others and face the consequences.[59] As the first female agent of the American Anti-Slavery Society, Angelina Grimké captured this sense of risk. Channing described how she spoke "before crowded assemblies, angry mobs," while she "sacrificed home, sundered the most tender ties of social life, and went forth."

By exposing the "crimes of the professedly free Republic" and forming public opinion, Grimké actively participated in the public sphere.[60] In terms compatible with Arendt's definition, heroic Christian antislavery women such as Grimké gained "immortality" through the public force of their "works and deeds and words."[61]

Paulina Wright Davis's view of women's public role in the churches echoed Channing's comments. Her definition of equality was drawn from Galatians 3:28, the paradigmatic passage for conversion and sexual equality: "There was neither bond nor free[,] neither male nor female[,] for all were one in Christ Jesus."[62] Equality implied transcendence, the elimination of sexual differences or social ranks, which paralleled the necessary neutrality—or the suspension of social distinctions—required for disclosure and deliberations in Arendt's vision of the public sphere.[63] Equality existed among peers, or the fiction of the public sphere that all members shared the same universal political identity. Public disclosure and appearance involved the ability to represent one's views, as in testifying and standing trial, and it included the more powerful role of standing in judgment of others, as in jury service. In the nineteenth-century public sphere, these dual roles were implicit, since true equals not only spoke and disclosed their opinions, but they judged others for what they said and how they represented themselves.

The argument over true equality became another crucial way to distinguish between the legal rights of men and women. Roman law provided one precedent, in which women could represent themselves, but they lacked the right to speak for others, except in special cases, such as the defense of their parents.[64] American law required that women had to stand trial for their crimes, but women did not have the right to represent themselves as voters in the polity. Davis made this central to her argument for suffrage in her 1852 speech when she stated that "no man can vote by proxy or delegate the power to another. . . . The right is personal and sacred."[65] Davis's argument was important because it suggested another problem with the myopic focus on the Declaration of Independence as the only source of rights theory. Modern historians have ignored Davis's usage of the "sacred right of suffrage," the phrase found in all the nineteenth-century histories, and they instead have highlighted the concept of inalienable rights, which inevitably has masked the range of rights traditions and the nuanced meanings of concepts available to antebellum feminist advocates.

All three authors of the nineteenth-century histories—Stanton, Davis, and Channing—identify central themes of the early women's rights campaign. *Prophesy* connotes the political force of words to "create anew." *Risk* represents the ability to assert oneself in the public sphere and insert one's legacy in the pages of history. *Distinction*, or the ability to gain immortality, or a transcendent public voice, is a sign of representative participation not only as a voter but as a cosovereign ruler in the government.

Stanton's portrayal of herself as a first- or twice-born feminist tells us a great deal about the politics of historical interpretation. Stanton's various accounts of the origins of the movement are not distortions of the truth, but her narrative retelling cannot be divorced from certain ideological imperatives that influenced the meaning she gave certain events. By concealing the religious and figurative nature of early feminist theory, contemporary scholars lose sight of one essential dynamic of how antebellum Americans defined political action and discourse. Rather than reducing the movement to the one issue of voting rights, a focus on the language of rights expands our understanding of gender as a critical component of political behavior and speech. The exclusion of women from the polis did not make gender irrelevant or invisible but instead exposed a central feature of antebellum political theory, one that drew distinctions between publicity and privacy, identified the masculine marks of citizenship, and revealed the fundamental difference between the symbolic whole claimed as "the people" and the dominant part (enfranchised white males) that in fact characterized "the people." The early movement is significant not for its mythic tales of origins but for the way it exposed the gendered construction of American democracy.

2

Citizenship Understood (and Misunderstood)

On April 19–20, 1850, a convention of women was held in Salem, Ohio, for the express purpose of securing equal rights to all persons "without distinction of sex or color."[1] Although the 1848 Seneca Falls convention gained notoriety as the first women's rights convention, the Salem convention evoked more clearly the political culture that gave rise to the antebellum women's movement. The timing of the Salem convention was crucial. Less than a month later a statewide convention undertook the task of revising the original Ohio constitution.[2] By sending a memorial with 8,000 signatures to the state convention, Salem activists employed political channels already in place, and they succeeded in making woman suffrage an issue of constitutional debate.[3] But as a "Convention of Women," the Salem forum stood apart from American political tradition. Activists used the meeting to critique politics as usual. Women occupied the floor and debated resolutions and gave speeches, while the men sat quietly in the gallery. Through a poignant reversal of gender roles, the women engaged in constitutional deliberation, and the men were relegated to the sidelines of political action.[4]

Antebellum feminists imagined that such conventions allowed them to participate in the political process of constitution-making. Founders such as Thomas Jefferson had endorsed constitution-making as a vital and ongoing part of the machinery of American government.[5] A less optimistic John Adams made a more dire prediction, contending that "the fabrication of constitutions will be the occupation or the sport, the tragedy, comedy, or farce, for the entertainment of the world for a century to come."[6] Notably, Adams revealed the dual nature of constitution-making by treating the framing of fundamental law as both performative (ceremonial, ritualized, and enacted through word and deed) and fabricated (invented, created, and fictionalized or mythologized through figures of speech).[7] The two theatrical stages of any constitutional convention were the actual political body of the convention and the final written text, script, or public document produced from the proceedings. Similarly, antebellum feminists published their proceedings to disseminate their views before a wider audience and document their acts for the public record.[8]

It can be assumed that a women's convention would have shocked if not mortified both Jefferson and Adams. Nineteenth-century constitutional reformers, however, carved a space for women through the recognition of "spontaneous conventions." Viewed as "efficient manufactories of public opinion," spontaneous conventions were unofficial bodies that existed outside the state and the party system. In the 1867 study *The Constitutional Convention*, John Alexander Jameson argued that these forums generated "public opinion in the making,—public opinion fit to be the basis of political action, because sound and wise, and not a mere echo of party cries and platforms." Such conventions had a constitutional precedent derived from the right of the people to assemble and petition the government. The common law provided another justification known as the "*conventus publicos propria authoritate*," or the voluntary meetings of the people.[9]

Historians have not paid close enough attention to the deeply political meaning of conventions. By classifying women's rights conventions as social events, scholars generally have ignored the structure, language, and theatrical form of the conventions.[10] These features surfaced as important concerns for the women's rights campaign in light of American constitutional development. Between 1830 and 1860 almost every state revised its constitution, and state and spontaneous conventions contributed to the democratization of the language of rights.[11] More importantly, constitutional revision legitimated the right of the disenfranchised to demand their political rights. In an age when democracy relied on the vote of the common man, women's rights activists saw the convention as perhaps the best stage for fashioning women into political actors.

Women's rights conventions, however, were never simply forums for securing the vote. In the first place, traditional theories of political participation continued to sustain the cultural barriers against women gathering in convention. The very idea of women appearing in public forums or delegated assemblies was deemed unconventional. While intellectuals such as Judith

Sargent Murray and Mercy Otis Warren actively engaged in the republic of letters during the revolutionary generation, they never crossed the threshold into the highly visible world of public deliberation.[12] Their exclusion was not surprising within the context of eighteenth-century political culture, where power remained in the hands of social elites, or to use Jefferson's phrase, the "natural aristocracy."[13] Even the 1787 federal constitutional convention had been held in secret, closed to observers, and issued no reports to the outside world while in session. The people had not been invited.

Rule by the few over the many remained standard practice until the early decades of the nineteenth century. Between 1818 and 1821 Massachusetts, New York, and Connecticut established public forums that were separate from the legislature for revising their state constitutions. By 1830 Virginia reformers, in part influenced by George Mason's Declaration of Rights as well as by Thomas Jefferson's Declaration of Independence, introduced a new principle based on the right of the people to reform, alter, and abolish the government. The Ohio constitutional convention of 1850–51 continued this practice of revision and set another trend by debating the right of women to vote.[14] Still, Ohio convention delegates rejected the proposal for woman suffrage, and most remained uncertain about whether the issue should even have been debated. By a 72-to-7 vote, they resoundingly defeated the motion to strike the word "male" from suffrage qualifications in the new constitution.[15] Delegates then agreed to another textual elision. The complete discussion of woman suffrage was cut from the official record on the pretext that it was too vulgar for public dissemination.[16]

Although the Ohio convention delegates refused to acknowledge women as full citizens, they retained two important speeches for the published proceedings. Before the vote on female suffrage, a delegate named Townshend defended women's equality on the grounds that "woman is man's equal in intelligence and virtue" and she "has the same or equal interest in all that pertains to civil government." Townshend believed that every woman must judge for herself the propriety of voting, and he further asserted that self-representation was necessary if women were to redress their legal disabilities. His longest digression covered the vexing issue of the sexes "mingling in politics." As Townsend stated, if "ladies can accompany their husbands or fathers or brothers to church, or public lectures, or entertainments," then "I do not see why they could not as safely accompany the same persons to the ballot box."[17]

On the same day, during deliberations on black suffrage, a delegate named Woodbury observed that the framing of fundamental law was essential to citizenship, contending that the word "people" should be stricken from the new constitution, because women and blacks had no voice in the proceedings. Woodbury offered a telling justification for the Salem convention, claiming that disenfranchised groups must assemble and establish their own constitution. By citing Jefferson's oft-quoted language, Woodbury asserted that when a minority trampled on the rights of the majority, then each generation had the right to "alter," amend, or "abolish" their government. As long as women and blacks were denied the right of consent, "the people" were not parties to the government, and thus their only recourse was constitutional revolution.[18]

Beyond the legacy of the American Revolution, there was something inherently new in this appeal for a full-scale constitutional revolt. Even Jefferson cautiously theorized revolution as a last resort to be pursued only after all the sanctioned channels of political redress had failed. Yet the meaning of revolution changed during the antebellum period. By 1833, constitutional reformers in Pennsylvania saw their efforts as the enactment of a "peaceful, tranquil revolution, effected by public opinion." Such a sober view would be severely tested in Rhode Island, where constitutional revolution led to armed conflict in the infamous Dorr War. In 1841 Thomas Dorr and his followers made the unprecedented move of calling a constitutional convention without the approval of the state legislature. In their "Declaration of Principles," Dorrites justified a radical reinterpretation of popular sovereignty that literally included "the people" in the process of constitution-making. Dorr's supporters widened suffrage in Rhode Island but still limited this right to white males, imposing the same racial and sexual restrictions on the vote as most other state constitutional conventions. The Dorr controversy nevertheless promoted the convention as a new kind of public and political forum and, perhaps for the first time, sanctioned revolution as a constitutional rather than a natural right. Other excluded groups, such as free blacks or women, now could assemble as "the people" and demand their right for constitutional revision. As one delegate at the Ohio constitutional convention succinctly declared in 1850, every individual had the "right to revolutionize—to dig up the whole structure of our old government and scatter it to the winds."[19]

Constitutional revolution circumvented the party system as well. In a climate hostile to what one commentator called "the detestable poison of party spirit," constitutional conventions offered an alternative to partisan politics and legislative reform. By 1840 both major parties ironically used antiparty rhetoric. The Whigs appealed to the superiority of constitutional reform over partisan concerns, and even some Democrats attacked the excesses of the second party system. For most Whigs the 1840 presidential contest between William Henry Harrison and Martin Van Buren seemed to define a new stage in the development of "modern democracy."[20] Not only were more voters pulled to the polls, but the people appeared more actively involved in the presidential campaign. That year a Whig convention in Ohio gathered 20,000 participants, and the delegates marched in procession while the band played the revolutionary French anthem "Marseillaise." The Whigs capitalized on the importance of their party conventions as public events, opening their doors to women as observers and describing their meetings as spontaneous, voluntary congregations.[21] Like the constitutional conventions, such party conventions blended the issues of popular sovereignty, peaceful revolution galvanized by public opinion, and popularly inspired principles used to check the power of party machines. Promoting what would become a familiar refrain in American politics, the Whigs claimed that the party that was above partisanship came closer to embodying the will of the people.

Partisan battles for the popular will generated political contradictions for women. Southern Whigs included white women in their conventions because it advanced their class-based pretensions to be regarded as the more civilized party. At their grand convention held at Richmond, Virginia, in 1840, the women seated in the gallery were described by Senator Daniel Webster as "beautiful ladies," whose presence ensured that rules of propriety would be maintained.[22] The presence of women did not domesticate as much as socialize the political sphere.[23] Having women in the audience upheld the masculine code of chivalry, in which male virtue required the display of social decorum and verbal prowess before the female gaze. In his letter to the 1850 national women's rights convention, "ultra" reformer Henry Van Amringe observed that women's presence in the capitol gallery merely served to "excite the love of display for some ostentatious Senator."[24] The Whigs assumed that women's attendance made their public conventions less partisan, because women were seen as nonpartisan; they could support candidates without expecting the spoils of office. Here the Whigs offered a radical reversal of the older sexual distinction of republicanism, arguing that women rather than men were better suited to sacrifice their self-interest for the public good. There was a catch, however. Women retained this vaunted position only as long as they remained nonpartisan.[25]

Certainly the Whigs had no intention of endorsing woman suffrage. It would take the radical wing of the Liberty Party, known as the Liberty League, to make female suffrage into a partisan issue in 1846.[26] One year later the same party added Lydia Maria Child and Lucretia Mott to their roster of potential nominees for the U.S. presidency.[27] In Ohio, Liberty and Free-Soil candidates supported women's rights, and they endorsed a vision of an educated public that included men and women.[28] Betsey Mix Cowles, the president of the Salem convention, was selected because she believed education, like suffrage, should be a constitutional right "without distinction of sex or color." In 1848 Cowles led the campaign against the Ohio Black Codes that discriminated against black children by refusing to protect their right to public education. Cowles was representative of the different coalitions that attended the Salem convention. She had ties to the Garrisonian abolitionists and the more moderate Liberty Party supporters, and activists from both wings of the antislavery movement attended the convention.[29] As a teacher and school principal, Cowles made the perfect convention president, as school elections provided the one public forum in which women were allowed to vote in Ohio.[30]

Liberty League and Liberty Party members described women and men as equals in "thought, advice, and suffrage," and they considered women eminently capable of voting in convention.[31] Civil liberty required the capacity to perform, think critically, and act responsibly, all capabilities that women exercised in schools, churches, and reform societies. In the words of Liberty Party supporter William Elder, political understanding had to be "periscopic," requiring a "viewing on all sides," which demanded the cultivation of critical inquiry in all citizens.[32] No longer mere observers or social arbiters of partisan activities, women instead possessed what Cowles described as an "extended vision" on all political subjects.[33] Neither more nor less partisan, women simply shared the same capacity as men for discerning the truth.

The radical Liberty League split from the Liberty Party to endorse a wider platform on human rights and move away from the single focus on antislavery. Although their first presidential candidate, Gerrit Smith, advocated women's political rights, members of the Liberty League could not reach a consensus on women's enfranchisement.[34] Their lack of commitment to woman suffrage would be passed on to the Free-Soil Party and the Republican Party, eventually reemerging after the Civil War in the failed attempt to include women under the terms of the Fourteenth and Fifteenth Amendments in 1868–70.

Thus the legacy of the antebellum women's rights campaign extended beyond the vote or even the terms of what was to be the Fifteenth Amendment. The larger contribution came from the varied and ingenious arguments for women's full entitlement as citizens. Women's rights activists developed a "rights discourse" that fit within the meaning of the later Fourteenth Amendment, raising issues related to equal protection, due process, and representation. Clearly, activism before the Civil War was not in vain. It is reasonable to suggest that the ability to organize a spirited convention was more important than the singular advocacy of suffrage. Between 1848 and 1860, organizers held numerous conventions in five states: Indiana, Massachusetts, New York,

Ohio, and Pennsylvania. During every year except 1857, national women's rights conventions convened in Worcester, Syracuse, Cleveland, Philadelphia, Cincinnati, and New York City. The conventions exposed some of the most fundamental contradictions inherent in antebellum democracy and gave women's rights activists a legitimate forum in the political order.

Three crucial developments shaped the antebellum conventions. Feminists recognized that constitution-making was more complex than simply demanding individual rights. Constitutional revolution created the possibility for antebellum activists not only to reframe the meaning of popular sovereignty but to question the sexual boundaries of citizenship and expose the state's failure to grant women equal standing under the law. The early women's rights conventions pursued three revolutionary goals, which can be summarized as follows:

1. *Entitlement*: the right to have rights, which employed the language of rights and challenged the gaps in constitutionalism that left women outside the logic of consent;
2. *National Citizenship*: the rights and privileges of political standing, which required redefining the nature of the contractual relationship between citizens and the state;
3. *Equality under the Law*: the right to equal treatment, which called for the state to redress civil disabilities and recognize women's claims to protection and due process.

These struggles could not be brought to the foreground through formal party organs. The rise of constitutional conventions and the challenges of third parties opened the door to political change, but these forums demonstrated more clearly how such new partisan developments failed to deal adequately with women's rights. In the antebellum period, reformers did more than demand suffrage; they contested the meaning of "consent of the governed." Constitutional revision meant a return to first principles, which exposed the tension between rule by descent and the right of consent, both of which still defined citizenship. Women best revealed this contradiction, finding their civil status defined by birth and descent, while men acquired all the rights of citizenship, legal protection, and the vote from their status as "common" men.

The Rite (and Right) of Passage from Descent to Consent

Jacksonian Democracy's most enduring image of the common man enshrined consent as the defining aspect of national identity. Unlike countries bonded through common ancestors, bloodlines, and inherited privileges, the United States generated a democratic ethos that celebrated chosen identities over inherited ones. The demise of primogeniture and property-based suffrage requirements unmoored the common man from his parentage and past.[35] Indeed, the common man became the quintessential self-made man; he read newspapers, listened to speeches, attended party meetings and conventions, and then voted for the candidate to whose party he gave his allegiance. Not only was his partisan support publicly affirmed and ritually enacted for all to see at the polls, but his embrace of citizenship was reconfirmed through his active participation in the political process.[36]

In 1848 Lydia Maria Child, author and a former editor of the *National Anti-Slavery Standard*, offered a less laudatory portrait of the common man in her fictional story "Home and Politics." In the story George Franklin is an ambitious lawyer who becomes intoxicated with the world of partisan politics. His future wife, Alice White, comes closer to the ideal of the self-made American. Although her parents are illiterate, Alice works in a factory, acquires an education, and eventually becomes a teacher. Through marriage Alice achieves her dream—a home of her own—a dream soon ruined by her husband's obsession with politics. Her husband's whole character changes. He becomes restless, frantically reading the newspapers, following the elections, and finally running for public office. As Alice watches the election-day procession, she observes that the two parties, Democratic and Whig, offer nothing for women and children, that is, nothing as important as granting women the political means for the "protection of homes." Alice's view of the election is an omen. When her husband loses the contest, gambling everything on his victory, she loses her possessions, her home, and her sanity— all set adrift on the "turbulent sea of American politics." The moral of the story for Child was that partisan politics had failed to foster a democratic culture based on choice or consent. Mass political participation thrived on the allure, the superficial excitement and the risk, involved in the "game" of electoral politics. While the common man appeared to have shed the chains of custom and tradition, he simply replaced them with a new political yoke as the party man.[37]

At the heart of this tale was an indictment of a political system premised on the idea that men could represent the interests of women. Universal white "manhood suffrage" was built on the interrelated principles that individual men, as heads of households, could understand their self-interest and protect their families. In fact Thomas Jefferson had offered the model of head of household—a man with familial dependents—as one basis for the right to vote.[38] Child's portrait of George Franklin reveals the fallacy of this approach, primarily because he fails to meet any of the idealized standards of the common man. George's behavior is marked by irrational rather than well-informed decisions; he is financially reckless rather than a competent guardian of his family's welfare; and he lacks a will of his own. According to Child, women had no security when men like George Franklin set their lives adrift on the "turbulent sea of American politics."

Yet even the most radical critics of antebellum political culture were not immune to the creed of the consenting community. Like the advocates of constitutional revolution, Child believed dissent through the conscious act of nonvoting was the truest form of consent.[39] Whereas constitutional conventions circumvented the legislature, nonvoting and disunion assumed that the national government eventually would have to reconstitute the social compact and form a new polity.[40] Lucretia Mott agreed, but she also observed that women first had to have the right to vote before they could choose not to vote.[41] In 1847 John C. Hathaway, abolitionist and women's rights supporter, explained how consent and dissent were both linked to social contract theories and national citizenship. Hathaway endorsed the view that government was a "voluntary association," in which every person had to claim political membership upon reaching adulthood.[42] Thus, voting or not voting fit within the logic of consent.

During the nineteenth century, legal adulthood had two stages: the age of consent (fourteen for men and twelve for women) and the age of twenty-one, when parental control over offspring ended.[43] Significantly, the age of consent implied the ability to use discretion and reason, while the arbitrary age of twenty-one presumed the acquisition of virtue derived from independence. Whereas women might reach the age of reason, they were never understood to have achieved full independence or adulthood, because married women, like minors, had their rights circumscribed by the legal guidelines for capacity. The courts judged children to be lacking the maturity necessary for self-representation, while wives were legally dependent on the consent of their husbands in all civil suits.[44] Legal capacity thus provided the rationale for denying women the right to vote. As John Adams had argued in 1776, women were routinely classified with minors and infants as legal dependents. When fused together as a political class, women and children provided Adams with the undeniable proof that consent was neither a natural nor a universal right.[45]

Women and men unquestionably followed very different paths on their separate journeys toward consent. In the eyes of the law, female and male children reached adulthood at twenty-one, but women who married were divested of their legal capacity. Women's political status never appeared to change from childhood to adulthood. Perhaps the best analogy is to be drawn with legal aliens. Women seemed doomed to political purgatory or limbo by moving beyond their legal dependence as children, sharing with aliens certain rights as residents but no political privileges, yet never acquiring full status as equal members of the consenting community.

From a historical perspective, women's status reflected the recurrent tension between chosen and imposed identities. Both legal capacity and political consent represented reverse sides of the same coin of citizenship. Derived from a republican model of citizenship, consent emphasized participation, deliberation, and free will as requisites for contracting into the social compact. In contrast, legal capacity stressed a passive model of citizenship, in which the state bestowed rights and privileges as an entitlement.[46] Both traditions emerged as part of the American experience during the formative period of the early republic. Almost by accident, consent preceded the original compact. In 1776 all residents within the borders of the United Colonies had to accept or reject their newly acquired civil identity. As Linda Kerber has shown, men and women were included under this definition of voluntary citizenship.[47] And as loyalty oaths were demanded of American residents during the Revolutionary War, both men and women often found themselves bound to declare their allegiance.[48]

As new states began to draft constitutions, legal capacity replaced consent as the essential prerequisite for full citizenship. Interestingly enough, New Jersey granted single, propertied women the right to vote from 1776 to 1807, and the U.S. Supreme Court ruled in 1809, "Single women have been allowed to vote, because the law supposes them to have wills of their own."[49] By granting a minority of women the right to vote, New Jersey never endorsed the doctrine of consent, since single women were the exception, not the rule, and their status flowed directly from their legal capacity.

Antebellum American society failed to close the gap between women's political consent and capacity. Single women still had wills of their own, but they could not vote in a single state. Unlike married women, single women earned and kept their own wages, made binding contracts, moved freely from state to state, and established their own place of residence. Women enjoyed education, and they sustained increasing rates of literacy compared with men. They displayed their moral virtue through church and benevolent activities, and women equaled men in civic virtue through the payment of taxes. Those opposed to granting women the vote either had to describe women as mentally inferior or deny women's common humanity, as Rebecca Sanford argued in her letter to the Salem women's rights convention: "It is improper for her [to] legislate, speak, and vote. Why? Because she is a woman. Ask man what legislates, and he will answer justice, knowledge, common sense; what it is that speaks, and he will answer, intellect, moral power; what it is that votes, and he will reply, understanding. To sustain his objections and his answers, woman is an idiot, or less than chattel. His position in reality upon this point is confused and ridiculous."[50] In these areas women were considered as capable or incapable as men. If this was true, as Sanford argued, then individual women and men might differ in degree, but there were no absolute differences when reason and common sense were viewed as universal human faculties.

Such lofty ideals about reason and virtue had little bearing on actual suffrage qualifications. The law presumed that adulthood conferred mental and moral capacities; but it had no method for testing actual intelligence, nor did the law distinguish between different grades of moral endowment. In his 1845 defense of women's right to the elective franchise, Judge Elisha Hurlbut of New York revealed that suffrage qualifications required competence rather than practical knowledge or understanding. The true measurement for the right to the franchise was the absence of any defects of character. According to Hurlbut there were four possible causes for exclusion: (1) immaturity in years, or the physical incapacity of an undeveloped mind and body; (2) disordered intellectual perceptions, or mental defects; (3) moral defects, evidenced by the commission of a crime; and (4) illiteracy, or the cultural incapacity to use language and participate in civil society. In addition to age and residency requirements, the state constitution of New York denied the ballot to idiots and criminals. At the very least, New York required mental and moral sanity from its voting population. Women as a group satisfied these basic requirements. Hurlbut believed that even the opponents of woman suffrage had to concede that woman "attains to the years of discretion—that she has clear intellectual perceptions—an admirable moral constitution, and is susceptible of the highest degrees of intellectual culture." Imitating but expanding the model that had been used in New Jersey, Hurlbut devised a three-step plan for gradual enfranchisement, first incorporating single women who paid taxes, then adding all other adult single women, and eventually allowing all adult women, single or married, to vote.[51]

According to Hurlbut, suffrage was based on a minimal measurement of civic competence. As early as 1816 Thomas Jefferson had anticipated this ideological shift when he suggested an alternative to property qualifications, proposing that militia enlistment and taxation be used as evidence of civic capacity for acquiring the right to vote.[52] Jefferson linked classical republicanism to modern democracy by making full citizenship a conscribed or conscripted status for white men. The Latin root for conscribe is *conscribere*, which originally applied to all men enrolled to serve in the Roman senate, and like military conscription, it emphasized an obligation to serve the state. Conscribe and conscription further underscored the imposed equality of the common man, since eligibility meant being enrolled "identically" in "common."[53] Quite literally, with their names on tax and company rolls, taxpayers and militia men represented the democratic equivalent of enrolled citizens.

Capacity allowed for any permutation of suffrage qualifications, but the exclusion of adult women became the only truly universal application of the rule. By 1851 the "principle of universal suffrage," stated the *United States Magazine and Democratic Review*, meant that "white males of age constituted the political nation."[54] There were exceptions. In New York, black men were permitted to vote if they owned $250 worth of real estate.[55] Race and gender at times seemed like fungible categories. During the 1846 New York constitutional convention one delegate contended that the differences between the races were too great to allow for "co-citizens," and thus blacks and whites could only exercise equal rights in their "respective spheres."[56] Anson Bingham, New York lawyer and regular contributor to the women's rights paper the *Lily*, observed that while black men paid for the privilege of voting, women's political nonexistence reduced them to the level of "serfs" and "slaves."[57] Bingham, however, missed the true irony of the situation. Strangely enough, given the property qualification for the franchise, property-owning black men had taken the place Hurlbut had proposed for single women.[58] Both single women and black men who owned property represented a compensatory class; that is, autonomy for single women and wealth for black men compensated for their presumed disabilities of economic dependence.[59]

Even if capacity provided the excuse for discrimination, then consent should still have promised a theory for universal suffrage based on fundamental rights. Yet consent like capacity evolved in ways that separated suffrage from its original premise of "consent of the governed." Most early state constitutions guaranteed a narrow range of absolute rights, generally limiting natural rights to life, liberty, and property. More importantly, property rights trumped all other natural rights. Property qualifications extended suffrage to those citizens seen as having a vested stake in society. At the 1820 Massachusetts constitutional convention one delegate argued that property holders surrendered a greater portion of their rights and, in return, they purchased a vested interest in the government.[60] Vested rights were not natural but alienable, and some rights, like property, required special protection. Instead of instituting consent of the governed in order to protect natural rights and ensure a just government, state constitutions acknowledged that the right of property superseded natural law and all other fundamental rights. If the vote was considered a privilege rather than a natural right, property requirements reinforced the rule that some citizens were more equal than others.

Property had a long-standing relationship to consent. It was, as most seventeenth-century social contract theorists believed, the very reason for government. But the consent they had in mind was consent to the rule of law, which was necessary for establishing civil society and granting government the police power to protect private property. The common-law prescription for women's economic dependence under coverture fit within the logic of protecting private property. As Thomas Hobbes contended in the *Leviathan*, next to a man's property right in his "life and limbs," men were most interested in having the state protect those "things held in propriety that concern conjugal affection."[61] Women and children fell under the rubric of things concerning conjugal affection. By the antebellum period this relationship between property and conjugal affection continued to serve as a reason for excluding women from the polity. As male guardians of private property, fathers, husbands, sons, and brothers carried women's wishes to the polls and the counsels of government. As her "charmed representatives," Judge Hurlbut sardonically recounted the conventional paternalism he disputed, "will not he who has smiled upon her infancy, fostered and protected her youth, and viewed her with the exulting pride and deep affection of a father, ensure to her an adequate legal protection? Will not her chosen husband guard her rights? Can the son forget the mother than bore him—and when he is performing the highest function he can execute in society, will he fail to consider and protect the rights of that being who loves him most?—Will the brother allow his gentle sister's rights to fail of protection?"[62] In this pre-Freudian model, every man replaced the father, providing women with paternal protection. Conjugal and familial affection placed married women and minors in the same class, reinforcing the idea that women's political standing remained constant from childhood through adulthood.

Property interests surfaced in another popular rationale that women's political exclusion was a matter of choice. Antebellum politicians and constitutional theorists argued that at marriage, women agreed to give up their property—their rights—and then to retreat from politics. Somehow a woman's choice to exercise her legal consent in marriage erased her right to political consent. If this theory had any credence, men and women stood at opposite ends of the civic spectrum between capacity and consent. While men secured the vote on the strength of their imposed rank of manhood attained automatically at adulthood, women were accorded their disenfranchised status from consent by choosing marriage over participation in the social compact.

It is clear that consent of the governed played a rhetorical rather than a constitutional role in defining the boundaries of democratic participation. Universal manhood suffrage relied mainly on the framework of legal capacity by using white male adulthood as the minimum requirement for the right to vote. The emphasis on manhood demonstrated the extent to which descent instead of consent ruled the day. By making sexual and racial status the essential suffrage qualification, white men were still born to their station as citizens, for descent implied one's race, caste, bloodline, and gender classification.[63] Family position and civic manhood also mattered, because the vote as a vested right clothed men with the rank of full citizenship in exchange for their possible service as heads of households, soldiers and militiamen, and productive, taxpaying citizens. Under these terms the state discriminated against all women and some groups of men, especially those who failed the meet the standards of manhood, which included slaves, free blacks, Mexican Americans, Native Americans, and immigrant, illiterate, poor, working-class men.

Natural Law and National Citizenship

Because American democracy changed the gender dynamics of national identity, citizenship for men meant something quite different from what it meant for women. Despite the trend toward participatory democracy at mid-century, women occupied an ambiguous legal and political position that made them appear as both citizens and noncitizens. For Paulina Wright Davis, in her speech at the 1852 Syracuse women's rights convention, the problem for women paralleled the dilemma of Eve and Pandora, two powerful mythic figures who symbolized Woman as the "enigma."[64] While it was assumed that women were citizens, the evidence proved otherwise—thus the enigma. Women as a group failed to match the characteristics normally identified with citizenship. Although citizenship did not have a definitive guideline in the United States until after the passage of the Fourteenth Amendment in 1868, its broader parameters could be traced to the antebellum period. According to the *Oxford English Dictionary*, a citizen is defined as "a member of a state, an enfranchised inhabitant of a country, as opposed to an alien; in U.S., a person, native or naturalized, who has the privilege of voting for public offices, and is entitled to full protection in the exercise of private rights."[65] As James Kettner has concluded, by 1820 the central assumptions about citizenship followed more loosely defined guidelines. The citizen was entitled to fundamental privileges and immunities; his membership in the federal community required allegiance to nation and state; and aliens had to meet certain standards of fitness to be admitted into the ranks of the sovereign people. Status was based on individual consent, and political participation was implied if the citizen met state qualifications for the franchise. It was presumed that the status of citizen was conferred on native-born Americans, although the volitional nature of this definition of membership remained purely theoretical and unexamined.[66]

How did women fare under these general rules of citizenship? In the first place, women were not members of the state, because membership implied standing, which was denied to women through their imposed incapacity. Second, women were not enfranchised inhabitants, nor could they exercise the political privileges of citizenship, because individual states had made it clear that women were denied the right to vote. Through coverture, married women were divested of their private rights, especially the right of property, which was considered one of the most crucial rights to be protected by law. Women were not entitled to full protection, because they were excluded from the consenting community. Thus, women's status as native-born citizens did not guarantee them the same rights as similarly situated men born on American soil.

When the Seneca Falls convention gathered on July 19–20, 1848, supporters called the meeting to discuss the "Social, Civil, and Religious Condition of Woman." Most of the participants came from the town of Seneca Falls, the neighboring village of Waterloo, and the nearby city of Rochester. Lucretia Mott, the only nationally known woman speaker at the meeting, gained recognition as "the moving spirit of the occasion." The sparse proceedings, not published before 1870, reveal that the convention produced two major documents: (1) a preamble and eleven resolutions, debated and drafted during the deliberations, and (2) the Declaration of Sentiments, written earlier by Elizabeth Cady Stanton and read during the meeting. With a touch of irony as well as ritualized performance, the Declaration of Sentiments was signed by the members of the convention much as the celebrated founders did in Philadelphia in 1776.[67]

At the Seneca Falls convention the meaning of citizenship was tested. By inserting the word "women" into the Declaration of Independence, Stanton made her Declaration of Sentiments a political document that posed a number of simple and complex questions. Could women appropriate the enlightened "rights of man" without changing the meaning? Or did the mere mention of women as full-fledged rights-bearers demonstrate, as English political philosopher Edmund Burke believed, that the "abstract perfection" of rights was "their practical defect"?[68] The Declaration of Sentiments sought to prove that women's citizenship was an enigma, or at least at odds with the universal claims made in the Declaration of Independence. If women were citizens, as Stanton attempted to show, they should logically be able to claim the language of rights as their own. Every abstract principle should apply to women, beginning with the idea of human equality, followed by inalienable rights and consent of the governed. But if women shared nothing in common with their abstract inheritance, if instead every principle was not binding when applied to women's status and condition, then women's citizenship was more a fiction than a reality.

The Declaration of Sentiments did not simply acknowledge women's omission from the Age of Rights. The real question it raised was whether the discourse of entitlement could be stretched not only to include women as citizens but to revise the tradition of rights and consent so that each could play a more active role in antebellum constitutional reform. There were signs that citizenship needed a new foundation that explicitly and legally connected suffrage to the idea of national citizenship. The Declaration of Sentiments insisted that women "have immediate admission to all the rights and privileges which belong to them as citizens of the United States."[69]

Was Stanton projecting the Nineteenth Amendment? Not exactly. Stanton's national orientation reflected the influence of Lysander Spooner, perhaps the most creative constitutional theorist of the antebellum period. In *The Unconstitutionality of Slavery* (1847) Spooner argued that the federal constitution guaranteed citizenship to every man, woman, and child born in the United States.[70] Spooner also looked to the Declaration of Independence as a source of constitutional principles, advocating that natural law and natural rights provided the only infallible test of the constitutionality of citizenship.[71] For this reason Blackstone's definition of natural law appeared in the preamble of the Seneca Falls convention: "The law of Nature, being coeval with mankind, and dictated by God himself, is of course superior in obligation to any other. It is binding over all the globe, in all countries, and at all times; no human laws are of any validity if contrary to this, and such of them as are valid, derive all their force, and validity, and their authority, mediately and immediately from this original."[72] How did natural law change the citizen's relationship to the vote? In Spooner's words, rules for exclusion had to be explicit and "expressed in terms legally competent" in order to "authorize or sanction anything contrary to natural right."[73] To reinforce this point, Stanton declared that suffrage had to be treated as an "inalienable right."[74] The burden of proof for women's exclusion now required a constitutional justification. Voter qualifications simply could not be imposed on citizens, because suffrage had to comply with the force of natural law and constitutional rights.

Spooner's theory was also appealing because it was not as radical as it seemed. His ruling assumption was that citizenship must be guaranteed through the constitutional right of protection. Judge Elisha Hurlbut had offered a similar proposition, arguing that the sole purpose of government was to protect natural rights rather than to create or invest rights.[75] Essentially, this emphasis on protection limited the role of capacity in defining citizenship. Capacity assumed that someone acted as a proxy: the parent for the child, or the husband for the wife.[76] If Spooner was right, such mediation was invalid, because every man, woman, and child had a direct and individual relationship to the state. Spooner interpreted the social contract as a binding legal contract.[77] Disenfranchisement now implied fraud and criminal deception, that is, the use of false representations in order to injure the rights of another.[78] In the Declaration of Sentiments Stanton agreed, describing women as "fraudulently deprived of their most sacred rights."[79] Under these terms, entitlement followed a different logic, one that measured rights not by their abstract perfection but by their ability to protect citizens against the "defects" of legal misinterpretation.[80]

It is not surprising that Spooner's interpretation influenced the Seneca Falls convention. Liberty Party leader Gerrit Smith, who was Stanton's cousin, sponsored the research and publication of Spooner's book and promoted its ideas among third-party reformers.[81] Ansel Bascom, one of the most vocal discussants at the Seneca Falls convention, shared Spooner's passion for legal reform.[82] Bascom had been elected as a delegate to the 1846 New York constitutional convention and published a paper, "The Memorial," which primarily focused on "finding fault with lawyers and criticizing legal weakness."[83] Throughout the 1840s Stanton and Bascom had been challenging the common-law fiction that fathers and husbands were the protectors of women by working for married women's property rights and temperance reform.[84] They also argued that politicians were rarely their "charmed representatives," as the women of New York learned in 1844 when a petition dealing with sexual violence in marriage was laughed out of the state legislature.[85]

Spooner's critique was attractive to Seneca Falls reformers, moreover, because natural law paralleled the religious framework of higher law that made "inalienable rights" and "sacred rights" interchangeable terms.[86] One of the longest convention resolutions, most likely written by Quaker minister Lucretia Mott, pointed to God alone as the author of rights. Every woman was "invested by the Creator with the same capabilities, and the same consciousness of responsibility for their exercise."[87] It is important to point out that over one-fourth of the participants were Congregational Friends, a group that had formed a month earlier and had included this view of rights in their "Basis of Association."[88] Thomas McClintock, the author of the "Basis";

Mary Ann McClintock; and their daughter, Elizabeth W. McClintock, all spoke at the Seneca Falls convention.[89] In addition, Mary Ann McClintock had joined Stanton, Mott, and Jane Hunt, another Congregational Friend, in planning the convention.

The Congregational Friends, like Spooner, believed that natural or sacred rights could not be transferred or surrendered. In the "Basis" McClintock wrote that the individual stood in conjunction to God to be virtually inseparable from God, implying that sacred rights embodied the very being of the divine.[90] The direct relationship between the individual and the state, which was the main feature of Spooner's definition of national citizenship, paralleled what the Congregational Friends saw as the direction relationship between God and the individual. This perspective was reinforced by Blackstone's assertion that natural law was "dictated by God." To the Congregational Friends, dictation translated as divine inscription, which meant no woman should rely on secondary sources for the law of "her nature." Even if this law "were unrolled from the heights of Sinai," they declared, "she must herself ascend the mount, and there receive the law—not written on tablets of stone, but engraved on her very being."[91] Higher law or natural law acquired physicality, no longer an abstract principle but a constituent part of every living person. The contrast between inherited law and inscribed rights served still another purpose. A woman did not have to rely on tradition, custom, or laws imposed by men; instead she had to judge for herself the validity of man-made law, consenting only to rules consistent with the natural law of her very being.

It is clear that the Declaration of Sentiments ushered in a new conception of citizenship, for its crucial themes included natural and inalienable rights, suffrage and national citizenship, and legal protection derived from the right of contract. But the Seneca Falls convention still did not fully establish women's status within the context of currently accepted constitutional views. The Declaration of Sentiments asserted what women's entitlement should be, and it listed the "facts" proving their exclusion; but it left unspecified where women stood in relation to constitutional interpretations of the antebellum period.

Women as Disabled Castes and Equality under the Law

Two years later the first national women's rights convention was held in Worcester, Massachusetts, on October 23 and 24, 1850. In her presidential address Paulina Wright Davis described the movement as "radical and universal," with the revolutionary potential for the total reorganization of "all social, political and industrial interests and institutions." A wider scope of issues emerged in the more formal organization of this gathering, which not only elected a full slate of officers but made appointments to several different committees, including a central committee as well as committees on education, civil and political rights, social relations, and avocations.[92]

But the approach to entitlement was also different at this national meeting. Davis pinpointed the problem when she described women as a "disabled caste." By calling for the "emancipation of a class," Davis turned to the constitutional principle of due process of law.[93] During the antebellum period several states used due process to redress "class legislation," which subjected individuals or groups to unjust treatment. Due process addressed the issue of divestment, since it imposed legal limits on depriving individuals of their natural rights of life, liberty, or property. Due process also complemented the right of protection as a constitutional safeguard by protecting citizens from the state and by ensuring equal treatment.[94]

Davis adopted an approach very different from Stanton's Declaration of Sentiments, placing less emphasis on abstract rights and more emphasis on two "maxims" of political science: "Equality before the law, and the right of the governed to choose their governors."[95] Davis's constitutional analysis reflected the legal context in Massachusetts. In 1849, a year before the Worcester convention, Chief Justice Lemuel Shaw offered a ruling in *Roberts v. City of Boston* that demonstrated how descent and capacity limited the application of equality before the law. Although the case addressed racial segregation, the plaintiff was a black girl, which probably influenced Shaw to use a common-law formula normally applied to women and children. Shaw ruled, "But when this great principle comes to be applied to actual and various conditions of persons in society, it will not warrant the assertion, that men and women are legally clothed with the same civil and political powers, and that children and adults are legally to have the same functions and be subject to the same treatment; *But only that the rights of all, as they are settled and regulated by law, are equally entitled to the paternal consideration and protection of the law, for their maintenance and security*."[96] Shaw created a two-tier system for equal protection: one that entitled competent male adults to full protection and another that subjected those identified as incapable—women and children—to paternal consideration. According to this precedent, women were a "disabled caste."[97] Shaw also assumed that the courts acted as a surrogate father or guardian for legal dependents. This approach fit within the standard interpretation of legal capacity, but it allowed the judge to act as a proxy and to decide in the best interest of the plaintiff.[98] Of course, this entire transaction occurred without the consent of the plaintiff. Women and children could neither give their consent nor demand full constitutional protection, because such rights were granted only to full citizens. At best the courts remedied the needs of women and children according to their station in life.

For Shaw, women's disabilities were treated as a reflection of their "actual" condition, and their status as a caste was justified because men and women were not "clothed with the same legal and political powers." Dependent classes and disabled castes could only voice their needs, while independent and consenting adult males had the capacity and legal recognition to claim rights. Implicitly, Shaw saw suffrage as a vested right, and he quite intentionally invoked the alternative interpretation of due process that emphasized the protection of vested rights. Shaw was not alone in his opinion. During the same year a New York judge ruled against the 1849 Married Woman's Property Act on the grounds that it violated and failed to protect the vested rights of husbands.[99]

Paternal consideration reinforced a static conception of women as legal dependents as it emphasized one unchanging political pattern of female representation-by-proxy. Vested rights relied on a property-based definition of citizenship, in which consenting members of the social contract had to have a material stake in the nation-state. As Jefferson had suggested in his vision for democratic suffrage qualifications, those deemed worthy of the title of citizen had to be willing to sacrifice their property, their lives, and even their families for the good of the nation. Women could not meet this fundamental requirement.

Women were subject to paternal consideration because they were, in theory, political subjects in the miniature government of the family. They were not only seen to be lacking a will of their own but were treated as though they were suffering from the same disability as resident aliens; that is, they were classified as having a partial or dual allegiance. According to the common law a woman's first allegiance was to her husband and family, which made it impossible for women to be entirely loyal to the state. Even a wife's marriage vows imitated an oath of allegiance, since she pledged to obey her husband. Consequently, women failed to adhere to the common-law formula of citizenship, in which full allegiance was exchanged quid pro quo for the guarantee of full constitutional protection.

Given that consent and the right of protection were closely intertwined, the problem of women's allegiance contributed to the political rationale that women retreated from politics by choice. Political observers found the common-law concept of a wife's obedience to her "lord and master" quite reassuring in the antebellum period. In particular, opponents of female suffrage argued that political equality represented a danger to the home, wherein equality threatened to undermine the chain of command existing between husband and wife. At the 1850 Worcester convention Abby Price readily discounted this argument. As a member of Hopedale, a self-proclaimed independent "Christian Republic," Price observed that women had little difficulty engaging in public deliberations while caring for their families.[100] In her letter to the Worcester convention, Stanton further exposed how this issue affected women's political rights: "Some tell us that if woman should interest herself in political affairs, it would destroy all domestic harmony. What, say they, would be the consequence, if husband and wife should not agree in their view of political economy? Because, forsooth, husband and wife may chance to differ in theological sentiments, shall women have no religion? Because she may not choose to worship at the same altar with her liege lord, must she of necessity do up all her worshipping in private, in her own closet?"[101] Lucretia Mott aired her own view on this issue. At the 1848 Rochester convention she agreed it was true that woman could not have two masters, but her only true "master" was God and not man.[102]

There was little room for women to maneuver within the existing framework of equal protection. Every principle raised in the Declaration of Sentiments faced a series of constitutional barriers that restricted women's full entitlement, for as Shaw had demonstrated, natural or actual conditions easily displaced natural rights, and paternal consideration compromised the rights of protection and due process. When women were defined as outsiders in their own country, women's partial allegiance undermined their claim for national citizenship. Women's status as a disabled caste sealed their legal dependence and political disenfranchisement. The constitutional reasoning was almost circular. As a disabled caste, women were divested of the right to vote, and they remained disenfranchised because the Constitution protected the vote as a vested right of men.

Reformers at the Worcester convention had good reason to be concerned with equal protection in advancing women's educational and professional opportunities. The first two resolutions focused on the infringement of women's equal rights through their restricted education.[103] Paulina Wright Davis, the key organizer and president of the convention, was a health lecturer devoted to medical education, and Marian Blackwell, the secretary of the education committee, was the sister of Elizabeth Blackwell, the first American woman to gain professional training as a physician. Although she was not present at the convention, Elizabeth Blackwell was appointed to the avocation committee.[104] Perhaps the most interesting appointment was that of Quaker Eliza Barney as chair of the education committee.[105] A close friend of Lucretia Mott, Barney had played a major role in the campaign against racial segregation in the Nantucket school system. Barney had ties to Sarah Earle, a cousin of Mott, who was one of the most important figures in the Worcester County Anti-Slavery Society from 1841 until her death in 1859. Earle also assumed a crucial position as a regional organizer of the Worcester convention. Not surprisingly, John Milton Earle, the husband of Sarah Earle, had established an earlier political alliance with Nantucket reformers. While serving as a state legislator, Earle worked for the 1845 passage of House bill number 45, a legislative reform that prohibited racial segregation in schools and gave parents the right to sue for damages.[106]

At Worcester, Harriot Hunt brought together the issues of educational discrimination and equal protection of the law. In her speech at the convention, she called for "equal medical advantages" and no "*separate medical colleges.*" She further argued that mind, not sex, should determine abilities.[107] In 1847 Hunt had requested permission to attend lectures at the Harvard Medical College but was denied as a matter of "expediency." By 1851 she had begun a new campaign against "taxation without representation" and aimed her attack at the two high schools in Boston that only enrolled male students.[108] More than revolutionary rhetoric, the constitutional meaning of equal protection had expanded through legal disputes over equal taxation rights during the antebellum period. Taxation was one measure of the quid pro quo relationship between the state and the citizen.[109]

Hunt's protest revived the contradiction in civil status between single and married women. As a single woman, property owner, and self-supporting professional, Hunt embodied all the capacities for citizenship. In accord with the terms of the 1809 Supreme Court ruling, she had a will of her own. As a taxpayer Hunt contributed to the public weal and demonstrated her economic competence and independence. Hunt had no father, husband, or brother to act as her proxy at the polls, and she never consented to retreat from politics or transfer her allegiance to a husband or male head of household. At the same time, taxation without representation had a revolutionary appeal, highlighting how women were the functional equivalent of a colonized caste, as they had no voice in the government. At the Worcester convention Henry Van Amringe compared women's colonized condition to England legislating for Ireland, for a "class of people, cut off from the right of voting, cannot bring their grievances, with any effective power, before the public." In other words, in a colonial empire or a democracy, "no people can safely be permitted to legislate for another."[110]

Suffrage and the Right of Self-Protection

The Seneca Falls and Worcester conventions followed different but related approaches to women's entitlement. While New York reformers elevated the importance of natural law and inalienable rights, their Massachusetts colleagues placed greater emphasis on the constitutional principles of due process and equal protection. Such differences were subtle but crucial for how they defined the significance of suffrage. Seneca Falls activists, especially Stanton in her Declaration of Sentiments, attempted to test the universal quality of natural rights by claiming that in theory women had the same entitlements as men. If women were denied their natural rights, then they were fraudulently deprived of their national citizenship. Worcester reformers started from a different premise, that women's status gradually devolved into a disabled caste. For women to exercise their rights, they needed equal protection in the law and the ability to challenge their legal and social disabilities. The vote, then, served as a tool for empowering women as a class so that they could secure entitlements from the state.

By 1851 both strategies appeared side by side in the resolutions presented at the second national convention held in Worcester. In the opening resolution a stirring invocation to the Declaration of Independence of the United States linked natural rights to national citizenship. Through a reference to taxation without representation, the next resolution emphasized the "tyranny" of class legislation. The third resolution, then, combined the two theoretical approaches, calling for suffrage not to "protect woman, but rather to place her in a position to protect herself." Thus the vote was established as an individual weapon, by which self-protection allowed every woman to guard her natural and sacred rights as a constituent part of herself. Suffrage also empowered women as a class, allowing them, as the fourth resolution stated, to make all the "unequal laws, relating to marriage and property, speedily vanish from the statute-book."[111]

The theme of self-protection offered the truest expression of due process, capturing its fundamental premise that all citizens deserve the right to bring their cases before the public. In a legal sense a citizen had to be empowered to defend and to protect herself from a miscarriage of justice. Two conditions were necessary: individuals required legal standing so that the courts would recognize their claims, and they needed resources that neutralized the excessive authority of the state. Self-protection suggested that the same rules should hold true for gaining the vote, by granting all citizens a hearing before the public, acknowledging their political standing, and defending them against abuses of state power.

Self-protection used an adversarial model—the courtroom trial—which shifted the foundation for suffrage from a passive entitlement to a necessary civil right. The state no longer bestowed the vote on those deemed worthy of the privilege or title, but instead the state acknowledged that a quid pro quo relationship existed between itself and the governed. Rather than exchanging protection for allegiance, the new formula exchanged due process or justice for obedience to the laws. Added to this emphasis on due process, more-over, the relationship between citizens and the state came closer to Spooner's vision of a contractual model. While the protection/allegiance formula relied on a hierarchical relationship between ruler and ruled, the due process version treated the government and citizens as equal parties agreeing to an equitable exchange. By 1852 women's rights activists recognized the connection be-tween due process and rules of contract. At the national convention held that year in Syracuse, Elizabeth Cady Stanton, Clarina H. I. Nichols, and Eliza-beth Oakes Smith called for civil disobedience by advocating that women refuse to pay their taxes until they had equal rights and the vote.[112] Until representation accompanied taxation, women should refuse to obey the laws. Consequently, they argued, women should break the social contract until the state established a quid pro quo relationship with women that recognized their citizenship.

The exchange of obedience for equal treatment placed less emphasis on legal capacity and instead reestablished consent as the logic behind the right of suffrage. Women required the right to frame laws, and they could do so only if they were allowed to exercise their consent and dissent through vot-ing. Ultimately, as most feminists believed, consent had to be based on the "courthouse of conscience," in which women made decisions and were held accountable for their choices.[113] This religious model of standing informed how activists understood consent. In her speech before the West Chester women's rights convention in 1852, Quaker physician Ann Preston eloquently captured this perspective, stating that women, like men, were vested with the same responsibility for their actions: "In all life's great extremities she is thrown upon her inward resources, and stands alone. Men cannot step in between her and the 'accusing angel' of her conscience; alone in the solitude of her spirit she must wrestle with her own sorrows; 'none can walk for her the valley of the shadow of death!'"[114] If women could stand before the bar of justice at the final judgment and be treated as equals before God, then they deserved the same treatment under civil law. The protection of her sacred and inalienable rights rested upon every woman's ability to stand alone in the solitude of her spirit, as well as her political right to stand alone in the ballot box as a responsible and accountable citizen.

Self-protection, however, also returned to the material concern raised by Lydia Maria Child in her story "Home and Politics," because self-protection offered a solution to the problem of home protection. Alice White, as a single woman, made the transition from childhood to adulthood by pursuing her education and by achieving her independence as a schoolteacher. Child emphasized that the schoolhouse was White's "sanctuary," where she defined herself. Yet Child saw the contrast between Alice White and the married Alice Franklin, in which the single woman lacked the wealth to have a home of her own, and the married woman lacked the power to defend it. How could women secure a fair hearing before the public, especially when they remained voiceless spectators in the partisan system?[115] Alice Franklin's sense of alienation as she watched the election-day parade demonstrated in vivid terms what Van Amringe had claimed, that "no people can safely be permitted to legislate for another."[116] This notion of self-protection was not merely concerned with self-interest but stressed how the government's duty was equal protection. By failing to allow one class to bring its grievances before the public, the state fell short of protecting that class against its own authority. It tipped the scale of justice by enabling those with the vote to decide the fate of others who had no means of self-protection or self-defense.

Child demonstrated the practical relevance of suffrage for the average woman, but women's rights activists developed a profound theoretical strategy that worked irresistibly within the context of antebellum constitutionalism. Suffrage was not merely an individual right that viewed women as atomized individuals, each of whom determined her own fate unmediated by social or political conditions. The theme of self-protection recognized that women first had to acquire a relationship with the state, a quid pro quo relationship that acknowledged their civil standing in return for civil support. Protection required a constitutional relationship between citizens and the state, and self-protection made the vote one of the means for ensuring that women grasped and did not lose that relationship. Self-protection also redefined the meaning of the consenting community, in which both men and women as citizens assumed a more active role in defending and securing their own protection. As Caroline Dall eloquently argued at the 1855 women's rights convention held in Boston, the vote was not only an entitlement, but "we consider the ballot woman's sword and shield."[117]

3

Visual Politics

In 1840 the Reverend Charles Giles published *The Convention of Drunk-ards*, mocking the idea that all citizens could engage in public deliberation. With characters such as Mr. Harddrinker, Mr. Cogitator, Mr. Foolhardy, Mr. Imitator, Mr. Rumhead, and Esq. Loveliberty, this gathering of incompetents gave resonance to John Adams's nightmare of political conventions as mere entertainment and perhaps something worse—a farce. Calling themselves the "sons of freemen," this odd assortment of sots and freethinkers was determined to decide their fate regardless of the consequences. Acting in defense of their rights, convention members instead ensured their own political demise and self-destruction. Addressing the assembly, Mr. Harddrinker thus reasoned,

> 'Tis freemen's right, it is no treason:
> We love our drams more than our reason. . . .
> So drinking makes our nature better,
> Breaks every useless, moral fetter; . . .
> Its hidden virtue makes us stumble,
> And knocks us down to keep us humble;
> So, oft we've lain, to fate resigned,
> A meek example for mankind.[1]

The Convention of Drunkards raised several familiar themes about the nature of political man, as it ridiculed men's ability to rise above their nature and rule themselves. Above all, the drunkard had none of the qualities needed to gather in convention. He lacked reason and virtue, and his speech and presence were devoid of merit or public greatness. Civility and manhood were missing as well from this comical collection of boozers and buffoons. There was little chance of having intelligent discussion and debate without civility, and there was no manliness without self-mastery—the rational control required to make independent judgments. Symbolizing the inverse of self-mastery, the drunkard traded his freedom for an enslavement to appetite; his actions celebrated weakness rather than strength, and he forfeited political progress in exchange for complete inertia.[2] Hence, a convention of drunkards ironically portrayed a public assembly of citizens totally incapable of political action.

Women's rights activists inspired similar fears of social disorder. Political women defied the rules of civility by behaving like men in convention. In one of the few references to women in *The Convention of Drunkards*, the author decried the drinking of Mr. Hardcast's helpmeet as he emphasized the connection between sexual disorder and drunkenness. Giles's account of the intemperate wife was brief but revealing:

> My wife was once a modest lass,
> But now she leads a scorner's class;
> Her part she plays, like Fanny Wright,
> And in wild doctrines takes delight.[3]

Women who indulged in drink were promiscuous, shrewish, and tempted by the "wild doctrines" of sexual equality and free love. Instead of "angels of the home," female drunkards and feminist reformers were considered to be primitive and closer to animals on the political scale of creation, in which rational and sober men ranked the highest.

It is evident that self-mastery required control over one's body, a degree of physical discipline that was considered well beyond the reach of both drunkards and women. Rum made the body rather than the man a master, while sex—epitomized by pregnancy—held women under the sway of their reproductive organs. Classical political theorists compared a woman's body to a prison or a cage, a powerful allusion later used by antebellum physiologists to describe women's enslavement to the "womb."[4] In 1852 the *New York Herald* satirized the unpredictable nature of women's bodies. The author asked his readers to imagine what would happen if women's rights activists suddenly started giving birth in public:

> How funny it would sound in the newspaper, that Lucy Stone pleading
> a cause took suddenly ill in the pains of parturition and, perhaps gave

birth to a fine bouncing boy in court! Or that Rev. Antoinette Brown was arrested in the middle of her sermon in the pulpit from the same cause, and presented a "pledge" to her husband and the congregation; or, that Dr. Harriet K. Hunt, while attending a gentleman patient for a fit of gout or *fistula in ano*, found it necessary to send for a doctor, there and then, and to be delivered of a man or woman child—perhaps twins. A similar event might happen on the floor of Congress—in a storm at sea—or in a raging tempest of battle, and then what is to become of the woman legislator, the female captain of the ship, or the female general of the army. The bare idea is ludicrous beyond measure.[5]

According to this unflattering view, a woman's rational side always lost in the struggle to subdue her physical and sexual nature. One message seemed clear: a woman, despite the appearance of respectability, intelligence, or virtue, concealed a body that she could not master on her own.[6]

Antebellum politics remained grounded in the ideology of publicity or the public sphere. Publicity ensured that individuals had certain civil liberties, such as freedom of the press, opinion, and association, all of which facilitated open communication and political debate. Publicity also reinforced suffrage and other political rights, such as the right of petition, because the essence of publicity was the act of private citizens exercising their freedom of speech and assembly for the purpose of changing laws and government policy. By constituting a gathering of private citizens, the convention enshrined a more formalized version of the public sphere.

In *The Structural Transformation of the Public Sphere*, Jürgen Habermas has theorized that publicity in the age of Enlightenment rested upon a contradiction. Although premised on universal access, the public sphere limited participation to educated citizens deemed capable of understanding the "public good." Equality was possible only because participants shared a common moral and legal vision, which was derived from their class position as bourgeois property owners.[7] Early state constitutions made citizenship compatible with the public sphere through property qualifications for the vote. By the 1840s Americans understood the public sphere to be both more and less restrictive than citizenship. Satires about drunkards captured the tension between political rights and publicity. Drunkards were not denied the franchise, despite their lack of reason or moral commitment to the public good. Drinking and democracy went hand in hand in the nineteenth century, with votes regularly being sold for drams, taverns used as polls, and hard cider recognized as a campaign tool since the 1828 election of Andrew Jackson, if not before.[8]

By conjuring images of chaos and disorder resulting from the presence of public women, male writers branded them, like drunkards, as the most unlikely candidates for political leadership or professional office. Despite their disenfranchisement and restricted property rights, educated women were not excluded from the literary public sphere. Their ability to participate in the world of letters depended on their disembodiment, the appearance that their bodies remained separate from the realm of partisan politics. To the extent that women remained anonymous readers, or authors whose reasoned arguments appeared only in print, they could influence public debate. But publicly and politically active women symbolized a special danger, because through their physical presence what once was public degenerated into a form of private desire associated with the state of nature. Ostensibly, sheer animal instinct ruled rather than the calm, deliberate consensus meant to characterize the public sphere. Women introduced sexual desire and natural weakness into the public arena, thereby subverting the intellectual and emotional discipline needed for rational deliberation and political debate.

The conflict between publicity and private desire returned to the philosophical problem of what constituted "the good society." This question was more complicated than the notion of separate spheres, for there was no absolute or fixed boundary dividing the sexes into two domains definable as public and private. Habermas has argued that the bourgeois public sphere was dependent on the subjective identity of the individual formed inside the family. Publicity required a class awareness among private citizens who were educated property owners, because their status as bourgeois citizens provided the foundation for belief in a common human nature and the fiction of universal equality.[9] Additionally, while private desire had the potential to undermine the public good, the bourgeois public sphere could not exist without it. As Thomas Hobbes and John Locke had realized in the seventeenth century, "conjugal affections" were crucial to generating the need for the social compact as the foundation for the protection of private property, and this was still true in the nineteenth century. Ideally publicity tapped and tamed private desire, utilizing its positive attributes and controlling its worst excesses, which meant disciplining both men and women for the public good. Moral sentiment and benevolence, combined with the rules of civility and middle-class manners, contributed to a complicated code of conduct not only for women but for the eighteenth-century and nineteenth-century political man as well.

Publicity continued to define the realm of politics, although according to

Habermas, the bourgeois public sphere reached its peak in the eighteenth century and disappeared by the early nineteenth century. One cause for its demise was electoral reform, the elimination of property qualifications for the vote, which ushered in the shift from republicanism to democracy.[10] Despite this political transformation, publicity remained a viable force in society for at least two reasons. In the first place, the creation of public debate among educated private citizens still had a political function, and it assumed an important role in reform societies that relied on the press and public meetings. Second, the vocabulary of publicity continued to define the terms of political action, which explains why the convention became such a popular forum in the nineteenth century.

Publicity, Promiscuity, and the Problem of Private Desire

In 1850 the *Lily* published an extract from English intellectual Harriet Martineau's *Society in America*, which addressed whether publicity had changed in the early nineteenth century. Martineau observed how Thomas Jefferson had stressed that even in a "pure democracy" three groups would continue to be excluded from public deliberations: infants, slaves, and women. From his perspective, children lacked reason, slaves lacked property and will, and women lacked publicity. In Martineau's account Jefferson had contended that women, "to prevent depravation of morals, and ambiguity of issue [rampant sexual behavior leading to out-of-wedlock births], could not mix promiscuously in the public meetings of men." Martineau scoffed at Jefferson's view. His implication, she argued, was that men and women could not meet "for worship, for oratory, for music, for dramatic entertainments,—for any of the thousand transactions of civilized life!"[11]

Jefferson and Martineau defined publicity quite differently. Whereas Jefferson imagined the public sphere to be dangerously similar to the state of nature, Martineau saw publicity and political business to be part of civil society. For Jefferson, public women were often akin to prostitutes, intriguing women that lured men to indulge in moral dissipation and reckless passions.[12] From the eighteenth through the nineteenth centuries, public and promiscuous women were considered "loose," women who were too visible, coarse, and vulgar and disconnected from the protection of friends and family.[13] In Jefferson's mind, promiscuity also evoked the sordid image of men and women commingling in the streets, theaters, and taverns of Europe—public places where rules of decorum were not enforced.[14]

Rather than describe a division between public and private, Jefferson defined the public as part of the "world" that he contrasted with "society."

During the eighteenth century both middle-class and aristocratic citizens associated the world with the temptations of the flesh and sin. Full of strangers capable of deceit and seduction, the world was similar to the state of nature, where Man was prepolitical and presocial, gratifying sexual desires at will.[15] In comparison, society referred to "polite intercourse," which included friendly visits from social equals and letters of civility between social acquaintances. By encouraging exchanges of ideas over public concerns, men and women engaged in courteous and frank social intercourse on the basis of their shared class interest.[16] Yet men and women acquired different benefits in relation to one another from society; men developed reason and the ability to control their sexual desire, while women internalized a sense of modesty that allowed them to restrain yet not master their natural appetites. As Jean-Jacques Rousseau had theorized, the natural differences between the sexes, especially women's physical disabilities, reinforced women's greater need for the moral and legal protection of society. Women's physical weakness made them dependent on men, and men in turn protected women to make sure that their children were their own—or as Jefferson put it, that there would be no "ambiguity of issue."

The concern over publicity did not disappear during the antebellum period. In 1837 Angelina and Sarah Grimké toured New England as agents of the American Anti-Slavery Society. The General Association of Congregational Ministers of Massachusetts issued a pastoral letter rebuking them for lecturing before mixed and "promiscuous audiences." This reaction was not unusual. It was quite common for antislavery women to be libeled in the press, portrayed derisively as harlots, miscegenationists, or spinsters shamelessly shopping for husbands. During the 1838 Convention of American Women Against Slavery, the Philadelphia newspapers helped to incite a mob that disrupted the meeting and then destroyed Pennsylvania Hall by setting it on fire.[17] When the national women's rights convention was held in Philadelphia in 1854, the *Sunday Times* published an editorial that employed similar racial and sexual slurs. Female activists were described as consorting with "big burly negroes and negresses," and such open displays of female licentiousness were condemned for forcing the virtuous public to "gaze on their prostitution."[18] To critics women's unchecked freedom of assembly mocked all the restraints of civilized society.

Promiscuity rested on more than fears of sexual deviance. A larger concern was that society might condone the idea of women without men. The Massachusetts pastoral letter made this connection, linking women's unnatural behavior with their independence from men, declaring that "when woman assumes the place and tone of man as a public reformer, our care and protection of her seem unnecessary; we put ourselves in self-defense against her, and her character becomes unnatural."[19] Here the fear was that women might discover that they could survive without male protection. Granted too much liberty and left to their own devices, women might imitate men or, worse, ignore them.

Two caricatures of women underscored the fear of female independence. American political commentators borrowed the image of a corrupted European society, filled with fashionable ladies of the court, "blue stockings" of the salons, and whores abounding in every class, high or low. Political satires of the Enlightenment created a scandalous portrait of aristocratic women, attacking them as pompous, sexually promiscuous, and consumed with their own political power, which they wielded in the royal court and the salons. At the same time nineteenth-century America had inherited another image of women, one associated with deception or even witchcraft, that developed into the political symbol of a woman "passing" for a man. This elusive and hidden figure appeared at promiscuous gatherings, mixing inconspicuously with strangers—because here a woman could assume male form without detection. In spite of the powerful imagery that each evoked, these caricatures of women, distortions of publicity, represented two vastly different worldviews. The first arose from a fear of overexposure; the second, from a fear of concealment. The vanity of the aristocracy caused elite women to demand a threatening degree of exposure, assuming airs of social importance and intellectual superiority, thus turning all social or political events into public spectacles. In contrast, women dressing like men implied insufficient visibility, conjuring the possibility that any woman might assume a dangerous disguise and pass unnoticed through the streets and public haunts found in "the world."

Throughout the nineteenth century, spectacles and secret meetings symbolized dangers to democracy, often providing a convenient justification for mob violence. Newspapers, political parties, and mobs attacked Catholic priests in monasteries, and Anti-Masons hounded followers of fraternal organizations, after both were accused of engaging in secret, even sexual, rituals behind closed doors. In 1850 a writer for the prominent *New York Globe* echoed these sentiments, arguing that the people had the right to protect themselves against a public meeting of abolitionists, described as a "gang of traitors."[20] To rationalize mob violence, the *Globe* editorial argued that the common law authorized the principle of "self-preservation" against political and social conspiracies. The community had the right to take the law into its own hands and to suppress the actions of anyone who threatened the natural or organic law of society. The private act of self-defense was used to legitimize a collective act of self-preservation.[21] Significantly, the Massachusetts pastoral letter relied on the same theory, contending that unnatural displays by a woman forced men to collectively "put themselves in self-defense against her." By claiming to restrain what was unnatural, the community could subdue traitors pretending to be patriots, infidels disguised as moral citizens, and women assuming the autonomy of men.

The satirical portrait of pregnant professionals in the *New York Herald* drew on this tension between exposure and concealment. Although a woman might attempt to be a professional or a politician, inevitably her body would reveal the deception. A woman could not transcend her sexuality; at best, as Rousseau had contended, through fashioning a modest and feminine demeanor a woman could cultivate but never conceal her female nature. Inculcating modesty in women also protected men. It guarded young and old men alike from the intrigues of dangerous women, who might succeed in seducing, manipulating, or fooling them through clever disguises. Occasionally a woman might pass for a man, and one example served as proof for the generalization. In 1853 a woman dressed in male attire voted in an election in Cincinnati, Ohio, only to be sentenced to twenty days in jail for the crime of impersonating a man—in essence pretending to be a citizen.[22]

DRESS REFORM AND DECEPTION IN THE PUBLIC SPHERE

In 1850 the feminist journalist Jane Swisshelm wrote a scathing satire on "women's dresses." With excessive padding added to the backs of dresses, the latest fashion, "the bishop," transformed women into "dromedaries" with humps on their backs. Swisshelm mocked the style for forcing women to "wriggle" as they walked, likening them to a "parcel of eels" or a "ship with all her sails and no rudders." By making "normal" attire appear ridiculous, Swisshelm emphasized, fashion turned women into a public sideshow. She proposed a simple reform: women should begin to dress like "responsible beings," wearing simple, comfortable, healthy, and practical clothing. Repeating the Enlightenment's critique of aristocratic women, Swisshelm, like other dress reformers, believed fashion made women into ludicrous spectacles.[23]

Dress reform captured the attention of feminists in 1849 when the *Lily* published an article on the "up roar over the male attire of Fanny Kemble."[24] During the next two years the "new costume," an outfit comprising a Turkish tunic and trousers, gained the avid support of Amelia Bloomer, Elizabeth Smith Miller, and Elizabeth Cady Stanton. While Miller developed the initial design for the short dress, Bloomer's name became publicly identified with the new costume.[25] In her first endorsement of "our costume," Stanton also echoed the enlightened theme that fashion thwarted women's ability to "be honest and virtuous, to lead simple, pure, and holy lives."[26]

Stanton saw dress reform as one avenue for replacing feminine modesty with virtue. Two issues prevailed: first, that modesty exaggerated women's dependence on their sexual attraction, and second, that women's fashion placed them constantly under the "watch tower" of public opinion.[27] The act of dressing to please men or to copy another woman, as health reformer Mary Gove Nichols argued, stood in stark contrast to virtue and moral accountability.[28] The danger of fashion was the weakness instilled through imitation and the physical dependence on luxuries that made women prone to sins of the flesh. Fashion stifled self-mastery; it forced a woman to cultivate a contrived appearance, which reflected the whims of society rather a will of her own. Feminine fashion was a disguise par excellence, pure surface without substance, which concealed any natural traces of a real identity.

This critique of fashion was double edged. Rousseau and other enlightened thinkers had ridiculed fashion for promoting a world of false appearances in which only surfaces mattered. Yet the enlightened alternative of feminine modesty had merely replaced one disguise with another. The only difference was that modesty went beyond the external image of women, demanding that middle-class women fashion both their appearances and inner selves. Rousseau had made it clear that women still depended on the "good opinion" of others and that modesty projected a carefully designed demeanor that had the appearance of being "natural."[29] Women's rights advocates, by using the term "new costume," recognized that clothing conveyed a staged presentation of the self. Women, they said, had to reject the artificiality of fashion and the equally debilitating illusion that modesty was a truer expression of the natural feminine self. Was human nature, then, paradoxically, a disguise?

Antebellum feminists, influenced by Romanticism and Transcendentalism, acquired a very different understanding of humanity's relation to nature. In place of a domesticated nature, which Rousseau imagined best resembled a garden, activists looked to the sky, mountains, and forests—the constantly evolving, ever spontaneously changing habitat of the physical world.[30] Nature was as vast and unfettered as the unbounded starlit universe. This shift in perspective went hand in hand with the democratic rejection of enclosed spaces. Rather than accepting a pastoral re-creation of nature, feminists assumed that there should be a direct correspondence between nature and all human representations of it.[31] The body, moreover, could be an enclosed and artificially cultivated space. Women's dresses, fitted with corsets, decorated with padding, and weighted down by layers of petticoats, constrained and constricted the human body. Nature should celebrate natural movement, and beauty should correspond to the actual shape, dimensions, and physical properties of the female body. At an 1851 "Bloomer Costume Meeting," Abby Price applied this theory to women's dress, arguing that popular fashions enveloped women in "useless drapery," while the bloomer outfit was "better adapted to human form."[32]

Behind this conception of nature was a new aesthetic: the purpose was to transform how men and women perceived beauty, especially the connection between visual pleasure and desire. The Enlightenment had discovered beauty and virtue through two kinds of visual experiences. "Taste" could be developed in the intimate interiors of the home and garden, or it could be enhanced by an appreciation for the "wonders of nature" through visual displays in museums, books, and paintings.[33] On the other hand, nature could afford sublime vistas, yet true beauty was rendered more nearly perfect when represented through painting or gazed upon from a safe distance as in a landscape, in which nature reflected harmony, tranquility, and a peaceful order of things in the world. According to this enlightened aesthetics, pleasure came from control, the ability to regulate the senses and subdue sensual desires. The same visual rules were applied to women's dress and feminine modesty. The nineteenth-century ideal of placing a woman on a pedestal implied turning a woman into a statue, elevating her beauty but keeping it at a safe distance, and cultivating the proper visual pleasure from viewing her. Feminine modesty adhered to similar expectations. A woman was encouraged to display a demure countenance and to refine and restrain the movement of her body; she was advised to inspire men's admiration but to discourage their lust to see what was hidden behind the layers of drapery.

Fashion, even modest female attire, did not eliminate male sexual desire. Women, as Rousseau believed, had to attract men's attention, fix their desires, and encourage their affections. The tension between concealing and revealing women's sexuality through fashion continued into the nineteenth century. Because it exposed women's ankles to public view, the bloomer costume was attacked in the press for being vulgar and indecent. Acknowledging the hypocrisy, dress reformers noted that the concern for women's ankles did not apply to their arms and bosom, for both were exposed to view in the latest fashion.[34] A correspondent in the *Water-Cure Journal* captured the contradiction, demonstrating how arbitrarily the rules of female modesty were enforced. Ultimately, whatever fashion was considered normal was then treated as natural and modest, as she explained: "I might walk the streets unmolested, with my waist laced to one half its natural dimensions, and my skirt sweeping the pavement every step, and should I appear with a dress but four or five inches shorter than usual, the voice of insult and scorn would attend me, as though my dress were a badge of disgrace, or the State prison uniform."[35] The emblematic quality of women's dress for symbolizing what was natural was far more important than actually allowing women to wear practical clothing.

Practical and sensible dress had another connotation for antebellum Americans. It harkened back to the rhetoric of the revolution, which praised American simplicity as a manner superior to European decadence. Versed in the austere ways of republican virtue, women had made material sacrifices, had worn homespun cloth, and had not idly stood by when needed for the patriotic cause. In 1851 the Lowell Bloomer Institute echoed these sentiments, pledging to secure independence from tyranny and avoid enslavement to "Dame Fashion."[36] Stanton agreed, observing that to be tied down by corsets or drapery, "one might as well work with a ball and chain."[37] Her complaint was not exaggerated. A dress could weigh as much as fifteen pounds, and tight lacing and heavy petticoats seriously inhibited a woman's movement.[38] Stanton believed that "for us, common place, every day, working characters, who wash and iron, bake and draw, carry water and fat babies up stairs and down, bring potatoes, apples, and pans of milk from the cellar, run our errands, through mud and snow," the pristine image of womanhood enshrined on a pedestal was a far cry from the reality of most women's lives.[39]

Stanton assumed that a woman's virtue was not corrupted through action but by the lack of exposure to danger and responsibility. By her definition virtue implied self-mastery, which was contrary to the socially imposed regime of feminine modesty and fashion. In 1853 she extended this theme to its logical conclusion, suggesting that women must not only appear more natural in their movements and dress but should be capable of taking "a solitary ramble in communion with great Nature and her God." Two tasks awaited women, according to Stanton: they should "enjoy the majestic forest and sunny dale, the glorious sunrise from some mountain top," and they must also venture into the streets.[40] Here, again, Stanton appropriated the rapturous language of the sublime, the sense of awe and transcendence, which came from confronting nature. Philosophers such as Edmund Burke had discovered the sublime and the beautiful in the natural landscape, and politicians such as John Adams had used nature, portrayed as a mountain, to symbolize civic virtue.[41] Unlike her predecessors Stanton did not identify sloth with the female body as found in nature, as Adams did in his proposal for the design of the Great Seal of the United States. Instead, if women were passive, imbued with physical and spiritual torpor, then the source of their enthrallment was society.

By changing the meaning of nature, feminists found themselves questioning the false division between society and the world. The eighteenth-century understanding of the world saw the streets as an environment filled with unsavory characters, including prostitutes, class pretenders, paupers, and working-class women and children. Antebellum America did not dramatically alter this portrait of urban culture, still concerned with confidence men, painted ladies, street urchins, and the disorderly activities of working-class women.[42] The Enlightenment's glorification of rural society simply ignored the existence of laboring men and women by generating pastoral images of landscapes devoid of people, except an occasional shepherdess or country squire.[43] If fashion represented the corruption of aristocratic women, then laboring bodies stood at the other extreme. Working women symbolized the curse of women without rank driven by necessity and the base instinct to survive, while reproductive labor continued to be associated with the curse of God that women must suffer during childbirth.[44]

The divine prescription of pain and penance carried little sway with antebellum activists, because "the pursuit of happiness" implied rights to physical health and freedom. Feminist and health reformers alike called for women to exercise, to gain medical knowledge about female physiology, and to imagine that women's bodies were capable of hiking through the forests and hills and walking down any city street without a male escort. In her lecture to young girls, Stanton challenged them to try an experiment: walk alone in Seneca Falls, and if you are harassed, probably by a drunk, then rise above the fear and run. Women, she believed, were generally more fleet of foot than the average man.[45] The Bloomer costume made women more mobile. Shortening dresses, eliminating petticoats, and wearing Turkish pants allowed women to walk with greater ease, to traverse the streets without collecting mud or dirt on their skirts, and to run, ride, or scale mountains.

Neither the streets nor the world were places that women could avoid, despite the paternalism inherent in the prescription for feminine modesty. In her lecture on women's dresses, Mary Gove Nichols noted how ridiculous it was to equate modesty with helplessness when widows, working-class wives, seamstresses, and teachers had to fend for themselves in the world.[46] Harriet Torrey offered a similar portrait of women's work on the farm, highlighting the contradiction between female labor and "modest" fashion: "Aside from their excessive labors, they do not take half care of themselves; neither do they dress with any regard for health, comfort, or convenience. Encased in tight bodices, and encumbered by a good many pounds of draggling skirts, they waddle through door-yards and barn-yards, accumulating dirt, and planting the seeds of disease in a most luxuriant soil."[47] Modesty and labor were at odds, as Abby Price observed, since the drapery of women's dress required "two hands," implying that modest women never had any real labor to perform other than lifting their skirts.[48]

Bloomers were intended to alter the perceptions of the viewer and the viewed. The new costume challenged the symbolic language of dress that identified men with active, aggressive, independent behavior, and it thwarted the desire to see women as soft, weak, frivolous, and stationary. Of course, critics attacked the Bloomer outfit for such sexual transgressions. Political cartoons depicted feminists in bloomers as a promiscuous breed, appearing as cross-dressing hags and men in drag, wearing a mismatched and tasteless attire of plaids and dots, and standing or sitting in graceless and unladylike postures.[49] Newspapers, such as the *Arkansas Intelligencer*, portrayed women as dangerously mobile: a "committee of twenty-four women, dressed in bloomers, mounted on horseback like gentlemen, with a omnibus driven by a woman, met Mrs. Bloomer in the environs of Worcester, and escorted her to the 'Woman's Rights Convention.'"[50] The reception and ridicule of the Bloomer costume was played out in the streets. Women's rights activists found that children followed, harassed, and insulted them when they attempted to wear the Bloomer costume outside their homes. Martha Wright recounted a story in which several activists in Philadelphia were pursued by children calling out, "Shanghai, Shanghai," comparing them in this way to exotic women of the Orient.[51] Far more telling were the "Bloomer balls" held in 1851, where women were dared to attend in their reform costume, and the staged burlesques in Boston, where prostitutes, dressed in bloomers, paraded in the streets.[52]

Not so surprisingly, the Bloomer also emerged in the popular press as a fad rather than a revolutionary change in women's public image.[53] Even more positive descriptions of the new costume, such as the account of Amelia Bloomer and Susan B. Anthony at the temperance convention in New York City in 1853, as reported by the *New York Tribune*, inevitably sounded like excerpts on the latest fashions from the society page. Every tasteful detail of Bloomer's outfit was described, from the black velvet trimming on her skirt and pantaloons to her flowing sleeves, diamond stud on her chemisette, and black lace mitts. Anthony's plainer attire of black brocade silk with white collar and cuffs gained equal attention.[54] While some feminists believed that any defense of the Bloomer outfit as elegant and tasteful protected them against charges of mannish imitation, such language in effect resorted to the use of taste as an alternative to feminine modesty. Many activists refused to adopt the costume, and their own aesthetic judgment demonstrated that they still clung to some idealized view of feminine beauty. In 1854 Martha Wright confided in a letter to her sister Lucretia Mott that Susan B. Anthony should "leave off the Bloomer," since Anthony was the "least graceful of anyone who adopted the dress."[55]

The Bloomer costume began to fall out of favor by 1855. Stanton, Anthony, and Lucy Stone decided that they had endured their martyrdom in the press long enough. Stanton's well-known cousin, Gerrit Smith, who was also the father of Bloomer advocate Elizabeth Miller, publicly criticized the movement's loss of commitment. Stanton and Smith engaged in a debate waged in print, publishing their exchange of letters in the newspapers and circulating both as broadsides in 1855. Stanton defended dress reform, but she rejected partial solutions like the Bloomer costume, arguing that for women to have complete liberty, they must adopt male attire. This position was not entirely original. As early as 1851 Paulina Wright Davis included in the published proceedings of the Worcester convention a letter from H. M. Weber, a French woman, who had adopted male apparel not to be "eccentric" or to "pass for one of the male sex," but mainly as a "convenience to her business." Stanton cleverly praised George Sand, whose disguise as a man permitted her to speak at political meetings, travel by land or sea, walk through the streets by night and day, and earn more money as a teacher than the average woman. Freedom had less to do with liberation from useless drapery or corsets, Stanton decisively argued, and more to do with the social rights granted to any person in male attire. Gerrit Smith agreed, and he emphasized that changing woman's dress would transmute her in the eyes of men and prepare her for the "battle of life." The strained arguments for gender difference would lose their political foundation when deprived of the visual reminder of how fashion separated the sexes.[56]

The Bloomer costume disappeared as a prominent issue of the campaign, but the women's rights movement remained divided over the best strategy for dealing with modesty and publicity. During the same period that activists donned their Bloomers, a related dispute developed around the appropriate outfit for feminists to wear as public representatives of the movement. In 1852, at the national women's rights convention held in Syracuse, Elizabeth Oakes Smith provoked a minor furor among some supporters. Her choice of dress was considered far too sexually revealing for a mature woman. Susan B. Anthony lobbied against her appointment as president of the Syracuse convention, and in 1855, at the women's rights convention held in Boston, Anthony again privately chastised Smith for making a spectacle of herself.[57] Clearly, women's rights activists became increasingly aware of the image they wanted to project to the public. As they retreated from the Bloomer costume and continued to find disfavor with Smith's apparel, they signaled their desire to direct the media away from their physical bodies and toward something less visual—the message inherent in their words.

Social Circles and Women's Place in the Literary Public Sphere

That Stanton and Smith decided to close the debate on dress reform (which they chose to conduct in print and not in person) revealed their awareness that publicity was shaped by its medium. The bourgeois public sphere imagined by enlightened thinkers glorified the reading public and considered that public far superior to those who privileged oral culture; in the former, educated citizens were guided by reason to the acts of writing and publishing. This community of readers, often personally unknown to one another, created the foundation for an imagined national identity generated through newspapers, pamphlets, tracts, published letters, magazines, and novels. Less clear was the precise place women occupied in this general readership and the impact their literary engagement had on changing their political identity.[58]

Unlike Jefferson's division between the world and society, the literary public sphere elevated print communication over ordinary conversations. The bourgeois public sphere made possible the proliferation of print communities, literary coteries, and reform societies, which defined their membership and boundaries primarily through the exchange of letters and a shared readership of published writings. Although dress reform carried its battle to the streets and to conventions in addition to print media, the public discourse of dress reform remained focused on the tension between exposure and concealment, between natural and unnatural behavior, and between modesty and promiscuity. Essentially, the struggle over female fashion centered on the dangerous effect of women's bodies on civil society and bourgeois publicity. In contrast, the literary public sphere highlighted the positive features of social circles and the national value and necessity of generating women's associations, social networks, and sympathetic bonds through a print culture. But the literary public sphere was hardly gender neutral, given that women could engage in political debate in print but were restricted or criticized for discussing the same political issues in public forums. The bourgeois public sphere brought out certain contradictions: between rational discussion in print and formal deliberation, between print culture and political culture, and between women's participation in the domain of letters and their exclusion from the male world of politics.

Horace Greeley, editor of the *New York Tribune* and a women's rights supporter, agreed that reading and especially writing had a direct impact on women's new political consciousness. "Woman has grasped the pen," he wrote in 1848, and "few would now seriously deny that man has been instructed and the world improved by her writings." On a deeper level of consciousness Greeley asserted that knowledge existed only through written language, postulating that "first to Write, then to Think, seems to be the natural order." Such speculative knowledge sparked women to ponder the vital questions, as posed by Greeley, that made their participation in the literary public sphere possible: "'What am I? What are my relations to others? Are they entirely just? Do they afford scope for all the good of which my nature is capable?'"[59] For Greeley, like other proponents of the bourgeois public sphere, the shift from observation to interpretation gave way to self-knowledge. To know oneself was the first step away from petty "female" complaints and toward the comprehensive understanding needed to recognize the universal concerns of justice and human nature.[60]

Publishing his article one month before the Seneca Falls convention, Greeley had in mind Margaret Fuller as the best example of an American woman of letters. Indeed, he not only quoted Fuller's writing verbatim, but he sponsored her career as a public intellectual by encouraging her to move to New York City from Boston and to write social commentary on the mores and manners of American society for the *Tribune* from 1844 to 1846. Later, from 1846 until her death in 1850, she served as a foreign correspondent in Europe, expanding her role as a public critic to encompass international issues such as the revolution in Italy. Called the "American Corinne" after the Greek lyric poet, and a great admirer of French writer Madame de Staël, Fuller planted herself firmly within the enlightened tradition of letters.[61]

Fuller's success as a woman of letters reflected in part her failure as a poet. Among Boston Transcendentalists or the New York literati, Fuller never received praise for her poetry, which held the contemporary distinction as the only genre for the expression of true genius. Yet she did make a mark through criticism, especially her book reviews, which Fuller viewed as an important and, at times, a higher art that demanded a discriminating intellect and a comprehensive knowledge of the world.[62] When serving as editor of the *Dial*, she considered her reviews a means of widening the range of reading material put before the American public. She also challenged the practice of reading literature didactically, contending that literature should be evaluated for its intellectual rather than its moral content.[63] Her famous "conversations" directed toward women in Boston used a similar method for developing critical reasoning. As Fuller remarked in the first of these salonesque conversations, her duty was "not to teach" but to "provoke the thought of others," which returned to the model of the eighteenth-century salons. She clearly rejected the female tradition of ornamental education, of dressing women's minds in fancy phrases as if adorning them in the latest fashions. Fuller contended that women learned without any attempt to "reproduce" their knowledge, developing little mastery or intellectual creativity, while men, at a very early age, were called upon to use what they had learned.[64]

Given her career in letters and her educational philosophy, Fuller bridged the eighteenth and nineteenth centuries in her understanding of a reading public as well as in her view of criticism. Literature for her was not a source of entertainment but an essential tool for training the reading public to develop more discriminating minds. In an 1840 letter to William Henry Channing, Fuller criticized the "superficial diffusion of knowledge" in America, arguing that although the multitude believe "themselves capable of judging what they but dimly discern," they in fact "see a wide surface, and forget the difference between seeing and knowing."[65] She had little respect for the "ladies magazines," and she shared Greeley's assessment that this kind of public writing offered little more than "amusement, fancy, sentiment, flattery, fashion."[66] Her critique of display as the fundamental flaw of women's education paralleled the dress reformers' disdain for fashionable surfaces and female modesty. Fuller dismissed this feminized style of learning, arguing that women, like men, needed to envelop their minds in critical thought.

Despite her unique emphasis and public reputation, Fuller could not escape that she was just one woman among the literati. How, then, did she compare to her male peers—what another publicist and women's rights supporter called "Our Public Men"? In 1843 John Neal published an editorial assessing whether Edward Everett met the standards of "great men," and here he identified five fields of public accomplishment: preacher, scholar, writer, orator, and statesman.[67] Fuller matched Everett's career; she had served as a teacher instead of a preacher, a writer and an editor, a powerful speaker in the salon tradition, and a "citizen of the world" as a foreign correspondent. But her contemporaries did not equate her with an Everett. Although women could inscribe a public figure in print and generate public opinion about political issues, they were not to engage in the open, visible, decidedly more exposed domain of public speaking. Teaching in a private school did not possess the same public meaning as preaching in a church, and speaking in a salon held in a private home was vastly different from giving a speech in the halls of Congress. Fuller's career revealed that public speaking and writing were not comparable as forms of publicity, illustrating the gendered distinction between the mastery of letters and the forensic art of political oratory.

Fuller's career represented a much larger trend toward adapting the republic of letters to the democratic political culture of the nineteenth century. An idealized image of women's place in the bourgeois public sphere was refashioned for its democratic audience. In 1839 the *United States Magazine and Democratic Review* published a review of Elizabeth Sedgwick's *Means and Ends, or Self-Training*, using the book as a platform to discuss the public role of American women. The reviewer explained that women deserved a practical education and legal reforms, especially in the area of property rights, but this critic drew the line when it came to granting women the franchise or the right to full political participation. Soon, the reviewer predicted, the enlightened "sense of justice and affection from fathers, husbands, sons and brothers" would result in legislation in favor of the rights of women. Through the "perpetual war" against injustice in print, persuasion rather than political participation was the key to women's progress. According to this representative piece, women could change the opinions of men, but they could do so more effectively in print and in person than as politicians or voters.[68]

Considerations of class and gender informed this democratic variation of the bourgeois public sphere. The reviewer returned to the same concerns raised in the eighteenth century, contending that women either fell prey to the "pseudo-aristocratic" habits of luxury and fashion, or they were educated to resist the "imaginary classification" of rank and urban gentility. While Americans did not inherit their class positions, the commentator enlarged, it was the credit system that in fact represented the source for the "rapid accumulation of imaginary fortunes." In such an atmosphere, fashionable women promoted the "deceptive appearances" of class distinctions. They bore responsibility for "pseudo-aristocratic" habits that generated an antidemocratic spirit among women and "exerted a powerful influence over the opinions and character of men."[69] Consequently, political equality rested on the inclusion of women in the bourgeois public sphere, because, this reviewer claimed, women's more active involvement would temper their lust for luxuries and channel their energies toward more profitable projects for the public good.

Women could only find a place in the public sphere in an environment that fostered civilized gatherings of the two sexes. To conceive of this political possibility, the reviewer devised another clever adaptation of an eighteenth-century model of virtuous citizenry for antebellum America. The democratic equivalent of the pastoral environment had become an idealized version of public life in a typical New England community. In this region education did not place everyone on the "same level" but at least "within the same orbit of social life." The exclusiveness of class distinctions gave way to "social circles" based on the "spontaneous action of natural affinities." In such circles, moreover, "all select their intimate associations according to respective tastes and inclinations; meeting together, however, occasionally, in general and promiscuous assemblages on a footing of entire equality and ease."[70] Education and taste could bind readers as well as residents who shared common interests, and courteous and frank exchanges allowed men and women to engage in social intercourse in the public sphere.

BENEVOLENCE AND THE BOURGEOIS
PUBLIC SPHERE

The bourgeois public sphere had its place in the ideological landscape of antebellum democracy. Early nineteenth-century women used the spontaneous action of natural affinities to organize Sabbath schools, orphan asylums, charitable and cent societies, maternal associations, and female missionary societies in cities and towns across the United States. As several women's historians have demonstrated, most early benevolent societies relied on social networks in which members shared not only the same tastes and inclinations but similar class and religious backgrounds. Members of benevolent societies relied on intimate associations to form contacts with elected officials, which suggested that their social circles gave them access to the government.[71]

By incorporating, benevolent societies also expanded women's ability to exercise certain legal rights, allowing them to own and manage property, to make legally binding contracts, and to control their finances. In essence, the benevolent society constituted a private association of educated citizens who shared common public interests. Such societies permitted married women to meet the requirement of the bourgeois public sphere as property owners. Finally, almost all of these societies engaged in the domain of letters by publishing their constitutions, reports of meetings, and circulars in an attempt to persuade the educated public to donate funds and to support their efforts. In conclusion, the benevolent society was called a society because women served "the interests of civil society."[72]

Female antislavery societies were not a radical departure from this reform tradition. As the 1833 constitution of the Philadelphia Female Anti-Slavery Society stated, the purpose of the society was to "collect and disseminate correct information" about slavery, and "any female uniting in these views" could become a member.[73] Also in Philadelphia, supporters established a school for black children, and in Massachusetts the Quaker feminist Sarah Earle founded the Worcester Anti-Slavery Cent-a-Week Society, both of which were no more radical than earlier benevolent organizations.[74] Antislavery activists also pursued their public purposes through fairs and bazaars held in Boston, Philadelphia, New York, Providence, and Worcester from 1834 to 1861. Crucial in raising financial support for the movement, these fairs subsidized both regional and national antislavery societies, which in turn channeled their proceeds into agents' salaries and publications. Most of the fairs sold locally produced "fancy goods," and the demand for needlework led women to form sewing circles that met on a weekly basis. All of the fairs sold "gift books" and antislavery literature, and the Boston and Philadelphia fairs in particular displayed printing presses, serving to highlight their place in the literary public sphere.[75]

Antislavery fairs were appealing because women could reach the public through "the silent, unobtrusive, and extensive dissemination of antislavery truth."[76] The fairs allowed women to preserve women's demeanor of respectability and modesty within the context of bourgeois publicity. Mary Grew, for example, praised the Philadelphia fairs for the "moral effect on the community" that resulted from the organizers' efforts to conduct them in accordance with "correct taste."[77] At the same time the fairs tapped into the symbolic meaning associated with women sewing for their political principles. Indeed, the local production of fancy goods demonstrated a commitment to a moral economy that eschewed all the extravagant habits of fashion and luxury.[78]

Antislavery societies were united through a literary public sphere. The Philadelphia Female Anti-Slavery Society devoted most of its revenues to purchasing multiple subscriptions to antislavery journals and to keeping afloat the financially troubled *Pennsylvania Freeman*. They also elected a librarian to manage their small but growing collection of antislavery books and pamphlets.[79] Reading and writing for the same publications created meaningful bonds among women of different regions. Equally important, the antislavery movement depended on writers and lecturers, such as the Grimké sisters of Charleston, South Carolina, to narrate their firsthand observations of slavery in action. Devoted to old and new methods of communication, antislavery supporters promoted language reforms such as phonography (an early form of phonetic spelling and writing intended for use in educating blacks), and they used visual images quite effectively to simultaneously educate and inspire "heart-felt" responses from their audience.[80] This strategy explained why southern defenders of their "peculiar institution" did everything possible to censor and curtail the spread of abolitionist materials through the mails. Astutely aware of the power of print, female antislavery activists developed a literary and iconographic genre about the female slave that was directed toward a female readership. Even at the fairs known for the "unobtrusive" dissemination of literature, supporters sold medallions and drawings of a female slave in chains, kneeling, praying, and pleading for redress, thus encoding their trademark public symbol of the "oppressed and downtrodden."[81]

Antislavery activists shared different conceptions of women's proper place in the bourgeois public sphere. Having an unobtrusive presence and meeting in circles and fairs, female reformers could adhere to the rules of social decorum and feminine modesty. Speaking at public lectures and acting as elected agents, however, extracted women from their social circles and placed them before the public eye in a different way. Open lectures that included men and women gathered an audience of spectators who were not necessarily intimate associates, nor did they all share the same class background. Public assemblies extended beyond the safe boundaries of social circles. Female lecturers had to engage in verbal exchanges with the masses, people from the streets, in which courteous discussion easily digressed into a barrage of insults, coarse language, violent fights, and even riots.

In 1840 the issue of women's public presence in the movement divided the American Anti-Slavery Society into two factions. The catalyst for the dispute was the appointment of Abby Kelley to the Business Committee of the American Anti-Slavery Society. Kelley became a controversial figure, not because she was a woman, but because she failed to meet the gendered expectations of bourgeois publicity. Her style of self-presentation sharply contrasted with that of two of her peers, Angelina Grimké and Lucretia Mott. Always introduced as a native of Charleston, South Carolina, Angelina Grimké had an appeal that rested on her reputation as a woman from a wealthy and respectable slaveholding family. Mott's background offered a northern version of Quaker respectability, because she had received her education from one of the finest Friends' schools, and her husband, James Mott, was a wealthy manufacturer in Philadelphia. In contrast, Kelley's family came from Irish Quaker stock, and her father had suffered financial setbacks that had forced Kelley at an early age to support herself by teaching. Kelley's husband, Stephen Foster, whom she married in 1845, came from a large farming family in New Hampshire, and he offered little promise of wealth or status.[82] Before her marriage Kelley refused payment for her services, and she lived on donations and a meager income derived from the sale of her family's land.[83] In a letter to the Grimké sisters in 1838, Kelley expressed her class awareness and observed how it affected her prospects as a lecturer: "I have nothing to start upon, nothing to commend me to the notice or favor of any, no name, no reputation, no scrip, neither money in my purse."[84] Kelley fashioned a public image of herself as a modern Christian martyr, following an ascetic lifestyle by wandering the countryside as a prophet of truth. At the 1851 women's rights convention she described how her "bloody feet" had worn the path clear for her sisters.[85]

Class differences among these women emerged through their speaking and literary styles. Angelina Grimké's lectures followed the tradition of letters, evidenced by her three most famous publications, *Appeal to the Christian Women of the South*, *Appeal to the Women of the Nominally Free States*, and *Letters to Catharine E. Beecher in Reply to an Essay on Slavery and Abolitionism Addressed to A. E. Grimké*. Addressing women and relying on carefully crafted biblical and historical arguments, she modeled and mastered the style of the essayist. Mott had a somewhat different relationship to writing; she was extremely well read and maintained an extensive personal correspondence, but she gave her lectures extemporaneously, following the Friends' tradition that rejected the clerical practice of reading written sermons. Several of Mott's speeches were published, but they were recorded and transcribed from her public addresses, demonstrating that she did not write and publish polished essays.[86] Kelley never published her lectures, except as part of the proceedings of antislavery meetings and conventions. Yet her career began in the world of letters; she served as the corresponding secretary of the Lynn Female Anti-Slavery Society, for which she drafted the yearly reports.[87]

Kelley and Mott had different approaches to public address. A letter from Martha Wright to her sister Lucretia Mott in 1852 underscored their contrasting styles of self-presentation. Kelley used confrontation. She pricked the consciences of her audience, harshly criticizing and rebuking their sins.[88] Kelley believed she was far more effective in gaining converts than Mott, and she described Mott's style as "the gentle zephyr, or the small summer rain," while her own impact as a speaker could be compared to "the rushing torrent and the wild Tornado." "People would listen with pleasure to the gentle words and go and forget them," Kelley remarked, but her viscerally charged language made a "great impression," even when she made "the hearers angry."[89]

Wright presented a contrary perspective. Kelley, she confided, displayed a "coarseness which is revolting to my taste. . . . While I didn't care how severely she rebuked the pious indifference of our people, I thought less swearing at them would be better, that it was not well for the children to listen to such words."[90] Rather than perceiving Kelley as having the effect of a "wild Tornado," Wright ridiculed Kelley's speaking style, classifying her expletives as a sign of poor taste and condemning her harangues of the audience as vulgar, coarse, and offensive expression. If she affronted the sensibilities of her middle-class audiences, Kelley defended such aggressiveness. She saw herself to be unmasking the falseness of bourgeois publicity, exposing the superficial concern for taste over truth.

The infamous London antislavery convention of 1840, in which all the female delegates were refused official recognition, continued the controversy on an international stage. Significantly, Abby Kelley was *not* selected to be part of the American contingent. Instead, the American women came entirely from respectable, affluent Quaker families. William Lloyd Garrison foresaw a fight over the female delegates and supported women who met the standards of bourgeois respectability.[91] In the *History of Woman Suffrage*, Stanton recalled these sentiments by describing the women from Philadelphia as dressed in "modest Quaker costume" and the Boston female delegates as "women of refinement and education."[92]

Considered the leader of the delegation, Mott had acquired a reputation among antislavery activists as a woman who spoke "modestly, in such sweet tones" and had a countenance that was "not only interesting, but exceedingly lovely." When she spoke at the 1833 convention that formed the American Anti-Slavery Society, one male observer noted that her remarks were so pleasing that they failed to offend, and that the chair encouraged her to express her opinions, despite the fact that she was only a spectator.[93] Mott and the other women delegates sent to the 1840 convention also bridged the two traditions in the movement; they all belonged to either the Philadelphia or the Boston Female Anti-Slavery Society as well as their respective state societies in Pennsylvania and Massachusetts. All of these women had achieved positions of influence, even appointments to the executive board of their state societies, without any fanfare or complaint.[94] Clearly, the delegates were selected for their activism and what they represented to the movement, since they could be portrayed as respectable women or they could be idealized as women capable of rising above the limitations of their sex. William Lloyd Garrison claimed that Mott was well suited for the task of serving as a delegate at the London convention because she virtually transcended her sex as an "almost peerless woman."[95]

Tributes to Mott veiled the eulogists' gender biases. One male reformer praised Mott for her charming manners, moral features, and dignified simplicity and grace, yet he carefully qualified her mental powers, describing her reasoning as "unsystematic" and questioning her failure to appreciate the sublimity of poetry—the mark of true genius.[96] In addition to her value as a symbol of modesty and simplicity, Mott stood for something heretical when situated within English society. British antislavery activists followed the rules of eighteenth-century sociability, and Mott found herself invited to several soirees where men and women gathered for tea and conversation. At one such gathering Mott displayed her acerbic wit when she refused to discuss the free produce movement, commenting that on politically charged issues she had better get her husband to speak for her.[97] She found herself snubbed by a clique that Philadelphia Quaker Sarah Pugh labeled "aristocratic Quakers," comprising English Orthodox Friends who viewed the Hicksite branch as heretical.[98] Even the artist hired to paint the historic convention refused to give Mott a prominent place in the portrait, and he instead chose an English "beauty" for center stage over the female heretic from the United States.[99]

The issues of gender and class surfaced in the arguments raised for and against seating the female delegates. American delegate George Bradburn noted how class pretension had little place in the antislavery cause, remarking that while the "men of property and standing" had rioted against abolition meetings, the women had defended the true meaning of liberty by protecting the male antislavery lecturers. English activist Elizabeth Pease nevertheless astutely observed that the dispute over the female delegates rested on an "enigma." In England, Pease contended, "class restrictions, religious disabilities, landed property monopolies" created the most formidable kinds of political oppression, whereas in the United States institutional prejudice was relegated "into distinctions of sex and color."[100] Pease assumed that if her English peers saw the similarity between disabilities based on class, religion, and sex, they might see the paradox of their protests over the female delegates. Yet Pease's evaluation missed the similarity between the political cultures of the two countries. Class and religion in English society had to do with issues of feminine modesty and social manners, and gender in the United States was defined through bourgeois publicity, relying on the class features of property ownership, education, and, most assuredly, the proper conduct of women in social and reform circles.

PETITIONING AND THE POLITICAL
PUBLIC SPHERE

Through the antislavery petitioning campaign, the uneasy balance between women's literary and political publicity was further exposed. In England, women's efforts for gathering signatures on petitions had contributed to ending the slave trade, but it had not stirred much debate over the intrusion of women into politics. The right of petition was open to any British subject.[101] In the United States, women also collected petitions, and they worded their complaints in the same deferential language of a subject pleading for a hearing from the "Fathers and Rulers of our Country."[102] But the impact was different. American democracy translated the petition into the right of constituents, which meant that women addressed the complaint to their representatives without relying on fathers, husbands, or sons. The exact meaning of female petitioning became blurred. Did a collective petition drive imply something more political than an individual grievance for the redress of a wrong? Could the gathering of men's and women's signatures on a petition be viewed as a social transgression—the promiscuous commingling of the sexes in print? Was the petition pure literary expression? Or did the act of demanding a hearing suggest that women were requesting public recognition and equal political standing in order to express their political views?

Many arguments emerged after the "gag rule" was passed that tabled all antislavery petitions sent to the House of Representatives between 1835 and 1844. John Quincy Adams's unrelenting criticism elevated him into a provocateur for the right of petition. When in 1838 the representative from Maryland contended that women belonged in domestic, social, and benevolent circles but that petitioning was part of the "fierce struggles of political life," the ex-president responded with a series of rebuttals. He began by defining the female petitioners as his constituents and an anonymous public, since he disavowed knowing the women personally who had signed the petition from his district. Adams then proceeded to demonstrate how women could not be categorized by one form of publicity or one kind of political relationship to the state. Referring to the Revolutionary War, he cited examples of women sewing for the cause, an exhibition of their patriotism, sacrifice, and direct political involvement. He cleverly pointed to Deborah Gannett, whose husband had received a pension from Congress as a result of her service as a soldier during the Revolution. Adams also employed humor. He read a petition that called on Congress to end all negotiations with England and request that Queen Victoria abdicate the throne, adding the sarcastic comment that some members of Congress, given their view on women's proper sphere, might take his proposal seriously.[103]

Adams's defense of the right of petition stemmed from his belief that southern opposition threatened fundamental civil liberties. He did not wish to expand women's rights but to preserve existing rights against what he saw as a conservative backlash. Adams maintained a very narrow definition of women's right to petition, declaring that women had this right if their "motive be pure, the means appropriate, and the purpose good."[104] For Adams, petitioning flowed from women's involvement in benevolent societies. They had a duty to petition as long as they worked within the appropriate circles, demonstrating that their character, motives, and purpose adhered to the standards of bourgeois respectability.[105] Adams compared the petition to prayer, which perhaps best suited the feminine version of the anonymous public.[106] Women's publicity remained unobtrusive and disembodied, communicating through prayer rather than engaging in direct political action.

Ultimately, Adams did not conflate the right of petition with voting, nor did he view petitioning as outside the bounds of bourgeois publicity. Petitioning still required male mediation, as the elected male representative presented the petitions and interpreted their meaning. In his 1842 lecture, *The Social Compact*, Adams applied this logic to demonstrate that women should not have the right to vote, because the husband acted as a sponsor for his wife at the polls.[107] Although he assumed that women had political opinions, Adams could not accept any better than his southern colleagues that women might embody and represent those opinions as independent voters.

Adams's position was no different from that of the reviewer for the *United States Magazine and Democratic Review* whose essay "American Women" resolved the controversy over women's engagement in politics in a similar fashion. Both acknowledged women's contributions to certain areas of political reform, but they confined women's influence to social circles and reserved legislation and deliberation to male politicians. Women's social circles nevertheless led to societies, their writing gave them entrée to the literary public sphere, and their social networks generated petition drives, all of which allowed women to move easily from social to political reform. Yet the class dimensions of civil society still curbed women's political involvement. Rather than restrict women to the home or family, the democratic variation of the bourgeois public sphere rationalized gender inequality by making sure women were seen first as social rather than political beings.

In *The Social Compact* Adams provided a theoretical framework for the origins of society, and he did so to link explicitly women's exclusion from politics to their social nature. Adams contended that Adam and Eve introduced civil society into the state of nature, and that their union symbolized the universal model of bourgeois society. Eve's introduction of dissension into the Garden of Eden suggested why partisan rivalries could not exist in the society of men and women, and Adam's punishment for listening to the "voice of his wife" offered a cautionary tale about allowing women too much political influence. In the garden of Eden, the ideal pastoral environment, men and women viewed each other with chaste affection and respect and shared a civilized communion. Adams warned that female societies such as the mythical Amazons, known for removing one breast and killing their sons, represented the antithesis of civil society. In a world without men, women reverted to being the enemies of men, lost their maternal affections, and disfigured their bodies, becoming, as in the case of the Amazons, nothing more than a grotesque caricature of men.[108]

Adams was not alone in this view. It had become quite common to equate the mythic union at creation with the meaning of national union and to compare partisan strife to the petty jealousies of married couples. In his 1829 published letter William Ellery Channing echoed this perspective, emphasizing that physical distance between factions preserved national harmony. Channing also believed that communication through letters facilitated shared sympathies, while face-to-face conflicts promoted jealousies, slander, and irreconcilable differences.[109] If shared sentiments and a common language united the nation, then women actually made civilized political deliberation possible. In other words, women countered the worst aspects of partisan strife by knitting society together through sympathy and social circles and by remaining aloof from contentious political squabbles.

Elsewhere, an observer wrote in the 1831 *Ladies Magazine and Literary Gazette* that women played a special role in uniting the nation through their letter writing. By transforming strangers into friends through correspondence, women had the ability to awaken intense emotions for unknown places and people, thereby elevating sympathy into an almost sublime experience.[110] Ironically, female abolitionists used the same argument to encourage disunion, claiming that women's sympathy for the slave forced them into political action. Mary Grew likewise compared the antislavery petition campaign to a flood of sympathy pouring from the hearts of women into their petitions.[111] By 1850 this theme surfaced as a justification for woman suffrage. As one advocate claimed, women's vote would benefit society because it would express the "soul of the nation."[112]

Despite attempts to expand the range and power of sympathy, the political meaning of sympathy was constrained as long as it remained associated with women's language. The curiosity for details and minutiae in women's letters, although capable of opening new horizons to readers, still fell short of the greatness invoked by a memorable historical occasion, a powerful speech, or an overwhelming natural landscape. Sympathy came from personal and subjective feelings, which often blinded the person from gaining a comprehensive understanding of universal laws. Sympathetic feelings, even those tempered by print, lacked the necessary rational detachment for judging political issues dispassionately. Consequently, women's petitions to Congress were dismissed by one representative as apolitical because they were identified with the "warm imagination of an enthusiast" and the "characteristic tenderness of the philanthropist." Such petitions lacked the perspective of a statesman who—without partiality and sentiment—looked at a political issue in "all its bearings." [113]

For women's rights activists the tradition of letters and sympathy fell outside the theoretical categories normally associated with the public realm of the polis. As Hannah Arendt later made clear, the public realm had to be "great." A truly sublime understanding came from an overwhelming sense of awe and recognition of triumph over a human adversary or even an invincible foe such as death or nature.[114] Antislavery activists were aware of the difference between sympathy and the sublime. Lydia Maria Child described Angelina Grimké's speech before the Massachusetts legislature as "a spectacle of the greatest moral sublimity I ever witnessed." [115] Child described this moment according to a traditional view of the sublime, which celebrated grand exposure over intimate revelations, an authoritative and commanding presence over the compassionate pleading of a warm enthusiast, and a display of strength over weakness. For this reason feminists found the language of sympathy less useful for elevating women into political figures and would develop another image of the transcendent politician, as evidenced by Antoinette Brown's admiring description of Gerrit Smith in 1852: "I saw Gerrit Smith on the morning of his election. His face was literally radiant with a lofty enthusiasm which sat sublimely upon him. He reported the progress of pure, free principles. Said he: 'I shall be elected; I have not a doubt of it.' He spoke of himself as he would have talked in the third person, reminding me of the transcendent vision of a newly disembodied spirit, which is represented as standing by the side of its body looking upon it, and participating in the emotions of friends, and yet beholding all as an impartial and disinterested spectator." [116]

This description of Smith as a public man offered a telling comparison to the *Herald*'s editorial that had satirized Brown as a pregnant professional. One unanswered question was whether women could ever completely transcend their bodies. This theme shaded all the attempts by feminists and female reformers to find an acceptable ground for engaging in their public activities. During the 1850s, activists pondered whether their attempts to deemphasize their bodies trapped them in the ideological couture of feminine modesty. They also had to wonder if donning the Bloomer costume represented a defiance of fashion or drew more attention to women's external appearance. Not only did the meaning of transcendence create difficulties for women, but greatness eluded them as well. Anson Bingham believed that women's superiority or greatness was seen by opponents of women's rights to diminish men's worth in the eyes of the world, because women were commonly considered less worthy foes in the struggle for public distinction and glory.[117] Indeed, women were valued for avoiding competition and political strife and cultivating sympathy and friendship, which acknowledged their contribution to civil society but reinforced their inadequacies as actors in the political public sphere.

Creating a Critical Public of Women

From 1846 to 1849 women's rights activists made a decisive break from the gendered expectations of bourgeois publicity by challenging the distinction between the literary and the political public spheres. In Philadelphia activists organized a series of "public meetings of women" around the most pressing political issues of the day, such as peace, capital punishment, liberty laws, prostitution, and women's rights. These meetings constituted a public gathering of women completely divorced from any female reform society. In March 1846 a public meeting of women assembled spontaneously, protesting the campaign in the press against Dr. Frederick Hollick. As a health reformer and New York physician Hollick lectured on human sexuality (and most likely on birth control) to a female audience, and his lectures were attacked as "indecent and libellous." The reputation of women and the public were at stake, according to his accusers, who orchestrated his arrest and trial but failed to convince the jury, which found him not guilty without ever leaving the box. In reaction a group of 300 women organized a meeting from a sense of "duty they owed the public and themselves," and they passed several resolutions that refuted the charges raised by "one or more anonymous writers." [118]

Informal meetings such as this were repeated. In June 1846 a similar meeting was organized to protest the Mexican War and to defend women's influence in their "more extended sphere." In a published letter that same month Lucretia Mott and several other antislavery activists called upon women to "look with an attentive eye upon the great events" and to use their "enlightened judgment, as well as their feeling hearts." The letter was signed "Women of Philadelphia, U.S.A.," and the local coalition did not identify themselves as members of the Philadelphia Female Anti-Slavery Society.[119] By 1847, when a meeting was called on the topic of capital punishment, this group explicitly rejected the boundary between women's social circles and their involvement with political legislation. Paulina Wright (she would marry Thomas Davis in 1849) was appointed chair, and Madame de Staël was quoted to make the point that if women could be put to death, then they had the right to know why. As a critical public of private citizens, they had the right to refute the reasons that justified state authority. This gathering called all women to attend, and the committee of correspondence voted to replace the word "women" with "inhabitants" in their memorial to the state legislature.[120]

The subsequent 1848 Seneca Falls convention on women's rights attempted to build from these developments. Women were called to meet alone on the first day, and then the forum was opened to men. Yet the organizers had not entirely escaped their observance of social decorum. In the *History of Woman Suffrage*, Stanton reminisced how "James Mott ascended the chair, tall and dignified, in Quaker costume," but she failed to mention the general concern about having female officers preside over men.[121] At the next women's rights convention, held in Rochester the same month, Abigail Bush was selected as chair, but not without provoking a controversy. Lucretia Mott and Elizabeth Cady Stanton voiced their disapproval of a female chair and threatened to boycott the convention.[122] Both women believed that a poor showing by female officers would threaten the public reception of the nascent movement. By 1849, when another public meeting was held in Philadelphia on women's rights, activists dismissed the need for "gentlemen officers," and subsequently they elected a woman as president at the next two conventions held in Salem and Worcester in 1850.[123]

Such public meetings, mobilizing around political issues, went beyond social circles. From intimate associations gathered according to respective tastes and inclinations, the developing movement featured gatherings of private citizens intent on disputing state authority and demanding a public hearing. In these meetings modesty was pitted against the dissemination of useful knowledge about women's health and the people's right to know, deliberate, and decide matters of life and death such as war and capital punishment. The pursuit of truth triumphed over matters of taste, public criticism prevailed over courteous social intercourse, and political concerns outweighed compassionate pleadings for the oppressed and downtrodden. Women were not speaking in the interests of the less fortunate or petitioning as deferential subjects; instead they voiced their opinions as concerned citizens, inhabitants of the city, and they eventually represented themselves as women.

Publicity, however, was never simply about appearing in public places. It revolved around visibility, or how people in public forums fashioned their reception for a wider reading audience. To a significant extent publicity remained a joint fabrication, constructed by the viewer or spectator as much as by the actual participants. Public gatherings, to be great, transcendent, or sublime, had to intensify reality and invite metaphysical certainty. Conventions had to be larger than life, address abstract principles, and represent the vital interests of all the people, just as public meetings were called in reaction to a violation of rights. While the Seneca Falls convention reenacted the signing of the Declaration of Independence, the conventions that followed it refashioned the meaning of civil society. By reclaiming and reconfiguring the state of nature, feminists sought to justify women's political equality and their public presence.

In 1849 the state of nature became the subject of public dispute. Richard Henry Dana lectured on "Woman" in Philadelphia, and Mott found herself forced to offer a lengthy response that was later published as her "Discourse on Woman." Her critique focused on Dana's contention that woman was created to "stand in awe and reverence of man," a powerful allusion that underscored the traditional notion of greatness.[124] Borrowing from John Milton's famous rendering of Adam and Eve in *Paradise Lost*, Dana had revived the view that women could only behold the sublime through their reverence of men. Adam and his descendants secured their claim to self-mastery within the state of nature because the "first man" demonstrated his natural superiority over all creatures, including Eve. Mott argued that because true greatness could only exist among equals, male and female were created simultaneously, and woman did not stand in awe and reverence of man, but both stood as "co-equals" before God.[125]

At the 1850 Worcester convention Abby Price, who gave the longest speech, quoted the same biblical verse, and she used the word "co-equal" to expand the meaning of equality in the Declaration of Independence.[126] At the Salem convention Elizabeth Wilson, who had spent ten years exploring this issue for her 1849 book, *A Scriptural View of Woman's Rights and Duties*, confirmed that women secured their "co-sovereignty" during creation.[127] Wilson and Price also agreed that women's political exclusion was contrary to the biblical verse that detailed woman's creation: "It is not good for man to be alone." As Price explained, " 'It is not good for man to be alone' were words of wisdom, and he had better not divorce her from any sphere of humanity. She has various capabilities, and with them, a charter for their use, from God."[128]

By rewriting the social contract, early feminists did far more than argue for individual rights. In what has to be seen as a conceptual revolution, they carved a theoretical space for women within the imaginary script of the "original contract" in the state of nature. Activists were well aware that the real value of the creation story was its "symbolic representation."[129] Their strategy served many purposes, for the creation story and the state of nature played a continuing, vital part in antebellum political discourse. The meaning of creation provided a seemingly endless variety of political paradigms for defining sexual difference. Coequality, then, offered an ideological critique that was both political and ethical. Simultaneous creation challenged the gender asymmetry that enlightened thinkers had firmly rooted in the state of nature.

Coequality dismissed the divine sanction for male dominance derived from the "one flesh" trope or the marital metaphor of Adam and Eve that was used as a foundation in family and property law. Coequal creation undermined the idea of a greater "penalty" against Eve that served political theorists and moralists who wished to legitimate the divestment of women's political and legal rights. But the creation story also addressed shame, modesty, and the loss of innocence, all of which represented the ways in which the state and the rulers of civil society could reinforce their powerful prescriptions for the public "dress" of both male and female citizens. As a writer in the *United States Magazine and Democratic Review* observed in 1846 in response to the New York constitutional convention, "For 'government like dress,' as has been happily remarked, 'is the badge of lost innocence.'"[130]

Coequality, however, indicated something very specific about the failure of democratic politics to alter the public sphere for women. It addressed the issue of making women the peers of men, which remained vital to democratic notions of participation. Suffrage, when granted to the common man, preserved the republican belief in a common identity. Partisan politics, however, retained a faith in greatness; candidates still had to prove their superiority, sometimes in debate, occasionally through their military prowess, but mainly through their mastery of the party system. Service on juries demanded that members judge their peers, deliberate, and reach a conclusion that rested on a consensual agreement. Jury service further symbolized the gender division between female sympathy and the objective and dispassionate reason needed to evaluate the facts and testimony presented in legal cases. In 1852 Paulina Wright Davis and John Neal acknowledged that jury service was pivotal to the democratic ideal of "embodiment" in the public sphere. Davis saw jury service as another arena for political transcendence, for members had to see one another as equals capable of judging without regard to race, sex, or religion. Juries had to act as one, a public body of peers, who simultaneously stood apart from their personal biases but together as participants in the public sphere. The trenchant theme "It is not good for man to be alone" underscored that women must receive as well as dispense just treatment.

Some proponents of women's rights, such as Cyrus Eaton of Maine in his poem "Woman," published in 1854, contended that the real distortion of "*public* walks of life" resulted when the sexes were separated and alone and women were trapped in isolation "in this frozen zone." Reversing the terms of the older debate, in which masculine women pretended to be men or consorted illicitly and promiscuously in public spaces as prostitutes or disorderly women, Eaton shifted the focus to the dangers of "men shut from Women." If left to their own devices, men

> soon turn to brutes, or like demons act,—
> grow coarse, obscene, smoke, gamble, and carouse,
> Fight duels, treason plot, or wear a blouse.[131]

The highly specialized masculine arts—warfare and politics—also carried the stigma of disorderly conduct. Eaton implied that men, too, were prone to excesses, thus blurring the boundaries between civility and brutish behavior, loyalty and treason, and sexual surfaces and natural identity.

Tension between the literary and the political public spheres did not entirely disappear. Activists debated whether women should display their greatness through their verbal skills or follow the model of Margaret Fuller by making their literary marks with their pens. At the 1852 Syracuse convention Susan B. Anthony and Elizabeth Oakes Smith were the focus of disagreement when Anthony moved that no woman should be able to speak whose voice was not strong enough to fill the house. Paulina Wright Davis rebuked this motion, claiming that she would not tolerate a "gag" placed on her sisters' or her lips. Davis also observed that the movement was divided between "speakers" and "writers." The attempt to silence Smith, a popular author and member of the New York literati but not a dazzling orator, was a spurious effort to privilege extemporaneous deliberation over the reading of written addresses. Davis found that "speakers" were comparatively less interested in convincing the "public mind" through the use of polished published essays. This split in the movement became evident when Davis tried to win support for her periodical, later titled the *Una*, which the convention refused to endorse as the organ of the movement.[132]

As Habermas has made clear, quoting the words of Immanuel Kant to extend his definition of the bourgeois public sphere, "The only qualification required by the citizen (apart, of course, from being an adult male) is that he must be his *own master (sui iuris)*, and must have some *property* . . . to support himself."[133] By the early nineteenth century, manhood and civil mastery retained their force as ideological markers of citizenship and public distinction. Self-mastery in democracy had less to do with using reason and more to do with being seen as reasonable. As women's rights activist John Neal observed in 1843, congressional deliberation often digressed in streams of monotonous words, rambling or ranting without purpose, while representatives monopolized the time, hoping to have their speeches reprinted or their names mentioned in the papers. Mastery eluded women because their efforts to obtain distinction always could be reduced to mere display, and women's political embodiment, if ridiculed as a sexual transgression, could be maligned for breeding dissension and social disharmony.

Coequality promised to change the appearance of women in men's eyes and to change how women viewed themselves, uniting men and women as mutual allies who "rise and sink together." When men and women "sit side by side . . . self-reverent each and reverencing each, distinct in individualities," then a sublime understanding of sexual relations would be possible.[134] Or, as Harriet Martineau contended, when the "principle of the equal rights of both halves of the human race" was acknowledged, then democracy would see the "remarkable transmutation of the ludicrous into the sublime" by treating women as equals in all spheres.[135]

4

Conscience, Custom, and Church Politics

At the first two conventions in Seneca Falls and Rochester, New York, in 1848, supporters had felt obliged to defend their gatherings against the combined charges of religious and political infidelity. The most vociferous attack came from a Seneca Falls minister who asserted that the existing government was "established by God" and that women's rights mocked both Christianity and democracy. Elizabeth Cady Stanton and Elizabeth McClintock wrote a lengthy defense of women's rights founded on religious liberty that rejected "fetters that bind the spirit of woman," and they called as well for ministers to engage in open and public debate on women's rights.[1] At the Rochester convention Stanton asked the unsympathetic clergy who might be present to speak out at that moment, rather than "as at Seneca Falls, [to] keep silent through all our deliberations, and afterwards, on the Sabbath day, use the pulpit throughout the town to denounce [women's rights activists], where they could not, of course, be allowed to reply."[2]

The alliance between church and state contributed significantly to cultural perceptions of women's civil status. Throughout the nineteenth century, as Carol Weisbrod has argued, "a special role for Christianity was at times conceded by the state," and their "systems of authority were sometimes cooperative, and even overlapping."[3] In 1833 Supreme Court Justice Joseph Story endorsed this position, writing in his *Commentaries on the Constitution*, "The general, if not the universal, sentiment in America was, that Christianity ought to receive encouragement from the state, so far as was not incompatible with the private rights of conscience, and the freedom of worship."[4] Other jurists shared Story's constitutional faith that religion and law made civil society possible.[5] Yet public sentiment did come into conflict with the rights of conscience, especially over Sabbath laws, and this constitutional struggle was revived after an important Pennsylvania Supreme Court decision in 1848.[6] The same year, an anti-Sabbath convention was held in Boston, garnering support from prominent and controversial figures such as Transcendentalist minister Theodore Parker, abolitionist William Lloyd Garrison, and Lucretia Mott, who made an appearance. Held four months before the Seneca Falls convention, the anti-Sabbath convention influenced the women's rights movement by charging, among other things, that Sabbath laws served as a bastion of clerical and male authority.[7]

That the Sabbath ensured a "Christian people—*and state*," as its proponents claimed, nevertheless raised the more complicated issue of what created the bonds of nationhood.[8] In 1841 the Pennsylvania house of representatives declared unanimously that a petition to revoke all Sabbath laws was "destructive, not only of all the ties which bind men together as civilized beings," but dangerous to public order and morals as well by giving "countenance and currency to infidel opinions and principles, which strike at the foundation of civil government."[9] A similar complaint was raised against the anti-Sabbath convention, claiming that such infidel opinions went beyond the pale of common sense and moral decency, as one critic declared in an angry letter in 1848: "They have denounced the ministry, the church, and the Sabbath; what will they next assault? Scarcely anything is now left untouched, but the '*family*' as an institution of God."[10] The Reverend Justin Edwards, secretary of the American and Foreign Sabbath Union, agreed that the Sabbath and the family were overlapping "parts of one whole, [which] mutually aid and sustain each other."[11]

If the Sabbath served as a touchstone for defining the religious fundamentals of society, then the movement to protect Sabbath laws was a reaction to popular discussions about sacred rights. If infidels could gather in convention to criticize the Sabbath, and women could debate their rights in public, then anyone could engage in deliberations over rights. For avid defenders of Sabbath laws, the language of rights appeared dangerously open to negotiation, subject to change, and seemingly divorced from the guidance and supervision of clerical interpretation.[12] To counter this trend Edwards stated that the Sabbath was not about the rights of men but about "THE RIGHTS OF GOD," and therefore beyond the control of individual men and women.[13] Such an attitude was more than a desperate attempt to preserve moral knowledge from the uncertainty of public discussion. In his massive study of American democracy Alexis de Tocqueville observed that religion contributed to a shared consensus of public opinion that discouraged dissent from moral fundamentals. The same restraints applied to the "fairer sex." For Tocqueville, a consensus of opinion curtailed American women from ever imagining to challenge the social restraints on their lives.[14]

Religion had a distinctive influence on the women's rights movement, not only as a set of ideas about morality and sacred truths, but as a crucial medium for debating such pivotal concerns as public opinion, the ethical foundation of rights, and the need for heresy and dissent when challenging the irrefutable authority of "common sense" and majority rule. A strong connection was established between the church and the state through the concepts of public opinion and representation. According to Tocqueville public opinion created "spheres" or "circles," which directed influence and behavior by establishing an internalized set of rules about propriety.[15] In a democracy public opinion acquired two positions: it could be used either to defend and demand rights or to discipline certain members of the polity as "moral subjects."

Women, as Elizabeth Wilson contended in 1849, exposed the cross pur- poses of public opinion. Restricted from the pulpit and the church hierarchy, women did not exercise the same rights or have equal standing with men because a female member could not act as a representative "head" of the con- gregation. She was seen as a "part" of the church polity but still could not embody or constitute the public opinion of a whole congregation as its figu- rative head. Through an increasingly dominant role as members of the laity, women had come to symbolize perfect moral subjects—a caricature of what Wilson bitingly called "conspicuous moral sublimity"—who continuously projected the image of a docile and obedient public audience. Men professed religious truths; women merely reflected them.[16]

Antebellum feminists recognized that the church itself was a religious public that assumed political and moral duties. Churches were neither power- less nor domesticated entities marginalized after disestablishment, nor were church members only interested in moral issues and unaware of the political consequences of their religious beliefs and practices. In fact, churches repre- sented the religious lens through which congregations viewed political issues; the clergy used the pulpit for decidedly political purposes; and male and female church members and ministers used a formidable religious press to instruct, discipline, and create opinions for their religious reading public. By obliging all citizens to treat Sunday as a holy day, Sabbath laws represented a larger debate about custom and consensus and demonstrated the limita- tions placed on liberty of conscience by the state in the name of majority rule. By understanding how jurists used the language of custom, antebellum feminists highlighted the dangerous and unholy alliance between church and state. They did not reject religion or turn to purely secular solutions, but as activists they sought to reclaim the church as a "true public." The church could not be ignored, and women's rights activists hoped to replace clerical rule with coequal representation. And rather than treat church and state as separate spheres, activists fully recognized that rights discourse and religion remained inextricably linked within American political culture.

Holy Time

In 1844, just two years after the American and Foreign Sabbath Union had organized, the Reverend Justin Edwards published his *Permanent Sabbath Documents* and within a period of seven years traveled 48,000 miles, distributing no less than 600,000 copies of his Sabbath tracts.[17] His actions were not extraordinary. Edwards had honed his marketing skills as a leading member of the American Tract Society, an organization that helped make the religious publishing industry into an aggressive and influential wing of the evangelical empire.[18]

For Edwards the Sabbath was a truly national American institution that defined the "bone and sinew of the American character."[19] From their first campaign to restrict transportation of the mail on Sundays in 1810, Sabbatarians linked national character to methods of public communication.[20] Like the efforts of the American Tract Society toward unifying Americans through the diffusion of religious knowledge from the "sanctified press," Sabbatarians inevitably pursued similar aims for promoting national habits of religious worship and faith among *"all the people."*[21] In this battle for the mind and soul of the American people, Sabbath reformers felt that constant supervision—not censorship—was the solution. By fixing reading habits and encouraging the public to attend Sunday worship and take their interpretative cues from ministers, they could, in the words of Justin Edwards, instill disciplined minds with a "sense of obedience before a knowledge of God."[22] By treating Sunday laws as a fundamental component of the national character, Sabbatarians built their campaign around the use of religious publicity, civic and moral education, and the aggressive construction of public opinion.

The Christian religion found ample support from early state constitutions, most of which endorsed religious oaths for officeholders as well as Sabbath and blasphemy laws.[23] In his 1796 Farewell Address, George Washington contributed importantly to the popular view that "religion and morality are indispensable supports" of republican government, and that "national morality" cannot "prevail in exclusion of religious principles."[24] In the post-revolutionary decade the most comprehensive program for elevating the role of religion in civil society came from Benjamin Rush, who in 1788 called for a "moral congress," with representatives from various denominations, for the "advancement of morals in the United States."[25] By the antebellum period "Christians of the nation" assumed they had extensive public power at their disposal, as one Massachusetts conference of churches reported in 1848:

> Besides, the sources of *moral* influence and power are great. The evangelical sects have nearly all the colleges and other seminaries of learning, of the land, under their control; nearly every chair of instruction and authority, being filled by those professing godliness. They have compiled nearly all the school books and have a far more than equal share in the management of our common schools. Then, they have all the power of religion, so far as it acts purely and legitimately, on their side. They have 30,000 ministers, who have access to the ear and the conscience of the nation a hundred times a year. And there is the Religious Press, with its weekly, monthly and quarterly issues, scattered broad-cast over the land, entering our Christian families, conducted with much ability and thus capable of exerting a tremendous influence in favor of those positions which are deemed worthy of it advocacy. Standing at such avenues of influence, who can gainsay our position that the Christians of our land have had the power to exert a paramount influence on the *politics* of the nation?[26]

As if to echo Rush's wishes, they proclaimed, "There should be *Conventions*—religious convention—for the specific purpose of entertaining and deciding upon the civil duties of Christian Citizens."[27]

Few disputed that publicity was indeed power. Originating in the eighteenth-century celebration of the literate public and freedom of the press, publicity nevertheless recognized the need for moral discipline.[28] American defenders of republicanism often placed more faith in moral vigilance than in civil liberty.[29] Literacy was related to liberty, however. The issue was not only that "knowledge is power," but that power derived from the disciplined dissemination of knowledge.[30] Over two centuries earlier John Milton had highlighted the two kinds of moral discipline that ensured supervision under the guise of civil liberty: the exhortation of ministers, which censured the disorderly conduct of the people, and the instructed conscience, which encouraged the self-disciplined and internalized compliance from each individual.[31] Consequently, if in theory overt censorship no longer existed in the enlightened polity, then in its place appeared publicity, which depended on moral persuasion—just short of compulsion—from the mighty engines of the pulpit and the press.[32]

NATIONAL CHARACTER AND THE MORAL
AUTHORITY OF COMMON SENSE

Publicity was therefore a matter of having the right opinions and compelling people to obey moral prescriptions in a manner that appeared natural and voluntary.[33] Of course, education had the capacity to "turn the mind right," and early advocates of female instruction accordingly tailored their programs to fit the republican ethos of restraint and "discipline for its own sake."[34] By 1828, when the Reverend Lyman Beecher established the General Union for the Promotion of the Christian Sabbath, his daughter Catharine Beecher pursued a campaign for female education along similar lines.[35] While both mastered the art of generating an "efficient public sentiment" and worked to create the widest base of popular support, they believed that both reforms reinforced the "duties of subordination," which ultimately served the "general good" of society.[36]

In *An Essay on the Education of Female Teachers* (1835), Catharine Beecher clearly echoed the concern of Sabbatarians for forming habits, opinions, and national character. Describing a nation on the brink of a crisis, comparing the United States to France, which had "once declared that Christianity should be banished, and the Bible burnt, and the Sabbath annihilated," Beecher contended that a corps of female teachers could protect society by extending a systematic program of instruction across the country. Women in particular had to acquire "virtuous intelligence" because information was useless, if not dangerous, in a "weak, undisciplined, unregulated mind." Beecher's strident emphasis on disciplined instruction advanced a new kind of Lockean pedagogy decidedly more aggressive in nature, in which the imprint of experience would not be left to chance. All the traits once associated with "female loveliness," such as "fainting, weeping," and the image of the "vapid, pretty play-thing," had to be systematically eradicated from the female character. According to Beecher this formidable task would only be accomplished when women were drilled in the habits of "order, neatness, punctuality" as well as "patient attention, calm judgment, steady efficiency, and habitual self-control." No longer left to its own devices, the female character would be recast with a vengeance into a new American and Christian mold.[37]

The debt to Locke cannot be overstated, both in the way he explained character formation and for what he omitted from his empirical theory of knowledge. Locke sketched the blueprint for two very different linguistic scenarios about character formation. Whereas the carefully instructed individual mastered the world of false appearances, his or her alter ego was seduced and misled by virtually all forms of verbal deception.[38] Locke separated the individual from the moral content of words; that is, all language was inherently corruptible regardless of the intentions of the speaker, writer, or teacher. It was imperative, then, that the observer, reader, and listener learn to discern the differences between true and false representations. For Locke, religion was a form of human knowledge and therefore subject to the same epistemological rules. By defining the mind as tabula rasa at birth, Locke not only removed predestination and the idea of an innate source of divine intelligence, but he also made religion contingent upon verifiable truths. Revelation was not a higher source of truth but only another form of probable knowledge that carried the same weight as secular beliefs or opinions.[39] False representations of religion, whether conveyed through words, visual images, or personal examples, posed exactly the same dangers as any other kind of erroneous opinions or information. Any medium of language could distort the message regardless of its original religious or moral content. In Locke's theory knowledge was inherently unstable, in part because moral truth had no sure hold on the human mind or the moral character of the individual.

Such indeterminacy of religious meaning undermined what many reformers felt was the imperative for national unity. If America was a "logocracy," a government created and constituted through words, then meaning could not remain ambiguous.[40] A "national language" was needed, as Noah Webster contended in 1789, in which all words, even the Scriptures, "ought to be explained in plain, intelligible language." Plain style, Webster believed, strengthened the bond among readers by leading "the reader, without study, into the same train of thinking."[41] Webster was not alone in his reliance on common sense—or a "common mental dictionary"—as the best vehicle for securing a moral foundation for the national character.[42] In full agreement, Elias Boudinot of New Jersey, the first president of the American Bible Society, argued in 1801 that the "rules of common sense" could defeat the forces of infidelity. Boudinot and other orthodox clergymen believed that to dismantle the threat of Deism, they had to meet their enemies on the same ground by application of reason.[43] Both Webster and Boudinot, while contesting Tom Paine's anticlericalism, echoed his powerful appeal for a reliance on "simple facts, plain arguments, and common sense."[44] And by adopting this premise on a wider scale, the American Tract Society sent forth didactic literature that contained "pithy" arguments and "plain" facts.[45]

But there was a decisive difference between the clerical and Deistic perspectives on common sense. For ministers and moral reformers, common sense provided a foundation for sustaining customs and even creating moral conventions, because it checked the ability of the individual to place freedom of thought before the shared consensus or will of the people. In language and society, received customs could not be rejected by the citizen until, as Webster assumed, she or he had "convinced the nation that the custom was a mistake."[46] In 1817 the Reverend Lyman Beecher voiced this perspective when he explained the duties of a minister through a pointed contrast between liberty and common sense: "Dare to think for yourself; but do not imagine . . . that, to be independent, you must of course despise antiquity, and differ from the vast majority of the wise, great, and good."[47] Beecher's advice was paradoxical: to dare to think for oneself while remaining constrained by custom and moral convention was potentially confusing.

Common sense offered a bridge between knowledge and faith, not only as a basis for understanding and judging according to ordinary or generally acknowledged principles, but as a conceptual domain for normalizing existing rules of authority.[48] By relying on a sense of community, ministers and reformers wanted to establish universal standards through the certainty of "rules of common sense" and yet simultaneously preserve a place for opinions, probable truths, and customs. The Bible could become a "storehouse of facts" or, for Lyman Beecher, a "code of laws" that accorded with Locke's "probable knowledge" based on the authority of rational evidence. At the same time, opinions were not considered a lower order of knowledge unless proven to be "erroneous opinions" or the habits of a perverted understanding.[49] If reason provided the basis for judging simple facts and plain arguments, then common sense added the moral dimension needed for evaluating the often ambiguous realm of opinions, beliefs, and customary practices.

MORAL CONSENSUS AND THE ILLUSION OF CONSENT

In 1829, one year after Beecher launched the General Union for the Promotion of the Christian Sabbath, William Ellery Channing offered a telling critique of a national moral consensus. In his "Remarks on Associations," Channing noted the dangers of public opinion generated by religious union. By harnessing various means of communication, men of "one mind," he claimed, concentrated their power with such efficiency that they achieved the "uniformity of a disciplined army." Rather than embodying or expressing the genuine religious sentiments of the people, associations manufactured a public consensus. By substituting the "consciences of others for our own," public opinion created standards of moral conformity that penetrated all aspects of society: "Its legislation extends even to our dress, movements, features, and the individual bears the traces, even in countenance, air, and voice, of the social influences amidst which he has been plunged. We are in great peril of growing up slaves to this exacting, arbitrary sovereign; of forgetting, or never learning, our true responsibility." Channing was persuaded that public opinion created a moral state within the political state: "They [moral associations] are a kind of irregular government created within our constitutional government."[50]

Channing's observations also reflected how the courts and the government forged a national and legal consensus on Christian morality. In blasphemy and Sabbath cases throughout the antebellum period, judges reinforced the precedent that "Christianity is part of the common law" and that the courts had a duty to uphold "moral discipline" and "public decency." In the important decision reached in the 1822 Pennsylvania case of *Updegraph v. Commonwealth*, the judge argued that the "Christian audience" or majority had a right to be protected from behavior or words that it found offensive or insulting to its religious values. By equating "general Christianity" with the general will, the judge in the Updegraph case further contended that the most genuine expression of a national moral consensus came from "the calm and mild accents of customary law." Religion, as a mixture of the general will, custom, and moral convention, was the "cement of civil union," and its deep foundations were "laid in the authority, interests, and affections of the people."[51]

The courts assumed a more important role than simply enforcing prohibitions against public denials of Christianity or ensuring religious conformity through Sabbath laws. American jurisprudence approved the use of the common-law tradition to create the illusion of general consent. This fiction of consent came from both the common law and common sense. The legal and linguistic reasoning of antebellum jurists closely paralleled the method of biblical interpretation employed by evangelical reformers. Lyman and Catharine Beecher believed that biblical verses had an "obvious" meaning. Like Noah Webster's view of a plain, intelligible language, the Beechers argued that words "always signify that which they are commonly *understood* to mean."[52] Yet opponents of this kind of reasoning, such as Thomas Herttell, a critic of the common law and religious conformity, rejected the proposition that general usage automatically implied general consent. What was obvious was not always right, and what was persistent was not always just. In 1828 Herttell argued that words such as common law and *"true and holy religion"* could be easily accommodated to "bolster up erroneous opinions, or to sustain acts of palpable injustice."[53] He mocked the contention that members of society might willingly consent to customs that reduced them to victims of injustice. Hence, custom was rarely based on actual consent, even if the common law made it appear so.

Custom and consent had a direct bearing on women's civil status. In his influential pamphlet on married women's property rights, which he drafted in order to promote legislative reform in New York, Herttell applied the same criticism to the common-law fiction of coverture. Common-law disabilities were applied to married women regardless of whether they consented to the divestment of their rights. In 1837 Herttell wrote, "Their assent is no more necessary to give effect to that law, than their express *dissent* could be to prevent or evade its operation."[54] As a general theory of the law, customary usage undermined the possibility for equal rights between the sexes and threatened the rights of conscience for members of different religious faiths. Sabbath laws violated equal protection and religious liberty because without the equal right to choose the day and time of worship, some people, Herttell observed, "not only [have] the right to choose for themselves, but also for their neighbors, and to *coerce* them to keep the sabbath chosen by another." In effect, the fiction of general consent conferred "double rights" on a particular class and left "others destitute of any."[55]

By the mid-nineteenth century the courts had reached a consensus that the government had a civic duty to protect the religious beliefs and practices of the majority.[56] Legal precedent and legislation invoked custom or the "conscience of the mass" as a higher authority that superseded individual or minority rights.[57] The 1848 decision of Judge Coulter rendered for the Pennsylvania Supreme Court case of *Specht v. Commonwealth* confirmed this position, and he claimed that the Sabbath offered the one day in the week when "all men, meet in equality at the Christian altar."[58] According to Coulter, Sabbath laws promoted equality and national unity instead of divesting rights.

The opposite was closer to the truth. Most churches replicated—rather than transcended—social distinctions. Pew ownership, rentals, and fees remained a feature of Protestant churches, especially those with an elite or middle-class clientele.[59] Divisions were drawn within the congregation, placing the wealthiest and most prominent families in the front rows. It was not uncommon for the church elders to be seated at the head of the church; in many Orthodox Quaker meetinghouses, the elders actually occupied a separate bench in front of the assembly. Even less elitist denominations such as the Methodists separated a special class of twelve men from the rest of the congregation; members of this group had the privilege of making their way through the fraternal ranks of class leader, exhorter, circuit preacher, and minister.[60] Location not only marked class and moral authority, but it could, as in the case of the Friends Society, divide the sexes. A system of sliding panels was used to divide the meetinghouse into two rooms used separately for men's and women's business meetings.[61] In 1843 Lucretia Mott observed that churches were hardly gatherings of equals but were riddled with caste divisions, which she aptly described as the "partition walls of prejudice."[62]

The moral geography of the congregation contributed to moral conventions. Custom trained people to look only at the "surface of things," to pay attention to the form—the image—rather than the substance or truth.[63] In 1856 Sarah Grimké astutely observed that the power of custom was to make social distinctions or prejudices so common that it "*seems* right."[64] Yet religious traditions, like the Sabbath, had the added potency of "undue veneration," or what Lucretia Mott described as consecrated authority, the ability to make something right and inviolable because the belief was "kept and guarded as a sacred thing."[65] The Sabbath consecrated space and time, representing an otherworldly, timeless wisdom that was beyond human control or criticism. As one defender of Sabbath laws declared in 1843, "The time never was, is not, and never will be in the present state, when we shall not need the sabbath."[66] For Justin Edwards the fixed and habitual devotion needed to keep the Sabbath holy uniformly trained church members to honor obedience before knowledge.[67] Of course, William Ellery Channing had a very different interpretation of "passively molded" parishioners. By instilling an "unresisting simplicity" of thought, he wrote, the Sabbath conditioned men and women to think, act, and behave according to custom and not from a sense of true conviction.[68]

Channing, Grimké, and Mott all believed that a customary range of thought suppressed the right to exercise liberty of conscience. This tension between custom and consciousness was the centerpiece of the arguments raised during the anti-Sabbath convention in 1848. Religious conventions, as Channing had implied, regulated dress, speech, and mannerism, which a leading "ultra" reformer, Charles Burleigh, later ridiculed as legislating "civility" and the "laws of etiquette." Sabbath observance was measured by a reticence that called for complete mental stasis and the restraint of all human agency. Burleigh declared that one minister had advised him, "We must not think our own thoughts; we must not speak our own words, or do our own acts; we must engage in no secular conversation."[69] Lucretia Mott told of a woman who read novels all week but on Sunday studied only the Bible and Hugh Blair's sermons and then looked with a "pious horror" on anyone who violated her rigid guidelines for the "consecration of the Sabbath."[70] Some ministers forbade the exchange of words on the way to church, encouraging a code of silence for chance encounters with neighbors or friends.[71] These rules required the force of habit and law to persuade individuals to "yield to the prejudices and feelings of the community." Conformity had to be upheld, as Burleigh put it, if Sabbath defenders were to be satisfied, for such people were consumed with the suspicion that even a complete stranger on the next street, or half a mile, or two miles from the meetinghouse might be desecrating the Sabbath.[72]

Thus the "partition walls of prejudice" worked on several levels. Distinctions drawn between the Sabbath and the rest of the week had a dual character. On one hand, church attendance provided for a more ritualized form of supervision, which encouraged the laity to master the unspoken rules of Sabbath etiquette as a mark of what Mott called "demure piety." On the other hand, the religious public extended its authority beyond the church through the enforcement of the legal and moral sanctity of the day. The Sabbath not only celebrated the "holiness of time" and the devotion for "outward authority," but the rules of Sabbath etiquette attempted to short-circuit the regular flow of information.[73] In the words of Theodore Parker, the Sabbath provided a "safe" and familiar sign, which shielded the public mind from competing views or an "excess of truth." He claimed, "I heard a man say, that if he had the whole of God Almighty's truth shut up in his left hand, he would not allow a man to unlock even his little finger."[74] Such a closed system ultimately granted the Sabbath a special power as an abstraction that elevated surface appearances into carefully coded gestures. More importantly, the Sabbath as gesture or affectation reduced religion to a mere "cloak of religion," eviscerated of real meaning, but a sign that nonetheless had the legal and social authority to divide the public through its regulation of surface appearances.[75]

Critics of the Sabbath used poignant and irreverent references to cloaks, sanctified coats, holy hats, and wooden shoes on the bound feet of Chinese women to lampoon religious rituals. The form should follow the substance, not the reverse. Thus the Sabbath, like "garments[,] are made for men, and not men for the garments."[76] These distinctions of dress accentuated the importance of sexual surface appearances. Elizabeth Wilson demonstrated how ministers used the biblical allusion of the veil to reinforce women's subordination in the church and all public assemblies. Women without their veils jeopardized the very existence of Christianity, the Sabbath, and the entire social order by placing men and women "on a level."[77] Encoded in the law, the metaphor of sexual difference predicated on surface appearances became extremely relevant. It should not be surprising that as late as 1891 one judge summarized this position. He argued that it would be as impossible to abolish laws of Sunday observance as it would be to abandon the custom of "clothing ourselves with garments appropriate to our sex."[78]

MORAL SUBJECTS OR ACCOUNTABLE CITIZENS?

The timing of the anti-Sabbath convention and the Seneca Falls convention was hardly a coincidence. Both political campaigns shared certain fundamental assumptions about the "unhallowed union of Church and State."[79] Opponents of the Sabbath laws argued that not only was it the "right of every class of citizens to be protected in the enjoyment of their religious sentiments," but the majority should not have the power of "binding and coercing our consciences"; nor should the legislature have the authority to enforce the "moral duties of civility."[80] Four months after the anti-Sabbath meeting, the members of the Seneca Falls convention passed their first eleven resolutions, which echoed similar concerns; their second grievance called for the repeal of all laws that prevented "woman from occupying such a station in society as her conscience shall dictate." Participants further acknowledged that man does not "accord to woman moral superiority," and they resolutely rejected woman's "circumscribed limits which corrupt customs and a perverted application of the Scriptures have marked out for her."[81]

The debate surrounding Sabbath laws revealed the extent to which the state relied on moral discipline to enhance its authority. By creating a "Christian state," one critic claimed, the government granted itself a "soul," which it used to impute the "righteousness" of its citizens.[82] By 1851, at the Worcester national women's rights convention, Wendell Phillips noted that the state had to resort to religious custom in order to deny women equal rights. Politicians and jurists found it far easier to trample on justice and liberty through the "alleged necessity of helping God govern what he has made."[83] Equality was reduced to a conditional right, for as Elizabeth Wilson remarked, "constitutional guarantees of rights, are like ropes of sand with respect to women," since *"custom* and *usage* are all that women had to depend upon."[84]

As a constitutional principle, the courts could use the power of moral guardianship to uphold the division of citizens into two classes, one as moral subjects, the other as fully accountable citizens. Women, of course, were refashioned into the best of all possible moral subjects. Their precarious political status demonstrated that women were not viewed as morally superior to men. After reviewing the terminology used in the Massachusetts state constitution of 1853, one feminist concluded that women fit into none of the categories for political accountability. A woman was "no *individual*—no *citizen*, does not belong to the *public*" but instead was "a *subject* of the *State*." As a subject, woman had the "power of being punished—and of causing the punishment of others," which at most made her responsible for committing or averting her own crimes.[85] The law assumed that women had consented to the social compact, at least as far as making them accountable for criminal action or immoral behavior. Yet their moral accountability, as Elizabeth Wilson acknowledged, existed purely on the level of exercising restraint, for they had "no positive authority whatsoever." Even this degree of accountability was limited. Although women were drilled in the "habits of self-control and self-government," they rarely were permitted to exercise them, because as Wilson noted, women were always destined to be "governed by others."[86]

The lesson taken from the Sabbath movement was the state's role in ascribing to women a particular place as moral subjects. The Sabbath symbolized the kind of moral authority the state endorsed. The moral expectations underlying female restraint, however, were more demanding. As Catharine Beecher advised, women were meant to stand in the shadow of men, reacting, reflecting, and influencing their moral virtue but never outshining them in the public spotlight.[87] For Mott this kind of demure piety rewarded false displays of righteousness. Consequently, if the Sabbath encouraged a false veneration of appearances, transforming genuine conviction into habits and gestures, then the same dilemma faced women more generally. The task for women was to "'break the image of man's lower worship,' as so long held up to view," as Mott argued, and for women to "stand out in heresy" rather than hide behind a veil of moral restraint. To accomplish this, Mott and other activists realized that the church as an institution had to be radically changed as a religious public. Dissent had to displace customary rituals of devotion, a conviction for right action had to replace the fear of censure, and women had to be certain not to "shrink from being such an iconoclast."[88]

Pillars in the Same Temple and Priests of the Same Worship

As the Sabbath debate revealed, public opinion—derived from the ability to constitute a public gathering and generate political opinions—conjoined secular and religious meanings. Protestant congregationalism, particularly after disestablishment in 1833, emphasized the voluntary nature of church membership as the basis of freedom of worship. Religious liberty, however, still required a disciplined moral freedom. While theologians and ministers stressed volition as essential to salvation, they just as readily saw humanity as willful, obstinate, and resistant to the "moral government of God." Moral accountability required choice—the will to sin or to be saved—but it also heightened the demand for what Lyman Beecher called "coercive necessity," the restraining power of church cooperation with the state. At the heart of this system of cooperative Christian action, which came to define the evangelical empire, was an educated ministry. Pious, enterprising, and intelligent ministers, Beecher believed, would create "a sameness of views, and feelings." The clergy were the "moral stewards" and pillars of society, preaching, teaching, and making their "official influence" felt through a "system of means" designed to ensure conformity.[89]

If Sabbath laws acknowledged the state's role in protecting a moral consensus, then ministers and elders—as pillars and priests of the church—defined the moral boundaries of a Christian democracy. The church not only provided a moral geography of society, but it embodied a public forum, which generated "public opinion in the making"—the beliefs, views, and conscience of the people. Yet ministers and the people did not always agree in their religious opinions. Most Protestant churches established rules, bylaws, and creeds that spelled out the rights and privileges of church membership. Lay members could be excommunicated; they also could bring grievances before a church session or trial. Congregations often divided into factions that led to schisms, and such defections and disputes demonstrated how churches mediated controversies as a public forum.

Mott's powerful image of woman as an iconoclast celebrated heresy and dissent. Public opinion required deliberation, gatherings among equals; the partition walls of prejudice that divided men and women into different castes had to be surmounted. Antebellum women's rights activists thus imagined a radically different kind of religious forum or *ecclesia*. Unlike Beecher's ideal church, which ensured the authority of the clergy and defined membership through creeds and a moral consensus, women's rights activists believed that dissent was the key ingredient of religious assemblies. Invoking the New Testament model of *ekkesia* as being "called forth," antebellum feminists translated this to mean being called out of conventional society. In this climate many women's rights advocates left their churches, formed new religious organizations, or in the case of prominent activists such as Lucretia Mott, were critics and provocateurs within their established religious institutions. Mott maintained her position as a minister in the Hicksite Society, and she supported the New York Congregational Friends and the Pennsylvania and Ohio Progressive Friends, all of whom seceded from the Hicksites. Members of these new religious assemblies and comparable "free churches," which attracted dissenters from evangelical and Unitarian churches, constituted the majority of reformers that attended women's rights conventions before the Civil War.

The political implications of dissent were obvious. Religious liberty for women's rights activists implied the dual rights of consent and dissent, the capacity to express one's fundamental beliefs and criticize those views that stood in contrast to one's personal faith. Dissent in the antebellum period also accorded the right to revolt and demand full representation. Dissent catalyzed constitutional reform, as individual states called conventions or public forums to revise their constitutions. Religious dissent tapped the same impulse among antebellum reformers as they critiqued existing religious institutions and practices, revolted and seceded from churches, revised creeds (or eliminated formal church laws) and rules for membership, and created a new public forum or new *ecclesia*.

Within this context women's rights activists eagerly and conscientiously applied the language of dissent to critique masculine models of representation in both religious and political forums. They compared the clergy to castes, whose authority came from vested privileges—especially their coveted monopoly over religious "truth" acquired through public speaking and preaching. At the same time activists challenged the existing church as a sect, a bureaucracy that had lost its public function as the embodiment of religious liberty. In its place they called for the church as a true public to promote a revolutionary kind of public exchange between men and women that was premised on the ideal of coequal representation. As president of the West Chester women's rights convention in 1852, Mary Ann Johnson declared that only then would the day arrive when "woman and her brother are pillars in the same temple and priests of the same worship."[90]

FETTERS THAT BIND THE SPIRIT OF WOMAN

When the women's rights convention gathered in Seneca Falls in 1848, over one-fourth of those in attendance had ties to the New York Congregational Friends. Religious liberty, moral accountability, and the exercise of conscience were closely intertwined with how the Congregational Friends understood religious and political assemblies to be public forums. Lucretia Mott became the "moving spirit of the occasion" after having come to the area to visit the McClintocks of Waterloo, New York, who, along with Mott, had played a decisive role in promoting the secession from the Hicksite Society. Thomas McClintock wrote the "Basis of Association" for the Congregational Friends, and his wife, Ann, and daughter, Elizabeth, worked with Mott and Stanton in organizing the women's rights convention.[91]

The church served as the perfect forum for enacting the politics of dissent, and not only for the Congregational Friends. Five years before the Seneca Falls convention, the local Presbyterian church had ignited a public controversy when Rhoda Bement was brought before a Session—the ecclesiastical equivalent of a trial—on charges of disorderly and un-Christian conduct.

Bement was placed on trial because she challenged the authority of her minister, the Reverend Horace Bogue. For two years she had refused to drink the communion wine as a temperance protest; she had attended an antislavery meeting led by Abby Kelley that had not been approved by her minister; and she had urged Bogue to read reform announcements from the pulpit. Prior to the trial Bogue had attempted to punish Bement through threats against her husband, warning that if his church attendance record was not improved, he would be disciplined. It was Bogue's refusal to read the announcements that finally led Bement to contest his actions in public. This verbal confrontation resulted in a charge of disorderly conduct against Bement. Her principal transgression, Bogue claimed, was that she had stepped out of her place by "publicly affirming," "declaring," and "asserting" accusations against him in the vestibule of the church before members of the congregation.[92]

Amid the trial proceedings the broader implications of Bement's protest— the divestment of her rights as a church member and a woman—emerged as issues crucial to her defense. Bement was obliged to defend herself against charges of "exhibitions"; her critics claimed that she represented all women who dared to declare their dissenting views in public. In response the defendant contended that Bogue had misused his clerical authority by censuring her opinions and threatening to punish her husband as a proxy for her alleged misconduct. Her rights had been violated, she asserted in her testimony, for Bogue had sought to "bind [my] conscience & deprive me of christian liberty." When faced with expulsion if she did not recant her accusations, Bement left the church and rejected all man-made authority, remarking in her final trial statement, "I appeal not unto Caesar but unto God." Eventually Bement and her supporters joined the Wesleyan Methodist Meeting, a free church that served as a public forum for many religious dissenters in Seneca Falls and later hosted the 1848 women's rights convention.[93]

Bement did not attend the convention, leaving town before the event took place. Yet her protest paralleled similar acts of defiance and dissent in New York, Ohio, Pennsylvania, and Massachusetts, that fueled the women's rights movement. Congregational Friends seceded from the Hicksites in 1848 because members felt their religious liberty had been unfairly restrained by elders trying to silence their testimony. Whereas Bement faced the charges of her minister and the censure of the elders, women in the Hicksite Society contested the gender hierarchy embedded within the Quaker ecclesiastical government. In the first place, the Congregational Friends rejected the ascending series of meetings that made the Select meeting of ministers and elders the "Head or Supreme Controlling Power," the pinnacle of authority— the supreme court or ruling body—for the entire network of societies in what can best be described as a federated system similar to the U.S. government.[94] Female members of the Hicksites suffered from a comparable imbalance of power, which Mott explained as the "assumed authority of the men's m[eeting]s, and the admitted subordination of the women's m[eeting]s." Women, despite their ability to act as ministers and hold business meetings in the Hicksite Society, still found themselves unable to participate in certain proceedings and to make crucial decisions about the policies of their local and regional societies.[95]

The bureaucracy of the church remained a pivotal problem for female dissenters. As in the Bement trial, the system of authority in the church imitated patterns of political hierarchy. In the Presbyterian Church the elders acted as a governing body or committee, making business decisions, enforcing bylaws, and mediating disputes. The minister's duties covered instruction, pastoral guidance, and moral discipline over errant members of the congregation. A recurrent theme in most struggles between the laity and the clergy was the tension over control of information. Bement felt that Bogue had prevented members from knowing about certain reform meetings, arbitrarily deciding not to let the laity judge for themselves. Bogue, in turn, had argued that Bement repeatedly defied his pastoral guidance, which he felt included the supervision of knowledge. On a larger scale the trial highlighted the institutional regulation of public opinion and the inevitable bureaucratic restraints on freedom of worship through the loss of "christian liberty."[96]

Antebellum women's rights advocates assumed that the church functioned as a bastion of either liberty or censorship. The key issue centered on whether the church remained a public forum. When ministers rewarded conformity and curbed public criticism and when members kept silent for fear of reprisal, then, as the Bement trial revealed, Christian liberty was sacrificed for church order, and ecclesiastical rules were legitimated at the expense of the rights of the laity. As one reformer astutely noted in 1845, antebellum churches often sacrificed the life of the forum in the church to the bureaucratic needs of the institution, especially when churches mobilized all their "ecclesiastical machinery" to make the "church into a state." To be a public forum the church had to create an environment in which members exercised consent and dissent, developing a critical perspective toward the abuses of state power. Consequently, the greatest danger for the laity was spiritual paralysis or alienation, which Stanton and Elizabeth McClintock described as the "fetters that bind the spirit of woman."[97]

This kind of criticism resonated among reformers. In 1848 Gerrit Smith voiced what many other antebellum dissenters believed to be true as well, namely, that most churches or religious societies had been reduced to "the soul-shrivelling enclosures of sect." The term "sect" and the political and denominational development identified as "sectarianism" reflected an intellectually and emotionally charged understanding concerning church-state relations. Having adopted the eighteenth century's contempt for political factionalism, critics were newly claiming that sectarianism resulted in the corruption of the public sphere through self-interested competition. The ambitious efforts of Protestant denominations to build the "evangelical empire," and factional struggles within churches over policy and creeds, indicated to dissenters a dangerous climate. Proliferating sects vied for members, institutional power, and public influence. Antebellum dissenters gave sectarianism a modern meaning when they focused on the control of information and the closing of the American mind. Seen as too preoccupied with theological squabbles and petty rivalries, sectarian churches were portrayed by dissenters as exclusive enclaves that carefully circumscribed members within their "respective circles of theology." By withholding the flow of public information, as Bogue had decided to do when he censored Bement's public announcements, these churches sought to deter their members from confronting the social and political issues of the day. Devoted to building denominational strength while isolating itself from open public debate, the sectarian church, one woman remarked, "has tended to make me a Methodist and nothing more."[98]

The public nature of the church had a direct bearing on women's capacity for political action. Lucretia Mott echoed Smith's allusion when she described the "sectarian enclosure on woman's mind."[99] Overall, activists believed that sectarianism constrained women's knowledge, undermining personal control over their fate by preempting their rational decision making. Church creeds called for "blind obedience," in effect consolidating inherited law that "enshrined the wisdom of the fathers as a yoke on posterity," thereby keeping women distant from the active production of truth.[100] As Progressive Friend Jane Trescott explained in her statement of withdrawal from the Society of Friends in 1849, months before she attended the Salem women's rights convention, "No sectarian shield can absolve us from our individual duty to God and man, which implies not merely *belief* but *action*, and you as a Society being unwilling to let me serve as according to the dictates of my own conscience, (believing myself the best judge,) I hereby withdraw my right of membership."[101] To ensure liberty of conscience, a democratic ecclesiastical order that placed the right of dissent at its center could counter the process of alienation and provide women with a model of political action. If church members replaced "assent to lifeless creeds" with the "living spirit" of dissent, then sectarian enclosure would give way to public disclosure.[102] Indeed, women would secure their rights when the church became a public forum, allowing each female member, according to Abby Price, "to contemplate her position under the full blaze of Christian dispensation." [103]

Price brilliantly captured the meaning of public disclosure. Her phrase "under the full blaze of Christian dispensation" implied open deliberations, scrutiny from different perspectives, and truth derived without "fetters" or "trammels" on the mind of woman.[104] Her understanding grew from participation in the Hopedale Community in central Massachusetts, considered a "practical Christian republic" that paralleled the goals of other dissident associations by allowing women to vote in all local political elections and church proceedings.[105] As one supporter explained, "It is not to be a mere Church or ecclesiastical communion; nor a mere civil government; nor yet duplicate organization of Church and State in mutual alliance; but a perfectly homogeneous organization, at once religious, social and civil in its structural characteristics. It is a new order of human society, properly called 'The Practical Christian Republic.'" [106]

Price was engaged as a lecturer for the Practical Christian ministry, speaking at Hopedale and pulpits in nearby towns in Worcester County. Developing a friendship with Paulina Wright Davis, she helped organize the first national women's rights convention in 1850, giving the longest address there, and later served as an assistant editor of the *Una*, Davis's women's rights periodical.[107] Davis and Price shared a similar religious outlook in that, by 1850, Davis had ties to the Religious Union of Associationists, which rejected sectarianism and even religious divisions among Catholics, Protestants, Jews, or any partial or exclusive religion. William Henry Channing, who also played a prominent role in the Worcester convention, was the minister at the Boston Religious Union of Associationists.[108] This band of reformers, along with other Unitarian and Transcendentalist dissenters such as Theodore Parker and Thomas Wentworth Higginson, developed ties to the Pennsylvania Progressive Friends, sharing that groups critique of sectarian churches.[109]

For antebellum dissenters the solution to sectarianism was what they called a free church or "people-church." Like the Congregational Friends or Religious Union of Associationists, membership was open to anyone in the community, and the goal was to attract men and women from a wide range of religious faiths to discuss moral and political questions. In 1843, the year of the Bement trial, Gerrit Smith had organized a free Presbyterian church in Petersboro, New York. In 1842 William Henry Channing had established a "free religious society" in Brooklyn, New York, followed by a Christian Union the next year in New York City. After his censure by the Unitarian Association, Theodore Parker and his supporters organized the Friends of

Religious Thought in Boston in 1845. Thomas Wentworth Higginson led a free church in Newburyport after his ordination in 1847 and, later, in 1852, accepted the post as pastor of the free church in Worcester, Massachusetts.[110] These radical new assemblies all experimented with a more democratic church polity and in some fashion blended the constitutional fiction of popular sovereignty or rule by the people with their notion of a religious public forum. Gerrit Smith believed that a "simple democracy" was modeled on the "primitive churches," or the New Testament version of *ecclesia*, in which Christians of a town or place joined together in worship.[111] The Congregational and Progressive Friends looked to George Fox for their ideal model of the *res foras*, for the founder of the early Quakers had also used the primitive Christians as his precedent. Fox had argued that a "meeting" came into being without regard to either time or place whenever "two or three are assembled together." Here, the people assembled constituted the church.[112]

Women's rights advocates recognized that a "simple democracy" raised the question of whether women had an equal place in such assemblies. As Presbyterian dissenter and women's rights supporter Elizabeth Wilson asked in her comprehensive study *A Scriptural View of Woman's Rights and Duties* (1849), "If women were collected together to hear the word of God, would they constitute a church?" Wilson's query went to the heart of the issue. Could women as "two or three gathered together" constitute a public assembly for worship? The answer was "no" for most denominations, because incorporation required that trustees and elders possess the legal standing of property holders and that ministers be put in charge of instruction and pastoral guidance. J. William Frost, for example, discovered that in Pennsylvania during the antebellum period, the state issued no charters to separate women's churches but did incorporate women's benevolent societies. A church as a public body required the presence of men, which Wilson sardonically acknowledged. She wrote that for a typical congregation the ideal church required a "fine" meetinghouse and minister in the pulpit addressing a "large assembly of people ornamented in *beards*." [113]

PRIESTCRAFT AND THE PRESENCE OF PUBLIC SPEECH

Wilson's allusion to "people ornamented with *beards*" recalls theme of public appearance. Manhood could be symbolically encoded through physical emblems. Even intangible signs of male superiority, such as public speech, acquired a physical image. One distinctive mark of the clergy was their carefully crafted "pulpit eloquence," which one writer described as "vesting" the man with a public presence. Public oratory had a gendered meaning, and women seeking equality in "christian, public, religious assemblies" were, as Wilson phrased it, lampooned for "putting on the pantaloons." In the 1850s fears of sexual inversion, cross-dressing, and "hybrid" mixtures were all common tropes for castigating public women.[114] Women who attracted too much public attention were condemned for making an "exhibition" or "spectacle" and, in the case of Rhoda Bement, charged with "disorderly and unchristian conduct."[115] Those women who commanded a public audience, daring to preach or to teach men, as one minister claimed at the 1853 women's rights convention in New York City, inverted the order of creation.[116] In fact, it became quite common to resort to the Pauline injunction "I suffer a woman not to teach," which the editor of *Harper's* used to attack women's rights conventions. This was presumed to offer sound evidence that women should be prohibited from preaching, teaching, or "engaging in the life of the forum" or the *"res foras."*[117]

The same *Harper's* editorial also attacked the women's rights movement for its "hybrid conventions" and rebuked the women present for hiding behind their "Quaker bonnets." It was one particular bonnet—that of Lucretia Mott—that probably inspired this angry harangue. During the previous decade Mott had emerged as a highly visible public woman by traveling thousands of miles, attending hundreds of meetings, and speaking before large and small crowds on such topics as women's rights, antislavery, sectarianism, peace reform, and land monopoly. She was considered the principal speaker at the Seneca Falls convention in 1848, and Mott either served as president or gave extemporaneous addresses at later conventions.[118]

As a popular figure Mott served as a prism for competing images of public women. Her public presence was either praised or rebuked, and her abilities as a speaker were either celebrated or trivialized. One newspaper account portrayed her as a quaint matron (rather than a great orator with a commanding presence) whose style of public speaking was comfortably domesticated in a telling metaphor: she was stitching together propositions as if she were knitting a pair of socks. Yet at the Unitarian Association meeting in 1846, she was lauded as the model of eloquence, described by the Reverend William Henry Furness as calm, dignified, and self-possessed in her manner of speech and presentation. Her most outspoken critic among the Hicksites, Quaker minister George White, previously had expressed disgust with her public appearances, comparing Mott to a disorderly shrew or "imperious woman," roaming "over the country from Dan to Beersheba, spurning the protection of man."[119]

Mott, however, saw herself mediating between her religious tradition as a Quaker minister and the idealized version of disclosure she associated with the public sphere. Although she wore the Quaker garb, Mott did not imitate the "singsong" style of female ministers, which caused some devout Friends to question her religious credentials. She spoke at public assemblies as a private citizen and what the Quakers called a Public Friend, a minister granted formal recognition to represent the society by traveling and speaking before other societies. She relied on her "conscientious reason" when addressing matters of general interest. Mott adopted the term "conscientious reason" from her "pet author," Blanco White, a dissenter who began as a Spanish priest, converted to Anglicanism, studied and absorbed the views of George Fox, and eventually joined the Unitarians. "Conscientious reason" bridged the moral category of conscience and an enlightened belief in progress by application of reason, demonstrating for Mott how rationality and an ethical or religious understanding could be combined.[120]

Mott also described herself as a public critic, succinctly illustrated by her favorite saying borrowed from Thomas Hobbes: "truth for authority, not authority for truth." A *New York Times* report published in 1855 described Mott as an exemplar of public opinion in the making. Here she was portrayed as a speaker without artifice, impassioned more by the power of thinking than feeling. She even symbolically exposed her character for the audience, the report noted, by "laying aside her bonnet and shawl." An austere presence of "stern intellectuality," she appeared wholly unaffiliated with sect, caste, or sexuality, disclosing herself through words that induced "prejudices to entirely vanish." Here Mott was not portrayed as a Quaker minister in her bonnet or a woman in her shawl, but as a public speaker whose sense and purpose could be gleaned through the honesty of her arguments.[121]

This characterization of Mott celebrated the idea of the "transcendent public," in which universal truths supplanted particular, narrow, and self-interested concerns. In general women were not perceived as the purveyors of monumental truths, since they lacked what most antebellum Americans associated with the masculine stature, voice, and authoritative presence of a powerful orator. Women lacked this "presence" before they spoke one word. As one women's rights supporter contended, "Do they suppose that truth, in falling from female lips, changes its nature before it reaches the ears of its listeners? One would suppose, although they deign to class truth with the feminine gender, that she must have a masculine exponent, or she would appear ridiculous and absurd."[122] Comprehensive and universal truths required depth and authenticity, two traits normally reserved for men, as Abby Price observed at the 1852 women's rights convention in Syracuse. She noted caustically that "women may speak when the themes are only trivial" but that they must remain silent when "the gathering is presumed to be from high and noble motives—to consider the truest and most important issues of the soul." Because women could not encompass the mind and soul of men, they could not presume to represent them. Such views recalled the biblical verse "Let them learn in silence; Adam was first formed, then Eve." If woman was an imperfect variation of man in the order of creation, this logic went, then any woman who dared to speak for men must be misrepresenting their interests.[123]

For women's rights advocates the church had to eliminate all caste privileges, most particularly the exclusive monopoly that men had over clerical offices, which elevated public speaking as the preeminent symbol of their vested authority. Dissenters and free church advocates criticized Protestant clergymen for clinging to certain traditional badges of personal distinction and physical display: the sacred text signified knowledge, the "drab coat and surplice" designated caste, and the pulpit was their exclusive platform for expressing words of wisdom. Given the legacy of the Quakers in rejecting a professional ministry, it is not surprising that the Congregational Friends revived the term "priestcraft" to encompass what they saw as the continuing abuses of a clerical caste. Priestcraft signified the artifice and duplicity involved in creating an office that elevated ordinary men above the rest of humanity. It was a term synonymous with "corrupt aristocracy," conveying the feudal image of courtiers and bishops pretending to please the sovereign while vying to win favor and power for themselves.[124]

Accordingly, the most telling sign of priestcraft for Mott was the "appropriation of the pulpit by one sex." Apostolic authority offered the most common reason for women's exclusion from teaching and preaching, especially the dictum borne out in the biblical verse that women remain silent in church and ask their husbands for instruction. Elizabeth Wilson summed up this credo by noting how ministers called for "woman always to be a learner" and "novice." Sarah Owen made a similar comment at the 1848 Rochester women's rights convention, sarcastically remarking that priests and husbands shared the same faith that a woman's opinion must always echo their own.[125]

Coequality, then, required that the church create a public forum that acknowledged men and women to be equally vested with the right to preach and that both encompassed and represented the opinions of the congregation. Dissenters promoted this idealized forum, encouraging a deliberative meeting of "so many different minds," where the public mind "presents itself without waiting to be re-presented." In this environment one was neither ruler or ruled. Men were not masters, and women were certainly not novices, because there were "fewer orators, but more speakers; fewer speeches, but more talk; less spoken, but more said." By engaging in what Abby Price described as "intercourse purified by a forgetfulness of sex," women and men could now recognize each other as coequal sources of the truth. Indeed, men and women could view each other as two corresponding parts of the whole, each contributing a partial understanding of the truth.[126]

"Of the parts the whole is formed." These were the words of an anonymous writer in the *Anti-Slavery Bugle* in 1849, and they stood along with a commitment to the "correspondence of the sexes, in true and rational relations." The writer concluded that women's presence must be felt not merely by "proxy" but personally in the church and the councils of the state. This premise, though it sounds simple, was hotly contested when the issue of coequal representation moved to center stage in the women's rights campaign. During the 1853 World Temperance Convention held in New York City, the Reverend Antoinette Brown captured the limelight when she presented her credentials as a delegate, appeared on the platform, and tried to speak. She was never given the chance. For nearly an hour she was hissed at and finally shouted down. From the audience there came repeated outbursts forbidding her to speak. One minister pointed his finger and called, "Shame on the Woman!" The controversy Brown generated continued for three days, as Horace Greeley aptly summarized in the *Tribune*: "The first day, crowding a woman from the platform; second day, gagging her; and the third day, voting that she should stay gagged." Prepared for Brown's inevitable exclusion, reformers organized the Whole World Temperance Convention, which they believed would expose the hypocrisy of the so-called half-world convention. In the same week feminists decided to add a women's rights convention to the roster of events to further foreground women's lack of public representation.[127]

A vital principle was at stake. Brown's presence on the platform had a double meaning because she appeared as both an elected delegate and a minister. Less than two weeks later she was formally ordained at the Congregational church in South Butler, New York, an occasion endorsed by two prominent free church advocates, Gerrit Smith and the Reverend Luther Lee of the Wesleyan Methodists. But on Sunday during the week of conventions in New York City, Brown gave a sermon, for which she was attacked by the religious press for falsely claiming the "title of Reverend." The mainstream press resorted to a wide range of sexual slurs. The *New York Times* compared Brown and her followers to an "Amazonian troupe." One paper described the Whole World Temperance Convention as "The New Barnum's Museum," noting that the main attraction was a freak show of transvestism with women clad in bloomers and abolitionist Charles Burleigh adorned in his long hair and curls. The *Express* depicted "Mr. Burleigh—a woman down to his shoulder blades, but a man, if pantaloons be the insigne, below." Burleigh was mocked and slandered for his feminine disguise, which was seen as a ruse for garnering him special "license" with the ladies on the platform. All the negative press coverage contributed to the mob of rowdies led by a Captain Rynders that invaded and disrupted the women's rights convention held that week. But the use of sexual innuendo and ridicule was not restricted to the media or mobs. When Brown left the platform at the World Temperance Convention, she noted a man's comments to her that "he had no objection to receive gentleman on the platform, provided they wore the garb of gentleman." With a touch of irony, Brown added, "You may gather your own inference from the *very gentlemanly* remark." [128]

The religious assumption that a divine edict ordained the offices and public calling undertaken by men proved to be a powerful metaphor of male representation. The life of the forum could invest men with special duties and distinctive skills as orators; thus men became a privileged caste. Borrowing from the biblical verse, men could retain their place closer to God as first formed, while women as eternal pupils and novices were obliged to remain outside the sacred circle of professional and public standing. In this traditional blueprint for gender relations, the church provided only one ideal for women's civil standing. Consistent with their position in the state, women could be members but not representatives. They could be limited rights-bearers but not among the privileged few chosen to assume public office. Nor could women be elevated to positions such as head of state or judge. Clerical authority and the divine sanction for a male monopoly over speech offered an overlapping formula of church and state authority for male representation. Not surprisingly, in 1853 the same battle between religious liberty and male representation appeared in the proceedings of the Massachusetts state constitutional convention, demonstrating the powerful political resonance of the struggle for coequality.[129]

Antebellum feminists saw the contradiction between abstract rights and the dominant political discourse defining representation as a masculine enterprise. Gender was never peripheral to the meaning of representation and was especially vital in explaining the masculine marks of presence and speech that were crucial to a nineteenth-century understanding of the public forum. Consequently, it was the "fetters of the law, both sacred and secular," as

Antoinette Brown claimed, that had placed a "thorny crown" on the brow and "leaden scepter" in the hands of woman. To untangle this unholy alliance between church and state, women had to be welcomed onto the same public platform, literally and figuratively, in constitutional terms, and vested with the right of coequal representation.[130]

5

The Political Fall of Woman

Skeptical of the claims of popular sovereignty, G. W. Knapp, a regular contributor to the *Lily*, cleverly parodied the political rhetoric of the day. In his 1854 article he renamed American democracy a "*man*-ocracy," a government that sidestepped the "*people*" and placed power "in the hands of . . . *men*." The fundamental reason for women's subordination rested, he wrote, on the "fall of man" that by the "grace of God" granted man the "right 'to rule over woman.'" At times provoking, in other instances castigating, his readers, Knapp revealed why this biblical ordinance prescribed civil death for the daughters of Eve. For their mother's transgression, women had forfeited the right to citizenship. With their "self-constituted proxical telescope," men had assumed the task of representing women; they not only voted in the "best" interests of women, but they literally became women's public eyes unto the world.[1] Women's loss of vision translated into invisibility. They had no public presence because a divestment of civil standing placed them beyond the protective arm of the state.

Knapp's comic retelling of the Fall broadcast a dual message, at once condemning and praising Adam for his bold defiance and deliberate action. In this construct, Eve "must be deceived," and she acts "hesitatingly, reluctantly, doubtingly," while Adam "looks Heaven full in the face and sins, boldly, deliberately, willfully, bidding the defiance to its degree."[2] Adam represented the quintessential public person, which Knapp captured through a celebration of his singularity, in sharp contrast to Eve's almost inert reaction.[3] Adam may be wrong in violating the command of God, but his strong will and presence, daring to look his accuser in the eye, demonstrated superiority. Adam earned his punishment with masculine honor, while Eve appeared vulnerable, cowardly, and therefore less capable of acting out her own will. In a most extreme act of defiance, Adam displayed his refusal to give himself to anyone, even God.

Several of the themes captured in this parody of the Fall detail the complex foundation of the "political non-existence of women."[4] Adam's exercise of will joined the distinctly male traits of indomitable resolution, risk, self-reliance, and personal control. All of these characteristics eluded the daughters of Eve, who lacked the masculine *virtù* of the republican tradition.[5] If Adam represented the idealized public man and citizen-soldier, then Eve and her descendants, as weak-minded beings, were potentially the enemy within. Political protection thus meant guarding the interests of men against the dangers posed by women as the "weaker vessel."[6] It was on these grounds that the state placed legal restraints on women's civil liberties and permitted the transfer of their property and person to male control. Women's provocative and seductive sexuality, another mark of weakness, called for greater chastity and chastisement. Male virtue and honor required that men ought to be granted the right to defend themselves against the sexual misconduct of women; self-defense was intimately connected to the power of men to avenge their reputation against accusations of female infidelity. During times of war, masculine virtue and valor assumed a larger, national purpose of reaffirming the state's power to protect the strong over the weak. Military protection translated male valor into a rationale for the use of force, even deadly force, against all enemies, regardless of sex, age, or status, and patriotic duty justified this use of force.

New democratic theories celebrated rather than concealed this decidedly masculine understanding of state power. In the decade before the women's rights movement, activists focused their attention on several nationally prominent issues—fugitive slave laws, capital punishment and prostitution, and the Mexican War—all of which addressed the use of deadly force and divestment. The fugitive slave law relied on recaption, the use of physical restraint, and the right of search and seizure against the body of the slave. The same common-law rule traditionally applied to runaway wives. This kind of force indicated the absence of personal liberty, as the state could transgress the bodily integrity of the female slave, and she had no right to defend herself against such violation. While slavery undermined personal liberty, capital punishment divested the citizen of the right to life. Prostitution similarly treated fallen women as civilly and morally dead, punishing women as traitors exiled from civil society. Finally, the politics of war promoted the glory of conquest, the condemnation of weakness, and the exclusion of women from the spoils of victory—full citizenship. Although women were viewed as passive objects or ciphers in the march of conquest, and occasionally were even taken as the spoils of war, they, too, became dangerous enemies if as political dissidents they placed themselves beyond the protection of men.[7]

This chapter explores these basic developments, beginning with the fugitive slave laws and ending with the impact of the Mexican War on women's civil and political rights. The common thread among them is the consistent designation of women as "civilly dead." It was in this way that women were denied constitutional protection and, as a class or caste, identified as outcasts or traitors.

The story of the Fall of Woman contributed to the overall political understanding of divestment. Women had been placed under a "primal curse," and as Antoinette Brown observed in 1853, the curse became a "blessing" of authority for men.[8] This unequal transaction fit neatly within Jean-Jacques Rousseau's rules for the social contract. While man secured added power and patronage from the state that enabled him to conserve his superior rights and rank, women found themselves reduced to what Lucy Stone called a "blank" and Lucretia Mott described as a "cypher."[9] In fact, women were not the only ciphers. Outside the corporate state and body politic were other outcasts or ciphers: children, blacks, slaves, infidels, Indians, resident foreigners, lunatics, convicts, and paupers—all the dregs, drudges, or dependents who lacked political value.[10]

State power and authority clearly relied on a gendered understanding in which force, aggression, risk, and self-defense were celebrated as both democratic and masculine virtues. Antebellum democracy incorporated these assumptions of male authority into its exclusive definition of full citizenship. Strangely enough, freedom and subjection were grafted onto the rhetoric of the natural right to "life, liberty, and the pursuit of happiness" found in the Declaration of Independence. Fugitive slave laws, capital punishment and prostitution, and the Mexican War exposed the democratic tensions inherent in life and death and slavery and liberty, and in military aggression and a "pursuit of happiness" measured by the acquisition of land, wealth, and security. This matrix of political and legal values was related both to women's rights and to the evolving meaning of constitutional protection. Female slaves were pivotal to the critique of fugitive slave laws, just as female prostitutes were essential to shaping criminal codes, and female traitors or conquered women were crucial to the enforcement of martial law and military conquest. Consequently, ciphers on the boundaries of the social compact contributed to the discourse of democratic citizenship just as much as its core membership of valiant white male voters did.

She Is Dead and Gone to Heaven

Through her discussion of the slave auction in *Uncle Tom's Cabin*, Harriet Beecher Stowe captured the sentiments of female abolitionists toward the shocking treatment of slave women. By openly selling women on the court-house steps, the slave auction transgressed every rule of justice and signified for Stowe a public "inquisition" that both mocked and mimicked the judicial system. Her chapter on the Russell sisters portrayed the precarious position of mulatto women sold at auction. Despite their cultivated upbringing and temporary protection as the property of a northerner, the sisters fell prey to the forces of the market. In response to the demands of creditors and aided by the advice of lawyers, the "respectable" firm of B. and Co. "made over" the two girls as part of a lucrative real estate transaction, sending them south into slavery. The cool calculation of the attorneys and astute business practices of the New York merchant had much in common with the callous dealings of the slave market. Both traded in slaves and souls, and both marketed women as first-rate articles sold for profit and pleasure to the highest bidder.[11]

Though Stowe borrowed heavily from the conventional plot of the "tragic mulatto," she slightly altered the characterization of white slavery by reveal-ing flaws in democracy.[12] Ironically, the enslaved Russell sisters invoke the image of disinherited daughters whose divestment cost them not only social status, moral rectitude, and freedom but their womanhood as well. Although a life of shame and prostitution awaited slaves like Susan Russell blessed with a beautiful and fair complexion, the loss of sexual virtue had as much to do with the public auction itself. Placed before the public eye, the two sisters were transformed from innocent women into spectacles for the male gaze.[13] Subject to "handling, examining, and commenting," the sisters, "fitted out for the auction" and paraded before a "crowd of commonplace men," shed the veil of respectability and civil immunities that protected them "body and soul."[14]

When exhibited in this fashion, the fallen slave became a victim of manoc-racy, revealing, in part, the cruel paradox embedded in this peculiar mixture of mass politics and male domination. A gathering of commonplace men did not create a realm of equals but a disorderly assembly of spectators in which passion and private interest ruled. Publicity of this kind betrayed not only true womanhood but distorted the quest for a sustainable personal liberty in the public sphere. Rather than placing women on a pedestal, the slave auction symbolized women's "civil death"—the systematic and silent surrender of life and liberty without due process of law.

Not surprisingly, the theme of civil death assumed a prominent place in the "list of facts of Man's Tyranny over woman" included in Stanton's Declaration of Sentiments. While marriage provided the means for women's divestment, the law enforced women's civil death. As Stanton declared, the husband became her "master—the law giving him the power to deprive her of her liberty, and to administer chastisement."[15] Through this transaction women not only lost civil liberties, but men garnered additional personal rights. In other words, slavery and civil death shared one crucial result: what slaves and married women lost in political protection and liberty, men and masters gained in personal power.

The comparison between women and slaves was more than hyperbole, for there was a common-law foundation for women's legal enslavement. Divestment, like slavery, relied on the alienation of rights, or the transfer of rights from one person to another. Jean-Jacques Rousseau had recognized this in *The Social Contract* when he argued that civil liberty could never coexist with slavery.[16] Nineteenth-century jurists agreed, according to legal historian Earl Maltz, that alienation stood in direct conflict with the principle of protecting inalienable rights.[17] In 1850 Paulina Wright Davis raised this principle of inalienable rights during the Worcester convention, declaring that the "rights and liberties of one human being cannot be made the property of another, though they were redeemed for him or her by the life of that other; for rights cannot be forfeited by way of salvage, and they are in their nature unpurchasable and inalienable."[18] But coverture and common-law rules did allow a wife to lose her civil life, liberty, and property, and as legal commentator Timothy Walker observed in the late 1840s, her status was the "exact definition of political slavery."[19] A husband's "gentle chastisement" implied the use of physical force, restraint allowed for imprisonment, and divestment meant that the most sacred rights could be suspended in the privacy of the home. Stanton asserted in 1852 that a married women, like a slave, could be robbed of her property, "stripped of her children," and "whipped and locked up by her lord."[20] Inside or outside the courthouse, property rights took precedence over the inalienable rights of women or slaves.

The connection between slavery and women's rights was far more complicated. Slaves did have the right of self-defense, although successful use of this argument for slaves in court cases was rare. Rape did not fall under the protection of self-defense, as evidenced by the 1855 Missouri trial of Celia, a slave women sent to her death for murder despite her attorney's expert attempt to prove that she had killed her assailant and master in defense of her sexual honor.[21] Physical restraint and force were accepted practices of slavery, and rape, according to southern law, was defined as trespass, implying that a master was not in violation of this right if the female slave being assaulted was his own property. By 1859 a Mississippi judge even concluded that the common law was null and void in cases involving the rape of a slave by her master. Indeed, this judge, like others, comforted himself with the legal fiction that slave law was a law unto itself and a slave's status was a matter of statutory law. In this manner judges found a rationale for the blatant disregard of a slave woman's right to due process and protection against sexual assault.[22]

But southern legal culture also demonstrated an unusual ambivalence toward the most intimate of sexual crimes—incest. Jurists condemned this shocking behavior as immoral, yet they withheld their outrage by treating the act as a rare occurrence. More importantly, incest was not considered an abuse of patriarchal power but as the opposite; it was so unnatural that the greatest degree of legal proof was necessary to prove that such a horrible crime had been committed. Even for this most dangerous disregard of family harmony, the courts remained reluctant to prosecute heads of households, primarily because their greater concern was for preserving the sanctity of male authority.[23]

In the North as well as the South, rape was defined as a violation between strangers, which made the law less likely to perceive domestic violence within the sanctuary of the household. Southern courts sanctioned the abuse of wives and slaves, claiming as Justice Ruffin of North Carolina did in the landmark case of *State v. Mann* (1829) that beating and chastisement were needed because "the power of the master must be absolute to render the submission of the slave perfect." It was the disapproval of society, not the force of law, Ruffin further believed, that would shame masters and husbands into treating their slaves and wives with kindness and "mildness."[24]

Despite the common concern for protecting male authority in the family, free and single women possessed basic rights that were denied slave women. Free women could own, inherit, and bequeath property; make contracts; and move freely, but such rights were circumscribed by coverture. Married women were not viewed literally as the political equivalent of slaves and could claim certain protections under the law. One telling difference was that women consented to the terms of coverture, while slaves had no capacity to choose or reject their status. Still, as Stanton noted, there remained an uneasy complementarity between the common-law reasons for divesting wives and slaves of rights. It was not that the law treated women exactly as slaves; the real problem, as Walker noted, was the illusion that women were not divested of fundamental rights. By being forced to see the connection between the status of women and the status of slaves, jurists would have to admit the flaws in the prevailing system of laws. Lifting the veil, they would be forced to recognize the dangerous similarity between married women's loss of personal liberty and that of slaves.

Stanton's critique reflected a growing concern among abolitionists over the violation of republican principles. In his 1844 *Views of American Constitutional Law*, William Goodell argued that slavery was contrary to every feature of a republican form of government. In addition to denying the well-known principles of a republic—life, liberty, and the pursuit of happiness—slavery, he believed, made it impossible for the sovereign power of the state to be lodged in the people. When "one fourth, one third, or one half of '*the people*' are held in slavery," Goodell claimed, there was "no 'common interest,' no 'commonwealth,'" which meant there was no "'public.'" Instead of forming a more perfect union, as the preamble of the federal Constitution stipulates, one-half of the citizens were permitted to "trample" on the rights of the other half, transforming one portion of the population into "despots" and another into "enemies."[25]

If the practice of representative government was lodged on a faulty claim, then exactly what kind of public sphere existed in the southern states? For Goodell the South was at best a war zone in which military force regulated the conduct of slaves. "Military patrols" combined with "acts of outlawry" allowed the states "to hunt down and shoot, without judge or jury, a portion of the people."[26] Goodell echoed the arguments of Alvin Stewart, William Jay, and other antislavery constitutional theorists who asserted that slavery contradicted the basic premise of the "due and equitable process of law."[27] This argument gained greater currency during the 1840s because of repeated disputes over fugitive slave cases. In the 1842 Supreme Court decision of *Prigg v. Pennsylvania*, Justice Story defended the constitutionality of the 1793 fugitive slave clause, which provoked lawyers, legislators, and reformers to challenge the ruling.[28] Much of the controversy over fugitive slave laws centered around the common-law right of recaption. Even at an earlier date, in the 1828 revision of the New York laws, the right of recaption had been limited by granting fugitives the traditional writ of *homine replegiando*, which required that slave catchers demonstrate claims to ownership of the slave by appearing before the courts.[29] When in 1837 several states passed personal liberty laws, antislavery activists argued that fugitives and free blacks had to have the right of redress for the violations of life, liberty, and property as a matter of equal protection.[30]

The right of recaption evoked the image of kidnapping and abduction, two violations that combined the crime of robbery with the threat of domestic violence. Goodell argued that the Constitution guaranteed protection from domestic violence and that it should "*ensure domestic tranquility*." In his careful definition of the words "domestic" and "violence," he suggested that the nation and one's place of residence could be considered "domestic"; "violence" encompassed several meanings but mainly connoted some kind of action, such as "to outrage, to force, to injure," or to commit "ravishment, rape."[31] The extent to which the theme of domestic violence applied to women emerged in the Prigg case. A fugitive slave, Margaret Morgan, had married a free black, had lived in Pennsylvania for five years, and was forcefully removed from her family. Story's decision, however, contained a complicated and possibly contradictory rationale for the right of recaption. Although Story endorsed recaption through the self-help rule, granting the slaveowner the entire authority to seize his or her property, he also ruled that this must be done "without any breach of the peace, or illegal violence."[32] Given the nature of the action, the use of physical force to invade the family and forcibly abduct the individual was implied. There was thus a double edge to Story's decision: he endorsed slave recaption but made it extremely difficult to accomplish without violating the requirement of a peaceable use of self-help.

Yet antebellum Americans also understood domestic violence in purely sexual terms, a pattern evidenced by the passage of the antiabduction laws in Massachusetts in 1845. In *Commonwealth v. Cook* the statute was tested, and the court offered a narrower definition of abduction that applied only to women forcibly brought to a house of prostitution.[33] This ruling recognized the possibility of white slavery and the threat of abduction. According to the terminology developed by Goodell, kidnapping implied domestic violence.[34]

But another form of recaption firmly rooted in the common-law interpretation of marital rights gained the attention of women's rights activists. The issue for activists was whether wives, either those who fled from their husbands or those forced to abandon their homes, could face the same treatment as fugitive slaves. After reviewing the case of an "orphan lady," in which the husband deserted, kidnapped, and then robbed his wife of her possessions and children, Ohio feminist Adeline Swift concluded, "that proves that the husband can compel his wife to leave her home and children, or he can compel her to return; and if she refuses to go with him, he can call men to aid him to securing her, and she has no redress unless she can prove extreme cruelty. Does not that show the husband is master of the wife?"[35]

Swift's commentary demonstrates that feminists were reinterpreting the meaning of recaption. While no published case in American law existed after the Revolution in which a wife was forced to return to her husband's house, an 1856 case in Rhode Island indicated that one husband had at least tried to assert this right. The trial judge dismissed this interpretation of the husband's authority, and the husband was convicted of assault.[36] Obviously, the real point was that women faced material consequences for leaving their families; they could lose support, property, and the custody of their children. "Orphan lady" served as an apt term for describing the conditions of runaway or deserted wives, especially given the legal terminology applied to married women during the antebellum period. In his 1845 treatise *The Legal Rights, Liabilities, and Duties of Women*, Edward Mansfield sought to clarify that the law placed the wife in the *"custody"* of her husband. Upon marriage, Mansfield explained, the *"personal control"* of the wife passed to her husband, which likened the legal standing of wives to that of fugitive slaves. Through his custodial authority the husband had the right to his wife's "services." He could "reclaim her when absent" and use "gentle means of restraint," and he had the "right to claim aid from the law and its officers."[37] Mansfield's explanation was important insofar as he used restraint and recaption to uphold the principle of custodial authority. Thus, although there was no legal way to make a wife return, and fugitive wives only on rare occasions faced the same treatment as slaves, the notion of marital custodianship was an assumption that could be applied to punish wives who left their husbands by denying those women claims to alimony, custody, or their property.

CUSTODY AND THE RIGHTS OF PERSONS
UNDER THE LAW

This classification of custody introduced new twists in the understanding of wives and slaves as "civilly dead." Whereas coverture had worked to rank women as aliens (nonconsenting subjects) in republican discourse, the term "custody" reflected a general shift away from "volitional allegiance" and the move toward "birth-right" entitlements as the basis for citizenship.[38] The question was no longer whether a citizen chose his or her national identity, but whether he or she could claim personal title to the exercise of civil and political rights. The condition of both slaves and women created conceptual difficulties because their status could change: slaves could become freemen and freewomen, while women could become wives. In either case few jurists were willing to acknowledge that free black men or single women should gain full political entitlements. Somehow jurists assumed that the state should retain partial custody. A Georgia Supreme Court judge had little difficulty ruling in 1848 that free blacks were the "wards" of the state, while a delegate to the 1853 Massachusetts constitutional convention likewise claimed that single and married women relied on the political guardianship of male representatives.[39]

During the antebellum period most discussions about citizenship consistently ignored the status of black women. One reason for this omission was that the civil standing of black women transgressed the boundaries of two distinct civil classifications. To consider the legal rights of black women would have vividly revealed the degree to which arbitrary discrepancies were drawn among different groups of citizens, suggesting that the political order perpetuated distinct ranks or castes. Jurists preferred to retain a sharp dichotomy between two kinds of standing rather than indicate the possibility of various gradations.[40] In an antislavery newspaper, *Emancipator and Republican*, one political commentator did note the strong similarity between the status of white and black women.[41] While this may have been true in Massachusetts, where free black men shared more civil and political rights than black and white women, in other states, such as Ohio, two Black Codes clearly distinguished women by race. One law prohibited free black men and women from migrating into the state, and another statute permitted the racial segregation of public schools.[42]

At the same time, constitutional theorists struggled to find some common ground for identifying native-born Americans as the "people of the United States." In part, the issue rested on finding a suitable category to designate what basic rights belonged to individual members. It became increasingly clear that the word "citizen" failed in this purpose because its meaning was constantly contested in the courts, the legislatures, and the state constitutional conventions. Such ambiguity encouraged legal theorists to identity some intermediary status that distinguished legal from political entitlements.[43] As William Goodell demonstrated in his treatise, if the most fundamental legal right was due process of law, then the language used in the clause offered some point of departure for determining essential civil entitlements. Given his penchant for etymology, Goodell concluded that the clause offered the one suitable definition of "person" as the basic individual unit of civil society.[44] In a similar fashion Mansfield developed a comparable category, listing what he considered to be the "absolute rights of persons."[45] Women's rights advocates such as Elisha Hurlbut used this claim to critique a husband's custody over his wife's "person," because, as he asserted unequivocally, "She must remain a distinct person, as by the civil law."[46]

The growing focus on personhood moved the discussion beyond the notion of purely abstract or innate rights and toward the assumption that these rights were somehow physically displayed through the action of each person. The body represented a new location for the exercise of rights. Women's status as partial wards of the state or their husbands severely jeopardized the extent to which a woman was recognized in the law as a person. When placed under the custody of their husbands, wives lost the rights of "personal control" and "personal independence."[47] Although civil death was still "life without speech and without action," custody offered a new vocabulary that highlighted how wives and fugitive slaves lost their right to personal security because their words and actions could not be used to defend their bodies. Fugitive slaves surrendered not only the right to bear witness before an impartial jury, but if subject to recaption, they sacrificed their bodies and souls to what abolitionists described as "inquisitorial" and "unreasonable searches and seizures." These violations emerged most visibly in the treatment of slave women sold at auction and rendered slave women as one of the most potent symbols of domestic violence. As women and slaves, mothers and daughters, they were publicly divested of their personhood through three transactions: they were placed in custody, stripped of everything, and subject to the scrutiny of the public eye. Not merely fettered and bound in chains, these women lost the right to control their bodies and their movements, and the right to shield themselves from physical violation. Unable to defend their bodies from a hostile invasion and captivity, slave women on the auction block failed to disclose themselves as persons, appearing instead as mere bodies incapable of displaying the marks of citizenship or personhood.

ORPHANS AND OUTCASTS

This view of personhood directly informed the political agenda of the early women's rights movement. In February 1847 a Meeting of Women was held in Philadelphia to discuss the subject of slavery and petitioning. Paulina Wright acted as president, joined by Hannah Stickney as secretary, and Lucretia Mott addressed the audience "in an eloquent and a forceful manner." Organized three days after the Pennsylvania Liberty Law was introduced as a bill before the state legislature, the meeting was aimed at safeguarding free blacks from abduction and limiting the effectiveness of recaption under the terms laid down by the *Prigg* ruling.[48] At the annual meeting of the American Anti-Slavery Society in 1848, Mott again gave a speech that focused on personal liberty, domestic violence, and the duty of the government to protect all of its inhabitants. As Mott declared, the "great principles of human freedom" required that "every man had a right to his own body, and that no man had a right to enslave or imbrute his brother, or to hold him for a moment as his property—to put his fellow-being on the auction-block, and sell him to the highest bidder, making the most cruel separations of families."[49] Invoking the language of custody, Mott defined slavery as the exercise of "irresponsible control, this legal right to their persons."[50] During the same year, a female abolitionist in Ohio called for the "Free daughters of America" to recognize how the despotism of slavery crushed their slave sisters, and she cited the outrages perpetrated against slave women as the loss of "ownership of self," "bodily torture," and sexual "submission." Furthermore, female slaves suffered from the lack of legal protection through their the loss of will, wages, education, and mobility, and "even to use her own feet *ad libitum* would be called the highest crime."[51]

The same concern over irresponsible control surfaced during the early women's rights conventions as well. In her letter to the 1850 Salem meeting, Elizabeth Wilson described the husband as "a licensed woman-whipper," whose right to use force stripped wives of their dignity and deprived them of liberty without due process of law.[52] Ernestine Rose offered the most dramatic rendering of the slave analogy, contending that the wife subjected her "body, mind, and soul, unconditionally to the husband." Marriage also implied the cruel separation of families. Coverture did more than extinguish women's legal personality; it severed the wife from her birthright entitlements, cut her ties to her family, and even forced her to relinquish her surname. A woman's former existence "died," and the wife's new, partial if not impaired, identity was incorporated into the husband's. As Rose further asserted, women were subject to the control of men from the cradle to the grave, because their father, guardian, or husband conveyed them "like some piece of merchandise over to the other."[53]

It was particularly fitting that Mott's summary of "great principles" in 1848 also repeated the words from the 1838 antislavery society constitution, a document drafted only a year following the passage of the Massachusetts Personal Liberty Act. In 1836 the Boston Female Anti-Slavery Society had initiated the proceedings of *Commonwealth v. Aves*, perhaps the most important fugitive slave case relative to the evolving legal arguments of antislavery advocates. Known as "little Med's case," the Massachusetts court disputed the status of a young female child in order to determine what restrictions the state could enforce in opposition to the 1793 federal Fugitive Slave Act.[54] Abolitionists, fully aware of the effects of slavery on family rights, long had recognized that slaves "are denied the enjoyments of domestic life, being liable at any moment to be separated."[55] If domestic unity defined one meaning of the family, then "separations" signified the hostile "tearing asunder" of sacred family ties.[56] In the Aves case the theme of separation centered around the relationship between mother and daughter. The attorney for the slave-owner argued that the child Med was not the property but the ward of the master, and as her legal guardian the slaveowner gained custody that denied the mother any legal recourse to protect the child. Any "natural" entitlement to the child was "void," and the oath of the mother as to her parental status carried no legal standing, because mother and child were legally separated at birth.[57]

The political implication of this kind of separation created a far less paternal picture of the legal guardianship of slaves than that which the attorney for little Med's master was claiming. Civil death made slave parents the equivalent of political outcasts, and slave children had more in common with orphans than with wards. Abolitionists emphasized the strong similarity between fugitive slaves and "outcasts" by conveying fugitive slaves' status as exiles shorn of a national identity and seeking political asylum.[58] Indeed, fugitive slaves lacked any lawful place of residence that entitled them to the full protection of the law. Goodell best explained the legal connection. The word "outcast" invoked the "spirit of caste . . . founded on circumstances of *color*, of *blood*, or *race*, or of *descent*," and descent defined the legal practice that the slave "child shall follow the condition of mother."[59] Descent also led to the divestment of family heritage and civil status, because the slave code operated as a "bill of attainder" that stipulated for Goodell that "*Slaves can not take by descent*. They can not be heirs. They can not inherit, or hold lands. They can receive and hold nothing by will or bequest. The slave can hold no property."[60] To Goodell this bill of attainder sentenced slaves to a "judgment of death" and "a corruption of blood," which was why the slave mother was civilly dead, receiving all the penalties of treason and criminal conviction: political exile and the loss of liberty for themselves and "their *posterity*."[61] In turn, slave children as political orphans were fully divested of their constitutional inheritance of birthrights. As most female abolitionists agreed, this practice of descent and divestment placed women at the center of a slave system "which robs mothers of their children, and children of their parents."[62]

The Aves case raised important considerations about divestment and personal custody that applied to the area of substantive due process. Did the federal government's protection of slavery under the fugitive slave clause enforce a legitimate state interest, such as the right of property, or did the government exceed its authority and promote an interest that was too burdensome to other civil rights, such as the right to personal liberty? By employing the writ of habeas corpus, which literally meant "you have the body," abolitionists used the writ in a civil context for challenging child custody. Since the writ of habeas corpus provided redress for illegal or improper deportations, abolitionists drew another legal link between political exile and the condition of the fugitive slave. The plight of the slave mother and child nevertheless went to the heart of the dispute over birthright entitlements, primarily because the mother's natural entitlement to have children was declared null and void. By 1851, in another decision in Pennsylvania, Judge Kane ruled that the state actually had claims on slave children while in the "womb."[63] Slave law not only protected masters' right to claim slave children upon birth, but their custodial rights gave them "personal control" over the fetus and, of course, the body of the slave mother. By demonstrating how the law invaded the body of the mother and separated her from her child, the custody of slave women implied that a woman's womb—her interior space—could be subject to "unreasonable searches and seizures" and the right of recaption. Civil death thus meant the child "died" in the womb, and as the state severed the legal umbilical cord, it simultaneously alienated the "rights of person" from both mother and child.

SELF-PROTECTION AND PERSONAL LIBERTY

By 1851 women's rights advocates had incorporated the critique of the fugitive slave law into their own political perspective on women's divestment of civil liberty. At the second national convention held in Worcester, Lucy Stone opened her address with an attack on the new 1850 Fugitive Slave Law, asking her audience if the "men who passed such a law are sons of worthy mothers!" Stone further remarked that women were political fugitives, "outlawed" in government, with neither a voice nor a part in its public deliberations. Ernestine Rose likewise cited the stain on the statute book, and she drew a parallel between women and slaves as outlaws. Both had their homes invaded and ransacked, the escaped slave's refuge by federal marshals, the widow's household by cold and calculating executors. Clarina H. I. Nichols offered another comparison between fugitive slaves and runaway wives, detailing the plight of a mother flying from her *"legal protector,"* who pursued her relentlessly from place to place, collecting her wages and personal belongings. Denied legal redress, the wife fled the state to regain "possession of her alienated property rights," seeking sanctuary just like the exiled fugitive slave on the run from the law.[64]

For antebellum feminists the fugitive slave law illuminated the connection between self-protection and personal liberty. The legal definition of personal liberty contained three features: first, the ability to move, to change one's residence, or to follow one's inclination without restraint; second, the right to speak, write, or publish one's beliefs freely; and third, the right to engage in useful employment or any pursuit that was not contrary to the welfare of society. In 1854, as the anonymous writer "Civis" claimed, all of these rights defined the husband's power to choose his residence or domicile, engage in any occupation, and provide for his wife and family "as his own judgment, or his own whims or caprices may dictate."[65] The husband had the liberty to keep his family together, which was implied by the self-help rule that empowered husbands (in theory) and slaveowners literally to use their own force to recapture runaway wives or slaves. Liberty served as a positive power to preserve the household, in which the government recognized the husband's right as a private citizen to reestablish his domicile. Husbands had a claim to privacy from state intervention when the sanctity of the "master's house" was at stake.

Crucial to this view of the master's house was the husband's economic freedom in preserving his property. The common-law rule of recaption assumed that the wife had unlawfully seized her own body and transported this possession against the law, making the fugitive wife a robber, thief, and outlaw. As Lucy Stone argued in 1852, the theory of marital custody divided the wife against her own person, for the husband "has a right to her, even against herself."[66] For activists the husband could legally kidnap his wife's children, usurping her right to protect and care for her offspring. He might deny his wife any freedom, carefully supervising her every action or denying her any privacy for her own thoughts. If he did compel his wife to leave through threats of physical violence, he could follow her, harass her, and still demand his rights as her guardian. On all counts, then, the wife's personal liberty was devastatingly curtailed, and her ability to have a "personal existence" was seriously restricted.[67] Without liberty—the ability to control one's livelihood, protect one's health and children, and disclose one's view—a woman lacked a civil life.

Feminists realized that the law placed severe restrictions on the husband's right to restrain his wife in cases of separation, but occasionally some men relied on this common-law right, if without the support of the courts.[68] The greater problem was how recaption reinforced the husband's power of restraint within the household. Many women, "Civis" observed, failed to leave their husbands because of economic need or their desire not to be separated from their children.[69] Such restraints reflected the custodial authority of the husband, which assumed a material and physical form (control of money, children, and household) as well as the internalized authority of the husband that paralyzed women out of fear or "constant vigilance."[70] In 1853 at the convention held in New York City, Lucy Stone raised this issue when she described a woman who had been locked in her house for years.[71] Less than a month later at the Cleveland convention, Abby Kelley Foster offered an explanation for such behavior. "Woman is always in the presence of her master," she explained, and "therefore she does not confess she wants to be free," because her dependence breeds a reluctance to "utter herself" and voice her "inalienable desire for freedom."[72] Stanton agreed, for the lack of privacy and legal dependency made the average married woman incapable of "thinking and judging for herself" and ultimately fitted the wife, if not for auction, then for her custody as the "ward of man."[73]

By 1856 another fugitive slave case commanded the support of women's rights activists, particularly Lucy Stone and Henry Blackwell. In Cincinnati Margaret Gardner was tried for attempting to kill her children in an effort to protect them from slavery. Stone remarked in a public speech that this woman's "love of liberty and her children was so great, that she would rather kill her children (and herself) rather than return to slavery." With emphasis Stone added that she herself "would give the woman the knife."[74] The Gardner case clearly reflected the earlier fascination generated by the Russell sisters, whose case also had focused on the way slavery stripped mothers and daughters of their personal liberty and civil protection.[75] Yet the later case emphasized more vividly the underlying issues of self-protection and self-defense, for Margaret Gardner had decided to use physical force to defend her children. Like the heroic Spartan or Roman mother, she decided that real death was better than civil death, and she took control of her destiny by refusing to surrender to the brutal system of slavery. At the heart of this case was a dramatic rendering of how the alienation of rights rested on brute force, and how slaves had to surrender their freedom or resist unto death itself.[76]

Unlike the story of the Russell sisters, the Gardner case accentuated brute force and physical resistance and thereby called for a fundamental redefinition of personal relations in the family. Rather than treat the father and husband as the center of the family and master of his private domain, antebellum feminists rejected the wife's status as an "appendage" or part of the husband's legal personhood.[77] Three years before the Gardner case, Henry Blackwell had challenged the traditional definition of the family, arguing that the bond between mother and child was just as important, since the mother's child was "bone of her bone, flesh of her flesh, a very part and parcel of her being." Quite cleverly, Blackwell countered the metaphor of marriage as "one flesh" or "one person" with the same biblical allusion, yet with a very different meaning. Mother and child deserved the same legal protection as father and family, for a woman had a stronger personal bond with her child. Men could not sever this tie without violating the mother's personal liberty and divesting "a very part and parcel of her being."[78]

In the end the issue of personal liberty returned to self-protection, and even suffrage. Adopting the first person in her appeal for woman suffrage, Clarina H. I. Nichols claimed that "I am deprived of the power of protecting myself and my children."[79] By restructuring power relations in the family and domicile, women would move from the margin as appendages to the center as equal guardians. On a personal level women's legal personality and liberty would no longer be defined through their husbands, for the law would recognize women as "distinct person[s] in the law."

In 1848 Frederick Douglass identified the same feature in the master-slave relation, noting that the law obscured the boundaries between their bodies, as he explained in his "Letter to My Old Master": "I am myself; you are yourself; we are two distinct persons, equal persons. What you are I am. You are a man, and so am I. God created both, and made us separate beings. I am not by nature bound to you, or you to me. Nature does not make your existence depend upon me, or mine to depend on you. I cannot walk upon your legs, or you upon mine. I cannot breath for you, or you for me; I must breath for myself, and you for yourself. We are distinct persons, and are each equally provided with faculties necessary to our individual existence."[80] Ernestine Rose echoed this position, concluding that the legal fiction of husband and wife as "one person" ignored the obvious fact that their still-distinct physical bodies were not merged. In spite of their civil death, women when married had not "ceased to feel pleasure or pain."[81] Henceforth, she argued, women had to secure the same freedom of privacy and self-protection as men at the level of the body—their flesh and bone—and not to be forced to endure either private or public divestment of their bodily integrity. Given their full measure of personal liberty through equal protection, women would come one step closer to appearing publicly as citizens, rather than exercising—as Jane Swisshelm ironically contended in 1848—the more "common privilege women enjoy in this land of being publicly sold at the auction block."[82]

Crimes against the Heart

It was not only the fugitive slave but the equally powerful image of the prostitute that appeared in the deliberations of the early women's rights conventions. Ernestine Rose, at the 1853 national women's rights convention held in Cleveland, stated emphatically that she refused to acknowledge a sexual double standard of morals, and then she summarized how the unwritten laws led to the degradation and dishonor of fallen women. Addressing her audience, Rose asked if the "mark of Cain" had been placed on their "foreheads." *"If she the victim, is cast out of the pale of humanity, shall the despoiler go free?* (Cries of no! no! no! [from the audience]) *And yet, he goes free!*"[83] Rose's rousing appeal to the plight of the prostitute came directly from the seduction novel in eighteenth-century sentimental literature. This convention was so popular that Rose's audience clearly anticipated, almost in a call-and-response tradition, her climactic statement of injustice—that the seducer "goes free!" By 1853 the fallen woman had achieved an iconic meaning. The familiar portrait of the female seduction victim not only permeated the speeches of women's rights activists but had become a common refrain among moral reformers, politicians, and even lawyers, who used fictional narrative to defend clients in rape cases.

Postrevolutionary treatments of wronged womanhood adhered to a predictable biblical formula of prelapsarian innocence followed by the fall from grace and, finally, virtue reclaimed though moral atonement and death. Popular novels such as Susanna Rowson's *Charlotte Temple*, which was first published in America in 1794 but maintained a devoted audience well into the nineteenth century, translated this religious plot into a morality tale. Lured from the safe haven of the family and her parents' protection, Charlotte Temple is first deceived by her French schoolmistress, kidnapped, and conveyed to the bed of her seducer. Poor and forsaken, Charlotte eventually finds herself pregnant, friendless, homeless, and cruelly dispatched "to a premature and dishonored grave."[84]

In many ways the seduction novel stood in sharp contrast to the antebellum feminist pursuit of women's rights, liberty, and real happiness. Seduction was as much a sign of female weakness as male tyranny. A persistent feature in novels such as *Charlotte Temple* was the unresolved tension between that sympathy which the innocent female victim evoked and the divine retribution demanded to expiate *her* sin. Throughout *Charlotte Temple* Rowson portrays Charlotte as a character worthy of compassion, yet culpable for her sexual misconduct and parental disobedience. Her loss of virtue results in physical suffering, punishment, death, and the "curse" of her mother.[85] While promoting the enlightened themes of reasonableness and sympathy, Rowson still emphasized the equally powerful and familiar dictate that family honor be avenged. Like the penalty placed on Eve and the mark of Cain, the curse on Charlotte evoked the Old Testament command of an "eye for an eye," or the moral law that sin must be redeemed through an equivalent physical punishment. According to this biblical law, moral wrongs were not merely forgiven but repaid through pain. The seduction novel counterbalanced sympathy with the punitive demands for sacrificial atonement.

Antebellum women's rights advocates were fascinated with the seduced victim, because seduction revealed the gross inequities embedded in the common- and criminal-law definition of the right of "self-defense." According to its most basic definition, the right of self-defense implied the ability to defend oneself against bodily harm or injury. As a corollary, criminal law recognized the rule of necessity, in which murderers were exempt from criminal prosecution and liability when acting in self-defense. Women, however, did not have the same right to self-defense; the common law placed wives and daughters under the protection of husbands and fathers, whose duty included the physical protection of female dependents within their families. Traditionally, seduction was treated as a crime that concerned men; seduced daughters had to seek redress through their fathers. It was the father's right to his daughter's services that had been stolen, making seduction a crime of theft. Seduction demonstrated the similarities and subtle differences between the rape of a slave and the rape of a daughter. Raping a slave was trespass, whereas for a daughter it was theft; a slave's body was treated as property and an inanimate terrain, while the daughter's body was domesticated space that housed a valued treasure: a woman's chastity. This view nevertheless reduced the daughter to the status of a servant, whose sexual value, according to the common law, could only be redeemed through her paternal guardian. According to the English common law, women had no standing in such cases, nor did they have the right to defend themselves or represent their interests before a court of law.[86]

These legal guidelines became hotly contested in the area of criminal law, as reformers, lawyers, and politicians debated the "unwritten law," that is, the right of husbands, relatives, or even seduced women to defend their sexual honor by killing the offender. Underlying the unwritten law was the belief that bodily harm applied to personal reputation and social honor. During the antebellum period the unwritten law gained a new legal meaning, for as New York jurist Elisha Hurlbut contended in 1845, such offenses constituted "crimes against the sentiments and affections." Seduction now had emotional costs that demanded legal redress.[87]

Yet as Hendrik Hartog has demonstrated for the postbellum period, the unwritten law allowed aggrieved husbands to escape conviction for murdering their wives' lovers. At stake in these criminal cases was the court's attempt to defend the "husband's rights," in which the husband's emotional sanity was inextricably linked to his masculine honor. As women's rights advocates realized, this understanding of masculine honor was an integral part of male civic identity. The unwritten law was predicated on the idea that the state had an interest in protecting men's right to defend, and if necessary avenge, their honor against sexual infidelity.[88]

Still, for antebellum feminists the route to unmasking the unwritten law emerged through their combined concern over capital punishment and seduction during the 1840s. Rose's reference to prostitutes and the mark of Cain was important. She recognized the contemporaneous impact of those strident defenders of the death penalty for whom murder was nothing less than fratricide and invited divine retribution. Numerous supporters of women's rights participated in the anti–capital punishment campaign, convinced that law and society treated murderers and fallen women as traitors, outcasts, and scapegoats. Most importantly, the unwritten law relied on a framework of moral thinking informed by the language of vengeance and atonement. Murderers in the image of Cain and prostitutes in the tradition of Eve, the first fallen woman, imposed the values of the covenanting community onto the social contract. Cain was the biblical model of the traitor, who broke the covenant, violated his allegiance to the law, and deserved punishment. Eve and her daughters were "unredeemables," who violated the sexual mores of the community, bringing shame on their families, and they, too, deserved to be ostracized. On these grounds, seduction not only contributed to a criminal defense of "husband's rights" but to the political meaning of sexual misconduct by women. Sexual infidelity thus constituted a crime against the heart of the state, which placed fallen women outside the social contract and beyond the full and equal protection of the law.

RETRIBUTIVE JUSTICE

The first place to encounter the range of understandings of fallen women is within the heated campaign to abolish capital punishment, which grew into a socially prominent issue during the decade leading to the women's movement. In 1841 the sensational murder trial and anticipated hanging of John C. Colt in New York City spurred politically prominent men such as John O'Sullivan to work for passage of an antigallows bill in the state legislature. Colt, the brother of Samuel Colt, inventor of the revolver, had murdered New York printer Samuel Adams.[89] Writers such as Walt Whitman joined the campaign by penning social criticism of clergymen and journalists who stirred public passions for social vengeance. Equally prominent female activists such as Lydia Maria Child attacked the "Christian community," which she described as devoid of sympathy, "swelling with revenge, and eager for blood."[90] Divisions between opponents and defenders of the death penalty became entrenched by 1843, when O'Sullivan faced the Reverend George B. Cheever, an influential moral reformer and Presbyterian divine from New York City, in a series of popular debates at the Broadway Tabernacle.[91]

Cheever's arguments provided the most polished defense of the death penalty, because he encapsulated all the fundamental biblical and legal reasons for "retributive justice," which he believed to be the "cornerstone" of government. Upstaging O'Sullivan, who had identified self-defense as an individual right, Cheever claimed that the death penalty was a "matter of self-defense" that belonged to nations as well. He further justified the right to self-defense as a male prerogative, observing that "if a man's wife and child be set upon by a murderer, he has the right to kill the murderer." Vengeance was also a right of divine justice that originated after the fall when Cain murdered Abel, because, Cheever asserted, the mark on Cain symbolized his "monstrous wickedness" for future generations. In a rather telling comparison drawn during his 1843 debate with O'Sullivan, Cheever converted Colt's suicide in his prison cell before his execution into an admission of guilt that echoed Cain's confession to God that "everyone that findeth me shall slay me." Colt was not an exception to the rule of moral atonement which stated that a criminal feared retribution, even preferring suicide to the ignominious fate of a public hanging.[92]

The dispute over the death penalty contrasted two very different theories of criminal jurisprudence. Cheever, on one hand, reasoned that citizens who committed homicide surrendered certain rights and risked the penalty of death. Criminal punishment implied pain, the atonement for guilt demanded retribution, and if true to these principles, then the "eternal eye" of the state exacted justice and fulfilled its obligation to society.[93] On the other hand, antigallows reformers viewed due process as a means for redress insofar as the basic purpose of government was to remit, restore, and protect "original rights." Guilt, they believed, remained difficult to determine with any moral certainty because human, not divine, tribunals ultimately issued the verdict. Applying the unwritten law of "social vengeance" to the crime of murder further distorted the judicial process. Driven by the need to find a guilty party, the courts were swayed by the public desire for "blood" in murder trials, making the delegation of authority more important than the preservation of rights. By making one person suffer beyond his or her measure for the benefit of others, the government transformed the criminal into a "victim or martyr" and scapegoat for the sins of society. By extending the principle of "an eye for an eye" to its most absurd conclusion, antigallows reformers contended, the state "doubles the offense which was before single," maiming and blinding the criminal rather than remedying wrongs, protecting rights, and ensuring due process of law.[94]

The anti–capital punishment movement posed a fundamental paradox: Did the state have the authority to kill a citizen, or did due process protect the citizen from this extreme exercise of power? It also addressed whether the state did more than take a life, divesting the accused murderer of his or her civic personality, social reputation, and soul—all in the name of redeeming the authority of the state. Reformers further realized that retributive justice paralleled personal acts of vengeance, particularly acts of retaliation motivated by a tarnished reputation and the unwritten law. As Child observed in 1843, the impulses behind the principle of an "eye for an eye" or social vengeance came from the pervasive belief that "considered revenge a virtue, and named it honor."[95]

Child became an important critic in the campaigns against capital punishment and prostitution. The two problems were enmeshed because revenge and seduction both followed the unwritten code of honor. In *Letters from New York* Child detailed how women and men sought revenge, and the courts, prisons, and the law doubled rather than redressed the offense. Chance determined which person got caught, sentenced, and punished, and vengeance often directed its wrath against innocent victims. In one famous tale of seduction and revenge, Child wrote that the slighted woman secretly murdered her lover, and another man assumed the blame and later died on the gallows. Child applied the same critique of retributive justice to the famous case of Elizabeth Wilson, who was convicted of infanticide in 1786. Retelling Wilson's story as a romantic tragedy, Child described the desperate attempt of Wilson's brother to rush to the execution with a pardon in his hand, only to see from a distant hill his sister's "garments floating in the air." Rarely pursuing the truth or concerned with justice, the legal system for Child was what she called a "gallows-game," in which life and death followed the "diabolical" rules of blood lust, honor, and chance.[96]

Passions stirred by the gallows-game mentality blunted the capacity for sympathy, which Child and other reformers felt was necessary for an impartial hearing and due process. Child captured this theme in her 1849 fictional tale "The Juryman," in which the foreman persuades the jury to seek revenge and conviction. The foreman must then confront his conscience when he is brought back to court after his own son is put on trial for murder. Looking to the jury for mercy, he sees only the pale young face of the boy he helped convict. The cost of state-sanctioned murder was dramatically apparent to Child. The stern arm of the law might place any citizen on trial, and the jury might convict from a sense of rage rather than evidence, discovering the truth too late.[97]

As a fiction writer Child had little difficulty turning capital punishment into a vehicle for sentimental literature. The battle against defenders of the gallows was just as much a legal and religious contest as it was an attempt to persuade readers on an emotional level. Of course, the courts were not immune to such sentimental designs, and juries were a ready-made audience.

In the early republic lawyers had effectively used the narrative of seduction to gain convictions in rape cases, resting their pleas on the conventional plot of villainous scoundrels taking advantage of innocent and helpless young women. According to historian Marybeth Hamilton Arnold, New York lawyers routinely employed this portrait to their advantage before 1820. By demonstrating that the female victim had sought redress through her father, or that she had been rescued by a man in defense of her honor, lawyers stood a better chance of winning the case.[98] In civil suits, as Michael Grossberg has proven, jurists adopted a similar legal framework in breach-of-promise cases, allowing virtuous women to secure damages from libertine fiancés who ruined their reputations.[99] Robert Griswold also has shown that adultery trials in the nineteenth century followed comparable guidelines for evaluating the female character. Wronged wives, shown to be chaste and virtuous, were granted more favorable terms in divorce settlements.[100]

It is revealing that the Colt case blended murder and seduction. Although the murder was not committed as a crime of passion or revenge, the subplot of the story in the newspapers, and even in the personal letters of reformers such as Child, concerned Colt's mysterious affair with Caroline Henshaw. Her sketch appeared on the extra edition distributed by the *New York Sun* in 1842, and her story appeared in the closing remarks of the prosecutor. Henshaw was described as Colt's mistress, and the prosecutor used her to demonstrate Colt's callous behavior after his murder of Adams. Transformed into two characters of a romantic tragedy, Colt and Henshaw were married in prison, and Henshaw most likely gave him the knife that he used to commit suicide in his cell. Unknown to the public, Henshaw was actually the mistress of Samuel Colt, John's more famous and married brother. So the issues of adultery, seduction, and family honor all contributed to the secret story in this celebrated scandal. Henshaw's fall from grace prefigured Colt's dishonor and death.[101]

TRAITORESS FIENDS AND CRIMES OF AFFECTION

Criminal jurisprudence added its own perspective to the changing meaning of social and civil death. The right to take a life still remained the most solemn power of the state, and capital and corporal punishment ritually enacted the full and violent force of legal interpretation. A modern constitutional understanding of state authority concealed the importance of this power through the social contract. Through the fiction of consent, any citizen convicted of a crime had agreed to his or her own punishment, thus making the convicted murderer the author of his or her own death sentence. This illusion of consent made execution seem reasonable as a punishment, as the convicted felon had consented to be subject to state authority.

In most trials, whether seduction, adultery, or murder was involved, the courts treated these acts of domestic violence as forms of civil infidelity. Vows or promises were broken, trusts were breached, and the moral sanctity of marriage, the family, and the social contract was transgressed. Both murder and adultery were categorized as acts of treason, which gave both crimes a decidedly political meaning. John Locke had contended that murder constituted an "act of war," the equivalent of fratricide, which demanded that the criminal be forced to forfeit his "right to life."[102] The common law imagined high treason as the most heinous crime possible, subjecting convicted felons to the most gruesome ritual of torture and punishment. Their bodies were dragged to the gallows, they were hanged and cut down alive, they had their entails removed while still alive, and they were beheaded. As scapegoats par excellence, traitors lost their lives, reputations, and moral connections to the community. Desecration of the bodies of traitors destroyed their social personalities, making sure there was nothing left that evoked sympathy.[103]

Infidelity continued to convey a deeply religious understanding of betrayal that made treason a crime against the heart and soul of the covenanting community.[104] Indeed, what made English treason so reprehensible was that the perpetrator consciously "delivered up" the life of his or her king, and the traitor was treated as devoid of remorse, motivated simply by political gain. Antebellum women's rights advocates realized that marriage was defined in the same terms. Nineteenth-century legal treatises continued to define marriage as a covenant, in which infidelity was seen as the principal moral offense, and the legacy of the common law involved treating adultery as a political crime. The wife's greatest transgression was that she willingly "handed over" her body to a man other than her husband, just as the traitor "delivered up" the life of the king. An anonymous legal expert and women's rights advocate further explained the connection between treason and marriage in the *Lily* in 1854. The writer observed that the traditional English practice stipulated that if a wife killed her husband, her crime was a "species of treason," known as *petit treason*. For this crime the wife could be condemned to the same punishment as if she had murdered the king, namely "to be drawn and burnt alive." Yet the same penalty did not apply to the husband, for if he killed his wife, the law treated the crime as though he had murdered a "stranger."[105]

The *Lily*'s invocation of treason was not irrelevant, especially within the context of the antebellum romantic fascination with feudal law. Although the crime of *petit treason* had been removed from the statute books during the early republican period, adultery was the one crime in which women were consistently subjected to greater punishments than those imposed on men.[106] In the 1850 Missouri divorce case of *O'Bryan v. O'Bryan*, Judge Ryland explained the serious consequences for a woman convicted of this charge: "The law deprives her of her property, her children, and all that is dear to her, and turns her as an outcast upon the world, a miserable and degraded being."[107] The image of the adulterer also haunted criminal proceedings in cases involving marital homicide. If the helpless and chaste wife or daughter symbolized the "good woman" worthy of redress and protection, then her alter ego was the fallen woman—seen as a coldhearted killer or shameless prostitute—that destroyed innocent men. In one of the most prominent murder trials, the case of Lucretia Chapman in 1831, the prosecution vilified her as a "traitress fiend" who consciously poisoned her husband. Her crime was threefold, for the motivating cause of her treachery was adultery, which the prosecution contended was all the proof needed to render a guilty verdict for murder in the first degree. Sexual misconduct provided the motive for marital treason and homicide. Adding to Chapman's list of character flaws, the prosecution argued that she had subverted male authority in the family by controlling her husband and behaving as an overbearing shrew, which only strengthened the evidence that domestic treason was the root cause in his murder.[108]

SELF-PROTECTION AND PERSONAL REPUTATION

The language of infidelity and treason created a range of problems for women's status and standing as citizens. Antebellum feminists realized that the right to self-defense came into conflict with a woman's right for self-protection. As Cheever argued, men assumed the right of self-defense in an effort to defend the sanctity of their homes against violence. The state likewise could retrain, punish, and if necessary, kill those individuals who endangered society and the social contract. The unwritten law followed the same logic. A man could redeem his personal honor and reputation by taking the law into his own hands and killing the immoral interloper who seduced his wife or daughter. Yet the problem for women and their standing as citizens was that their personal reputation and personal security remained in the hands of men. The contradiction, as Ernestine Rose observed, was that a woman was forced to look at a man, "her only assailant, as her natural protector."[109]

Rose's comments indicate how the unwritten law contributed to a sexual and legal double standard. Somehow women were both more and less accountable for their sexual misconduct before the law. As criminals, prostitutes suffered dearly for their fall from grace, serving as scapegoats for the sins of the community and legally paying the price for men's infidelity. But as seduced wives and daughters, women were less accountable and less liable, as they were dependent on men to redress their wrongs. Seduction was a crime against the hearts and sentiments of men, which meant that women were not acknowledged as active participants in the moral economy of male honor and social vengeance. Only men met as equals on the field of honor, and they redeemed the virtue of women deserving such protection while dismissing women who were considered outside their code of gallantry. In theory, self-defense remained a legal right that belonged exclusively to male citizens.

A woman's right to self-defense through revenge became a matter of debate during the trial of Amelia Norman for attempted murder in 1844. Child, present during the proceedings, wrote a detailed account for the newspapers, and Margaret Fuller, in *Women in the Nineteenth Century* (1845), noted the importance of the case in generating public interest about the rights of "our injured sisters." [110] Norman, in fact, fit the sentimental profile of the fallen woman: she was a young, unmarried girl who went to the city to find employment but instead fell prey to the enticements of a wealthy gentleman. Yet, by stabbing her seducer on the steps of the Waldorf Astoria Hotel, Norman rejected personal blame or suicide in favor of avenging her own honor and reputation. [111]

Despite the sensational nature of the case, the trial had more to do with prostitution than attempted homicide. Of course, the prosecutor compared Norman to Eve the temptress, and he drew upon the familiar allusion to Cain in order to highlight the sin and "horrors of murder." The most compelling issue focused on the conflict of interest between protecting a man against revenge and recognizing a woman's right to defend her reputation. The prosecutor maintained that society could protect itself against either seduction or social vengeance, but not both. In this zero sum tribunal, the jury had to choose between having "the virtue of their daughters ruined" or allowing their sons to be "stabbed by the hands of prostitutes." The greater danger, the prosecution added, came from New York City's 12,000 prostitutes, especially if they "were all armed, and abroad to redress their wrongs." Like a marauding band of Amazons, these prostitutes, armed with the legal right of self-defense, would ruthlessly slaughter any and all male citizens, and leave a bloody trail of "dead bodies" across the city. Child responded with "burning indignation" to this wild threat of sexual warfare in the streets, and she contended that fallen women already displayed battle scars from their hostile encounters in the courts and society. Rather than leave the city in a sea of blood and male bodies, prostitutes had slipped into exile and oblivion, incurring the penalties of a "blighted reputation, the desertion of friends, and the loss of respectable employment." [112]

The somber warning of the prosecution fell on deaf ears. Norman was not convicted. As Timothy Walker explained in the *Western Law Journal* shortly after the verdict, the jury used its "pardoning power" to "acquit her without hesitation, and their verdict was received with shouts by the spectators." The jury believed that Norman deserved redress and clemency, for a "ruined woman had nothing left but vengeance." This trial closely followed the particulars of the Mercer case in Camden, New Jersey, in which a brother had avenged his sister's seduction, had killed the seducer, and like Norman, had been acquitted through the insanity defense. At least in the eyes of the jury, Norman had the right to defend her reputation, if not on the field of honor, then on the steps of the Waldorf Astoria.[113]

But the verdict revealed only part of the impact of the case. The Norman trial exposed why women did not secure the same legal protection of their sacred rights. Seduction was not treated as a crime, as Walker noted, because the "woman is herself to blame for consenting." Consent distinguished seduction from rape. Walker argued that seduction should be compared to robbery, in order to shift the blame to the male seducer. Implicitly, the woman's real crime was in giving her consent, which invoked the issue of treason. She was not just equally at fault but had willingly given her body to another man, and her body and sexual services were not her personal possessions. By saying "yes" to her seducer, the woman had betrayed her solemn trust to remain obedient to the law of her father and the state, and she had proven her disloyalty through the exercise of the right of consent, a right she had no authority to exercise. The greater transgression of political infidelity explained the "infamy" of her crime.[114]

A JURY OF HER PEERS

The Norman case contributed to the emergence of the women's rights movement, resulting directly in the formation of the Female Department of the New York Prison Association in 1845 and the opening of the Isaac T. Hopper Home for discharged female convicts in New York City in 1846.[115] Abby H. Gibbons, founder of the home and daughter of Isaac Hopper, was related to Lucretia Mott by marriage. Both Mott and Paulina Wright Davis gave talks in support of female prison reform, and the Hopper home served as a model for reform efforts that followed in Philadelphia. In 1847 the initial step toward addressing women's rights and female criminals came when a Public Meeting of Women was called in Philadelphia for the purpose of petitioning the legislature to abolish the death penalty.[116] As at the fugitive slave meeting held two weeks later, Paulina Wright served as chair. Several women gave brief speeches, and the petition drive gathered 11,777 signatures. The newspapers claimed their petition drive had placed women in the forefront of the campaign against capital punishment.[117] But this meeting served an additional purpose: it provided a public forum for the establishment of the Rosine Society, which advocated the prevention of prostitution as a means for curtailing female crime.[118]

In her public address and proposal for the Rosine Society, presented at the anti–capital punishment meeting, Pennsylvania women's rights advocate Mira Townsend advanced a class and caste critique to further women's rights. Townsend, like Child, contended that society was the source of the prostitute's fall from grace through the "barriers of caste." From a deeply ingrained public prejudice, respectable women had learned to turn away in disgust from any prostitute encountered in the streets. Women were not automatically more sympathetic than men toward their fallen sisters.[119] To exercise genuine empathy, women had to see prostitutes as peers rather than as victims or unrepentant sinners. One goal of the Rosine Society was to create a community of women, a social and public space where respectable and fallen women could meet as peers, cultivating that sense of equality that eluded them when they met in the street or in private homes, or when they withstood the scrutiny of the courts.[120]

Public sympathy was not pity or compassion alone, but a comprehensive understanding of "the necessities of Woman's nature." Before any woman cast the first stone, she should search her past, Townsend declared, and stand accountable to the tribunal of her own conscience and the "eye of God." Matilda Gage echoed this sentiment in her speech to the 1852 Syracuse women's rights convention. If driven to secure the "necessities of life," such as food and clothing, could any woman remain completely chaste and virtuous? By understanding these "necessities," antebellum feminists argued, women would realize that survival rather than sin compelled their less fortunate sisters to become prostitutes.[121] At the Cleveland convention in 1853, Lucy Stone gave a similar description of a woman who needed to support her child. Forced to choose between two evils, the woman placed her duty as a mother before her reputation. Despite the loss of respectability, this woman possessed the "very soul of fidelity and purity."[122]

It is not surprising that prostitution appeared in the proceedings of all the national women's rights conventions from 1850 to 1856, and that necessity and coercion surfaced as reasons why a woman consented to sell her sexual wares in the marketplace. As Gage observed, women were driven into marriage by economic necessity, because all lucrative means of support were seized by men.[123] Virtuous women found themselves side by side with their fallen sisters, both racing to find male patronage and financial support in the contest of life. The struggle for survival followed women into the courts. In 1855 Paulina Wright Davis acknowledged that convicted female criminals and prostitutes had much in common, because "when a fallen sister is dragged before the public, exposed to the frightful executioner's platform, and her person rudely handled, it becomes time for us to ask how we are protected?" Although Davis admitted that some women might be treated as "petted children" by husbands or fathers, such privileges faded once they entered the criminal justice system.[124]

Prostitution underscored how sexual virtue reinforced women's unequal civil standing with respect to men. The rigid separation of women into sexual castes allowed some women to be raised to a "higher elevation" while other, erring women, fell farther and lower, leaving men altogether untouched.[125] As a class, men stood apart. This division of society into three castes resurrected earlier republican anxieties: fear of the aristocracy and the lower classes, both represented here by women, and the insistent celebration of a virtuous middling sort, implicitly understood to be exclusively male. In the idealized middle ground, men were equals and peers; weak, "petted" women on the pedestal and seductive and sinful women in the streets potentially threatened to upset this comfortable social order. Republican virtue required that men make themselves invulnerable to contamination from below and situate themselves beyond the corruption of an effete, pampered elite.

Writing to the Salem women's rights convention in 1850, Elizabeth Cady Stanton noted the inherent failure of this tripartite caste system to promote women's constitutional rights. By treating women as "antipodes," men lacked the ability to understand and empathize, let alone represent women.

> It is impossible for us to convince man that we think and feel exactly as he does, that we have the same sense of right and justice, the same love of freedom and independence. Some men regard us as devils, and some as angels; hence one class would shut us up in a certain sphere for fear of the evil we might do, and the other for fear of the evil that *might be done to us*; thus, except for the sentiment of the thing, for all the good it does us, we might as well be thought the one as the other. But we ourselves have to do with what *we are* and what *we shall be*.[126]

Sexual caste distinctions made it impossible for men to represent women, and Stanton even mockingly chided that the American system of government had not surpassed the English model, for American democracy had only substituted " 'Lords and commons' " with "Lords and women."[127]

A more serious proposal came from Jane Elizabeth Jones at the Salem convention. In her address, "Woman's Rights and Wrongs," Jones noted that women's treatment as a caste undermined the crucial precondition for the right of due process. The fundamental constitutional right of a trial by a jury of peers had been denied women. Instead of a lower house in the legislature, Jones claimed that women required a "jury of women."[128] In a hearing before the New York assembly in 1855, Antoinette Brown repeated this challenge. She argued that "no man was the peer of woman," and the assembly should either "take back the principle that man has a right to trial by his peers, or grant women the same; or at least, let each be tried by a jury of the race—men and women together." Brown raised the essential question: Did women have the right to judge men in matters of life and death?[129] Or, as Jones asserted earlier at the Salem convention, did men have exclusive authority to "sit in judgement" over women?[130]

For antebellum feminists, sexual discrimination in the courtroom undermined the very foundation of justice. The exclusion of women from juries tipped the scales, making women pawns rather than participants in the legal system. Jury service exposed the cruel irony embedded in women's lack of self-protection, as the law assumed women were accountable for their crimes but not responsible enough to judge the criminal behavior of others. "The only case in which her individuality is acknowledged by the law," Maria Giddings noted in 1851, "is in her punishment."[131]

As Child contended in "The Juryman," due process required accountability and empathy from the jury. Judicial empathy from a jury of peers implied reciprocity; the defendant and the juror—the judged and the judge—should be able to change places. Women clearly did not meet this standard, because justice was neither sex-blind nor impartial. In the eyes of the law, women would never be peers until they could acquire the public virtue and standing to see and to be seen from both sides of the bar. As Jones observed, justice called for a jury of her peers.

Ultimately, the right of self-defense and the "law of necessity" enabled this imbalance of power. A sexual economy of rights, or the belief that classes and castes competed for a limited amount of power and protection, provided the rationale for unequal treatment. Stanton employed this critique on several occasions. If women voted or served on juries, then men forfeited their right to self-defense and self-preservation. As long as the interests of man and woman remained "antagonistic," sexual equality threatened, in Stanton's words, "to drag man down from the responsible position which nature and necessity assign him."[132]

Neither anxious fears of sexual antagonism nor the exclusive reliance on male representation justified women's virtual exclusion from the adversarial process. Because the force of the law came from consent—the ability to know and to be held accountable to the law—women's rights activists accurately saw jury service as a crucial forum for defining democratic citizenship. A resonant quotation from Madame de Staël, first appearing in Child's writing in 1844 and later at the public meeting for women in 1847 and again at the seventh national women's rights convention in 1856, summed up this view: "Sire, when women have their heads cut off, it is but just they should know the reason why."[133] Only as peers would women be able to consent to the law rather than be subject to the coercive imbalance of power found in the zero sum sexual economy of rights. Justice required that the mark of Cain and the curse of Eve be replaced by an equal right of consent. In doing so, women, for the first time, could establish a civil reputation without paying the price for what Wendell Phillips saw as the "moloch of artificial delicacy"—namely, women's unequal protection before the eyes of the law.[134]

Empire and Glory

In 1846 Jane Swisshelm entered the "great political maelstrom" with the publication of her "war letters" on the impending military conflict with Mexico. As one of the few women to engage in the relentless and often savage debates waged in the newspapers, she rejected any "theories of politeness" and instead saw herself to be unmasking the "revolting crimes" of war with her "sarcasm, ridicule," and "solemn denunciations."[135] Although Swisshelm cast her most vicious aspersions on southern slaveholders, she had little difficulty blaming the Democrats in general for their expansionist policies.[136] Following the annexation of Texas in 1845, the Polk administration added Oregon, California, and New Mexico, which in the space of four years doubled the territory of the United States.[137] Yet Swisshelm identified the "pusillanimous" and covetous quality of war as the greatest crime, because the desire for unlimited power encouraged the strong to trample the rights of the weak. Rather than deserving the laurels of victory, most soldiers, politicians, and especially ministers disgraced themselves in supporting a war that stained their hands with the "blood of women and children." Through the expansion of slavery, manifest destiny and war transformed slave women into the booty of conquest. National honor and protection of women had little to do with the conquest of Mexico; it was a war waged for empire that Swisshelm compared to "a giant whipping a cripple."[138]

Conquest, domination, and the containment of women provided Swisshelm with the essential themes for detailing a political theory of war. If female slaves and Mexican women symbolized the spoils of war and sexual conquest, then wives and mothers on the home front were representative of the many internal enemies of the expanding nation-state.[139] Along with "Negroes" and "Indians" and other "inferior orders of humanity," women were shorn of political privileges and piled upon the "immense pyramid of fools" that served as the broad foundation of American society.[140] Swisshelm's harsh words suggested that building an empire did more than to carve out new national boundaries. The war promoted a distinct perspective, that the sovereign people were a corporate body unified by "one flesh," a virtually homogeneous population with a common heritage and shared manifest destiny.[141] The allusion to "one flesh" linked the civil standing of free blacks, Indians, Mexicans, and women. As a trope of marital unity, "one flesh" signified the political condition of women as dependents in which men by "proxy" represented their interests.[142] When used as a racial metaphor, however, it reinforced "natural" differences and the impossibility of any kind of political amalgamation among the various races.[143] Such crucial distinctions inevitably placed the scepter of dominion in the hands of white male citizens, making suffrage not a right but a mark of "superiority" and an "honor" bestowed by the state.[144] Without patronage and a polis, women and blacks, Mexicans and Indians, came to represent political casualties of the war for empire and glory.

At the women's rights convention held in Akron in 1851, Frances Gage referred to this view of nation-building and manifest destiny. In her presidential address she alluded to the conquest of the "wilderness," describing the "herculean task" of America's forebears to subdue the land and the savage beasts, and she recalled the "prophetic visions of their far-seeing powers in the new and untried country." Quite cleverly, Gage next shifted the metaphor of the frontier to the "wilderness of prejudice to be subdued," the "foe of selfishness and self-interest," and the "wild beasts of pride, envy, malice and hate" needing to be destroyed. Securing women's rights stood as the new challenge on the national horizon. Yet the legacy of conquest still haunted women's civil standing. If the wilderness represented another version of the state of nature, then the transition to civil society had subdued rather than incorporated women. Like Swisshelm, Gage identified the "power of the strong over the weak" as the motive force behind national expansion. Conquest and expansion justified rule by "dominion," the right to claim the land—all its human and natural resources—as the spoils of victory.[145]

Authority over the land introduced another condition of political sovereignty. Dominion implied sovereign control of the land through a natural hierarchy and, if necessary, through the use of force and violence.[146] Yet the old dictum "might makes right" undermined consent or rule by the people.[147] Gage perceptively pointed out this contradiction, arguing that woman never met in council with man; neither did she voluntarily agree to give up her claim to make the law nor place all the power in "his hands." [148] At the 1850 Worcester convention, Paulina Wright Davis made a similar point about the "masterdom of the strong hand" as a remnant of "barbarism." Equality before the law could not exist as long as one sex relied on "old time tyrannies," especially the tyranny of male dominion derived from the "battle-field and the public forum." [149]

MANIFEST DOMINION

By mid-century, Americans displayed both fascination and disgust for barbarism and conquest. Captivity narratives provided the foundation for romantic fiction, generating works such as James Fenimore Cooper's *The Last of the Mohicans* (1831), which provided alternating portraits of Indians as both noble warriors and vicious savages. Cooper granted his fictional Indians the traits of a lost heroic civilization—one that embodied bravery, honor, and chivalry—but, to justify white conquest, reinforced the Indians' ethical inferiority to the white race through vivid accounts of their acts of butchery and torture, and a primal lust for the scalps of white maidens.[150]

In 1843 William H. Prescott continued this trend with his timely publication of the *History of the Conquest of Mexico*, portraying the Spanish conquest of the Aztec civilization as epic history and a romance of chivalry. Despite being a "Conscience Whig" opposed to the annexation of Texas and the expansion of slavery, Prescott repeated the racist sentiments of his generation by terming Mexicans an effeminate and weak people. His *History of the Conquest of Mexico* showed the Spanish and Aztecs exhibiting the worst extremes of conquest and barbarism. He drew the Spanish leader Hernando Cortes as a cruel, deceptive, and immoral conqueror who treated Aztec women as concubines and spoils of war. Montezuma, the king of the Aztecs, was seen less as a tragic than as a pathetic figure of "pusillanimity," whom Prescott charged with changing his sex and becoming a "woman" in defeat.[151] For Prescott, neither leader embodied heroism or chivalry.

Nineteenth-century theories of civilization equated barbarian with "inertia," passivity, and subsistence, combined with a puerile temper, cowardice, and the selfish exploitation of women. The primitive male was the child-man. He was devoid of manliness, measured by self-reliance and heroic exploits, and emasculated by his physical and mental weakness. While primitive cultures engaged in warfare, sought glory, and created "infant states," they fell short in the scale of civilization when compared with the advances made by European nations.[152] Of course, race contributed to the gulf between savage and civilized societies. Mexico was portrayed as a racially mixed country and troubled republic, teetering on the brink of despotism. The one "black republic," Haiti, was identified as another country in stasis, forever trapped in an "immovable state of barbarism." In his 1848 *Considerations Upon the Nature and Tendency of Free Institutions*, Frederick Grimké described the "negro race" in Haiti as "emasculated" and incapable of progress:

> The inert and sluggish propensities of this people have already created habits which preclude all hope of substantial advancement. If they had found the island a wilderness, it would now be covered with wigwams. Instead of strenuous industry which carries the white man forward in the march of improvement, and makes him clear up the forest with as much alacrity as if he were subduing an empire, the negro is satisfied if he can appropriate one or two acres of land. All he cares for, is to obtain just enough to satisfy the wants of animal life. He has the name of freeman only: for liberty is of no account, unless it absolves us from the yoke of our own propensities and vices, which are far more galling and degrading than any physical disabilities whatever.[153]

Freedom required struggle, a far-reaching vision, and the desire to subdue the primitive encountered in the wilderness as well as the primitive encountered within—our "own propensities and vices." Gage identified the forefathers' "prophetic visions" and "far-seeing powers," just as Alexis de Tocqueville in 1835 had described democratic nations as motivated by an "unbounded imagination," their "eyes fixed" on their march across the wilderness, subduing nature and cultivating the land.[154] It was the romantic imagination that spurred progress, inspiring the conqueror to take risks, to rely on his impassioned conviction, and to make the land his own. Through mastery, the frontier became dominion, remade in the image of free white men.

Debate over the annexation of Texas centered around the issues of freedom, dominion, and democratic progress. Texas statehood became the major plank of the Democratic Party in 1844, and their presidential nominee, James Polk, avidly championed the cause. As an independent nation Texas posed a distinctive threat to the grand theory of national expansion, symbolizing a rival empire capable of conducting its own "mighty march" to the Pacific.[155] In 1841 Abel Upshur, President John Tyler's secretary of the navy and close adviser, raised two concerns: either Texas could generate a dangerous degree of economic competition with the United States if it expanded westward at a comparable pace, or it might suffer from such competition, making it politically vulnerable to the sway of hostile nations. The latter fear of "incursions" from hostile nations, aiming at inciting "revolution," reaffirmed Upshur's belief that the real the danger to democracy came from the primitive within the nation-state. Those members of society, the unfree, weak, and easily manipulated factions, threatened domestic tranquility and national security. For Upshur the most dangerous element was the "black menace," the free black population, always deemed capable of inciting rebellion and slave insurrections. Significantly, Upshur's views reappeared before the Senate in 1844 when Robert Walker introduced the argument that Texas could serve as a "safety-valve" for the "black menace." By luring free blacks to migrate south, Texas could contain what southern Democrats and Whigs had come to perceive as a deadly internal enemy: a large, mobile, free black population.[156]

The theory of unoccupied land acting as a safety valve for the nation was not new, and yet this plea became more urgent and shrill during the decade before the war. While southerners feared slave insurrections triggered by fanatical abolitionists and free blacks, northern politicians increasingly became concerned with labor unrest and class conflict. After the panic of 1837 and during the lingering depression that was not overcome until 1843, northern democrats saw "new homes in the West" as the panacea for "white slavery." John O'Sullivan, as editor of the *United States Magazine and Democratic Review*, condemned wage labor for degrading factory workers, making them "defective beings, with sallow complexions, emaciated forms, and stooping shoulders."[157] As a theory of political economy, however, white slavery not only invoked parallels with the South but with the European feudal order that divested workers of rights to the land and the value of their labor.[158] When he coined the term "manifest destiny," O'Sullivan argued that the people required ownership of the "soil" to sustain their productivity as well as their self-reliance.[159] A less sanguine view of the working class accompanied this expansionist philosophy, because those dispossessed of property held what O'Sullivan believed to be the greatest motive for fomenting rebellion and class warfare. His opinion was not unfounded, given the political turmoil surrounding the Dorr War of 1842. As a constitutional and armed conflict over the right to vote, the Dorr controversy addressed popular sovereignty, land ownership, and property qualifications for suffrage. The demand for popular sovereignty by labor activists in Rhode Island demonstrated quite vividly the enduring capacity of the "common people" to mount a revolution against a landed aristocracy.[160]

Hidden behind this concern for white slavery was not only a fear of discord but a feeling of contempt for the debilitating consequences of a life of drudgery and dependency. Unable to liberate themselves from the "sheer necessities of life," slaves—white or black—were subject to the rule of their bodies and the crippling effects of alienation.[161] To be deprived of vitality, strength, and spirit implied the loss of virility; to be crippled, lame, or enfeebled connoted castration; and to be prostrate, helpless, and cowardly—

cringing and shrinking in size—suggested emasculation. Women, of course, best reflected the defect of drudgery. Working women, portrayed as hapless drudges, consumptive, or creeping away to die in dark garrets or by suicide, offered one popular nineteenth-century image of the *"white slave of the North."*[162] Indian women as degraded, expendable "squaws" were described as menial drudges, abused and treated like animals, while their "braves" avoided labor, hunted, played the game of war, or lolled around the camp.[163] Mexican women did not escape such demeaning stereotypes, especially the "black Mexicans" of poor peon families who were classified as ignorant serfs. Although Americans viewed the lighter-skinned "Spanish" to be kind and attractive, they, too, lacked modesty, prudence, and domestic self-reliance.[164] If women's place in society was the measure of civilization, then democracy was equally endangered by a possible regression to a primitive stage of social organization and by the rapid advance of class divisions and the creation of a bloated aristocracy, which reduced women to wage slaves, peons, or in the southern planter economy, legal slaves. Clearly, great tension centered on the emasculation of "enslaved" white men, whose debasement made them more like women, while drudgery degraded women to subhuman beasts, lowering both sexes one rung on the ladder of evolution.

This classical view of slavery permeated the political theory of most expansionists who lauded the virtues of self-sufficiency as the cornerstone of American character and society. Sam Houston, the leader of the military campaign for Texas independence and the republic's first president, best captured this blend of contempt for dependency and exuberant celebration of conquest. In most of his writings Houston elevated the importance of freedom achieved through armed and willful action: the "soldier-citizen," like the "pioneers," engaged in a contest against overwhelming odds that displayed "unsubduable courage," "bold and generous daring," and independent "might." Texas, he claimed unequivocally, had gained its nationhood through sheer mastery with every military and political opportunity: "We made ourselves, by our acts, a free, sovereign, and independent nation."[165]

In embellishing the "privations of the wilderness" and the "perils of the soldier," Houston necessarily implied that physical sacrifices and the use of force "made" a nation. Oddly enough, the wilderness represented for him an almost pastoral version of Hobbes's state of nature. The strong conquered the weak, and then the victors transformed the uncultivated land into the "garden of America." This perspective diminished the importance of natural rights, because it was "instinct" that compelled a "superior" and "mighty people" to claim their "birth-right." The ability to conduct self-government required a kind of physical and cultural inheritance from a "kindred" people, tracing its lineage to the "glory" of the "Anglo-Saxon race." In addition, Houston believed that these instincts and desires needed to be "consecrated" in "blood"; risk and sacrifice, combined with the recognition of the sovereignty of the nation, converted the natural impulses of the people into a "holy devotion" to one's country. Although a common origin united the people, Houston argued that shared emotional and material investments in lives and property incorporated the sovereign people as a nation-state.[166]

Houston's views did not go unchallenged. Peace activists opposed to the encroachment of military authority rejected the basic premise of conquest and empire that "might makes right."[167] William Jay, who wrote a point-by-point rebuttal against justifications for the Mexican War, argued that the war represented a distinctly "dangerous foe of constitutional liberty." Jay realized that aggressive war curtailed the fundamental rights of life, liberty, and protection both outside and inside the country. "In its admiration of military success," the public mind had lost that "jealousy of military power," which Jay believed was the most powerful safeguard of republican liberty.[168] In fact, the same arguments used to advance the conquest of Mexico reappeared in the Supreme Court during the 1849 trial of Thomas Dorr; in the majority opinion, Chief Justice Roger Taney argued that state governments had the right to use unlimited military authority when threatened by an internal rebellion. Justice Levi Woodbury, in opposition to Taney, described martial law as turning the "whole country" into a "camp," suggesting that such unregulated power eradicated civil liberty in the public sphere. "Might makes right" justified military force for conquest, and it sanctioned martial law for the equally ominous purpose of containing political dissent.[169]

Two months after the declaration of war, opponents held a series of public meetings to voice their protest against this "act of unprovoked aggression and plunder."[170] Almost immediately such activities raised the specter of treason, a sentiment that Polk himself invoked in his presidential message before Congress. The *Washington Union* called for a war register in every city, town, and village for the purpose of listing all the names of "knaves at home, who give aid and comfort to our enemies." Some antiwar meetings encountered angry mobs that further reflected widespread and direct efforts "to stifle by brute force, all open denunciation of the war."[171] This explains why opponents of the war identified "brute force" and an infatuation with "military glory" as deadly consequences of the Mexican campaign.[172] While conquest and military domination gained political legitimacy as national policy, critics charged that the "spirit of war" on the home front replaced public virtue with "blind obedience" in the name of patriotism. Despite hostile reactions, antiwar activists dissuaded enlistments, circulated antiwar pledges and petitions, and called for "peaceable means" of civil disobedience, such as the refusal to pay taxes for war supplies.[173]

At the beginning of the war, Elihu Burritt, a leading reformer in Europe and the United States, enlisted the support of the women of Philadelphia to draft a letter "on the subject of peace." In response to an address sent from a group of British women, a public meeting was held on June 17. Lucretia Mott read the address during the meeting, Sarah Pugh served as president, and Sarah Tyndale gathered names for the final document that eventually was sent to England. The women included in their letter a familiar plea against "physical force" and the "false love of glory, the cruel spirit of revenge, the blood-thirsty ambition, swelling the breast of the soldier in the battlefield."[174] Others supported a campaign for "women *en masse*" to petition Congress to withdraw the army from Mexico, while many women's rights advocates attended antiwar meetings in Pennsylvania and Ohio and drafted the statements of protest.[175]

Most pacifists felt that annexation of Texas marked the "beginning of conquests" for the United States and concurred with William Ellery Channing's prediction that war represented the inevitable culmination of territorial "encroachment" and the "tragic" continuation of "deeds of rapine and blood." Yet land was not the only coveted "quarry" of war.[176] As Sumner Stebbins contended in his letter of protest to the *Pennsylvania Freeman*, the actuating motive of the war was the extension of slavery and Anglo-Saxon domination over the entire Mexican population.[177] Those who justified expansion referred to women as one of the "spoils of war," arguing that soldiers could intermarry with Mexican women and thereby "regenerate" and colonize Mexico by "gradually infusing vigor into the race."[178] Sam Houston made similar allusions to the "beautiful señoritas, or pretty girls" and claimed that their "annexation" would establish the "most powerful and delightful evidence of civilization."[179] Such views complemented theories of racial superiority associated with Anglo-Saxonism, as a new sexual dimension was added to the grand plan for manifest dominion. On one hand, marriage to Mexican women peacefully incorporated both women and land; as "one flesh" according to the law, these marital unions implied that civil authority would be placed in the hands of white men. On the other hand, the "laws of nature" and sexual breeding suggested that successive generations could be cleansed of "inferior" Mexican traits, and these future citizens would eventually "change back" to the pure Caucasian stock.[180] Thus a quiet revolution of sexual annexation laid the groundwork for the conquest of the entire continent.

It is quite clear that Mexican women provided expansionists with a convenient racial and gender model for subordination and extinction. The Anglo-Saxon myth of "Yankee chivalry" reinforced this view but masked the more violent features of military conquest with portrayals of U.S. soldiers as the noble and gallant "warriors" of a superior race. In the nineteenth century a revived usage of the term "chivalrous" described the ideal knight as "characterized by pure and noble gallantry, honor, courtesy, and disinterested devotion to the cause of the weak and oppressed."[181] When the term was applied to the war, writers claimed that American soldiers were the heroic defenders of the weak who sought to rescue the "Spanish maid" from her life of drudgery. Trapped in her exotic prison in a distant land and forced to marry her inferior and slothful "mate," Mexican women, as one poet claimed, longed for the "purer blood and valiant arms" of American men "to clasp" their "budding charms."[182] By making the female body an object of conquest and the male body an agent of valor, the code of chivalry accentuated physical prowess and bodily strength as the distinguishing mark of civil capacity. Significantly, white men represented the primary bearers of civilization; ultimately their actions alone could master the forces of nature and fulfill the destiny of the nation. Unable to protect their own women or their country, men of "inferior races" demonstrated their lack of "instinct" for action and risk as well as their inability for acquiring the necessary attributes of self-reliance and civic autonomy. Women likewise appeared as mere ciphers devoid of any intrinsic civic value of their own. Whether trophies of conquest or ladies fair, women perpetuated the Anglo-Saxon heritage but only indirectly, because men alone provided the "principle of action" in the "mighty march" of civilization.[183]

Even before the war, the language of chivalry already had foreshadowed the internal dangers that American women posed through resisting the march of conquest. In December 1844 an important legal case involving charges of conspiracy (and allusions to treason) gained the attention of reformers, primarily because it involved a female defendant.[184] Delia Webster, a schoolteacher from Vermont, was convicted, sentenced, and imprisoned for assisting the escape of a slave child from Kentucky.[185] Because Webster was treated as a political prisoner, her trial suggested how the state dealt with enemies within its own borders. As the *Emancipator and Republican* claimed, at first "gallant" Kentuckians slandered her "reputation for virtue" and then expected her to "convert" northern abolitionists "from the error of their ways." Female political dissent not only implied the loss of sexual virtue, but Webster's unsubduable courage emasculated the southern defenders of chivalry. By re-canting her antislavery views and confessing her error, Webster could redeem herself and the honor of the men of Kentucky.[186]

In 1845 Jane Swisshelm wrote a rather provocative poem titled "Chivalry" that satirized the handling of the case, especially the appeal for a pardon in which Webster had praised the "moral bravery, noble generosity, the zealous patriotism, and chivalry of proud Kentucky." In her caricature of the "chival-rous South," Swisshelm invoked the image of the medieval knight preparing for a tournament. Despite his armor and strong steed, the knight's glorious performance appeared ridiculous when set in contrast to the human suffer-ing wrought by slavery. Hardly the result of noble sentiment, the knight's mastery of the arts of warfare reflected a compulsion spurred on by his baser instincts of greed and cowardice. The profits from selling children supplied the gold for his "trappings fair," while his most daring acts involved whipping "an old woman" and "hunting down decrepit old men." Webster was another trophy for the brave knights who "hunted down a lady fair." In the most revealing lines of the poem, Swisshelm described Webster's view from her prison cell. Although she could "peer out through her prison grate, on the flowers of chivalry," she saw before her "nothing but men, mere men." Rather than a glorious and sublime vision of knighthood, she caught only a glimpse of "mere men," conveying a mere masquerade of masculine chivalry.[187]

In addition to sharpening their critique of the war, the unmasking of chiv-alry gave women's rights advocates another point of departure for explaining the anomalous position of women in the American polity. Aside from noting that greed rather than gallantry seemed to be the motivating impulse for mili-tary conquest, feminists argued that political privileges reflected the lingering remnants of a system of patronage that contradicted the constitutional tra-dition of rule by consent of the governed. "Self-interest," not sacrifice, drew men into the war, for as Ernestine Rose contended, "Rulers think they can acquire fresh territory, larger revenues, higher honors by war."[188] The forces of conquest threatened the public good by unleashing the desire for personal ambition at the expense of rights, as Betsey Cowles concluded in a playlet she wrote against the Mexican War. In her cast of characters, which included President Polk and Zachary Taylor as the two major pawns of American ex-pansion, she suggested that underlying the rhetoric of glory could be found more mundane concerns for territorial gain and the rewards of military hon-ors and political favors.[189] At the 1850 Salem women's rights convention, in which Cowles served as president, the twin themes of patronage and con-quest defined the position on suffrage. In the call for the convention, activists stated that the vote was treated "like government scrip or deed on parchment, transferrable, to be granted or withheld, made immutable or changeable, as caprice, popular favor, or the pride of power may dictate; changing ever as the weak and the strong, the oppressed and the oppressor, come in conflict or change places." [190] As scrip—payment for soldiers—suffrage was a reward for military service and a political spoil of the Mexican War.

The problem with chivalry, as Mrs. C. M. Steele wrote to the 1851 Akron convention, was that it was so interwoven with American culture that men and women assumed it was universally true, even when the evidence of the real conditions of war and political injustice proved otherwise.[191] Women were blinded by the gallantry of men in the same fashion that men were blinded by glory; the romanticized myth of national grandeur was always more appealing than the sobering reality of life.[192] Weakness remained a capacity or human trait that was impossible to valorize as a civic virtue, whether used rhetorically to condemn the inherited defects of inferior races or to idolize femininity. In her speech at the Akron convention, Emma Coe made this point perfectly clear, arguing that any attempt to cripple the mind and body of woman not only made her "weak" but reduced her to a "feeble, pusillanimous being." Dependency and drudgery did not discriminate in their effects on different "castes," Coe added, much as it might appear that white women were cherished and protected. When conquest turned to despotism and consent no longer was the rule of democracy, the "flowers of chivalry" faded for all women, equally divested of basic political rights.[193]

HERO WORSHIP

Chivalry and military valor became a crucial part of antebellum political culture. Expansion across the continent and conquest transformed the frontier for many into an imaginary place in which to define the cultural and political meaning of citizenship. For women's rights activists, however, the celebrated soldier-citizen praised by politicians such as Sam Houston failed to personify the civic qualities of self-reliance or patriotism needed for American democracy. The exaggerated language and hubris of hero worship subverted the basic principles of liberty, equality, and the pursuit of happiness. Manifest dominion was contrary to the right of protection, because brute force rather than justice determined rights and privileges as a matter of patronage. At the 1850 Worcester convention Henry Van Amringe demonstrated the hollowness of heroism as a model of citizenship. Military service, he asserted, was "by no means the greatest act of patriotism that a man or woman can render to their nation"; many soldiers and officers were inspired by the less admirable motives of ambition, love of glory, desire for carnage, and subsistence.[194] Noble sentiments had little to do with "murder and rapine." Two years later

John Neal addressed the more contentious issue of whether women could enter the militia. Regardless of their official exclusion, women were "found in all the armies of the earth—shamefully disguised," Neal wrote, and yet they were successfully acting as men in all ranks and assuming leadership roles.[195]

Both of these observations exposed the fallacy of assuming that actual military service determined civic duty or worth. Glory and ambition ran against the ethos of sacrifice required for patriotism. Not all soldiers were heroes or good citizens. Soldiers could be viewed as well-disciplined machines, even drudges, making military service into a mindless routine devoid of genuine patriotic feeling. Many soldiers simply wore the uniform, earned scrip, collected booty, or killed because it was part of the job.[196] In her playlet about the Mexican War, Betsey Cowles argued that the savage and survivalist code of the soldier was to kill or to be killed for the failure to carry out orders.[197] If neither heroism nor moral character mattered, then chivalry was just as irrelevant to the conquering soldier. Ironically, the fact that women, when disguised as soldiers, acted like men, implied that women could equal men in strength, aggressiveness, and courage. A woman passing for a soldier disproved the romantic myth of rigid and unchangeable sexual roles whereby the strong chevalier rescued the helpless maiden in distress. Not all soldiers were manly or exclusively men.[198]

Reaffirming the gulf between male valor and female weakness formed another layer to the debate over women's enfranchisement. In three articles titled "Chivalry vs. Woman's Enfranchisement," published in 1855 in the *Lily*, Anson Bingham disputed the views of a writer published in the *Southern Quarterly Review* three years earlier. The southern critic of women's rights claimed that female enfranchisement mocked chivalry and equality. By inverting the natural order of society and treating female and negro enfranchisement as one, northern women replaced protection from their Yankee knights with equal suffrage, and as the southern writer slanderously derided, "Mounted on [free black entrepreneur Paul] Cuffee's shoulders, in rides the lady!"[199]

Bingham responded with telling insights into chivalry and political rights. Tapping the popular refrain concerning conquest, Bingham contended that the idea of the eternal servitude of woman was rooted in age-old "Pagan brutalities." Chivalry had little romance for women when looming behind its glossy veneer was brute force and humiliation. The mistreatment of women, he insisted began with the first lesson of "manhood," which he compared to the savage custom of a son striking his mother with a stick. Brute force also could be used to impose the rules of manhood and the battlefield onto the public forum. The southern reviewer had offered a vivid description of "Miss

Caroline" vying with Cuffee for the vote, resulting in the weaker sex finding herself "thrust into the mud," ornamented with a black eye and bloody nose. If the polls had reverted to the state of nature, electioneering was equated, in the southern critic's piece, with a "boxing match." The "gentle Paulina, Angelina or Lucretia" would face defeat, the southerner had held, if pitted against the "valorous Houston" or any other patriot armed with "forensic power in the war of words." Strength, or the courage to face a blow or pistol in the face, determined the vote, Bingham harangued, unfortunately making brute power—the "law of physical might"—the basis of political rights.[200]

Inevitably, war made metaphors of the body politic decidedly physical and visual. Blacks could be excluded on the basis of skin color, while women as the weaker vessel lacked the bodily frame and physical might necessary for participation in the polis. In the words of the southern reviewer, " 'Sex and color are so essential to the being of the woman and negro—that it is impossible to imagine the existence of either without these distinctive marks.' "[201] The underlying message was that character was inseparable from flesh and bone, and that strength, energy, and heroic impulse all radiated from natural instinct. From this perspective leaders naturally took command, gallant soldiers instinctively displayed valor, the victors deserved the spoils of war, and the losers should just as naturally assume their assigned lot in defeat. The body politic reflected the natural order of the strong over the weak, and peace and tranquility could only be maintained when the dangers of sexual or racial inversion were averted.

Hero worship upheld this faith in rewarding the strong. According to Ohio feminist Jane Frolock, "hero worship" and the "love of rule" were best expressed through honors granted for feats of strength; this then allowed the warrior to scorn the weakness of his daughters and reward his valiant sons.[202] Frolock identified the connection between dominion and patronage, but more importantly, she addressed how military service and masculinity could be used to assign an entire class of people to superior or inferior ranks. Real strength or weakness came from caste position. At stake was ranking men and women according to their bodily makeup, treating all men as beings endowed with physical strength and all women in the context of what Bingham described as "her manifest destiny" as the "weaker sex."[203] Here, again, the state created an imaginary civic category that conflated masculinity with political strength and virtue. As Bingham mockingly noted, if physical strength was so valuable as a civic trait, then all men should be ranked from the strongest to the weakest, with the strongest man in power in every town across the country. The real purpose of the linkage of masculinity with political competence was to make the myth of the heroic citizen into a gendered reality by devaluing women's contribution to the nation-state. As Mott astutely observed, women became a "cypher in the nation." Barred from the battlefield and the "forensic war of words," women were excluded from the civic domains of political mastery and progress.[204]

In the rhetoric of manifest dominion, heroic impulse and hero worship rewarded men for seizing the moment and for mastering and subduing any obstacle, whether land or the nation's enemy. The rewards were not individual but were distributed as a bonus to a class, which as Charles Burleigh argued at the New York women's rights convention in 1853, defined the social compact: "It holds out a bonus to society, or rather, to its individual members,—'Give me this little, and I will give you in exchange this much.'"[205] But the bonus or political spoils granted to men necessitated a loss for women. Although women were expected to surrender the same rights as men in the social compact, they became one of the spoils being exchanged. Women were ciphers, it seems, for more reasons than their dependence and drudgery or their lack of strength. As Lucy Stone argued at the Cleveland women's rights convention in 1853, traditionally women had been exchanged among men for a bonus or reward (property and dowry), and this practice was reaffirmed through the social contract.[206] Women were not equal members to the social contract but part of the booty; both their land and access to their bodies were a political bonus. Thus, all women, not only slaves or Mexican women through "marital annexation," defined the sexual spoils of empire.

Feminists contended, then, that conquest upheld sexual slavery, placing all women in a servile and politically dependent position as the "victim of false gallantry" or "tyrannous subjection," crippled in either case by a "lordly and arrogant spirit, a love of dominion."[207] Activists denied that women lacked the natural power of "heroic action," and Stanton in particular claimed that if necessary, woman would "buckle on her armor and fight in defense of her country."[208] But civic virtue did not come from sacrificing the "blood of a brother," or by reducing nations or groups to helpless pawns, or from man's boundless capacity for extending his sphere to everyplace encompassed within his gaze.[209]

Nor did feminists believe that democratic citizenship could be based on brute force. Women did not benefit from male chivalry but were divested of the means of protection, because the narrative of national greatness required that women's lips remained sealed, their rights eclipsed. As Rose remarked, women's property could be taxed to support any unholy or unrighteous war, yet "she has not power to give veto against it."[210] Such savage remnants of conquest might be dressed in pomp and glory, but the "Anglo-Saxon head-splitters" who marched through Mexico pushed the nation backward rather than forward in the greater march toward enlightened civilization. Women were not minor characters in this narrative of nation identity formation, for their status justified manifest dominion. The logic of conquest relied on the pursuit of happiness—the acquisition of land and political aggrandizement. As Elizabeth Wilson remarked, the heroic impulse, the "strong arm of power," ensured that women were "vassals" and promoted only the "happiness" of men as a class.[211] The fall of woman secured the political patronage of the strong over the weak not only on the battlefield but in the social compact as well.

All Equal-Born and Free

The decade of the 1850s featured several political disputes that exposed the anomalous status of women as "citizens." Innocuously, and without arousing much notice, the definition of citizenship changed in 1855. That year Congress passed a law to "secure the right of Citizenship to Children of Citizens of the United States" born outside the jurisdiction and limits of the United States. This law enshrined the principle of birthright citizenship, insuring that all the children of American male citizens inherited their father's national identity. Adhering to a paternalistic formula, the law relied on male posterity and descent. It was fathers who secured the right to pass on the legacy of citizenship to their offspring. The same act of Congress, however, provided a different rationale for constituting women's relationship to the state. In Section 2 it stated that a woman who might be "lawfully naturalized" and married to a citizen of the United States "shall be deemed and taken to be a citizen."[212] Female aliens became citizens through their husbands, suggesting that naturalization for married women was the result of male proxy and custodianship.

During the same year, women's rights activists gathered in Boston, holding a convention and publishing "Reports on the Laws of New England." In her opening remarks Caroline Dall alluded to the marriage protest of Lucy Stone and Henry Blackwell that year, asserting that their declaration of coequality underscored the central problem of giving the husband "custody of the wife's person." Reviewing the laws of Massachusetts, Dall further noted that the "legal existence of woman is suspended during marriage, so that in many States, she neither has a legal part in the choice of her residence."[213] Ironically, the new naturalization law of 1855 repeated these concerns, implying that a married woman not only lacked any choice of residence, but a married alien woman did not necessarily have the right to choose her national identity. Marriage transferred the custody of the wife to her husband, and through naturalization the female alien found that his citizenship became her own.

Throughout the decade the themes of residency, dominion (paternal claim to land and persons), and birthright citizenship were intertwined in law and politics in strange and not so new ways. Debates about naturalization largely reflected the growing support for nativism, crystallizing in the formation of the Know-Nothing Party, which had victories at the local level in 1853 and 1854, sent forty men to Congress in 1854, and just as quickly faded after the failed presidential campaign of Millard Fillmore in 1856.[214]

The spirit of nativism emerged in a series of dramatic speeches in the House and Senate. Only weeks before the passage of the 1855 law, Congressman Augustus Sollers of Maryland addressed the potent theme of "Americanism." Two familiar chords appeared in his oration. Birthright citizenship was paramount, evidenced in his rhetorical question: "Why, I ask, shall we, born here, reared here, not be permitted to call it 'Our own, our native land.'" His vision of the "native land" encompassed the "lofty mountains and majestic rivers," the "stupendous forests and boundless plains," and he concluded that only native-born "Americans shall govern America." Dominion was implicit in his definition of full citizenship, for true Americans were "the offspring of civilization," nurtured from birth in the "sentiments" of liberty and manifest destiny, which came from the "boundless" land of the American continent.[215]

Sollers did not directly assess the place of women in the " 'land of the free, and the home of the brave.' " He did, nevertheless, theorize about the origins of nations as well as their demise.

> The nucleus of a nation is the family—the home.—Nomadic tribes have no home. From the family circle the community is formed—formed for mutual defense and for the protection of the weak against the strong; laws are made for the government; a government is formed, its jurisdiction is established, its boundaries marked out, and you have a nation, and a national sentiment is created. Now, invert all this—first break down one barrier and then another; the nation, government, the home, the family circle, and you have either barbarism or fourierism.[216]

The protection of the weak against the strong had been a consistent refrain in the doctrine of manifest destiny. Resounding support for continental expansion had been accompanied by the threat of amalgamation and unharmonious combinations of different racial and national stocks.[217] Nativism, often directed at immigrants in northeastern cities, just as easily registered fears over attempts to absorb immigrants and those people of the Mexican cession (cast by some as a "Catholic, dependent people") already residing in the newly acquired western territories of California, Utah, and New Mexico. Such populations had to be "*Americanized*"—incorporated and imbued with the proper national "sentiments." For nativists unsympathetic to assimilation, the un-American had to be subdued, displaced from the land, or carefully and securely contained as inoffensive "residents." Becoming a prominent member of the Know-Nothing Party in the 1850s, Sam Houston, ardent promoter of western expansion, easily adapted the democratic politics of conquest to nativism. An amorphous fear of foreigners corrupting the ballot box caused Californians, in their new constitution of 1849, to restrict the franchise to "white" male citizens.[218]

Five days after the 1855 law passed, naturalization was again the issue in congressional debate. This time the subject was Nebraska, and the discussion concerned whether the period of residency (before the granting of citizenship) should be shortened. Some advocates for the law proposed that residency alone could secure suffrage, a view rebuffed by others as a "monstrous doctrine" that "denationalized" citizenship and bypassed the process of acquiring the full rank of citizen.[219] In this regard citizenship was a prerequisite for suffrage, as membership in the national community had to precede the right to participate in the polity. The most hard-core members of the Know-Nothing Party believed that naturalization diminished the meaning of citizenship, and that the government should uphold permanent distinctions between native-born citizens and resident aliens. Naturalization, as one nativist wrote, was the most "unnatural of all proceedings." A feeling of home, of place, and an attachment to the laws required at least a twenty-one-year period of incubation for resident aliens or, as the hard-liners assumed, permanent restriction of political rights, because genuine and natural "sentiments" could never be cultivated in one who had been born in a foreign land.[220] Here, again, the 1855 law posed a contradiction. Birthright citizens could inherit their citizenship, despite having been born or raised in another country, far removed from those national "sentiments" that defined American identity.[221] Women, as well, could be more readily Americanized because as women they would occupy a status almost identical to that of resident aliens. Neither could vote, so the purity of the ballot box was protected from "corruption." Naturalized as unequal citizens, disenfranchised by sex, women's "sentiments" posed less of a danger because their husbands, as full citizens, voted by proxy for them.[222]

The 1855 law relied on a racial premise, limiting to Caucasian women the privilege of naturalization through marriage. By implication, American women who married foreign men faced another dilemma, namely, the possible divestment of their right to consensual citizenship.[223] The loss of national identity recalled the issue of personal custody. Did a child born outside the jurisdiction of the United States gain the birthright of citizenship because she or he was born in the custody (legal paternity established) of the father? And did a woman acquire citizenship through her spouse because the husband had a right to the "custody of the person of his wife?" At the same time, women's dependence complied with the nativist insistence that there was a natural evolution in nation-building, for which careful barriers and boundaries had to be preserved. As Congressman Sollers contended, distinctions between nations and between families were natural and required legal boundaries. Nations were bulwarks against "barbarism"; families were bulwarks against "fourierism [here meaning free love and moral decay]." By linking naturalization to marriage, the 1855 law reflected the older notion that wives could not share dual allegiances to husband and country, especially if those loyalties conflicted. Such a conflict erased the natural sexual distinctions found in the home and family circle that, for politicians like Sollers, represented the "nucleus of the nation."

Yet, much as Sollers and his compatriots tried, such clearly demarcated boundaries failed to define the policies for determining birthright citizenship in the antebellum period, particularly in cases involving slaves. Issues of personal custody, claims of political wardship, and the rights of residence all surfaced in legal controversies over the status of slaves living in free states. The highly celebrated Ohio case of Margaret Gardner, who aimed to kill her children to protect them from a life in chains, contrasted with an Illinois case in which the slave Jane sued for her freedom and her children. Having resided in Illinois for over two years and occupying a farm belonging to her owner from Kentucky, Jane was not a fugitive; she had remained in the custody of her master.[224] Masters who brought their slaves into free states, as in the case of Pierre in Pennsylvania, could find that their slaves turned free once they reached free soil.[225] But this practice was not universally adopted. Residence in a free state did not make slaves automatically free, just as nativists argued that residence in the United States should not make aliens into citizens. According to *Prigg v. Pennsylvania*, marriage to a freeman also failed to protect fugitive slaves or their children. This was what Margaret Morgan discovered. As a slave, she had no right to give her consent in marriage, to transfer her allegiance to her husband, or to choose her domicile, for her body and her posterity were not her own.[226]

Although married women were not the same as slaves, the law did generate analogous situations, which demonstrated why residence and custody had different implications for the civil standing of women compared with men. In

1858, in the case of *Hair v. Hair*, a South Carolina judge reaffirmed the legal constraints placed on the mobility and freedom of the wife. Although the wife contended that the husband had deserted her, the judge found that she was at fault. By refusing to move with her husband, she had violated his legal right to determine the family's place of residence. As the judge explained, "Certainly the husband, by our laws, is lord of his own household and sole arbiter on the question as to where himself and the family shall reside." The husband did not require the wife's consent in matters of residence: "The husband has the right, without consent of his wife, to establish his domicile in any part of the world, and it is the legal duty of the wife to follow his fortunes, wheresoever he may go." Clearly the wife was compelled to follow her husband, even if it meant leaving the country, and if the wife refused, she was guilty of desertion. In this case a married women did not have an equal claim to freedom of mobility, particularly when property was at stake; nor did her consent have the same legal weight, and her resistance was interpreted as disloyalty and disobedience. A married woman's place of residence was clearly with her husband, regardless of what part of the world he lived in.[227]

Making the husband the "lord of his own household" echoed the older, common-law notion of *petit treason*, which had been removed from American statutes following the Revolution but retained a resonance in certain controversial murder cases.[228] In 1833 Lucretia Chapman could be labeled a "traitress fiend" because she had usurped her husband's authority and had taken his life. The slave Celia, who killed her master in defense of her sexual virtue, was quickly sentenced to death in 1855. Southern courts had been less willing to eliminate the law on *petit treason* for this very reason: the act of murder and rebellion could be applied not only to husband and wife but to the relation of master and slave. The Missouri judge did not view Celia as a seduced woman protecting her honor but as a defiant slave whose punishment was the gallows.

Allowing female dependents to exercise the right of self-defense in the household posed a problem even for free women. It required that the woman had to assume the role of the protector of the family, assuming custodianship over herself and the entire family. In the 1843 case of *State of Indiana v. Hubbard*, in which a daughter killed her father in defense of her mother, for the killing to be treated as a homicide either the death had to be accidental or the killing had to be "in defense of the accused, his wife, husband, child, parent, servant or ward." Self-defense in the home, legally, was an action taken by the head of the household; it was a male responsibility. In the Hubbard case, self-defense implied that the daughter acted as a deputy husband (as well as deputy father and master), replacing the father in his duty to protect against an assailant in the home. While the jury found that Hubbard was justified in her act of self-defense, this decision demonstrated how the courts had reversed the legal roles of father and daughter, creating a tenuous legal fiction for rationalizing this deadly breach of authority.[229]

By 1859 another case of seduction leading to a murder trial provided women's rights advocates with an example of the abuses inherent in male custodianship. At the convention held in New York City that year Wendell Phillips lamented the sad state of affairs in Washington, D.C., by referring to the recent murder of Francis Key by Congressman Daniel Sickles after Key had seduced Sickles's wife. Most of the sympathy was directed toward Sickles as the wronged husband, Phillips noted, while his adulterous wife was ridiculed in the press. This tragedy demonstrated to Phillips the hypocrisy of "the chivalry that American Democratic Institutions produce." He railed that the trial was a farce: "Not one fair or considerate word from the lip of lawyer or judge. With malignant ingenuity, they dig up from the dust of two hundred years every atrocious judicial maxim, that made the wife a slave, and borrow it, though long since forgotten or exploded, for the defense of the assassin." In the same speech Phillips highlighted the recent hanging of Mrs. Hartung, a convicted murderer, claiming that to hang any woman was murder, for none had ever given her assent to the law. While men talked of "Nationality," of "empire," and "our destiny," such high-minded words failed to conceal that men were never as noble, courageous, or honorable as they wished to appear. The social ostracism and scapegoating of Mrs. Sickles in the name of male honor or the hanging of Mrs. Hartung provided all the evidence that Phillips needed.[230]

During the same 1859 convention Phillips had to distinguish between the status of women and aliens when a heckler from the audience asked (after Phillips had challenged the state's authority to hang a woman), "Have we a right to hang a foreigner?" His answer was interesting:

> Certainly, we have; because, when a man comes voluntarily into a country, he subjects himself, for the time being, to the laws which he knows to exist in that country, and that is the evidence of his assent. But a woman is born here, as we are. God gives her her place. We have no right to drive her from it. He gives her thought, he gives her moral being and responsibility to law. She has a right to them all; for our government rests on brains and thought, and not bayonets and power.[231]

His response revealed the difficulty inherent in a theory of female citizenship. As the 1855 law indicated, married women as aliens did not necessarily come voluntarily into the country. A woman's consent was not needed for her husband to determine where he and his family should reside. Women, as birthright citizens, did not acquire the same rights as men, nor did they secure the political rights that naturalized aliens as "free white men" could exercise. The citizenship of a woman still rested on her custodial and marital status, and the law placed limits on her right to self-protection when it denied her the same privileges of self-defense and consent. For Phillips this loss of rights was all in the name of conquest—rights derived from "bayonets and power."

Birthright citizenship did not resolve the divestment of rights faced by married women. Political consent was not deemed necessary for the state to exercise capital punishment, as Phillips's answer implied, and dominion (the husband's right to be lord of his own household) weakened a woman's ability to exercise resistance, whether she was protecting her life, liberty, or property. Lurking behind the theme of dominion, the pursuit of happiness through control of the land, was the ever present image of the soldier-citizen whose rights came from "bayonets and power." According to political rhetoric in vogue during the Mexican War, soldiers who married Mexican women annexed these women; by 1855 these women in all likelihood would have met the criteria for citizenship, which made them the subjects of American law and their husbands.

In a poem of 1854 titled "Woman's Warfare," Frances Gage offered one approach for displacing the image of the soldier-citizen. Using the metaphor of combat and self-defense, Gage contended that women had to meet the foe, face to face, eye to eye, defending their homes by

> Forming a phalanx, true and strong,
> Of mother, sister, wife,
> Around the loved ones of our homes,
> Our husband, sons, and sires.
> Ready to give our lives for *them*
> And for our hearthstone fires.

Gage believed that nonresistance, the antebellum term of passive resistance, would undercut the dubious goals of war. By inverting the traditional pattern of men defending their homes, Gage promoted the idea that women could assume custodianship of their lives and their families. Like Swisshelm, Gage's antiwar poem exposed the ruse of chivalry, forcing soldiers to see that murdering any woman (especially one who stood her ground as an equal) was akin to killing a member of their own families. Men could not at once honorably protect and murder women.[232]

Gage, in addition, presented a different model for legal standing. Women had to stand apart from men and

stand by his side, as *human souls*
All equal-born and free.[233]

If the family was the "nucleus of the nation," then a woman needed the same political prerogatives in order to defend her home and to consent to her place of residence and her choice of nationality. Birthright citizenship had to extend the same rights, privileges, and immunities to women and men, creating a balance of power in the family and not reverting to common-law fictions that transferred certain rights from the wife to the husband. Women were not property, ciphers, or trophies of war; they were, in Gage's words, "*human souls*." As activists such as Gage understood, dispensing with the illusion of masculine power began by resting citizenship not on dependence or custodianship, but on the principle that all are "equal-born and free."

6

The Bonds of Matrimony

As early as 1837 Thomas Herttell noted a glaring contradiction between common-law and constitutional rights. In his bill before the New York assembly, Herttell identified the divestment of married women's property rights as a suspect legal precedent for the State of New York. He noted that the law deprived a married woman of "her rights, her liberty, and her property" and "left her destitute of the means of seeking redress in a judiciary court." "Empty-handed, and powerless," she had no recourse in protecting herself against her husband—and her "antagonist"—to whom Herttell argued the law had given all her property and "nearly unlimited authority over her person." The legal identity of the wife had been stripped of any means of subsistence or power of self-protection and self-preservation. She represented at best a creature of the common law and a constitutional contradiction—a citizen without the basic rights of life, liberty, and property.[1]

Herttell was not the first or the last to criticize *feme covert* or to use political rhetoric rather than pure legal description to attack the common-law definition of marriage that erased a woman's civil identity. In her early eighteenth-century treatise *Reflections Upon Marriage*, Mary Astell had argued that custom and common law reduced married women to a state of submission and subjection.[2] Almost a century later in *A Vindication of the Rights of Woman* Mary Wollstonecraft asserted that wives were "suspended" under the "galling yoke of sovereign man."[3] Abigail Adams had lodged a similar complaint in her oft-quoted 1776 missive to her husband, John Adams, urging him to "remember the ladies" when drafting the Declaration of Independence, because "all men would be tyrants if they could."[4] English socialist William Thompson followed suit in his 1825 treatise, *Appeal of One Half of the Human Race*, contending that "each man yokes woman to his establishment" through marriage and "calls it a *contract*."[5] In 1838, not long after Herttell addressed the New York legislature, Sarah Grimké attacked the "peculiar rigor" of Blackstone's formulation of coverture, quoting his famous words in her *Letters on the Equality of the Sexes*: "*the very being, or legal existence of the woman* is suspended during the marriage, or at least incorporated and consolidated, in that of the husband under whose wing, protection and cover she performs everything."[6]

All of these writers identified the legal definition of marriage as the source of women's dependence, but they realized that Blackstone's "legal fiction" had several meanings. Herttell concluded that coverture made women into something remarkably similar to slaves, vassals, and servants, highlighting that coverture reduced women to "piece[s] of property," landless tenants, and docile laborers.[7] Herttell did capture the essential features of a strict interpretation of a common-law definition of the political economy of marriage. A married woman's wealth was consolidated into the husband's holdings, and the practice of dower in tenancy, which granted wives a life interest and not ownership of the land, potentially left widows or abandoned wives to become landless tenants.[8] Because marriage was a profitable and corporate venture, a husband's right to his wife's labor was part of the bargain; thus whatever the wife earned or produced, the husband could claim as his own.[9] Marriage granted sexual rights, which empowered the husband to have control over the paternity of his offspring and to command his wife's fidelity. The "unlimited authority over her person" gave the husband a right to the use of her body and the fruits of her womb, ensuring that the children became solely his custodial charges.[10]

But another message emerged in Herttell's contention that women's hands signified their peculiar state of dependence.[11] Traditionally, marriage was seen as a gift exchange between men, in which fathers placed their daughters figuratively and legally into the "hands" of their husbands.[12] Hands also represented the power of resistance, the right to self-defense, an active force that wives lacked because the courts expected women to "suffer in silence." The marriage vows—"till death" do us part—justified the legal assumption that "tolerable cruelty" had to be endured without redress.[13] Hands further connoted the capacity to produce, fabricate value, and control the fruits of one's labor by making and signing contractual agreements.[14] In 1848 one writer argued that the hands best explained the emblematic nature of marriage vows, or at least symbolically reflected human agency: "Intention, desire, motive—all suggest themselves figuratively by epithets borrowed from the action of the hand; and the marriage rite hath for its almost universal symbol, encircling the finger with a little hoop of gold."[15] Most vividly, this description illustrated the difference between husband and wife. While the husband enhanced his standing through marriage, acted on his own initiative, and satisfied his wants and wishes, somehow the wife lost her "intention, desire, and motive" for mastering the material world and imposing her will on the future. In other words, "empty-handed, and powerless," wives failed to secure full legal recognition, and the hoop of gold on their fingers registered their inability to imagine or prosecute a plan—or to act on their own.

This chapter explores the marital politics of antebellum feminists by reconstructing the legal implications of coverture and by investigating how activists turned this legal fiction into different narrative plots for exposing the economic and sexual conditions of the family. Reformers crafted arguments for divorce and for pecuniary and custodial rights, drawing their legal claims from a wide range of campaigns such as temperance, health, and labor and land reform, as well as married women's property rights. In part, this approach holds that marriage must be viewed not only as a private relationship but as a decidedly political institution. Despite popular mythology surrounding the "cult of domesticity," which identified the home as a haven of selfless affection that was shielded from the ruthless ambitions of the marketplace or politics, this rarefied view represented only one among a host of contending visions of the family.[16] Antebellum Americans regarded matrimony with far more skepticism, and jurists reinforced and refashioned older, more traditional beliefs about marriage as a commitment based on obligations rather than affections. Customary rites—combined with theories of social and natural rights—placed coverture at the center of reform efforts that attempted to replace common-law practices with a newer constitutional understanding of family, labor, and property law. By contesting the sexual and political economy of the family, feminists duly acknowledged the significance of marriage in shaping the legal contours of political authority in antebellum America.

The Twain Are Not One

The precarious position of the widow—torn from her home and husband—emerged as a persistent rallying cry for the supporters of both marital and temperance reform. In 1853 "The Widow's Appeal," a powerful story of trial and tribulation, appeared in the *Una*. By recounting the wretched tale of a "drunkard's hell," the author described a home destroyed by the effects of alcohol. Shorn of his strength and yielding in abject submission to his "deadliest foe," the drunkard, like Samson, was seduced and defeated by his own personal desires and weaknesses. "Thrice before God and man" the husband broke his solemn pledge to deny the "tempter," eventually dooming his family. His lack of personal control led to financial disaster, and his inflamed passions from alcohol resulted in "cruel blows" against his loved ones. Forced to salvage what was left of her marriage, the widow was compelled to seek "shelter where RUM could not invade her sanctuary." [17]

Crafted as melodramatic yet political in tone and style, this appeal made the private complaint of intemperance into a public matter of "life and death." [18] For the wife caught within this nightmare, the solution was not restoration of the family but recognition that the husband lacked the "fitness" to be head of the household. Whether the partner for life was a fit helpmeet addressed the larger question of the rights and duties of marriage. In "The Widow's Appeal" the author demonstrated that the drunkard had violated his duties for protecting the material happiness of his family. Because of his personal failings, he transgressed on the unwritten laws of conjugal love: respect, spiritual affinity, and mutual assistance through life. Yet marital fitness and happiness were not rights sanctioned by the courts. As Edward Mansfield explained in his 1845 treatise, *The Legal Rights, Liabilities, and Duties of Women*, such complaints involved "moral circumstances" that remained outside the province of the law. [19]

In the 1840s the temperance movement pursued a new direction that closed the gap between moral circumstances and legal redress. Through the field of medical jurisprudence, which was influenced by the moral theories of phrenology and physiology, legal and temperance reformers advanced the category of moral mania to explain the "morbid perversion" of the "affective or moral powers." As early as 1834 the courts had endorsed a similar principle of "irresistible impulse," which recognized that a person might engage in criminal behavior because "one vice or ruling idea" held "tyrannical sway over the entire man and his actions." [20] Clearly, the drunkard, with his "irretrievable bondage to alcohol," fit the diagnosis of a monomaniac. [21] What was significant about this kind of legal reasoning was that it divided the brain into two compartments: one half was used for reason, the other for moral action. By acknowledging the separate existence of moral disorders, the courts opened the door to redress of moral wrongs previously ignored in the law.

Within this political climate, the "unfit" spouse became a symbol of marital reform. By 1850 at least fourteen states agreed that "habitual drunkenness" was grounds for divorce. Contemporary legal writers such as Henry Folsom Page defined drunkenness as a temptation and a sin, relying on Lyman

Beecher's *Sermons on Temperance* as the authority on this subject. By wasting his property and destroying "his health, his reason, his usefulness, and reputation," the chronic drunkard displayed all the signs of an unfit head of household. Page also echoed the medical view that drunkenness "blunted" moral perceptions, making the husband unable to comprehend his "relations" as a neighbor, citizen, father, and spouse. Significantly, the drunkard subjected his wife to his "repulsive condition" even when they shared "the closest intimacy." Here the most basic conjugal right of fidelity was desecrated: the wife was forced to share her bed with a virtual stranger—a man devoid of any understanding of his duty as a husband because he lacked affection for her.[22]

THE NEW TYRANNY OF INTEMPERANCE

Temperance reform dramatically politicized the relationship between husband and wife, making the domestic sanctuary into a battleground. Marital discord was not merely a quarrel between an unhappy couple but a grander and momentous struggle between life and death.[23] The Washingtonian crusade, organized in 1840, took the lead in placing the marital duties of the husband under public scrutiny. A feature of this reform movement was the "experience" meeting, in which a former drunkard stood before an audience and confessed his sins. Creating a mock trial, the drunkard's confession cataloged all the crimes of an unfit husband. In a formulaic recitation the drunkard testified to his utter incompetence as a spouse, conceding that the demise of his marriage—separation from his wife—was caused by "that foul monster, rum."[24]

A nationalistic and patriotic flavor suffused the rhetoric of the Washingtonian campaign. Named in honor of George Washington, the movement readily drew comparisons between the "tyranny of British yoke" and the new tyranny of intemperance.[25] By 1842 the language of the movement had carved distinctive roles for men and women and encouraged the formation of female auxiliaries known as Martha Washingtonian societies. Several women also assumed editorial positions and wrote articles for the major temperance publications.[26] In their literature teetotalers (pledged to total abstinence from all intoxicating beverages) often embodied the virtues of model patriots, while drunkards assumed the part of embattled soldiers fighting their "deadliest foe," rum.[27] The drunkard's wife appeared as a patriotic heroine and war widow, a woman who performed the duties of a devoted helpmeet until forced to abandon her home when the enemy appeared at the door. Even single women became figures in this genre through their pledge never to marry a man whose lips had touched alcohol.[28] Total abstinence virgins imitated the patriotism of chaste maidens who refused to consort with the enemy. When the Daughters of Temperance organized a new reform organization in 1845, they continued to emphasize the war against temperance, even promoting the physical destruction of saloons by bands of women. In 1854 Abraham Lincoln defended such a group of women before an Illinois court, claiming that their noble impulse was modeled on that of the men of the Boston Tea Party.[29]

The patriotic zeal of the Washingtonians and the Daughters of Temperance gave their crusade what Robert Cover has called a "revolutionary constitutional understanding." The emphasis on the temperance pledge not only served as a ritualized form of initiation, but as a pledge of honor it echoed the solemn oath at the end of the Declaration of Independence: "We mutually pledge to each other our lives, our fortunes, and our sacred honor."[30] This kind of oath resembled the idea of covenant found in the Old Testament, in which commitment was staked upon nothing less than blood itself.[31] Female reformers were not averse to using the language of war and physical resistance for the temperance cause. When Amelia Bloomer organized the Ladies Total Abstinence Benevolent Society of Seneca Falls in 1848, she declared war against the "thirsty tyrant" and "foul destroyer."[32] Other activists, such as Ohio feminist Sarah Coates-Kinney, compared the temperance pledge to a blood pact. In her fictional story, "Love's Triumph by Stratagem," she described two solemn pledges. At his mother's deathbed the drunkard vows to give up alcohol. Failing to keep his promise, he violently beats his wife. As a strategy of self-defense, his wife devises a plan to disguise herself as her brother, retrieve her husband from the tavern, and force him— at knifepoint—to pledge on his sacred honor to renounce rum forever. For Coates-Kinney the powerful pledge between the husband and the wife (disguised as a man) superimposed the higher expectations of political fidelity onto their original marital vows. Through this new covenant, wives secured the right to self-protection, while husbands vowed to respect it. Thus they reaffirmed—as the founders had in 1776—the mutual pledge to safeguard their "lives and sacred honor."[33]

A revolutionary understanding meant that natural rights were grounded on the human impulse for self-preservation—an "instinctive dread of danger" and a natural right to resist all forms of tyranny.[34] The "natural right of self-defense," as Ohio feminists and temperance reformers resolved in 1853, empowered women to revolt against "indignities which no man would bear."[35] By fostering a moral revolution, temperance reformers claimed that the siege on the body politic came from two deadly foes. In the drive to pass local option laws, which restricted the licenses for taverns, activists likened rumsellers to both an invading army and plague spreaders. During the 1846 campaign in Pennsylvania, a common tactic was to vilify the rumseller and his "accursed poison" for dispatching drunkards to an early grave and for annihilating families, which, one report claimed, annually left 1,500 widows and 9,000 orphans.[36] Torn apart by disease, death, and destruction, the community was compared to a wasteland in the aftermath of war. Such allusions to contagion or the devouring element of a "fearful conflagration," according to the women of Chester County in 1848, vividly dramatized an invisible force raging across the community and decimating all homes in its path.[37] Some women, like Mrs. Margaret Freeland of Syracuse, New York, in 1853, took the "war into their own hands," destroying the rum and property of the local saloon.[38] Feminist and temperance supporters also endorsed legislation that made rumsellers liable for their "social debts." Like war widows requesting pensions, married women could seek compensation and damages for the loss of their husbands to that "foul monster, rum."[39]

THE PATHOLOGY AND POISON OF
DOMESTIC VIOLENCE

Seen as a concealed threat, something lurking beneath the surface, the disease pathology of drunkenness further underscored fears of moral disorder. It was not just rumsellers and grogshops that posed a danger to the community; it was an unseen intruder whose "cruel visitings" preyed on the living tissue of the drunkard.[40] This "fall of the house of Usher" portrait focused on ravages against the flesh, the unsettling image of the "once loved husband" as the enemy within whose insanity induced the downfall of his own household.[41] The invisible force that raged outwardly against friends and family wreaked silent horrors on the mind and soul of the drunkard. Intoxication, Amos Dean explained in his 1850 textbook *Principles of Medical Jurisprudence*, devoured the "strength and energy of the drunkard by feeding on the corruptions of moral death which has thrown its oblivious pall over the intellect and higher sentiments." Reminiscent of Edgar Allan Poe's 1843 poem "The Conquering Worm," Dean's analogy likened the pathology of alcoholism to that of a moral cancer. "Like the worm," he wrote, it was "increasing from the consumption of its coffined banquet."[42]

The symbolic decomposition of the drunkard's body allowed feminists to dissect the legal fiction of husband and wife as one flesh. His split personality made the merging of the couple as one flesh impossible, if not hypocritical, since the drunkard made his wife figuratively a bigamist—a woman fraudulently deceived into marrying two men.[43] "Dread and loathsome disgust" for the drunkard on the part of the wife implied that the marriage dissolved because it could no longer be consummated.[44] Physical affinities and aversions had a particular meaning in the symptomatology of medical jurisprudence. An unnatural aversion to a person inhibited the capacity for procreation, and vice versa: unnatural sexual acts such as rape induced an instinctive inability to reproduce.[45] If the drunkard came to represent a "loathsome corpse" and marriage a "living death," then gothic overtones of bestiality and necrophilia reconfigured marriage to a drunkard into the most unholy of legal unions.[46] As Elizabeth Cady Stanton claimed in her 1850 appeal for divorce, the radical transformation of the husband into a "coarse, beastly, and disgusting drunkard" inferred that the marriage bed was polluted with almost every conceivable crime against God and nature.[47]

By conjuring such images of marriage as a house of horrors, feminists demonstrated that it was perverse to insist that marital unity never failed to preserve "conjugal peace and tranquility."[48] Activists rejected the general assumption of the common law that the real danger to society was separation and divorce. Most American courts were upholding this ideal through the "one flesh" trope and by quoting the famous English jurist Lord Stowell, who had contended that separation created sexual disorder, for "the most dangerous characters" were "a wife without a husband, and a husband without a wife."[49] Given this emphasis on preserving unity at all costs, jurists treated domestic and sexual violence as a natural condition of marriage. Violence within marriage was defined as something distinct from criminal transgressions between strangers. For example, the common law had established a long tradition that marital rape was a misnomer. As a crime between strangers, rape implied that the offender had forced his victim to have sexual intercourse without her consent.[50] Marital sex was the exact opposite: it was legally sanctioned sex based on the voluntary consent of both parties. Throughout the nineteenth century no court recognized marital rape as grounds for separation or divorce.[51] In his *Principles of Medical Jurisprudence* Amos Dean mentioned the one case of marital rape in English law, in which the husband was convicted of "rape upon his wife, by assisting another person to violate her."[52] Rape was conceivable only when another man—not the husband— sexually violated the wife.

Rape was a problem because marital unity endorsed the idea of an instrumental use of the female body for procreation and as a moral restraint on infidelity and adultery.[53] Legal theorists and moralists believed that a sexual economy should be imposed on marriage, in which the wife constituted a vessel and conduit for the husband's passions. If the wife said "no" to sexual intercourse, the husband might seek release elsewhere through prostitution, by fixing his desires on other objects—children, men, or animals—or by wasting his imagination by engaging in "solitary pleasures."[54] This theory reinforced the binding nature of the social contract. Enlightened thinkers such as Jean-Jacques Rousseau had argued that in a state of nature man was uncivilized, preferring to engage in sex with many women, but in society his lusts were tempered because he directed his desire to fix on one woman.[55] Here again, the scale was tipped against the wife. While marriage claimed to protect society from men's sexual excesses, it subsequently objectified married women as the mere "vessels" of male desire.

In 1845 a rather prominent legal case suggested how jurists condoned marital rape as "tolerable cruelty." After the State of Connecticut passed two new laws in 1843 that granted divorce on grounds of drunkenness and cruelty, the legislation was tested two years later in *Shaw v. Shaw*.[56] The court ruled that the husband's repeated attempts to "force" and "compel" his wife to "occupy the same bed with him" did not constitute "by itself" extreme cruelty according to the statute. The husband's conduct did not demonstrate "intolerable cruelty," nor did it entitle the wife to a decree of divorce. During the trial proceedings the wife openly acknowledged that she was forced—against her will—to have sex with her husband. Several predictable lines of argumentation were used in this case. By treating sexual abuse as a singular condition, an exception to the overall conduct of the husband, the effect was to marginalize its significance as a cause for divorce. Sexual coercion within marriage was expressly distinguished from rape. The court ruled that the husband's actions were not subject to "criminal prosecution" because the sexual "act in itself was a lawful act." Although his actions were "harsh, if not cruel," the ruling qualified this criticism because the husband's intentions were seen as flowing from his "marital rights."[57]

Yet the rights of the wife did not carry the same weight, especially in her claims to legal protection. The husband's verbal abuse and his attempts to restrain his wife physically by locking her in the house and forcing her to escape by a window did not represent either excessive authority or cruelty. The court discounted the husband's jealous motives and irrational behavior. His jealousy was condoned as a measure of his attachment and affection, the normal desire and possessive devotion of a husband for his wife. If his jealousy did cross the line into momentary displays of "rage" or "evil passion," then his actions fell outside the law as a "moral offence." The husband's behavior, however, never constituted extreme cruelty, which required that his intention was to kill his wife. Thus the opinion of the court on domestic and sexual violence was neatly summarized in one phrase: "It may be intolerable, but is not intolerable cruelty."[58]

At the same time, the courts began to offer some compelling reasons for expanding the definition of legal cruelty. In 1849, in the Pennsylvania case of *Butler v. Butler*, while the decision stressed that the married state involved suffering, even "submission to great wrongs," and that separation posed the social dangers of a husband without a wife and a wife without a husband, the ruling offered two conditions that expanded legal cruelty beyond visible forms of physical violence. "Indignities to her person" could make life "intolerable" and force the wife to "withdraw from his house and family," and constant danger, which demanded that the wife choose the higher duty of self-preservation, could make it impossible for her to discharge her marital duties. Yet more importantly, the court noted that a "course of humiliating insults and annoyances," practiced with "malice," could "eventually destroy the life or health of his wife, although such conduct may be unaccompanied by violence, positive or threatened." This case highlighted the "system" or "course" of abuse and shifted the measure of violence to the long-term "effects" on the life or health of the wife. As stated in the decision, "The cruelty is judged from its effects; nor solely from the means which those effects are produced."[59]

Personal indignities could extend to sexual improprieties, which served as the grounds for divorce. The 1846 Ohio case of *Huldah A. Barber v. Hiram Barber* is illustrative in this regard. Drawing on the English legal precedent, spitting on one's wife, attempting to infect her with a venereal disease, having sex with a servant, or making a "brothel of his own house," all constituted brutal conduct. In this case the husband had attempted to have sex with his stepdaughter on repeated occasions. He also humiliated his wife by bringing false charges about her sexual incapacity. She was forced to endure a "distressing personal examination" by a doctor to disprove his accusations. The husband refused to cohabit with the wife or have conjugal relations with her. In the opinion of the court, it was "accumulated wrongs" against the wife that justified her claim of cruelty. To remain in his house (which was the husband's condition for support) would have been intolerable, for she was an "object of scorn" to his children and "of hatred and dislike" to him. The wife, moreover, was praised for her "propriety" during her trials, having borne her "griefs in silence" and having submitted to her fate "with uncomplaining resignation" until he filed against her for sexual incapacity. The husband's crime was his repeated personal indignities. He subjected her to public and private humiliation, flagrantly violated her modesty and that of her daughter, and placed her body (the most private sexual parts of her body) on trial before the public eye and the ears of the community.[60]

Both of these cases offered examples of how the definition of marriage unity had to be changed. In 1855 Francis Gage expanded on the themes raised in these cases, providing an astute analysis of domestic abuse. As in the Barber case, Gage stressed the "accumulated wrongs," writing that the long train of abuses, the mundane "agony of days and weeks and months and years of wretchedness," constituted the effects of cruelty. Hidden behind closed doors, the threat of violence might be constantly present. Gage surmised, "In the home, the sanctuary of both love and hate, that screen of both caresses and curses, the wife will become the recipient of . . . mortification, humiliation, degradation, and abuse that the world's eye will never see or hear." Such personal indignities threatened the health and safety of the wife. Gage further argued that abuse must be viewed as a permanent condition rather than a single transgression; it constituted a propensity or mania that could not be measured by isolated acts of violence. In other words, marital abuse resembled a "poison" that "slowly and torturously sapped the foundations of life."[61] Domestic violence had the same effects as intemperance, poisoning the home, the health, and physical integrity and spiritual affinities binding the family circle.

EQUAL RESTRAINT AND IMMUNITIES
IN MARRIAGE

"For better, for worse" had suggested that "prudent conciliation" rather than divorce or separation should resolve marital disputes.[62] Caresses and curses were part of the burden imposed by marriage, and endurance and pain were treated as normal and natural conditions of married life. But as Gage revealed, the burden of suffering or silent acquiescence fell disproportionately onto the wife. Most jurists assumed that it was the wife's duty to concede to her husband's wishes in order to avoid conflict. Even Huldah Barber was praised for her "forbearance," "uncomplaining resignation," and "humility" for having suffered in silence.[63] A wife's liberty vanished, however, Gage observed, when she checked her words and actions out of constant "fear of domestic reprisal."[64] The traditional emphasis on "prudent conciliation" slipped into patterns of physical coercion in marriage. Gage's clever application of the poison analogy invoked an invisible danger, but it had legal implications as well: real poisoning constituted an aggressive act that was seen in the law as inflicting visible bodily injury.

Undue coercion and restraint of his wife by the husband—based on the unchecked exercise of his marital rights—exceeded his authority and violated the wife's natural rights. As demonstrated in the case of *Shaw v. Shaw*, the wife might find herself with little protection against her husband's unreasonable demands. Submission was a slippery category, and a wife's health did not necessarily check a husband's sexual expectations. As one man confessed who had expected the "unconditional and unqualified" submission of his wife, "As long as she has her health, it is her duty to yield herself, unreservedly, to my wishes."[65] As Stanton commented, the imbalance of power and privileges in marriage led to abuses and underscored the practice that when the happiness of the husband and wife came into conflict, the wife's wishes were sacrificed.[66]

While feminists exaggerated the pathology of the drunkard's body, they did so, in part, to counter the emerging scientific discourse that designated women's bodies as prone to pain and created primarily to bear children. In 1853 Dr. Wiltbank gave an introductory lecture at the University of Pennsylvania Medical School that defined female reproduction as a pathology.[67] Most women's rights activists observed that medical science emphasized the pattern of "sexualizing everything outwardly," as Harriot Hunt concluded in 1849, and that women were taught to dread and fear their bodies.[68] A constant state of "penance" rather than preservation, Jane Elizabeth Jones observed, explained how most women approached a physical understanding of the laws of life and health.[69] Indeed, activists concluded that diseases could not be fixed outwardly as sexual laws, and physiology required "self-knowledge" that countered dangerous prescriptions such as sexual submission.[70] The sexual "wishes" of husband and wife required "equal restraint and equal privileges," making sexual intercourse into a pleasurable act of affection rather than a pathology or "erotic mania" marked by lust or violence.[71]

The drunkard posed a danger when he concealed his illness and insanity behind the veneer of marital rights. The state, in turn, ignored this danger by insisting that wives submit to their husband's wishes, arguing that the sanctity of marriage was more important than a wife's safety. Feminists noted how preposterous it was to quote biblical dicta that wives should "submit yourselves unto your husbands, as unto the Lord." As one writer in the *Lily* asked her readers, "Is it a woman's duty to 'reverence and stand in awe of' a licentious, brutal, or drunkard husband?"[72] Instead, wives needed "self-knowledge," for as Paulina Wright Davis claimed in 1846, "We have a right to know everything that concerns our life and happiness."[73] In this regard women's rights activists like Davis established female physiological societies and joined the corps of health lecturers, recruiting others such as Jane Elizabeth Jones, Sarah Coates, and Mary Ann Johnson.[74] Yet knowledge was not enough without recourse against cruelty and coercion. Divorce and separation had to be combined with physical sanctuary; that is, wives had to view their bodies as a sanctum sanctorum, a "holy temple," which transformed the body from an instrument or vessel into a place of worship and knowledge and an asylum from physical harm.[75] Here feminists acknowledged the shift from seeing the body as an object to defining the body as a subjective terrain in which a woman determined her own body's desires, uses, and means of protection.

Consequently, when feminists compared marriage to "legalized adultery" or "legalized prostitution," they emphasized how the implicit law of "unconditional submission" condoned marital rape.[76] Although the law could not enforce sexual intercourse, as stated in the Barber case, the law did not provide women with means of self-defense.[77] Women's inability to dissent from sexual intercourse denied that women had "intentions" or a will of their own insofar as they might choose when to have children or when to express their own desires.[78] From the perspective of the law, a wife's desire was irrelevant, as she was expected to mold her desires and feelings to her husband's wishes and wants. Submission nevertheless invoked the undemocratic images of tyranny and the loss of moral liberty. Both the drunkard and the wife of a jealous husband sacrificed their bodies to a dangerous impulse, a moral mania, and "morbid love." According to temperance reformers, marriage had to adhere to the ideals of honor and self-defense found in the Declaration of Independence. And for antebellum feminists, women's bodies demanded the same standard of protection from physical harm inside or outside the bonds of marriage. Divorce, then, was a civil right flowing from the natural right of self-preservation and the laws of "health and happiness."

The Devoted Drudge

While Francis Gage exposed the "mundane" agonies of domestic abuse, a similar concern arose for the health and welfare of the wife as a laborer within the sacred family circle. One such incisive rebuke of the household economy appeared in the *Lily* in 1852, appropriately titled "Every-day Life of Woman," in which the author intended to capture the pedestrian side of "life in all its reality." Rejecting the romantic portrait of marital affections, the author contended that marriage more accurately resembled an economic alliance for profit and material accumulation. Although the typical couple might share the same desire for acquiring comfortable property, the author stated without hesitation that the husband's "spirit of avarice" changed "the woman of his love" into "his most devoted drudge." Curiously enough, property alone was not the only reason behind this transformation of the wife into an exploited servant; the husband sought to use the money saved from his wife's labor to acquire more wealth. The calculated self-interest of the husband resulted in the wife's total divestment, for as the author remarked, the wife became "broken-down, twenty years before [her] time," only to die without reward and even to "give place to a second wife." Expendable and exchangeable, the wife—turned drudge—clearly failed to reap the fruits of her labor when ruled by the husband's "spirit of avarice."[79]

This tale emphasized how the husband pocketed the real assets of the marital economy. And rather than charting the demise of the family per se, the exposé revealed wives' oppression from the "division of labor" in a prosperous household.[80] A stark and ironic tone pervaded the "Every-day Life of Woman," for the anonymous author realized that little separated healthy ambition and acquisitiveness from the "spirit of avarice." As Frederick Grimké concluded in his 1848 *Considerations Upon the Nature and Tendencies of Free Institutions*, acquisitiveness was prudence in "making and saving money," and such "industry, sagacity, and enterprise constituted the principal capital of society."[81] When women's work was compared to "menial drudgery," domestic labor closely followed traditional property relations. According to coverture and common law, the husband's personal property came from the right to use the labor of his household dependents.[82] Yet even early advocates of manufacturing, such as Alexander Hamilton, adapted the household economy to theories of political economy, arguing that women and children would be "rendered more useful" if allowed to labor in factories.[83] Husbands and fathers would benefit from the surplus income derived from the wages earned by their family members. The enterprising husband, then, was both a master of old and a small-scale capitalist who consciously reaped profits from the labor of his wife.[84]

The compelling theme of drudgery mocked the sentimental defenders of domesticity by demonstrating that the home was not a private sanctuary untouched by forces of the emergent capitalist economy. This insight was correct for both legal and economic reasons. Following the panic of 1837, new laws for the protection of debtors and married women's property rights gained support in state legislatures, and the legal rights of wives and wage workers became an important area of civil litigation and discussion in legal circles. Also in 1837, Timothy Walker published his *Introduction to American Law*, a major resource for reforming the rights of married women that reflected the influence of the codification movement toward eliminating abuses of the common law.[85] Through debates about "pecuniary rights" antebellum Americans began to understand the interrelationship between property and wage labor in marriage. Legally, marriage channeled the profits of the family economy into husbands' hands and made wives into disabled servants (and possible drudges) for life.[86]

Paulina Wright Davis led the charge in the campaign for labor rights in the household. In her 1854 essay "The Pecuniary Independence of Woman," she defined the wife as a worker within the wage system, whose marital status most resembled the condition of an "upper-servant." Davis contended that marriage involved a "life-long engagement" in which wives accepted the promise of subsistence in exchange for relinquishing the right to control services they rendered.[87] Blackstone's definition of coverture, namely that the wife "performs everything" under the husband's "wing, protection, and *cover*," reinforced the husband's entitlement to his wife's services and time and the use of her person.[88] Wives could not negotiate a fair contract, and marriage law divested them of the capacity to protect the value of their labor. Neither consent nor dissent mattered in this marital agreement, because the state relegated to the husband the right to his wife's services.

The same legal inequalities that plagued wives informed the wage labor contract. In his 1832 *Commentaries on American Law*, James Kent invoked the euphemism of upper-servant in asserting that all persons "employed in husbandry, in manufacturing business, *or in any other manner*" were "hired servants." Because personal authority over an individual implied servitude, wage laborers did not simply sell their time and labor; they implicitly agreed to be directed and controlled by their employers. Labor contracts established a one-sided agreement that stipulated fixed hours and wages and at the same time constituted a status relationship.[89]

It was the blending of legal rights and social duties that made the modern wage contract resemble the contractual and economic alliance forged between husband and wife. The legacy of common law influenced how "the rules of propriety" regulated social behavior according to the mores of a "well-governed family." This was what William Blackstone had concluded in his *Commentaries on the Laws of England*.[90] Family and common law recognized a series of social hierarchies that had evolved from feudal custom and convenience, most notably the relations between master and servant, parent and child, and husband and wife.[91] These distinctions carefully circumscribed the rights of subordinates; through the force of law, moreover, these customary ranks compelled men and women to "know their place" and "move in it."[92]

Not surprisingly, legal reformers, especially those influenced by the codification movement—or those strongly drawn to theories of natural law or rights—had little respect for the "condensed wisdom of the ages" attributed to common law.[93] In the 1830s, legislators, lawyers, and reformers began to describe the common law as an "anomalous" remnant of the "dark ages" that stood in opposition to the rights tradition of American constitutionalism.[94] Advocates for the legal rights of women identified the "legal fiction" of coverture as the fundamental flaw of common law, and yet they further noted how "custom does not teach us so to regard it." As Timothy Walker suggested in his *Introduction to American Law*, common law remained appealing, even in a free and democratic society, because of its capacity to conceal inequities under the rubric of custom.[95]

Beyond challenging the persistence of common law, legal reformers returned their attention to the fundamentals of natural law. Although due process had always guaranteed the protection of life, liberty, and property, the theory of natural rights was taking a new direction in the antebellum period. One important development involved the recognition of social rather than purely political conditions as the source of rights. By the 1830s the meaning of the natural right to life had expanded beyond issues of punishment and death to include the natural impulse to survive, and hence, in the words of Thomas Herttell, individuals were "bound by natural obligations to sustain themselves" and thus were "naturally and justly entitled to the avails of their own labor and industry, and all other property honestly acquired."[96] Notions of "property" and the "pursuit of happiness" could be used to invoke the right to "the means of subsistence," just as liberty acquired a decidedly social function by protecting the right to make contracts, receive honest wages, and pursue employment unencumbered by the laws of the state.[97] Labor reformers embraced these sentiments in petitioning the state for shorter hours, as they defended their right to organize unions and challenged the "capitalist" tendency to secure "sovereign control over the prices of labor."[98] Whether criticizing the act of granting privileges or of imposing penalties on a select group of citizens, advocates of natural rights argued that class legislation posed the greatest threat to equal protection before the law. Whereas labor activists attacked the "*avaricious* MONOPOLIST and *purse proud* ARISTO-CRAT," women's rights supporters attacked husbands for acting the part of "lords and barons." In both cases critics believed that the common law subverted due process by granting capitalists and husbands class or caste privileges at the expense of the natural rights of wage workers and wives.[99]

Feminists versed in the socialist theories of Charles Fourier readily recognized the similar "antagonisms" between classes and the sexes. By bartering their lives for low wages, both workers and wives found themselves subject to the will and whim of their employers. As Charles Sears wrote in a letter published in the *Una* in 1854, men and women "solicit as a privilege" the right to work, and what should be a "right in birth" is granted as a "pleasure and convenience." Sears added that this power of treating workers as servants was used to "appropriate to private use the fruits of labor produced by other hands." [100] The failure to secure uniform wages for women, as Paulina Wright Davis herself pointed out in the *Una*, further augmented the power of employers by dividing male and female workers into factions competing over the price of their labor. While "capitalists" made "fortunes" from the "injustice, robbery, and fraud" of "low wages," the state was equally accountable for the "great gulf of separation" between the classes and the sexes. Despite the "great lie" that women would be "unsexed" if they dared step beyond the few menial employments open to them, the government—in conjunction with the marketplace—determined which citizens were "*enabled*" and "*entitled*" to equal protection. [101]

Government was in a position to correct the antagonistic social arrangement between the sexes, argued a petition sent to the 1853 Massachusetts state constitutional convention. Full legislative protection was "not based on the idea of one class or sect receiving protection from another; but on the well recognized rule, that each class or sect is entitled to such civil rights as will enable it to protect itself." To be "enabled" implied the right to be unencumbered by legal disabilities. Being "enabled," like the legal condition of emancipation, involved granting children or servants their independent status so that they could make contracts and secure their own wages. "Enabled," in the language of the Massachusetts convention (recall Davis's designation of "disabled" for women's "caste"), was the opposite of Hamilton's notion of women and children being "rendered more useful." "Enabled" implied the potential to secure a fair price and equal value for one's labor in all jurisdictions—public or private, at home or at work. [102] The status of wives and workers as upper-servants clearly represented a barrier to their emancipation and equal protection. As the Massachusetts petition asserted, "mother, wife, daughter, or laborer" all required identical protection of her economic liberty.

THE LEGAL FICTION OF UNREPAID DEBTS

Common-law rules for marriage, as for hired service, specified obligations and liabilities for each party. Husband and wife, like master and servant, agreed to certain limitations placed on withdrawing from the relationship. [103] The wage contract enforced these limitations through the assignment of liabilities for nonperformance. A wife theoretically incurred financial liabilities if she failed to perform certain domestic services. If a wife left her husband's household without sufficient cause or his consent, she forfeited any legal claim to "necessaries" from her husband for her "maintenance." [104] A comparable rule was applied to workers. In civil suits for the recovery of past wages, jurists argued that laborers were not free to break and make new contracts at their own discretion. Through the duties inherent in the marriage and the wage contract, wives and workers were placed under a similar obligation of "fidelity" and loyalty to their husbands and employers.[105]

This peculiar approach to liability was central to the common-law definition of marriage. The husband exchanged protection for his wife's obedience, and he entailed the greater economic risk by assuming responsibility for all debts acquired by the wife. Coverture stipulated that the husband had to cover two kinds of debts: first, the financial burdens accrued by his wife before marriage, and second, any bills contracted for her necessaries during the marriage.[106] In practice this rule of law all but ensured husbands' profit. As a legal fiction the rule transformed the wife into a debtor and indentured servant, which divested her of full civic competence in all pecuniary matters. In turn the husband became her guardian and creditor, and the wife's status as debtor implied that the husband paid a "bond" for her release. Importantly, the debt owed the husband could never be fully repaid, since the fictionalized financial transaction changed into a contractual obligation for service for life.[107] The husband assumed the payment of his wife's debts in exchange for her fidelity and loyalty, a theme captured in the wife's marriage vow "to love, honor and obey, till death do us part." And because this exchange of debt for obedience existed purely as a legal fiction, the law never considered whether wives had actually acquired any real debts. By the nineteenth century a husband could profit from this arrangement for the simple reason that he acquired his wife's property and services even if she came to the marriage without outstanding debts.

Regulating marriage according to creditor and debtor relations became a key feature of American law, particularly in periods of economic crisis and depression. In the wake of the panic of 1837, federal and state governments enacted bankruptcy legislation, abolished imprisonment for debts, and passed other reforms aimed at protecting the assets of debtors. The first wave of married women's property acts served a similar purpose, since the legislation made the wife's real and personal property exempt from the debts of her husband. Though they granted married women control over their separate property, the laws did little to alter the subordinate legal status of the wife. The New York act of 1848, for example, shielded the wife's separate property from creditors, but the statute left in place many of the common-law "disabilities" under coverture. Most of the new laws reinforced rather than challenged the role of the husband as the financial manager and guardian of his wife's assets.[108] Instead of emancipating the wife as a legal actor, the laws preserved the husband's custodial charge over his wife—and ward.

Yet the debates over married women's property rights generated a wider spectrum of arguments beyond the narrow interpretation applied to the statutes. Proponents as well as detractors realized that separate property for wives could alter the "pecuniary interests" of the family economy. For Elisha Hurlbut, separate property should transform the wife into a "distinct person," recognizing "her separate estate, contracts, debts and injuries." Any divestment of property and pecuniary rights undermined the wife's power over her own subsistence. Simply stated, Hurlbut believed, "The woman and the wife must remain one and the same. She must be deemed capable of moral and legal consent; capable of judging and acting; of willing and refusing."[109] At the 1846 New York state constitutional convention Charles O'Conor opposed separate property for wives on the grounds that it would introduce "the fiend, pecuniary self-interest" into the domestic sanctuary. Couples would be converted into "mere partners" and perhaps commercial rivals, because the wife gained a pecuniary interest of her own. As a "distinct person," the wife no longer needed patronage and protection—or viewed her husband as "her only source of power or distinction."[110]

MASTER OVER THE PROFIT OF HIS WIFE'S HANDS

Separate women's property and pecuniary rights inevitably addressed the cash nexus of the household. Common-law rules of marriage permitted the husband to "pocket all the cash," as one delegate declared at the New York state constitutional convention.[111] In the words of Caroline Severance as well, the husband was "absolutely the master of the profit of his wife's hands during coverture."[112] The new separate property laws regulated the family as a quasi corporation, particularly through the practice of sheltering marital assets from the husband's debts. Like Charles O'Conor of New York, a delegate at the 1850 Indiana state constitutional convention ridiculed married women's property rights for creating a "domestic corporation."[113] But even with the new laws, which preserved certain conditions of the wife's dependence under coverture, the husband reaped control of the financial dividends.[114] Most of the profits belonged to the husband, because of the common-law precedent for allowing the husband to retain the proceeds from his wife's property. In addition, husbands could pocket all the cash for another reason: wives could not claim cash as part of her maintenance, since the common law refused to treat money as "necessaries."[115] The new laws left this unchanged, since almost all cash and much of the disposable capital and credit remained securely vested under the husband's financial authority.

The limited scope of the new property laws emerged as a crucial issue at the early women's rights conventions.[116] At the Seneca Falls convention, held two months after the passage of the 1848 New York statute, those in attendance drafted resolutions and signed the Declaration of Sentiments, which expanded the issue of woman's economic vulnerability to her legal status in marriage and not just her lack of separate property rights. Blackstone's formula for coverture received the harshest rebuke, followed by a complaint against property rights, especially the "tyranny" of denying a wife "the wages she earns."[117] Less than a month later at the convention held in Rochester, participants rejected the husband's right to his wife's wages and resolved that the wife's promise of obedience reinforced her condition as a hireling servant.[118] In her letter to the 1851 Akron women's rights convention, Amelia Bloomer frankly noted how married women's property laws had accomplished "little." She observed that property rights offered no protection for the "great majority of girls," who "have nothing at marriage" but their "economy and industry."[119]

Bloomer's point revealed how resistant most legislatures remained to providing married women with the right to their wages. At the same time many states passed married women's property statutes, none, except Massachusetts in 1855, passed earnings acts before the Civil War.[120] The courts were equally conservative in separating property rights from wages, as Judge Woodward of the Pennsylvania Supreme Court ruled in 1853. In spite of the 1848 Pennsylvania married women's property act, Woodward ruled, the husband was "still entitled to the person and labor of the wife, and the benefits of her industry and economy."[121] The standard rule was that the wife could retain her earnings only if the husband consented to the arrangement. Recognizing that the husband could relinquish his right—and "emancipate" his wife—was a legal development that appeared later in the nineteenth century.[122]

The courts struggled over acknowledging the wife's right to her wages, for the most part because judges were torn between protecting the traditional marital rights of the husband and masking the divestment of the wife's pecuniary rights. In an 1858 case in New York, *Cropsey v. Sweeney*, the judge claimed that the marriage contract had little to do with the sordid business of profits and wages, ruling that the wife's "services were performed not as a servant, with a view of pay, but from higher and holier motives."[123] This case was striking as a civil suit, since the female plaintiff was seeking redress for nonperformance, arguing that her bigamous husband had failed to provide adequate maintenance. Nevertheless, as the judge realized, granting the wife back pay came dangerously close to endorsing the idea that domestic services could be translated into wages. Ann Cropsey in fact presented herself as the model employee and household manager, who had devoted herself to "the entire management of his domestic affairs, and labored by industry, economy, care and attention to her duties, to promote his interests and success." Rather than a hireling or servant, Cropsey claimed that she was quite the opposite: an efficient laborer whose work had'a wage value.[124]

For Paulina Wright Davis the denial of women's labor value explained women's position in the home and the marketplace. It was crucial to understanding why women received "half pay for the drudgeries" they performed either "in the menial occupations of the household" or in "the exhausting toil of the needle, and the ill paid labor of the cotton factory."[125] In the 1850s most women's rights advocates argued that women's lower wages reinforced caste and class differences by creating a pattern in which the working "woman's sphere extends downward instead of upward."[126] Husbands were not the only ones to benefit from this division of labor, for the economic advantages of controlling the profits of the wife's hands or the profits of any woman's hands also applied to employers. Women's rights and labor activists noted the "customary fraud" of unequal wages created a very different kind of woman's sphere.[127] Far from creating a separate sphere for women, the law augmented the system of private rights used to derive profits from women's services, either paid or unpaid. One labor activist from the Lowell mills complained in 1847 that the same economic motives affected work in the "kitchen and the factory," making the sphere of exploited labor impossible to escape.[128]

Antebellum feminists offered solutions that went beyond legislative reforms, although they continued to agitate for equal wages for women and for the passage of fair earnings acts for wives.[129] They realized that the corporate structure of the family needed to change by granting wives, in the words of Paulina Wright Davis, "a fair partnership of profits, as well as separate capital and its fruits."[130] Davis called for joint ownership and management of all the family finances; her vision extended well beyond the limited reform of relinquishing the husband's right to his wife's wages. Davis advocated that the traditional corporate model of the family become a "combination," substituting for the legal tradition by which the "annihilation of the wife's natural rights" allowed "aggrandizement" and "doubling of the husband."[131]

Davis was borrowing the vocabulary of socialist and labor reformers in accepting the idea that "combination" meant "combined capital" and "combined industry," a model attempted in cooperative households and businesses.[132] Capital and labor would be combined, she explained, to place control in the hands of employees, who would then become partners rather than wage workers. For Davis, the best solution for women involved a dual trans-formation of the economy: first, marriage laws would eliminate the division of capital and labor between husband and wife, and second, women would adapt the idea of combination to other branches of industry. In 1852 another women's rights advocate, Lydia Jenkins, repeated this view in arguing for women-controlled businesses, wherein women would be able to "invest, manage, gain capital," and even more importantly, "men would not have their profits." Instead "woman would secure to herself *the profits of her toil.*"[133]

Davis also invoked the notion of "emancipation," well aware of how this allusion addressed the larger of problem of "personal independence." The legacy of women as a "disabled caste" required change in women's legal status in the family. Consent would replace the premise of descent by which women were encumbered with imposed liabilities. By dismantling the legal fiction of coverture, marriage would become a very different kind of contract. In-deed, the social form of marriage symbolized in the exchange of vows would gain more validity by constituting the union as a partnership. Any public declaration of obedience would be excised from the ceremony, and the new vows would celebrate the equality of the couple. In 1855 Lucy Stone used her wedding to protest the existing marriage laws; according to Stone, these laws made "man and wife one, and that one is the husband."[134] Dr. Lydia Sayer, editor of the *Sybil*, redrafted her wedding vows to reject openly the statement of "undue subjection," and she declared exactly the opposite, vowing never to "renounce her individuality."[135] Such dramatic performances underscored a radical protest that marriage required not only two consenting adults but two parties who would be recognized as contracting adults after the ceremony. As Stone claimed, "Marriage should be an equal and permanent partnership." Women's legal identity, she added, should not be "suspended," nor should custody of the wife's person and property be placed in the hands of husbands or trustees, "as in the case of minors, lunatics and idiots."[136]

Personal independence required more than separate property, for the wife needed to make separate contracts without the consent of her husband. The right of contract was identified with the idea of self-possession. Women not only had to renounce their dependence, but they had to claim ownership of themselves through the public and visible transaction of making contracts. In her 1855 essay "How to Make Woman Independent," Elizabeth Cady Stanton explained succinctly the reason for recognizing a woman's capacity to make contracts, earn profits, and secure a "purse of her own." She stated, "A right over my *subsistence*, is a power over my thoughts and actions."[137]

Control over the value of one's labor had a direct impact on the mental content of work, and true happiness required that one's "credit and business talents" were not thwarted through the suppression of natural inclinations or alienated by another. Servants and slaves worked without full satisfaction. Their labor was exploited and their minds were numbed by the "monotonous drudgery" of tedious physical labor.[138] Pecuniary rights were monetary rights, and the extraction of the value of the domestic services of the wife served to barter away her self-ownership.[139] Trading her labor value for maintenance exchanged a woman's "rational freedom" for the "condition of infancy and wardship," as Davis caustically remarked, leaving all women as wives and workers dependent on the paltry "bounty" of men, in which "the reward for toil and trials of our service in matrimony is food and clothing, and for our work in your shops and houses, less than half the wages."[140]

In sum, Davis, like other antebellum feminists, did more than argue for the natural rights of life, liberty, and property. Pecuniary independence required the right to subsistence, and it also required the civil protection afforded from laws that guaranteed wives' wages, their right to contract, and their civil standing as adults fully emancipated from common-law disabilities. Wives required control of the value of their labor and the corporate profits of the household. The husband's rights to his wife's services had to be replaced with equal economic privileges. Invoking a powerful biblical allusion, women's rights proponent Elizabeth Oakes Smith declared that this situation called for a transformation of the intimate economic relationship between the wage contract and the marriage contract. When such a transformation occurred, Smith prophesied, "Woman will cease to [be] the Hagar of the household; she will not be the bond-slave of her master, dependent upon him for the scrap of bread and flagon of water, but she will earn these by the Angel of Labor, and she will be the honored and honorable companion of man, . . . as her *capacity* shall qualify her for all places."[141]

By refusing to recognize woman's status as an upper-servant, activists challenged the legal fiction that the husband paid a "bond" for her release from custody and was placed under his cover and custodial guardianship. Women had to escape their fictionalized bondage as debtors, which legally trapped them in eternal marital servitude as the "Hagar of the household." The marriage contract under these terms transferred more than the wife's time and service; it granted the husband a portion of her legal personality. Alienation of the value of the wife's labor meant that she lost control over her physical capital—her will to survive and direct the action and use of her body. The drudge sacrificed the right to subsistence and self-preservation, dangerously submitting the use of her body to the control of another person. Whereas the drunkard's tale called for sanctuary and equal immunities and privileges, the story of the domestic drudge highlighted a different reform. Neither men nor women were meant to surrender their right to subsistence, but as co-owners and partners of the family firm, they would share equal liabilities and profits. When the marriage contract was declared to be an agreement between two equal and competent individuals rather than a superior and an inferior, the power dynamic of the relationship changed. Woman's word on other contracts would be honored, her capacity duly recognized, and the privilege of reaping the fruits of the couple's combined labor would be jointly shared. Under these circumstances wives gained the value of their labor, and women workers secured a more "equal footing" in the capitalist economy of the home and society.

The Despoiled Wife

A wife's labor value extended beyond wages, as women's rights activists realized when they began to examine the impact of property, land, and material possessions on the rights of women to manage the household and the family circle. In an 1853 letter to the *Una*, Hannah Tracy Cutler reported a crime of "legal robbery" against the wife and widow. An independent business woman found herself divested of her property after marriage when creditors—through the sale of her personal belongings—collected the debts of her husband and his brother. While her husband failed in business and his health deteriorated, the wife assumed control of the family finances and proceeded to "amass a small fortune." Besides caring for her husband and paying his medical expenses, the wife again found herself "plundered" and despoiled of her property after the husband's death. Her brother-in-law "coolly pocket[ed] two thirds" of her husband's estate. With a touch of irony, Cutler concluded that this case demonstrated why "women's interests are not safe in the hands of men, notwithstanding the gallantry so often boasted." Cutler invoked an even stronger message through her contrast of "robbery" and "gallantry."[142] Divestment was tied to property rights, property in the sense of tenure, title, and trust, all of which secured the husband's prerogative to seize, manage, and dispose of property regardless of his wife's interests. Wives at best secured an "uncertain estate," since they were never fully entrusted with the spoils of the marital economy.[143]

This case indicates that disputes over married women's property rights raised issues other than the wife's domestic services and contractual liabilities. In fact, the word "estate" evoked several meanings, including capital, assets and liabilities, and of course the legal definition, which referred to the "interest, right, and ownership in land."[144] The legal relationship of couples to the family estate shared a complicated legacy of feudal and common-law rights that virtually reduced husband and wife to the condition of patron and client. While wives retained the title to and ownership of real estate they brought to the marriage, they not only lost "*personal control*," but all "*beneficial interest and power*" over their property, which went to their husbands.[145] Not surprisingly, legal reformer Elisha Hurlbut mocked the holy estate of matrimony when he described how the wife exchanged all her "worldly estate, for that most uncertain estate—*a man*."[146]

Antebellum feminists realized the integral connection between property and parental rights, noting that wives needed both rights to secure an equally beneficial interest in the family resources. One great discrepancy between the rights of the husband and wife related to the close of the marriage. At the husband's death, the tenuous position of the surviving wife was evidenced in the possibility that she and her children might inherit "*nothing*," as one writer to the *Lily* remarked in 1856. Yet the greatest "insult to injury" struck all wives when the courts required them "to *give bond* that they will not squander the property of their children." Such treatment reflected the law's preoccupation with "*his* intentions" about "*his* property" and the "property *he* left" his children; the law protected the husband's vested right "to dispose what he acquired." The husband's superior property rights, especially his claims to the family estate, determined his exclusive parental authority; he had the power to manage his children and will his property as he pleased. The wife at her death "leaves no children" if her husband is still living, whereas if her husband dies, she must go before a court to be appointed "guardian of *her own* children."[147]

Without equal title to the family estate, mothers had a rather "insecure tenure" over their children.[148] Anson Bingham concurred that the wife, like the widow, did not naturally assume guardianship of her children but instead gained it by default "whenever the husband deserts, or neglects to support," at which time society recognized that the "wife may support herself and her children." Such a grudging concession or "privilege," as Bingham noted sardonically, frequently "came with the additional burden of feeding and clothing her husband."[149] Wives received custody as a fiscal burden without any legal benefit, and wives turned widows gained only a contingent claim to the guardianship of their children.

THE PATERNAL GUIDELINES OF CUSTODY OF RIGHTS

At the heart of this issue was the "transfer of property across generations." Although many common-law powers vested in the husband ensured the transmission of property to rightful heirs, the husband's exclusive right to control and dispose of property had more fundamental consequences. To safeguard the rights of inheritance, the husband required the "certainty of paternity"; he had to know his own children, and he ultimately had to have exclusive title to his offspring, or at least custodial rights over his paternal heirs. Wives sacrificed through marriage their absolute property rights as well as their legal and financial authority over their children. As long as husbands retained the power to dispose of property at will, and as long as marriage existed principally for the purpose of protecting private property, then wives had few claims to their children, except in special cases where the husband forfeited his rights.[150] Nonetheless, the husband still had expansive powers over the destiny of his children even in his absence. He could override his wife's custodial claims by selecting another person to assume guardianship of his children. According to the common law, the father and not the mother was the legal "guardian and next of kin" to his children. Legal guardianship protected both the father's parental powers and the husband's property rights against those of his wife and the mother of his children.[151]

By the 1830s, American legislators and jurists had defined parental rights according to fundamental paternal guidelines. While the father still remained the head of the household, his authority and custodial rights became defined less in accordance with the rules of descent than with those of consent. Legal commentators increasingly agreed that a family was created not solely through bloodlines but through a tacit agreement between parents and children that stipulated the exchange of paternal protection for filial obedience. American jurists gradually promoted a standard for fatherhood based on guardianship that depended on two legal definitions of parental duties. First, the father as the natural guardian gained "custody of the person" but not the property of the child. Second, the father as the legal guardian had the responsibility to provide for the maintenance, education, and domicile of the child, along with his fiscal duties to manage the child's property. Significantly, however, the effort to place natural fathers under the same legal trust as appointed guardians inevitably gave the courts the power to evaluate the conduct of parents toward their children.[152] Despite this change, the courts did not recognize mothers and fathers as equal guardians, and state legislatures were slow to grant mothers the power to appoint guardians for the children. In Pennsylvania, where the state legislature in 1833 gave mothers a beneficial interest in their children's estates, and wives secured separate property rights in 1848, the same legislature did not grant mothers the power to appoint a testamentary guardian until 1881. Furthermore, throughout the nineteenth century the Pennsylvania legislature did not permit mothers to challenge a "responsible" father's selection of a guardian.[153]

In the standard formula for defining a mother's custodial rights, jurists recognized her duties as a natural but not a legal guardian. Edward Mansfield offered authoritatively that, according to the "laws of nature," the power and government over children was exercised "*by both parents jointly.*"[154] Some mothers were awarded custody of their children because jurists recognized the benefits of maternal care during children's "tender years." In South Carolina such a decision was handed down as early as 1811, and a Pennsylvania court in 1813 denied a father's request for custody. The judge in the latter case concluded that the two girls required "the kind assistance afforded to none so well as a mother." Yet the decision was reversed when the court decided that the mother might prove to be a bad example as her daughters matured, since it was the mother who had broken the marriage vow by committing adultery.[155] Jurists accommodated these changes within the distinction they drew between natural and legal guardianship. Echoing the views of Jean-Jacques Rousseau, maternal and paternal care could be summed up as follows: "As the true nurse is the mother, the true preceptor is the father."[156] The courts did not establish a legal precedent for denying a responsible father the company and custody of his children. The courts instead deferred his paternal claims until his children were older and he could best fulfill his duties as their tutor, preceptor, and legal guardian.

At stake in preserving the father's superior rights as legal guardian was the unified authority of the husband as the "head of the family."[157] Denied equal custodial authority and legal status as head of household, wives and widows found themselves hampered with a serious economic disability: they could lose title to and tenure within their homes. Unless the husband provided for his wife in his will, the widow would not only lose "her companion of youth" but most likely her house and home as well. Of course, if the wife died first, as Elizabeth Cady Stanton contended in 1854, "The house and land would all have been the husband's still. No one would have dared intrude upon the privacy of his house or to molest him in his sacred retreat of sorrow."[158] The common law enabled the husband to keep the family together through tenancy by courtesy, which allowed him to gain a life interest in his wife's real estate if the couple had children. Tenancy by right of dower provided the widow with a one-third life interest in the husband's real estate, but the widow was a tenant and was not given the power to will this land that she temporarily occupied until her death.[159] If husbands did not provide for their wives—or had outstanding debts—widows could be divested of the means to support a household after the death of their husbands. Widowers found their lives unchanged. They had their homes, land, personal belongings, and a possible inheritance from their wives that kept the family together.

The image of homeless wives and mothers highlighted the crisis over rules of tenancy and how these rules applied to the custody of children, property, and land. Anson Bingham aptly summarized the problem when he described the widow and the divorced wife as a "houseless wanderer" and "pauper." In reviewing an 1849 New York case in which a wife had been expelled from her home and her claim to separate property rejected, Bingham emphasized the striking similarity between the legal status of an evicted tenant and the ejected wife. He noted, "Her husband may turn her out, a wanderer and a pauper, although . . . *he* is left in the castle, and *she* is ejected; *he* is still the lord of the manor, and she is equally a houseless wanderer."[160] Bingham's metaphor had a more telling purpose, for he realized that the rights of tenants had a direct bearing on women's legal rights. At the 1846 New York state constitutional convention the same group of land and legal reformers supported separate married women's property rights and the elimination of feudal tenures.[161] Both land reformers and advocates of married women's property rights advanced a "personal safety net" through exemptions from debt that placed property beyond the grasp of creditors.[162] The economic crisis of 1837 made women and children the victims of coverture, unable to rely on the protection of men and liable to creditors for the sins of their husbands and fathers.[163] In words of Thomas Jefferson cited by William Henry Channing, land reformers found a resonant chord for protecting homes and widows through their legislative efforts to make "the homestead of every man a sacred thing, which no law can touch, juggle or wrestle from his wife and children."[164]

The lessons of land reform influenced the way feminists framed their political arguments. Antebellum feminists shared land reformers' desire to promote individual proprietorship through the free distribution of western lands. During her 1850 lecture tour Lucretia Mott came out boldly for "Homes for All" and commended the goals of the land reform movement.[165] In the same year at a meeting in New York City, land reformers endorsed women's rights, calling for "no right of lordship of the strong over the weak, no exclusive legislative power inherent in the husband, brother and son, over the wife, sister, and mother."[166] In addition, the homestead served not only as the model of individual and independent land ownership but of female proprietorship as well, since widows were granted title as "family head" of the household.[167] Women's rights advocates took special care to note how the policy for the custody, sale, and inheritance of western land grants offered a precedent where husbands and wives were placed on an "equal footing."[168]

However, land reformers and feminists realized that they had to challenge the right to "exclusive appropriation" inherent in the protection of private property. According to the common law, landlords had an exclusive right to the profits and rents from the lands occupied by their tenants, but they were not under any legal obligation for the maintenance of the property. Because maintenance was the tenant's and not the landlord's responsibility, tenants were liable for waste or damages, and they were not allowed to make alterations, even if those changes enhanced the value of the property. A similar imbalance defined the duties of husbands toward their wives. At most, husbands had to provide necessaries for their wives' support, but even here their duty for maintenance was a qualified rather than a strict legal obligation.[169] The same held true for children, as Timothy Walker surmised in his *Introduction to American Law*: "How can you compel a parent to maintain, protect, or educate a child? The law furnishes no means of doing it; and as the test of legal obligation, is the means of enforcing it, this proves the legal obligation does not here exist."[170]

Land reformers rejected the landlord's right to collect rent when a property was "unfit for human habitation." For the first time, land reformers argued that property had to be valued as shelter, which stood to make landlords responsible for maintenance.[171] Maintenance acquired the status of a right, in which nonperformance sanctioned redress and the contributions made by tenants carried financial and legal consideration. This subtle shift for recognizing "habitation" rather than possession had profound implications for distinguishing property rights issuing from the family economy.[172] Stanton clearly understood the connection in her address to the New York legislature in 1854. By acknowledging the "management, economy and industry" that the wife contributed to make the family home and property "their own," the law had to protect more than her claim to "sustenance" or dower rights.[173] Mutual justice required legal recognition of the joint investment of the couple and their shared custody in the "support of the family and the family government."[174]

This approach to maintenance highlighted another feature of the political economy of the household: wives often produced rather than received necessaries for their support, and the money they saved became ready capital invested in home improvements.[175] Such efficiency made independent proprietorship possible for small homesteads or farmsteads, because good management ensured self-sufficiency.[176] Prudent management exposed the long-standing bias in dower rights whereby the wife was treated as a "nonproducer."[177] Dower perpetuated the legal fiction that wives did not directly contribute to the family estate, despite the actual property and services they brought to the marriage.[178] According to the common law, the widow became a tenant in dower, and customary views of dower treated it as a "gift" furnished by the husband. This legal fiction allowed the husband to absorb the wife's property as "one person," suspend her rights, and then redistribute through dower a less substantial one-third interest in the property.[179] As a gesture of the husband's "bounty," dower transformed the wife's rights of ownership to an inferior claim for patronage.[180]

In place of dower rights, women's rights activists argued, separate women's property was not enough protection. A balance of power and interests had to be incorporated into the marriage contract. This is what Mary Mott argued in her letter to the 1852 West Chester women's rights convention: "In marriage, the man offers love for love and hand for hand, but what consideration for those personal rights of which he dispossess her? If a contract, why is there not a remedy for its violation, either in Law or Equity, as is the case with other contracts?"[181] Two conditions seriously hampered the wife's contractual rights. As Hurlbut argued, coverture treated the wife as a victim of conquest who voluntarily surrendered her rights. Unable to negotiate a fair contract, wives could not enforce a promise or make it a binding condition of the marriage contract. It is significant that dower rights were a gift, the exact opposite of consideration. Gifts were freely given, reinforcing the husband's role as a patron who bestowed his bounty as he pleased. In contrast, consideration meant that both parties agreed to surrender something in return for what they would receive, which made both equally liable for the performance of their duties. And as Mary Mott contended, through consideration of her rights, the wife gained the legal power to enforce a promise and demand redress or remedy if the husband failed to fulfill his side of the bargain.

CULTIVATION, EQUAL CONFIDENCE, AND LEGAL COMPETENCE

The feudal notion of tenure involved physical strength and a capacity to defend the soil. In return for contributing their resources or wealth to the state, citizens were granted protection of their private property. Lacking the strength to defend themselves or lend support to national solvency, "penniless beggars" and "paupers," and wives and widows, all fell outside this system of guaranteed protection. Physical and fiscal weakness invited political divestment, as one delegate to the 1844 New Jersey state constitutional convention argued when evaluating the political rights of paupers as citizens. A pauper "voluntarily surrenders his rights," he reasoned, and because "he parts with his liberty—he loses his control of his children and he labors for others."[182]

Timothy Walker acknowledged that lack of physical strength contributed to women's legal dependence in marriage. Neither women nor children could act as "sole providers" and protect the family estate from the onslaught of creditors or anyone else interested in despoiling the wife of her property. Walker explained: "The argument ran thus:—the husband is generally stronger. Policy therefore requires that he should have dominion, because in his hands the power supports itself. Give but the legal supremacy to the wife, and she would need external interference in order to maintain it. Or give her an absolute equality, and the effect would be the same."[183] Antebellum activists agreed that women often did not bargain from a position of equal power, but insisted that the source of their problem was legal rather than rooted in nature. If granted equal consideration, recognition of their joint investment in the family economy, and control over their "thrift, skill and industry," wives would acquire the strength to protect hearth and home. By establishing a mutual marriage contract, wives could manifest "mutual thrift" in contributing to the household economy and the value of the property, and they could develop "equal confidence" in directing the care of their children.[184] For Caroline Severance, this formula redefined equal protection, since women deserved the "*protection, cultivation, and manifestation*" of all their faculties like men, rather than having them "blighted through neglect . . . *because of the mere accident of sex.*"[185]

Severance blended equal protection with the theme of cultivation, returning to the land reformers' emphasis on measuring the value of property through habitation. It was the productivity of the soil—its capacity to secure wealth and self-sufficiency—that determined its total worth. Cultivation required care and maintenance, which as Severance noted, came from "mutual thrift" and "industry"—or savings and investment. Cultivation led to competence, which had a range of meanings. In its most formal usage competence originally indicated a bequest of property that allowed an heir to be self-sufficient. A story in the *Una* described a widow who inherited a "competence" (portion of property) but who lost it when she remarried and conveyed her property to her incompetent and greedy husband.[186] Another story described competence as a sum of money that provided a couple with enough capital to get married.[187] Competence also invoked the legal notion of sanity, or the ability to discern right from wrong, make contracts, and protect one's personal interests and finances. The common law, of course, treated wives as incompetent, even requiring that a legal official be present to make sure that married women were not coerced by their husbands to sell, transfer, or relinquish control of their property. Yet the most compelling use of competence came from Hannah Tracy Cutler, who argued that the cultivation of marketable skills secured for wives their competence as a form of "bank stock" for future use.[188] Cutler's definition stressed "self-cultivation" as both the source and means of active capital and "mental capital."[189] In other words, Cutler recognized that wives needed some reserve capital or stock that they could bank on later as widows, and they needed active capital that allowed them to bargain from a position of strength with their husbands.

Competence implied more than a financial safety net of last resort when the family faced a fiscal crisis. The cultivation and manifestation of mental stock and capital shifted the status of wives from passive to active agents in the household economy. Competence further revealed the inherent limitations of the married women's property laws that did little to remove the common-law disabilities of wives. If women did not assume an active role in managing the property, they might find themselves conveying their property to unreliable husbands. Or if they did not invest in their own skills and talents, wives—turned widows—might end up homeless wanderers. Wives had to break the pattern of dependence by contributing to the care and management of the family and by securing future dividends from their investment.[190]

Antebellum feminists raised the problem of competence as the most revealing illustration of the connection between the property and parental rights of mothers and wives. As long as the father retained the right to dispose of his children, the law protected his right of custody as a property right. Stanton thus reasoned, "By your laws, the child is the absolute property of the father, wholly at his disposal in life, or at death."[191] But the law dispossessed women of their children by treating wives as merely the "agents of their husband."[192] On a deeper level, mothers and wives needed full legal capacity to perform all their duties faithfully when acting as the sole providers and legal sponsors of their children. Without this legal recognition, the law would continue to treat the husband as the "substantive" and the wife as his "adjective" and therefore perpetuate the common-law tradition of female incapacity. As Timothy Walker neatly summarized, "In a word there is scarcely a legal act of any description she is competent to perform."[193] Without the combined recognition of economic and legal competence, women would never be treated as full legal guardians of their children, because the law would continue to "impeach her ability to manage property, her honesty and her maternal affection."[194]

While jurists and legislators refused to recognize wives as legally competent, they became more willing to acknowledge the incompetence of husbands as natural and legal guardians. Separate property laws were built around the possibility of the husband's financial mismanagement, his imprudent investments, or his excessive losses. Yet the law distinguished between a failed husband and a failed father. A husband's loss of property undermined the confidence and trust of his wife, but the mistreatment of his children violated a legal and public trust. By the 1840s the courts had begun to consider children's protection under the law and whether adequate provision and shelter was the legal duty of natural and surrogate parents. In the 1848 case of *State of Ohio ex rel. Stephen Ball v. Anna Hand*, the judge defined the right of custody as providing for the welfare and education of the children and the "bonds of natural affection" between parent and child. Because the father wanted his children to join him in a Shaker community, he abjured in his proper duties as their custodian; he sought his children, the ruling explained, "not to protect, and feed, and clothe, and educate them as a father, but to proselyte them to the peculiar faith, and place them under the care of the Shakers." Their maternal grandmother, Ann Hand, was capable of cultivating the proper sentiments in and maintaining proper supervision of the children; she kept a respectable boardinghouse, possessed ample savings to support the children, had sent them to Sunday school, and "teaches them to love and respect their father." The judge selected a curious legal metaphor to underscore the surrogate parent's role. She "has a sort of moral lien," implying that she had a moral claim, if not title, to the children. Her investment in raising the children was the equivalent of an encumbrance, deposit, debt, or security, which paralleled how land reformers viewed the maintenance of property: its value increased through careful custodial supervision.[195]

Legislative changes followed this pattern of punishing irresponsible fathers with a forfeiture of their rights. According to an 1853 Pennsylvania law, wives could obtain custody of their children if their husbands failed to support the family.[196] Two years later, Pennsylvania passed another statute that divested the "wasteful" or negligent father of three paternal prerogatives: the right to apprentice his children, the right to receive their wages, and the right to appoint a testamentary guardian in his will. The same 1855 law even barred an irresponsible husband from claiming his wife's wages, because she could use them to promote the welfare of her children.[197]

Given these developments, child custody was perhaps more affected by the concern over children's maintenance and support than granting wives separate property. The same logic of mutual consideration and protection appeared to influence how some courts might award custody to the more competent and responsible sole provider. Despite Stanton's assertion to the contrary, the child did not necessarily remain the "absolute property of the father," and yet the ruling premise of the father's superior rights were not abrogated. While jurists and legislators divested fathers for gross negligence, they at best granted wives only conditional rights that tended to offer temporary rather than permanent solutions. By making the wife's custody rights contingent on the husband's forfeiture of his duties, the law preserved disabilities that empowered the husband at the expense of the wife.

The reasons behind such legal changes were not surprising. Most legislators and jurists had no intention of developing radical innovations in the areas of marital or custodial rights. They borrowed from the well-established precedent derived from the wife's claims to necessaries and dower rights. Dower was a contingency that provided for the wife if her husband died intestate and had failed to provide for her in his will, while necessaries were a right of last resort that the courts enforced if the husband failed to support his wife. Necessaries were based on a husband's ability to pay his bills, which meant that the wife's right still flowed from the husband's economic condition. Both of these practices recognized that wives needed additional protection when their maintenance was at stake, but neither suggested that wives deserved "absolute equality" with their husbands.

According to one of the most important custody cases of the period, *People ex rel. Barry v. Mercein*, rendered in the New York Supreme Court in 1842, the husband's superior claim to his children was considered "paramount." John Barry, the plaintiff, had a "right to train up his child as he has his other daughters, with dispositions to serve him affectionately in the business of the household." As in the Ball case, the father's performance of his duties mattered, and the care and training of his daughters from a previous marriage proved that he was "eminently" qualified for the "moral and mental instruction" of children. Any intimation of household equality posed a dangerous precedent. Judge Cowen stated that the husband was considered the "legal head of the whole family, wife and children inclusive; and I have heard it urged from no quarter that he should be brought under subjection to a household democracy. All will agree, I apprehend, that such a measure would extend the right of suffrage quite too far." Judge Bronson reaffirmed this point, noting that the laws of marriage had not kept pace with civilization's push for greater liberty and equality. The conservatism of the law clearly avoided what he considered to be the obvious adverse results: "It may be best that the wife should be declared head of the family, and that she should be at liberty to desert her husband at pleasure and take the children of the marriage with her." By reducing the family to a political absurdity, a household democracy threatened to undermine male guardianship and elevate the wife over the husband as the legal head of the family. For both jurists, marital equality remained an impossibility, humorous at best and radically subversive at worst.[198]

Feminists hoped to push the law beyond its narrow and conventional interpretation. For activists the concern was not simply a matter of parental fitness or providing wives with contingent support for their children. Rather, the real issue was investing wives with rights and powers that fully acknowledged their mutual consideration and equal interests in the marriage. Equal tenure and title recognized that wives would be consulted on anything affecting those interests, whether it involved expenditures, savings, investments, or decisions relating to the care and management of the children or the household. Such obligations called for a comprehensive knowledge of the family finances and the authority to be held accountable for right and wrong decisions. Frances Gage made this point when she chided the woman who did not understand the family business and then had defended her indifference by "folding her hands" and remarking, " 'Husband knows all about it.' " [199] Without personal accountability, implicit in the meaning of legal guardianship, the mother would never secure equal standing in the eyes of the law. As another reformer wrote in the *Lily* in 1854, "*The right to the custody and control of her children*[—]for how can she be answerable for that which is not under her control? If another have a claim superior to hers and can command the children contrary to her will and pleasure . . . how can she . . . be made accountable for their loss?" To control her children, the same writer realized, the mother and wife needed control over herself—"*the right to her own person*," which came with full legal capacity as well as control over her livelihood— which meant "*the right to her own property and earnings*." [200]

Competence thus revealed a great deal about whether wives had control over their "capital and livelihood" and whether they were acknowledged to possess the court's confidence in their ability to provide equal care and discipline for their children. In adopting this strategy of combining legal and economic reform, feminists realized that parental and property rights could not be easily divorced. Of course, they realized, too, that wives faced real obstacles as long as the husband remained the legal head of the family. According to Sarah Coates, the wife who ran her own business and lived apart from her husband had perhaps the best chance of demonstrating her capacity as a "sole provider." [201] Contributions to the family economy were measured by concrete returns: selling land, earning wages, and managing a productive business or farm. The difference between having title and tenure to the land and contributing to the economy indirectly by producing goods without the right to their cultivated value left wives in a position of economic dependence. As Hannah Tracy Cutler observed, when the typical wife was mainly "engaged in the manufacture of those articles immediately consumed around her," she lost her claim to be a valued contributor to the family estate: "Her labor is rarely counted out in dollars and cents, and since it is coined in no mint, it is accounted of little value." [202]

Antebellum feminists learned vital lessons from the land reform move-ment, especially that because value was both tangible and intangible, wives needed both conventional rights and a new social identity. They needed prop-erty rights first, which meant an equal claim to land ownership and an equal title and tenure to all the material resources issuing from the family estate. In addition, wives needed personal rights—the right to a competence and a separate livelihood for investment. These rights would be won with the freedom to cultivate skills, mental capital, and a reputation for good credit and prudent judgment.

Ultimately, the notion of marital partnership went beyond dismantling exclusive possession and the notion that paternity was the foundation for all family and property rights. Mutual justice dictated a new legal order that finally placed women under the same rules of law as men without any civil disabilities—disabilities that reduced them to tenants, paupers, childless mothers, or wives despoiled of land and livelihood. For as Stanton asserted, the common-law legacy of " 'dower,' 'widow's claims,' 'protection,' 'incapaci-ties,' 'incumbrance,' is written on the brow of every woman." Instead of this legal inheritance, she proposed wryly, "We *ask* no better laws than those you have made for yourselves. We need no other protection than that which your present law secures to you."[203]

The Sovereign Body of the Citizen

Like the Athenians, we have bowed down and worshiped in woman, beauty,
grace, the exquisite proportions, the soft and beautifully rounded outline, her
delicacy, refinement, and silent helplessness—all well when she is viewed
simply as an object of sight, never to rise one foot above the dust from which
she sprung. But if she is to be raised up to adorn a temple, or represent
a divinity . . . then must the type of womanhood be on a
larger scale than that yet carved by man.
—Elizabeth Cady Stanton, National Woman's Rights Convention, 1860

When activists called their last convention before the Civil War, they recognized that their national campaign had generated a rights discourse of its own.
Their initial definition of citizenship, growing out of the grievances listed
in the Declaration of Sentiments in 1848, had expanded by 1860 to include
multiple narratives that spoke to women's legal, political and religious rights.
Ironically, women's rights conventions had come to face criticism for their re-
dundancy. Martha Wright, president of the Tenth National Woman's Rights
Convention, addressed this issue in her opening remarks. "What is the use of
these continual conventions?" she posed. "What is the use of this constant
iteration of the same things?" Reviewing accomplishments of the past twelve
years, Wright was caustic. Ministers had chided women who undertook the
"foolishness of preaching," and now Wright warmly applauded her comrades

for having learned the value of the "foolishness" of preaching. When opponents from the press praised women's "beneficent movement" and ministers shouted "Amen" from their pulpits, then, Wright allowed, women's rights activists might be able to depart the platform. This statement, followed by laughter and applause, suggested that the newspapers and the clergy had yet to be persuaded.[1]

Did the constant iteration of rights really matter? The promise of change seemed close at hand in 1860 though it still lay, of course, in the distant future. Over the next decade, as a result of the Civil War and the two critical constitutional amendments passed during Reconstruction, the United States finally established a uniform definition of national citizenship. Given the opportunity to remake the social compact, Republican legislators eliminated many of the ambiguities that had plagued citizenship in the antebellum period. Had they chosen to, they could have challenged one of its most glaring contradictions: the treatment of women as a "disabled caste."[2]

But coequality did not guide Republican legislators. Old and new barriers surfaced in the process of ratification of the Fourteenth and Fifteenth Amendments in 1868 and 1879. The Fourteenth Amendment established women's entitlement to federal protection, yet it continued to distinguish suffrage as a privilege of "male inhabitants." It was the first time the federal Constitution explicitly associated the words "suffrage" and "citizenship" with "male." The Fifteenth Amendment stated, "The right of citizens of the United States to vote shall not be denied or abridged by the United States, or by any State, on account of race, color or previous conditions of servitude," proving that Republican congressmen had ignored all other instruments of discrimination, such as poll taxes, literacy tests, and entitlements based on sex. The hierarchical division between the sexes was now universally practiced, if not national policy. It would require over a half-century of political struggle and constitutional wrangling before women finally secured the right to vote. Coequality remains even today a utopian dream, strikingly evidenced by rejection of the Equal Rights Amendment during the 1980s and its failure to revive in the 1990s.[3]

By 1860 women's rights activists already had begun to temper their hopes for a constitutional revolution. In the territory of Kansas, which historians have described as a "rehearsal" for the Civil War, the gap between feminist theory and constitutional reform became apparent. In 1859, after five years of political canvassing in Kansas, Clarina Howard Nichols positioned herself to observe the fate of women's rights at the state constitutional convention held that year. Like activists in Ohio, supporters had organized the Kansas Woman's Rights Association in anticipation of a state convention. Nichols had been asked to speak during the proceedings. As a political lobbyist, she understood the partisan division among delegates, enabling her to receive explicit support from Republicans and silent endorsements from Democrats.[4]

Initially, Nichols believed that Kansas held the greatest possibility for woman suffrage. It was a state in the process of making itself, seemingly freed from the weight of constitutional tradition. Her assumption proved wrong. Too many "old lawyers" dominated the constitutional proceedings, she later reflected, noting how little the Kansas gathering had departed from other state conventions. Despite the turmoil over "bleeding Kansas," delegates retained a faith in constitutional order. Neither the existence of two state governments vying for power, armed conflict among its citizens, nor illegal voting deterred members of the constitutional convention from drafting a conservative document in harmony with "organic law" and political guidelines found in other states.[5]

Nichols believed that this conservatism preordained the fate of woman suffrage. Popular sovereignty may have created the bloody conflict in Kansas, but the will of the people would not determine the state's constitutional definition of citizenship. As Nichols concluded, even if the electorate had endorsed women's right to vote, the members of the convention would have rejected such a radical reform. For her the lesson of Kansas was obvious. By 1860 constitutional conventions did not appear likely forums in which to enact revolutionary change. The radical implications of dissent were supplanted by a new consensus—that political rights were necessarily a male privilege.[6]

Dissent and popular sovereignty failed because the polity—the fictive people—were embodied, or engendered, as male. Abstract rights were never understood to be abstract enough to include women. And although natural rights relied on an imaginary framework of the universal man, not all men could lay claim to those rights. During the antebellum period unpropertied men, paupers, slaves, free blacks, Native Americans, and Mexican Americans were all excluded from full citizenship as flawed men.

During the same period, state constitutional conventions discovered that they had the power to invest and divest rights. Democratic citizenship was defined by the physical display of civic capacities and the ability to contribute materially to the state. Under Jacksonian democracy, in which value was measured through partisan loyalties, military service, economic freedom, and a traditional conception of republican virtue, the citizen had to meet the standards of the common man. Consequently, the *persona ficta* of the rights-bearer never could be divorced from manhood, because only a valiant individual was intended to symbolize sovereignty.

Feminist scholars of the 1980s and 1990s continue to grapple with this unresolved dilemma: Can political sovereignty, as legally defined, ever transcend the idea that "man is the measure of all things"? In her examination of pornography, sexual harassment, and other constitutional issues, legal scholar Catherine MacKinnon states unequivocally, "When [liberal jurisprudence] is most ruthlessly neutral, it will be most male; when it is most sex blind, it will be most blind to the sex of the standard being applied. When it most closely conforms to precedent, to 'facts,' to legislative intent, it will most closely enforce socially male norms and most thoroughly preclude questioning their content as having a point of view at all. Abstract rights will authorize the male experience of the world."[7] Though claiming to be neutral and sex blind, the interpreters of rights merely reify a male view of what is normative. MacKinnon contends that today jurists are still not capable of judging from an unbiased point of view what it means to be human, or to be a citizen. Instead they always begin with a concrete image of the idealized rights-bearer embodied with distinctly masculine virtues. If for MacKinnon "maleness is the original entitlement," then behind every abstract right is a person who is male.[8]

Her bold formulation has a historical foundation. Abstract or civil rights were always defined in relative terms, that is, in comparison to or in contrast with other rights. It was common practice in the nineteenth century to distinguish between "natural" or given conditions and politically imposed or artificially created conditions. This approach proved to be essential in determining whether a person's rights had been violated under the terms of due process. It allowed jurists the luxury of identifying select natural conditions understood to exist beyond the purview of the law. This was the reasoning used by Judge Lemuel Shaw in the *Roberts* decision of 1849, upholding racial segregation. Here, race, sex, and age were treated as differences derived from nature rather than as inequalities resulting from legislation or the law. Nineteenth-century jurists expected "reasonable" differences, rooted in nature (or, similarly, divine law and social custom) to be tolerated as "facts" rather than considered as forms of discrimination.[9]

Shaw's view that sexual and racial differences were natural was a view of human origins beyond the scope of the law. In her updated effort to explain the logic of legal reasoning, MacKinnon has observed that the classic paradigm for natural differences came from the creation story: "On the first day, difference was; on the second day, a division was created upon it; on the third day, occasional dominance arose. Division may be rational or irrational. Dominance either seems or is justified. Difference *is*." Other feminist scholars have criticized the reasonableness of "obvious" differences. Catherine Belsey has shown that "facts" in all discourses are shaped by ideology. From this perspective ideology is not always a deliberate distortion of the truth, but it acts as an imaginary framework that masquerades as a coherent and complete explanation of real conditions. It is a truism or commonplace belief often treated as obvious yet riddled by omissions and false generalizations about human behavior that smooth over contradictions. The unquestioned nature of sexual difference is as much a creation of ideology as the myth of the universal or common man.[10]

If the desire for coherence is rooted in the need for ontological certainty, then MacKinnon and Belsey have recognized the similar imperatives found in religious and legal systems of thought. Clarina Howard Nichols's allusion to "old lawyers" wanting to preserve the harmony of organic law was also based on the assumption that a natural (and agreed upon and fixed) coherence existed in legal tradition. Common sense arguments, as developed in the Sabbath law controversy, relied on the fiction of a moral consensus, a majority will, and the jurist's ability to speak for the "soul" of the state. A moral consensus and the appeal to custom gave the law a distinctly moral function for disciplining its civil subjects. Because compliance to the law was based on the fiction of consent, custom or the sense of the community imposed a fictive consensus in the name of the "public good." In this way, as Michel Foucault observed, power relations can be made tolerable and illusive, particularly when disciplinary power takes the form of internalized discipline and self-regulation. Consequently, behind abstract rights was not simply the universal man but a reasonable man embedded in an abstract community or *communitas*, representing the public order. The idealized political man had social relations, moral ties to the church and family, and bonds to the nation-state.[11]

For antebellum feminists the imaginary and symbolic nature of rights discourse explained both its appeal and its inherent limitation. As Hendrik Hartog writes, rights embodied "aspirations," almost a religious faith, an "intense persuasion that we have rights, that wrongs can be remedied, patterns of illegitimate authority can be challenged, and public power must provide the mechanism for undoing injustice."[12] Accepting this vantage point, Clifford Geertz's definition of religion as a "cultural system" of symbols associated with an "aura of utter actuality" could just as easily apply to rights discourse.[13] The concept of coequality was very much a metaphorical and metaphysical framework. It was intended to challenge the dominant theme of the creation story that "difference *is*," which reinforced the gender hierarchy upholding women's subordination in nature and society. Yet the battle of persuasion was a complicated task, and feminists often found themselves confronted by a cacophony of authoritative voices (ministers, journalists, jurists, politicians) drowning out their plea for coequality. Did, then, the constant iteration of women's rights matter?

If exposing gender contradictions was their purpose, then women's rights activists served an important function as a critical public. Through the concept of coequality, feminists tried to move the debate about women away from essentialist notions of femininity and sexual difference. And by dissecting the sovereign body of the male citizen, they demonstrated how manhood—or male privilege endowed by the state—was neither natural nor divinely ordained.

How else did manhood contribute to the sovereign nature of citizenship? If popular sovereignty transferred the body of the king onto the abstract people, then democratic politics eventually resuscitated the body of the sovereign and gave him life through the citizen. Antebellum democracy and constitutionalism vested the civic body through two imaginary frameworks, which were overlapping and reinforcing, and contributed equally to the dual identity of the male citizen as a political-social being and a transcendent ideal. In general, certain parts of the male body represented the civic and political capacities that women necessarily lacked. The head stood for reason, and the eyes—the organ of vision—represented foresight, an expansive, comprehensive, and universal understanding. The body itself symbolized strength and mastery, with the hands as a trope for self-defense and honor (soiled hands implied dishonor), or productivity, initiative, and invention. Speech referred to the ability to communicate, persuade, and engage in political action. None of these metaphors was new; each was simply refashioned for a modern, male-defined democracy.[14]

As the opposite of the embodied male citizen, women represented the lack of skill, the absence of virtue, or diminished capacity. When it came to jury service, men and women did not see eye to eye. Women's lack of public experience made their vision myopic rather than periscopic or judicious. Nor could men hear the truth from female lips, because a woman's speech lacked the masterful presence needed to voice the will of the people. Shrill and discordant, a woman's voice transformed the sublime act of representation into a sideshow or public spectacle. Women's hands, seen as busy but not productive in terms of the cash nexus, suggested another weakness. And the lack of strength that made women incapable of defending their homes against creditors, invaders, or seducers, ultimately provided another metaphor of civic incompetence.[15]

The focus on body parts emphasized that women were the "weaker vessel" and "the sex." As Nel Noddings has argued, evil is often projected onto women's bodies, portraying women as the inducers of male weakness. Undisciplined female sexuality threatened to lead to male political seduction and infidelity. Nineteenth-century political discourse divided women into two dangerous classes: a pretender class or faux caste of weak-minded women who represented luxury and weakness, and fallen women, prostitutes, or the debased masses who threatened to lower men into a morass of immorality. To protect his honor and integrity, the male citizen had to stand apart from both female classes, choosing to protect only those women deemed worthy of his gallantry.[16]

The language of moral superiority, however, came from yet another dominant trope of embodied male citizenship. The citizen was seen vested with rights and bestowed with the honorary title of national membership. In turn, he vowed to uphold his sacred trust to defend his honor and the nation as a whole. Military service provided a compelling route to honorific citizenship. Here the man faced his fears and faced death and, through the glory of battle or the shedding of blood, became "one flesh" with the nation. The transcendent ideal of ultimate sacrifice on the altar of the state agreed with the republican and covenant ideal that nations were consecrated in blood. True greatness required every member of the polity to be ritually initiated into the national community and clothed and civilly enhanced in the mantle of his national identity. Male citizenship was embodied and sacralized.[17]

Of course, the joint allusion to civic dress and a commanding presence was an old ideal. By the mid-nineteenth century, a dignified civic appearance (denoting vested rights) was an ornament of democratic rule. That is why, at the 1860 national women's rights convention, Wendell Phillips referred to suffrage as a "scepter," and why five years earlier Caroline Dall had described the franchise—enhanced citizenship—as a "sword and shield." Stanton perhaps provided the most lofty portrait of the democratic image of the political man. Part sovereign and savior, the voter was "crowned in the glory of his manhood," a creature and creation whose elevated status came from the state and not nature.[18]

While the state could grant additional powers to the civic body, it just as easily could strip the citizen of political identity. Simply put, citizens could be made or unmade. To be or not to be a citizen was the difference between having the civic body fashioned, crowned, and deemed worthy of the title, or having the body defrocked; given a "crown of thorns" and "leaden scepter," as Antoinette Brown had contended in 1851; and then ritually humiliated as a political outcast. To Stanton, female divestment best related to physical disfigurement. In her 1860 address she vividly described man's legal version of the "woman-citizen" as a "monster, half-human, half-beast." If all the legal doctrine, sermonizing, and political images were compiled into one being, the female citizen would appear as a Frankensteinian creature composed of mismatching body parts. The distortion was skin deep: the state had to transmogrify women's civic body into a grotesque public anomaly whose physical presence was at once dangerous, uncontrollable, supernatural, and unnatural.[19]

Was it possible to imagine a sovereign female citizen? Stanton attempted to provide this alternative. By drawing on a classical parable, she told the story of two artists who were asked to sculpt a statue for the temple of Minerva. One figure was life-sized, idealized, and beautifully refined. The other assumed "Amazonian" proportions, "so boldly chiselled that it looked like masonry rather than sculpture." The eyes of the public selected the first and contemptuously rejected the second. But when the statue was lifted upward to its intended place on the temple, its fine features faded. The public then demanded that the other statue take its place, and as it ascended, Stanton noted, "the rude hewn mass, that before scarcely appeared to bear even the human form, assumed at once the divinity which it represented, being so perfectly proportioned to the dimensions of the building, and to the elevation on which it stood, that it seemed as though Pallas herself had alighted upon the pinnacle of the temple in person, to receive the homage of her worshippers."[20]

Stanton's point was that man had created his own image of womanhood. She might appear soft, beautiful, delicate, and refined and embody a "silent helplessness—when she is viewed as an object of sight," but her presence and value faded when she was lifted up to the heights of citizenship. This weakened image was constant, fixed, and incapable of transcendence, for woman was "never to rise one foot above the dust from which she sprung." Tellingly, Stanton stressed the visual positioning of man and woman, suggesting that women could never look down on men or out on the people, which was a necessary condition for assuming the duties of public representation. Her metaphorical choice of the statue recollected the words of Lucretia Mott, who in 1849 had called for women to break the lower image of man's unholy worship and smash the false idols of womanhood that denied women's divinity. The reference to the "temple of liberty" returned to Mary Ann Johnson's powerful phrase that women and men must become "pillars of the same temple, and priests of the same worship."[21]

The perfectly sculpted goddess did not resolve the contradictions of male embodied citizenship. She could not represent real women, whom Stanton described as the "women who are called masculine, who are brave, coura- geous, self-reliant and independent." Stone was not real flesh and blood. And the monstrous Amazon was always lurking in the background. Yet another message can be drawn from this parable. Sovereignty itself was a political allegory. Despite all the rhetorical appeals to "birthright citizenship" as the hallmark of antebellum constitutional theory, one was not born a citizen but made one through the sculpting of the original body into a political form. There remained a dissonance between the ideal and the real. The configura- tion of the sovereign citizen might change and dress in a new style, but the fact remained that the citizen was a creature of law, public opinion, and the ontological desire for a gendered state.[22]

While Stanton tried to present a transcendent image of female sovereignty, in this speech at the 1860 national convention, she did not address the other half of male citizenship: the common man as a social and political being embedded in the community. Nevertheless, at the convention the socially embedded woman provoked debate and division among the reformers. Un- like the transcendent figure portrayed as a statue, the common woman was rigidly bound by the physicality of the body. This problem became strikingly clear when activists discussed the relationship of divorce to women's rights. In this debate Stanton provided a very different model of womanhood: she was not ethereal, divine, or invulnerable to the forces of the body, but just the opposite. To justify the claim for divorce, Stanton focused on the physi- ology of the body politic. The biological forces of reproduction determined the happiness or misery of women, and an "ill-assorted marriage" was a bio- logical "crime." Divorce was a social necessity that protected society against these "unhallowed connections" in which children were born as the "fruit of lust" and "not love."[23]

Stanton's extreme characterization made the family a realm of the flesh. By violating the laws of affinity, marriages ruled by lust and violence were noth- ing better than "legalized prostitution." It was here that the common man became a "monster and villain"; a woman's only recourse from this den of "debauchery" was to fly from him as she would "the hot breath of a ferocious beast." Marriage was a "living death," a hell on earth, making the family a dangerous environment infected with a contagious disease (like "small pox") that needed a social cure: legally sanctioned divorce.[24]

Antoinette Brown Blackwell countered Stanton's imagery of biological warfare. She rejected Stanton's underlying assumption that marriage was a contract just like any other business partnership. Instead, Brown Blackwell contended that "marriage is a *relation*," not simply a legal bond between husband and wife, but a three-way relationship among the parents and children. Marriage for Brown Blackwell was a covenant based on justice, devotion, righteousness, and peace.[25]

A rather obvious rhetorical tension quickly developed as the rights of justice/righteousness were contrasted with the duties for devotion/peace. Although Brown Blackwell refused to see women as dependent or absent a sense of "self-sovereignty," the covenantal emphasis on obligation created a contradiction that could not be resolved. As she tried to explain,

> Marriage is a union of equals—equal interests being involved, equal duties at stake; and if any woman has been married to a man who chooses to take advantage of the laws as they now stand, who chooses to subject her, ignobly, to his will, against her own, to take from her the earnings which belong to her family, and to take from her the children which being to the family, I hold that woman, if she cannot, by her influence, change this state of things, is solemnly obligated to go to some State where she can be legally divorced; and then she would be solemnly bound to return again, and, standing for herself and her children, regard herself, in the sight of God, as being bound still to the father of those children, to work for his best interests, while she still maintains her own sovereignty.[26]

Brown Blackwell's solution turned the marriage argument on its head. A woman had an obligation to get a divorce when her rights were violated, a duty to sever the legal tie, but she was still married in the "sight of God." She regained her legal sovereignty but sacrificed her moral autonomy by choice.[27]

Ernestine Rose found Brown Blackwell's reasoning convoluted and untenable. To her, marriage was not a covenant in which couples were compelled by a sense of righteousness or right action. To describe woman as "*she* ought to be," and man as "*he* ought to be," and marriage as "*it* ought to be," Rose reasoned, rendered the institution impossibly ideal. Brown Blackwell's presumption that marriage should be based on equality and the wife's self-sovereignty ignored the actual condition of most marriages. "According to the definition of our Rev. sister," Rose observed, "*no one has ever yet been married*, as woman has never yet been perfectly equal with man."[28]

Rose saw divorce as a simple acknowledgment of the real division between "true marriages" and "false ones," and she argued that partial solutions like separation penalized couples because remarriage was prohibited. It forced many women to stay married for economic reasons rather than a higher moral sensibility. "It is the indissoluble chain that corrodes the flesh," she believed, and not the dangers of "free love" or divorce that threaten the institution of marriage.[29]

This debate centered on issues of obligation. Were married women embedded in a network of personal obligations to their children and husbands that deprived them of self-sovereignty? Or, as Stanton implied, did the forces of the body oblige some couples to divorce, and was it in the interest of the state to enforce this obligation and protect society from such "ill-assorted" marriages? Or, as Rose suggested, if marriage and divorce were merely conditions of society, then should the state desist in trying to impose a higher moral obligation by penalizing couples that failed to meet the ideal?

The "flesh," whether one in marriage or divided in divorce, clearly changed women's civil standing. The sovereign male citizen and the female citizen had biological needs and social and moral relations that had to be reconciled with their rights. Obligation presumed a sense of duty, a willingness to make a sacrifice, but the obligation in marriage was not an equal but a relative relation. Both coverture and the "one flesh" trope of the marriage covenant presumed an unequal exchange of duties between husband and wife.

All three activists attempted to reconcile marital obligation and equal rights. Brown Blackwell tried to remove the stigma of the wife's allegiance to her husband, making it her choice to return after divorce. This solution failed, because wives did not really have a choice but a duty. Stanton tried to erase the higher-law condition of marriage as a divine covenant but came dangerously close to replacing the law of God with the law of nature. Rose followed a moderate course, noting that humanity was fallible and not perfect. Marriage was to be treated as a social rather than a civil relation, distinct from the sense of obligation found in either the ideals of the marriage covenant or political sovereignty.

The divorce debate was divisive in ways that suffrage was not. It was, perhaps, centered too much on the body, and too controversial, and so provoked attacks on the women's movement as one whose goal was "free love" and sexual anarchy. But it also heightened fears already generated by the demands for coequality and women's embodied public representation. Even Wendell Phillips attempted to have Stanton's resolutions excised from the proceedings, arguing that the topic of marriage lay beyond the goals of the 1860 convention. Although he claimed that divorce affected men and women equally, which meant it was not a women's rights issue, his real aim was to keep the movement focused on traditional political issues such as suffrage. His reaction, however, was not widely endorsed. Stanton found it difficult to imagine how Phillips could attempt to justify his claim that marriage was not a political issue. And despite her disagreement with Stanton and Rose, Brown Blackwell also defended the political nature of marriage.[30]

In the end it was Rose who had the most faith in rights. For her it was the public, endowed with a critical view of marriage in society, that had to shape the course of the law. Glorification of marriage relied on theological distortions that concealed the actual conditions of marriage. Rights could not be wrapped in biblical dicta, nor was the state to impose artificial and arbitrary standards on its citizens that made their lives worse rather than better. The state was constituted to promote the happiness of the people, offer redress when necessary, and safeguard natural rights. For Rose, then, the state had a compelling interest in protecting the rights of all its citizens, an interest that superseded any moral claims for insuring the marriage covenant as one foundation for political order.

On a national political scale the problems of divine authority, the marriage covenant, and sovereignty were forming a permanent constitutional legacy. In developing their strategies after the ratification of the Fifteenth Amendment, the National Woman Suffrage Association returned to the basic meaning of popular sovereignty. Francis and Virginia Minor advocated this constitutional theory, which was hardly original but fundamental to the older idea of an exchange of rights for protection. The people had entered the social contract only in return for the state's guarantee to protect natural rights. Popular sovereignty implied that political power, the vote, and full citizenship had to be derived from all the people.[31]

This observation aside, one of the strongest statements against woman suffrage and citizenship was the 1873 Supreme Court decision of *Bradwell v. Illinois*. A case addressing whether women could practice law, it also determined whether female lawyers could be the vested representatives of the state. In ruling against Myra Bradwell's claim to act as an attorney, the court made clear that the issues of gender and the sovereignty of citizenship remained unresolved. The concurring opinion issued by Justice Joseph Bradley reaffirmed the tradition set during the antebellum period. Coverture and the marriage covenant, he contended, placed authority in the husband, and the will of God sanctioned the divine order of sexual difference. Women were not equally endowed with the mantle of state power for two reasons. First, as a class, they were subordinate to men, which was based on both the "law of the creator" and the common-law dicta from "time immemorial" that the husband is the "head and representative" of the wife. Second, women lacked the bodily form of the sovereign citizen. They had neither the presence and mastery nor the physical attributes of "confidence," "decision," and "firmness" of the "sterner sex." A woman's representative body lacked that essential maleness deemed the normative requirement for the right to represent the people.[32]

Here, in its most classic version, divine authority was pitted against due process or equal treatment; the male citizen was contrasted with the female citizen, who was found lacking in virtue and public presence; and representation was treated as a special privilege rather than a natural or sacred right. Not surprisingly, in the arguments made for the plaintiff by Matthew Carpenter, the theme of coequality emerged. Carpenter stated, "When God created man, he announced the law of his being, that it was not well to be alone, and so he created woman as his helpmate and companion." But even here Carpenter reworked the feminist idea of coequality, arguing that it did not imply suffrage or political cosovereignty, but mainly social equality, which in the long run benefited men as much as women. He reasoned that the social equality of women was better for men, because it demonstrated the social advances made by Christianity and modern civilization. Good manners and good morals were the natural offspring of social equality, which could only improve the character and quality of male citizenry.[33]

A battle of words enveloped the Bradwell case, as the male perspective on women's equality and women's inequality was debated. Ultimately, the interests shown to be at stake were "men's rights." The sovereign authority of citizenship remained vested in the male body, the scepter of suffrage was placed in his hands, and it was his prerogative to decide the benefits of women's place in society. For Carpenter, as his companion she could improve his manners, but—and here is where Carpenter and Judge Bradley diverged— as his rival in the courtroom she could only display her obvious physical flaws. Divine authority might be used to justify both positions. The design of God could ordain women's subordination as a timeless and fixed feature of the universe, or God could provide a more benign system of sexual companionship and harmony between men and women. Both visions were compatible with marriage and women's political exclusion.[34]

The legacy of antebellum feminism was its ability to expose the contradiction between social and political equality, arguing that this was a false distinction denying women true equality. Activists offered the countervailing framework of coequality, which claimed that God and the law of the Creator endorsed equal rights rather than the subordination of women. And they effectively introduced a wide range of women's rights issues into public discourse, forcing community leaders to give serious responses to their reasoned complaints.

Although suffrage was a faint hope not to be realized for several more decades, and equal citizenship was to remain an unrealized vision through the entire twentieth century, the power of critique was still pronounced. If the masculinized civic body had not been transcended, at least the contradictions inherent in normative definitions of rights and sexual difference had been disclosed and dramatically contested. Antebellum feminism was significant not in its legislative victories, but because its mature critique was not confined to women's issues—it directly shaped the historical development of a language of constitutional sovereignty and American democracy.

Notes

The following reports and proceedings of women's rights conventions are abbreviated throughout the notes:

Akron WRC 1851
The Proceedings of the Woman's Rights Convention, Held at Akron, Ohio, May 28 and 29, 1851. Cincinnati, 1851.

Cleveland WRC 1853
Proceedings of the National Woman's Rights Convention, Held at Cleveland, Ohio, on Wednesday, Thursday, and Friday, October 5th, 6th, and 7th, 1853. Cleveland, Ohio, 1854.

New York City WRC 1853
Proceedings of the Woman's Rights Convention, held at the Broadway Tabernacle, in the City of New York, on Tuesday and Wednesday, Sept. 6th and 7th, 1853. New York, 1853.

New York City WRC 1856
Proceedings of the Seventh National Woman's Rights Convention, held in New York City, at the Broadway Tabernacle, on Tuesday and Wednesday, Nov. 25th and 26th, 1856. New York, 1856.

New York City WRC 1859
Proceedings of the Ninth National Woman's Rights Convention held in New York City, Thursday May 12, 1859, with a Phonographic Report of the Speech of Wendell Phillips, by J. M. W. Yerrinton. Rochester, N.Y., 1859.

New York City WRC 1860
Proceedings of the Tenth National Woman's Rights Convention, Held at the Cooper Institute, New York City, May 10th and 11th, 1860. Boston, 1860.

Rochester WRC 1848
Proceedings of the Woman's Rights Convention, held at the Unitarian Church, Rochester, N.Y., August 2, 1848, to Consider the Rights of Woman, Politically, Religiously and Industrially. New York, 1870. Reprinted in *Woman's Rights Conventions: Seneca Falls and Rochester, 1848*. New York: Arno Press, 1969.

Salem WRC 1850
The Salem, Ohio, 1850 Women's Rights Convention Proceedings. Compiled and edited by Robert W. Audretsch. Salem, Ohio: Salem Public Library, 1976.

Seneca Falls WRC 1848
Report of the Woman's Rights Convention, held at Seneca Falls, N.Y., July 19th & 20th, 1848. Rochester, N.Y., 1848. Reprinted in *Woman's Rights Conventions, Seneca Falls and Rochester, 1848*. New York: Arno Press, 1969.

Syracuse WRC 1852	*The Proceedings of the Woman's Rights Convention, held at Syracuse, September 8th, 9th & 10th, 1852.* Syracuse, N.Y., 1852.
West Chester WRC 1852	*The Proceedings of the Woman's Rights Convention held at West Chester, PA., June 2d and 3d, 1852.* Philadelphia, 1852.
Worcester WRC 1850	*The Proceedings of the Woman's Rights Convention, held at Worcester, October 23d & 24th, 1850.* Boston, 1851.
Worcester WRC 1851	*Report of the Second General Convention of the Friends of Woman's Rights, Wednesday, October 15th, 1851.* Boston, 1852.

Introduction

1. It was reported that about "four hundred persons, mainly females," convened at Cooper Institute for the Woman's Rights Convention. See *New York Times*, May 11, 1860.

2. See Pauline Maier, *American Scripture: Making the Declaration of Independence* (New York: Knopf, 1997), 136, 154, 190–91, 194, 204–6, and J. R. Pole, *The Pursuit of Equality in American History* (Berkeley: University of California Press, 1978), 144–51.

3. I am aware that some historians argue that the word "feminist" should be limited to a twentieth-century perspective, since the word was first coined in this century. However, I think that the theoretical framework of feminism has a longer history. The purpose of this study is to demonstrate that antebellum women's rights activists developed a coherent theoretical critique and philosophy that can best be categorized as feminist.

4. By "critical public" I am referring to the process of creating a rights discourse, which reworks old ideas into new configurations, challenging and deconstructing dominant or hegemonic beliefs. A critical public defines itself in opposition to the state, exposing the injustices or abuses of government power. See Alan Hunt's chapter, "Rights and Social Movements: Counterhegemonic Strategies," in *Explorations in Law and Society: Toward a Constitutive Theory of Law* (New York: Routledge, 1993), 227–48. The literature on "woman's sphere" or "separate spheres" is extensive, and this framework has played a dominant role in the field of American women's history. Scholars have argued that women created a distinct "woman's culture," beginning in the family and extending outward to include benevolence institutions, which contributed to the domestication of politics in the nineteenth century. Scholars also have noted the limitations of this approach, such as the tendency to essentialize all women's experiences, ignore racial and class differences, conflate "reality" with "ideology," and uphold a rigid dichotomy between "politics" and "culture." See Barbara Welter, "The Cult of True Womanhood: 1800–1860," in *Dimity Convictions: The American Woman in the Nineteenth Century* (Athens: Ohio State University Press, 1976) (this article was originally published in the *American Quarterly* in 1966); Nancy F. Cott, *The Bonds of Womanhood: "Woman's Sphere" in New England, 1780–1835* (New Haven: Yale University Press, 1977); Suzanne Lebsock, *The Free Women of Petersburg: Status and Culture in a Southern Town, 1784–1860* (New York: Norton, 1984); Paula Baker, "The Domestication of Politics: Women and American Political Society, 1780–1920," *American Historical Review* 89 (June 1984): 620–47. For an early discussion about the merits of and problems with "woman's culture," see Ellen DuBois, Mari Jo Buhle, Temma Kaplan, Gerda Lerner, and Carroll Smith-Rosenberg, "Politics and Culture in Women's History: A Symposium," *Feminist Studies* 6 (Spring 1980): 26–64. For more recent evaluations of the "separate spheres thesis," see Linda Kerber, "Separate Spheres, Female Worlds, Woman's Place: The Rhetoric of Women's History," *Journal of American History* 75 (June 1988): 9–39; Joan Scott, *Gender and the Politics of History* (New York: Columbia University Press, 1988); Joan C. Williams, "Deconstructing Gender," *Michigan Law Review*

87 (February 1989): 797–845; Nancy Isenberg, "Second Thoughts on Gender and Women's History," *American Studies* 36 (Spring 1995): 93–104.

5. It is important to note that, although 1920 served as a benchmark for middle-class white women, the Nineteenth Amendment still included loopholes that allowed states to exclude black, Native American, Mexican American, and poor women from voting. See Nancy A. Hewitt, "From Seneca Falls to Suffrage: Recasting the History of American Women's Activism, 1848–1965" (presented to the Center for Advanced Study in the Behavioral Sciences, Stanford University, January 23, 1997; personal paper in possession of author).

6. Hannah Arendt, *The Human Condition* (Chicago: University of Chicago Press, 1958); Jürgen Habermas, *The Structural Transformation of the Public Sphere: An Inquiry into a Category of Bourgeois Society*, trans. Thomas Burger (Cambridge: MIT Press, 1991).

7. Several scholars have reinforced the "secularization" argument. See Ellen Carol DuBois, *Feminism and Suffrage: The Emergence of an Independent Women's Movement in America, 1848–1869* (Ithaca: Cornell University Press, 1978), 33–35; Blanche Glassman Hersh, *The Slavery of Sex: Feminist-Abolitionists in America* (Urbana: University of Illinois Press, 1978); and for a recent emphasis on the secular nature of the women's rights movement, see Sylvia Hoffert, *When Hens Crow: The Woman's Rights Movement in Antebellum America* (Bloomington: Indiana University Press, 1995). Some scholars, such as Ann Braude, have looked at the connection between spiritualism and women's rights, defining spiritualism as a "crisis of faith" or scientific alternative to mainstream Christian theology. See Ann Braude, *Radical Spirits: Spiritualism and Women's Rights in Nineteenth-Century America* (Boston: Beacon Press, 1989). Others, such as Nancy Hewitt, have argued that women's rights activism emerged outside the evangelical Protestant tradition. See Hewitt, "Feminist Friends: Agrarian Quakers and the Emergence of Woman's Rights in America," *Feminist Studies* 12 (Spring 1986): 27–49. Elizabeth Clark has similarly pointed to the failure of historians to analyze how religion shaped the women's rights movement. See Elizabeth Clark, "Religion, Rights, and Difference in the Early Women's Rights Movement," *Wisconsin Women's Law Review* 3 (1987): 29–57. Traditional political historians, those that focus on the second party system, ethnoreligious political behavior, or the connection between religion and democracy, tend to ignore women's contributions or to treat women as part of the larger liberating impulses generated by evangelicalism. See Daniel Walker Howe, "Religion and Politics in Antebellum America," in *Religion and American Politics: From the Colonial Period to the 1980s*, ed. Mark A. Noll (New York: Oxford University Press, 1990), 121–45, and Nathan O. Hatch, *The Democratization of American Christianity* (New Haven: Yale University Press, 1989).

8. Keith Melder, *The Beginnings of Sisterhood: The American Women's Rights Movement, 1800–1850* (New York: Schocken, 1977). For the division among female abolitionists and evidence that antislavery did not automatically lead to women's rights, see Debra Gold Hansen, "The Boston Female Antislavery Society and the Limits of Gender Politics," in *The Abolitionist Sisterhood: Women's Political Culture in Antebellum America*, ed. Jean Fagin Yellin and John C. Van Horne (Ithaca: Cornell University Press, 1994), 45–66, and Hansen, *Strained Sisterhood: Gender and Class in the Boston Female Anti-Slavery Society* (Amherst: University of Massachusetts Press, 1993). Also see Nanch A. Hewitt, *Women's Activism and Social Change: Rochester, New York, 1822–1872* (New York: Cornell University Press, 1984), esp. 190, and Judith Wellman, "The Seneca Falls Women's Rights Convention: A Study of Social Networks," *Journal of Women's History* 3 (Spring 1991): 9–37. Wellman's influence preceded the publication of her article through her conference paper and unpublished essay written for the Seneca Falls History Project. Both of her papers were available at the Stanton and Anthony Paper Project, under the direction of Ann Gordon, at the University of Massachusetts, Amherst. Both of these unpublished essays, "The Mystery of the Seneca Falls Women's Rights Convention: Who Came and Why?" (personal paper in possession of author) and "Women's Rights, Free Soil, and Quakerism: The Seneca Falls Women's

Rights Convention" (paper delivered at the Society for the History of the Early American Republic Conference, July 1981), include information found in her later published article.

9. See Norma Basch, *In the Eyes of the Law: Women, Marriage, and Property in Nineteenth-Century New York* (Ithaca: Cornell University Press, 1982); Norma Basch, "Equity vs. Equality: Emerging Concepts of Women's Political Status in the Age of Jackson," *Journal of the Early Republic* 3 (Fall 1983): 297–318; Peggy Rabkin, "The Origins of Law Reform: The Social Significance of the Nineteenth Century Codification Movement and Its Contribution to the Passage of the Early Married Women's Property Acts," *Buffalo Law Review* 29 (Spring 1980): 683–760; Peggy Rabkin, *Fathers to Daughters: The Legal Foundation of Female Emancipation* (Westport, Conn.: Greenwood Press, 1980); Amy Dru Stanley, "Conjugal Bonds and Wage Labor: Rights of Contract in the Age of 'Emancipation,'" *Journal of American History* 75 (September 1988): 471–500; Elizabeth Clark, "Matrimonial Bonds: Slavery and Divorce in Nineteenth Century America," *Law and History Review* 8 (Spring 1990): 25–54; Jeanne Boydston, *Home and Work: Housework, Wages, and the Ideology of Labor in the Early Republic* (New York: Oxford University Press, 1990).

Chapter 1

1. In the Stanton and Anthony papers there is an early speech by Stanton on the history of woman suffrage. In an 1850 letter to Mott, she first reveals her plan to write a history of the movement. Two years earlier Stanton already had begun to collect a scrapbook of events about the women's rights campaign. See Elizabeth Cady Stanton to Lucretia Mott, September 30, 1848, and September 16, 1850; also see speech, originally from the Elizabeth Cady Stanton Papers, Library of Congress, Rare Books, Scrapbooks, now part of the Papers of Elizabeth Cady Stanton and Susan B. Anthony, Rutgers University, New Brunswick, N.J. I would like to thank Ann D. Gordon and Patricia G. Holland for allowing me to use the papers when the editing project was located at the University of Massachusetts. For one of her published versions, see Elizabeth Cady Stanton, "The Woman's Rights Movement and Its Champions in the United States," in *Eminent Women of the Age: Being Narratives of the Lives and Deeds of the Most Prominent Women of the Present Generation* (Hartford, 1869), 362–404.

2. William Henry Channing, review of *The History of Woman Suffrage*, by Elizabeth Cady Stanton, Susan B. Anthony, and Matilda Joslyn Gage, eds., *London Inquirer*, November 5, 1881 (reprint, New York: National Woman's Suffrage Association, 1882), 2, 18.

3. Elizabeth Cady Stanton, Susan B. Anthony, and Matilda Joslyn Gage, eds., *History of Woman Suffrage*, 6 vols. (New York, 1881; reprint, New York: Arno Press, 1985), 1:8.

4. Although Mari Jo and Paul Buhle claim that the *History of Woman Suffrage* is not "a historical interpretation," they do not assess its impact on twentieth-century scholarship about the early movement. See Mari Jo Buhle and Paul Buhle, eds., *The Concise History of Woman Suffrage: Selections from the Classic Work of Stanton, Anthony, Gage, and Harper* (Urbana: University of Illinois Press, 1978), xviii.

5. Fredric Jameson, *The Political Unconscious: Narrative as Socially Symbolic Act* (Ithaca: Cornell University Press, 1981), 9, 28–31; also see George Aichele Jr., *The Limits of Story* (Philadelphia: Fortress Press, 1985), 36–37.

6. Stanton, Anthony, and Gage, *History of Woman Suffrage*, 1:8.

7. Ibid., 53–54.

8. Keith Melder, *The Beginnings of Sisterhood: The American Women's Rights Movement, 1800–1850* (New York: Schocken, 1977), 118.

9. Eleanor Flexner, *Century of Struggle: The Woman's Rights Movement in the United States* (Cambridge: Harvard University Press, 1959; rev. ed., 1975), 71.

10. Stanton, Anthony, and Gage, *History of Woman Suffrage*, 1:420.

11. Ibid., 422; Mary Clemmer, "Lucretia Mott," in *Our Famous Women: An Authorized Record of the Lives and Deeds of Distinguished American Women of Our Times* (Hartford: A. D. Worthington, 1884), 490.

12. Stanton, Anthony, and Gage, 1:420; Clemmer, "Lucretia Mott," 478–79, 490.

13. Flexner, *Century of Struggle*, 72.

14. For example, Judith Wellman and Joan Hoff, although aware of the historical complexity of events leading to the Seneca Falls convention, still place Stanton at the center of the story of origins. Hoff identifies Stanton and Mott's first meeting at the London antislavery convention in 1840 and then discusses their fateful reunion in 1848. Both scholars rely on Stanton's autobiography to reinforce the idea that the convention served as her political debut. Wellman discounts Mott's role and calls Stanton the main organizer of the convention. See Joan Hoff, *Law, Gender, and Injustice: A Legal History of U.S. Women* (New York: New York University Press, 1991), 137–38, and Judith Wellman, "Women's Rights, Free Soil, and Quakerism: The Seneca Falls Women's Rights Convention" (paper delivered at the Society for the History of the Early American Republic Conference, July 1981), 12.

15. Flexner, *Century of Struggle*, 70, 72.

16. Elizabeth Cady Stanton, *Eighty Years and More; Reminiscences, 1815-1897* (New York: T. Fisher Unwin, 1898; reprint, New York: Schocken, 1971), 148, 150.

17. Melder, *Beginnings of Sisterhood*, 118.

18. Flexner, *Century of Struggle*, 72.

19. Anne F. Scott and Andrew M. Scott, *One Half the People: The Fight for Woman Suffrage* (Philadelphia: Lippincott, 1975), 9.

20. Ellen Carol DuBois, *Feminism and Suffrage: The Emergence of an Independent Women's Movement in America, 1848-1869* (Ithaca: Cornell University Press, 1978), 23.

21. Theodore Tilton, "Elizabeth Cady Stanton," in *Eminent Women of the Age*, 346.

22. DuBois, *Feminism and Suffrage*, 41.

23. Ibid., 28, 202, 19, 33–35.

24. See Mary F. Davis's letter in *Woman's Journal*, September 17, 1870, 296.

25. Channing wrote that "the most influential [convention], in giving form and direction to the movement, was the First National Convention, held in Worcester." Melder likewise concluded that the Worcester convention "climaxed the organizing process of the woman's rights movement," and "following this occasion, the movement took on the characteristics of an independent, organized reform crusade, much like antislavery agitation." See William Henry Channing review, 9, and Melder, *Beginnings of Sisterhood*, 153.

26. Davis wrote two drafts of the history of the movement. The earlier, unpublished manuscript, "History of the Woman's Rights Movement since 1829," includes these references. It is located in the Paulina Kellogg Wright Davis Papers, 1813–1876, Vassar College Library, Poughkeepsie, N.Y. The later published version appeared as *A History of the National Woman's Rights Movement, for Twenty Years, with Proceedings of the Decade Meeting Held at Apollo Hall, October 20, 1870, from 1850 to 1870, with an Appendix Containing the History of the Movement during the Winter of 1871, in the National Capital* (New York, 1871).

27. Davis, *History of the National Woman's Rights Movement*, 4–5.

28. Stanton, Anthony, and Gage, *History of Woman Suffrage*, 1:62.

29. Earl M. Maltz, "Fourteenth Amendment Concepts in the Antebellum Era," *American Journal of Legal History* 32 (1988): 308, 320; also see Linda Kerber, "The Republican Ideology of the Revolutionary Generation," *American Quarterly* 37 (Fall 1985): 475.

30. See Kerber, "Republican Ideology," 484; James H. Kettner, *The Development of American Citizenship, 1608–1870* (Chapel Hill: University of North Carolina Press, 1978), 180, 183–84.

31. George P. Parkinson Jr., "Antebellum State Constitution-Making: Retention, Circumvention, Revision" (Ph.D. diss., University of Wisconsin, 1972), 9.

32. Maltz, "Fourteenth Amendment Concepts," 320; also see Duncan Kennedy, "The Structure of Blackstone's Commentaries," *Buffalo Law Review* 28 (1979): 288, 290, 350.

33. See Linda Kerber, "'May all our Citizens be Soldiers, and all our Soldiers Citizens': The Ambiguities of Female Citizenship in the New Nation," in *Arms at Rest: Peacemaking and Peacekeeping in American History*, ed. Joan R. Challinor and Robert L. Beisner (Westport, Conn.: Greenwood Press, 1987), 16.

34. Although Suzanne Lebsock has noted the loopholes in common law that allowed women to exercise certain legal rights, the law did not perceive women as financial independents. Women's dependence represented the rule, not the exception, in marriage law. One telling example is that a husband retained a legal right to his wife's services throughout most of the nineteenth century. As the ownership of property became less important in defining citizenship, the status of men as heads of household and wage earners substituted as the new requirement for political status. See Joseph Warren, "Husband's Right to Wife's Services," *Harvard Law Review* 38 (February 1925): 421–46; Suzanne Lebsock, *The Free Women of Petersburg: Status and Culture in a Southern Town, 1784–1860* (New York: Norton, 1984); Norma Basch, "The Emerging Legal History of Women in the United States: Property, Divorce, and the Constitution," *Signs: Journal of Women in Culture and Society* 12 (Autumn 1986): 102.

35. Blackstone wrote that "by marriage, the husband and wife are one person in the law; that is, the very being or legal existence of the woman is suspended during marriage, or at least incorporated and consolidated into that of the husband." See Sir William Blackstone, *Commentaries on the Laws of England in Four Books*, 2 vols., 2nd ed., ed. Thomas M. Cooley (Chicago: Callaghan, 1879), 1:441.

36. Hannah Arendt, *The Human Condition* (Chicago: University of Chicago Press, 1958), 51.

37. Kerber, "Republican Ideology," 484; Rowland Berthoff, "Conventional Mentality: Free Blacks, Women, and Business Corporations as Unequal Persons, 1820–1870," *Journal of American History* 76 (December 1989): 755; Judith Wellman, "Women's Rights, Republicanism, and Revolutionary Rhetoric in Antebellum New York State," *New York History* 69 (July 1988): 353.

38. J. G. A. Pocock, "Virtues, Rights, and Manners: A Model for Historians of Political Thought," *Political Theory* 9 (August 1981): 359.

39. Berthoff, "Conventional Mentality," 766.

40. In the *New York Times* and the *New York Herald*, political commentators defended the principle of drawing distinctions across the population that could be applied to any class—based on age, sex, or color. Women's lack of experience as a "new and untried class" justified their exclusion; their political status was not defined by abstract rights, nor was there a quid pro quo relationship between duties (such as taxation and freeborn status) and rights. The newspapers mocked the idea of women's autonomy, claiming that women who stood apart from male protection would have to "stand by [themselves], act as firemen, or rather firewomen, perform military duty, chew tobacco, and drink rum as sailors." See "Woman's Rights Convention," *New York Herald*, November 1, 1851; "The Female Suffrage Question," *New York Times*, March 18, 1859; and "Impracticable Rights," ibid., February 6, 1860.

41. Hilda Smith, "False Universals of Human Experience" (personal paper in possession of author).

42. Political theorists have stressed the importance of self-ownership as a critical component of rights theory derived from Locke's writings. During the antebellum period this argument gained wider acceptance among lawyers, politicians, and even radical reformers, such as anti-

slavery advocates. See C. B. Macpherson, *The Political Theory of Possessive Individualism: Hobbes to Locke* (Oxford: Oxford University Press, 1962); Jonathan A. Glickstein, *Concepts of Free Labor in Antebellum America* (New Haven: Yale University Press, 1991), 11–12.

43. See Linda K. Kerber, *Women of the Republic: Intellect and Ideology in Revolutionary America* (Chapel Hill: University of North Carolina Press, 1980); Jan Lewis, "The Republican Wife: Virtue and Seduction in the Early Republic," *William and Mary Quarterly* 44 (October 1987): 689–721; Rosemarie Zagarri, "Morals, Manners, and the Republican Mother," *American Quarterly* 44 (June 1992): 192–215.

44. Linda Kerber, "Separate Spheres, Female Worlds, Woman's Place: The Rhetoric of Women's History," *Journal of American History* 75 (June 1988): 13–16; also see Nancy Isenberg, "Second Thoughts on Gender and Women's History," *American Studies* 36 (Spring 1995).

45. Nancy F. Cott, *The Bonds of Womanhood: "Woman's Sphere" in New England, 1780–1835* (New Haven: Yale University Press, 1977), 201.

46. Mary P. Ryan, *Women in Public: Between Banners and Ballots, 1825–1880* (Baltimore: Johns Hopkins University Press, 1990), 12.

47. Joan B. Landes, *Women and the Public Sphere in the Age of the French Revolution* (Ithaca: Cornell University Press, 1988).

48. Nathan O. Hatch, *The Democratization of American Christianity* (New Haven: Yale University Press, 1989); Daniel Walker Howe, "The Evangelical Movement and the Political Culture of the Second Party System," *Journal of American History* 77 (March 1991): 1216–39.

49. See John Christian Laursen, "The Subversive Kant: The Vocabulary of 'Public' and 'Publicity,'" *Political Theory* 14 (November 1986): 584–603; Catherine Zuckert, "Not by Preaching: Tocqueville on the Role of Religion in American Democracy," *Review of Politics* 43 (April 1981): 259–80.

50. John Dunn, *The Political Thought of John Locke: An Historical Account of the Argument of the "Two Treatises of Government"* (Cambridge: Cambridge University Press, 1969), 97.

51. For the most recent example of a study that completely ignores religion, see Sylvia D. Hoffert, *When Hens Crow: The Woman's Rights Movement in Antebellum America* (Bloomington: Indiana University Press, 1995).

52. See Paula Baker, "The Domestication of Politics: Women and American Political Society, 1780–1920," *American Historical Review* 89 (June 1984); also see Lori D. Ginzberg, *Women and the Work of Benevolence: Morality, Politics, and Class in Nineteenth-Century United States* (New Haven: Yale University Press, 1990).

53. Carole Pateman, *The Sexual Contract* (Stanford: Stanford University Press, 1988).

54. James T. Johnson, "The Covenant Idea and the Puritan View of Marriage," *Journal of the History of Ideas* 32 (January–March 1971): 107–18; Mary Lyndon Shanley, "Marriage Contract and Social Contract in Seventeenth Century English Political Thought," *Western Political Quarterly* 32 (March 1979): 79–91.

55. The "one flesh" trope is taken from three biblical passages: Genesis 2:23, 24 (creation story); Matthew 19:5, 6; and Ephesians 5:30, 31. This biblical allusion became part of the reasoning used to define marriage in ecclesiastical and secular marriage law. See Derrick Sherrin Bailey, *Sexual Relations in Christian Thought* (New York: Harper and Brothers, 1959). For an example from a popular nineteenth-century legal treatise, see Edward D. Mansfield, *The Legal Rights, Liabilities, and Duties of Women; with an Introductory History of their Legal Condition in the Hebrew, Roman and Feudal Civil Systems* (Salem, Ohio, 1845), 266. Mansfield wrote that since "marriage creates a unity," then "the husband is religiously the head of the family."

56. See William Henry Channing review, 11; also see the list of resolutions reported by W. H. Channing from the Business Committee, which emphasized women's "co-equal share in the formation and administration of law" and the "grand social reform of establishing woman's

co-sovereignty with man," in *Worcester WRC 1850*, 16. The idea of cosovereignty fit within Channing's Christian socialist philosophy that emphasized solidarity (revolution and reconciliation of class interests) and the transcendentalist notion of "correspondence," which stressed unity and harmony between the spiritual and material worlds. He endorsed women's "just co-sovereignty" in his paper, *Spirit of the Age*, in 1849. See "Topics and Their Treatment," *Spirit of the Age*, August 18, 1849.

57. William Henry Channing review, 6.

58. Ibid., 2, 5.

59. Arendt, *Human Condition*, 186.

60. William Henry Channing review, 2, 6.

61. Arendt, *Human Condition*, 18–19.

62. Davis, *History of the National Woman's Rights Movement*, 2.

63. Arendt, *Human Condition*, 18–19, 32.

64. Neil H. Cogan, "'Standing' before the Constitution: Membership in the Community," *Law and History Review* 7 (Spring 1989): 7.

65. Paulina Wright Davis, "Woman's Rights" (1852), in Davis Papers, 26.

Chapter 2

1. See the first call to the convention in "To the Women of Ohio," *Anti-Slavery Bugle*, March 30, 1850; the call has been reprinted in *Salem WRC 1850*.

2. The constitutional convention for revising the Ohio constitution opened its sessions on May 6, 1850. See Frances N. Thorpe, *The Federal and State Constitutions, Colonial Charters, and Other Organic Law* (Washington, D.C., 1909); George P. Parkinson Jr., "Antebellum State Constitution-Making: Retention, Circumvention, Revision" (Ph.D. diss., University of Wisconsin, 1972), 163.

3. Diane VanSkiver Gagel, "Ohio Women Unite: The Salem Convention of 1850," in *Women in Ohio History*, ed. Marta Whitlock (Columbus: Ohio Historical Society, 1976), 6.

4. The reference to "Convention of Women" appeared as the title of the article announcing the Salem convention published in the *Anti-Slavery Bugle*, March 30, 1850. In one of the later calls, the organizers emphasized that this "Convention has been called distinctly as a *Women's* Convention, we hope it will be such in fact, and that no patronizing *male* orators will be called to set copies for it, or in [any] way control the proceedings." See "The Women's Convention," *Anti-Slavery Bugle*, April 6, 1850. Immediately after the adjournment of the Convention of Women, the male spectators organized a meeting for "Universal Suffrage." See "Universal Suffrage," *Anti-Slavery Bugle*, April 6, 1850; also see *Salem WRC 1850*, 11, 19, 65.

5. Jefferson believed that each generation should revise its constitutions. See Jefferson to Samuel Kercheval, July 12, 1816, in Merrill D. Peterson, ed., *The Portable Thomas Jefferson* (New York: Penguin, 1977), 558–60.

6. See, Charles Francis Adams, ed., *The Works of John Adams*, 10 vols. (Boston, 1851), 10:397.

7. For a discussion of how the founders recognized the fabricated nature of drafting constitutions, see Robert A. Ferguson, "Ideology and the Framing of the Constitution," *Early American Literature* 22 (Fall 1987): 165.

8. Antebellum convention proceedings were published in both local and reform newspapers. The Seneca Falls convention proceedings, for example, were published in the *New York Tribune* and reprinted in the *National Anti-Slavery Standard*. But a separate publication of the convention proceedings was not issued until 1870, as part of the anniversary celebration for the origins

of the women's rights movement. Ohio women's rights convention proceedings (those held in Salem, McConnelsville in 1850, Akron in 1851, Chesterfield in 1851, and Massillon in 1852) were printed in the *Anti-Slavery Bugle*. The national women's rights conventions set a new trend by appointing a permanent publication committee during the first convention held in Worcester in 1850. The proceedings of several national conventions were published as printed proceedings: Worcester, Mass. (1850 and 1851); Syracuse, N.Y. (1852); Cleveland, Ohio (1853); and New York City (1856, 1859, and 1860). The publication committee also issued two collections of *Women's Rights Tracts* in 1853 and 1854. Other conventions had their proceedings published as well: New York City (1853); West Chester, Pa. (1852); and Boston (1855 and 1859). After the Ohio Woman's Rights Association was formed in 1852, the executive committee also distributed a series of tracts titled the *Woman's Rights Advocate*.

9. See John Alexander Jameson, *The Constitutional Convention: Its History, Powers, and Modes of Proceeding* (New York, 1867), 4.

10. Ferguson emphasizes the importance of "structure, form, and language," but he is more interested in the literary craft of constitution-making. See Ferguson, "Ideology and the Framing of the Constitution," 164. Given the importance of antebellum constitutional conventions and spontaneous conventions, I argue that the conventions had a decidedly performative, staged, and theatrical quality.

11. Between 1846 and 1851 eleven states held constitutional conventions, and there was typically a connection between state conventions and women's rights conventions. New York held a state constitutional convention in 1846, and two years later activists organized the Seneca Falls and Rochester women's rights conventions. In addition to the Salem women's rights convention, another meeting gathered in Akron in 1851, both organized in response to the Ohio state constitutional convention of 1850–51. Activists in Indiana held a women's rights convention in 1850, the same year as the state convention. And the first two national women's rights conventions held in Worcester preceded the Massachusetts state constitutional convention held in 1853. See "Constitutional Reform," *United States Magazine and Democratic Review*, July 1851, 3; also see Rowland Berthoff, "Conventional Mentality: Free Blacks, Women, and Business Corporations as Unequal Persons, 1820–1870," *Journal of American History* 76 (December 1989): 753–84.

12. Judith Sargent Murray published her "Gleaner" essays in serial form in 1792–94 and in book form in 1789, and she used the non de plume of "Constantia." Mercy Otis Warren wrote political satires and a history of the American Revolution and maintained an extensive correspondence with John and Abigail Adams. See Linda Kerber, "I Have Don . . . much to Carrey on the Warr'; Women and the Shaping of Republican Ideology after the American Revolution," in *Women and Politics in the Age of Revolution*, ed. Harriet B. Applewhite and Darline G. Levy (Ann Arbor: University of Michigan Press, 1990), 238–44. Also see Maud Macdonald Hutcheson, "Mercy Otis Warren, 1728–1814," *William and Mary Quarterly* 10 (July 1953): 379–402; Joan Hoff Wilson and Sharon L. Billinger, "Mercy Otis Warren: Playwright, Poet, and Historian of the American Revolution," in *Female Scholars: A Tradition of Learned Women before 1800*, ed. J. R. Brink (Montreal: Eden Press, 1980): 161–82.

13. Cynthia Jordan makes the point that Jefferson's advocacy of a "natural aristocracy" reflected his larger view of an intellectual elite serving as the "guardians" and interpreters of the "rights and liberties of the people." See Cynthia S. Jordan, " 'Old Words' in 'New Circumstances': Language and Leadership in Post-Revolutionary America," *American Quarterly* 40 (December 1988): 504–5, 510.

14. Although delegates at earlier conventions used women as foils for arguing against the extension of the suffrage, the Ohio convention had the first serious discussion of woman suffrage. The 1846 New York constitutional convention received three petitions for women's right to vote, while the Ohio state convention entertained numerous petitions from several counties for

women's right to vote and for the right to vote "without the distinction of sex or color." See Parkinson, "Antebellum State Constitution-Making," 12–13, 18, 20, 24, 28, 30–32, 37, 42, 170. Wellman notes that three petitions were sent to the 1846 New York state constitutional convention asking for woman suffrage. Yet the issue was used in the convention proceedings to discredit black suffrage, which followed the same pattern set during the 1821 New York state constitutional convention. See Judith Wellman, "Women's Rights, Republicanism, and Revolutionary Rhetoric in Antebellum New York State," *New York History* 69 (July 1988): 379–81. For the petitions sent to the Ohio state constitutional convention, see D. C. Shilling, "Woman's Suffrage in the Constitutional Convention of Ohio," *Ohio Archaeological and Historical Society Publications* 25 (1916): 167–70.

15. *Report of the Debates and Proceedings of the Convention for the Revision of the Constitution of the State of Ohio, 1850–51* (Columbus, Ohio, 1851), 555 (hereafter cited as *Proceedings of the Ohio Convention*).

16. Gagel, "Ohio Women Unite," 6.

17. *Proceedings of the Ohio Convention*, 555.

18. Ibid., 553–54.

19. Parkinson, "Antebellum State Constitution-Making," 48, 77–82, 167. For a nineteenth-century account of the Dorr War that covers the "mass conventions," suffrage associations, and their Declaration of Principle, see Francis Harriet (Whipple) Greene McDougall, *Might and Right: A History of the Dorr Rebellion* (Providence, R.I., 1844), 76–114.

20. William R. Brock, *Parties and Political Conscience: American Dilemmas, 1840–1850* (Milwood, N.Y.: KTO Press, 1979), 4–6.

21. John G. Miller, *The Great Convention. Description of the Convention of the People of Ohio, held at Columbus, on 21st and 22nd February 1840* (Columbus, Ohio, 1840), 3–4, 6, 10; A. B. Norton, *The Great Revolution of 1840. Reminiscences of the Log Cabin and Hard Cider Campaign* (Mount Vernon, Ohio, 1888), 48, 52.

22. See Norton, *Great Revolution*, 330.

23. Elizabeth Varon has noted the importance of women in the Whig election campaigns during the 1840s, and she writes how women's presence was portrayed in Whig propaganda as providing decorum, dignity, and disinterestedness. But she places this political view within the context of "true womanhood," or what she calls "Whig womanhood," describing how the women were seen as "fostering 'domestic' virtues." The problem with this conclusion is that antebellum Americans did not see women as always symbolizing domesticity, and it ignores how the language of "society," manners, and the civilizing role of women did not necessarily flow from their roles as mothers, wives, or homemakers. See Elizabeth Varon, "Tippecanoe and the Ladies, Too: White Women and Party Politics in Antebellum Virginia," *Journal of American History* 82 (September 1995): 503, 505.

24. See Henry H. Van Amringe, "Woman's Rights in Church and State," in *Worcester WRC 1850*, 48.

25. Varon also claims that women were "partisans," but she may be overstating her case. Women did not have the same political privileges inside the party system, and their real appeal (at least rhetorically) was their public cachet as nonpartisans. She notes that the same papers that endorsed women's partisanship referred to women's rights activists as "cackling geese" and "Amazons," but she fails to address how this view contributed to her notion of "Whig womanhood" and female partisanship. See Varon, "Tippecanoe and the Ladies, Too," 495, 514, 516–20.

26. See "Liberty Party and Woman's Rights," *National Anti-Slavery Standard*, August 6, 1846. This letter explains how the Liberty League had a new standard, bearing the inscription "Free Trade and Women's Rights." It further mentions that the Liberty League sent a petition to Con-

gress asking for the extension of suffrage, so that "women *may be represented* in the State and National Councils, it being their right."

27. At a Liberty League convention in Macedon, considered their national convention, all women present were invited to vote on the last ballot for president. Gerrit Smith received 66 votes; J. G. Birney, 6; Lucretia Mott, 1; Lydia Maria Child, 1; and another woman, whose name was not retained, 1. See "Liberty League and Its Nominees," *National Anti-Slavery Standard,* July 15, 1847.

28. Several newspapers wrote responses to the Salem, Ohio, Woman's Rights Convention, including a strong letter of support from the "Liberty Party Paper." They wrote, "We commend the doings of the recent Convention of Women in Ohio. . . . We hope that the influence of it may be felt upon the Ohio Constitutional Convention, not only, but upon the whole country. In an age and country where the exercise of human rights depends upon the ballot, not the sword, upon the ever active and growing intelligence and heart of the people, it is not surprising that the wrongs done to woman by civil government should attract attention." See "Liberty Party Paper," *Anti-Slavery Bugle,* May 25, 1850. Free-Soil candidates supported women's rights as well. Lucius Bierce, described as an "active and influential politician of the Free Soil Party, residing in Akron," wrote a letter of support for woman suffrage. Daniel Tilden, who served in the federal Congress from 1843 to 1847 and was nominated but declined to run on the Free-Soil ticket for governor, also endorsed women's rights and signed the call to the Salem convention. Martha Tilden signed the call and was described as "a radical without doubt, for we never heard of a woman insisting on her equal rights with man, that was not a thorough reformer all round the bush." Adeline Swift, another women's rights advocate, was married to Lucius Swift, a Free-Soil politician who was elected to the state senate and was a delegate at the Ohio state constitutional convention. See "The Women's Convention"; Lucius V. Bierce, "Rights of Woman"; and "Daniel R. Tilden: Free Soil Candidate from Akron," *Anti-Slavery Bugle,* April 6, 13, May 11, 25, 1850. Also see William Henry Perrin, *History of Summit County, with an Outline Sketch of Ohio* (Philadelphia, 1881), 307, 310–11, 333; *Proceedings of the Ohio Convention,* 5; Theodore Clarke Smith, *The Liberty and Free Soil Parties in the Northwest* (New York: Russell and Russell, 1897; reprint, New York: Arno Press, 1969), 336.

29. Cowles served on the business and fair committees of the Western Anti-Slavery Society and worked closely with Jane Elizabeth Jones, editor of the *Anti-Slavery Bugle,* who was a prominent women's rights advocate in her own right. In addition to her ties to the Garrisonian wing of the movement, she established a link to Liberty Party supporters through her campaign against the Black Codes. She served as secretary of the Ashtabula County Ladies Antislavery Society in 1846, where six Liberty Party ministers gave speeches against the Black Codes. By June 1847 she had distributed and published a circular against the Black Codes, and she wrote an even stronger appeal on the subject, "Outrage upon Human Rights," published in 1848. Cowles graduated from Oberlin's Ladies Course in 1840, served as a teacher and then a principal, and from 1850 to 1855 was superintendent of grammar and high schools in Canton, Ohio. See *Anti-Slavery Bugle,* August 14, 1846, June 18, 1847, and February 2, 1848. Also see Linda Geary, *Balanced in the Wind: A Biography of Betsey Mix Cowles* (Lewisburg, Pa.: Bucknell University Press, 1989), 50–59, 69–72; Keith E. Melder, "Betsey Mix Cowles," in *Notable American Women, 1607–1950: A Biographical Dictionary,* 3 vols., ed. Edward T. James, Janet Wilson James, and Paul S. Boyer (Cambridge: Belknap Press of Harvard University Press, 1971), 1:393–94.

30. For a discussion of women voting in school elections, see "Report of A. Brooke, on the Civil and Political Functions of Women, in the U.S.," which appeared in "Proceedings of the Third Woman's Rights Convention of Ohio," *Anti-Slavery Bugle,* June 12, 1852. Many of the supporters of the Salem and Akron women's rights conventions had ties to the local school boards

as well. Lucius Bierce was elected to the school board in 1847 along with Henry Spellman, and both signed the call to the Salem convention. The Salem school board was composed of Garrisonian and Liberty Party supporters, and all eight members had female relatives that attended the Salem convention. It is just as important to recognize that Liberty Party supporters used school districts to recruit voters in the 1846 election in Massachusetts, and that a similar pattern appears to have been adopted at the local level in Ohio. See Reinhard O. Johnson, "The Liberty Party in Massachusetts, 1840–1848: Antislavery Third Party Politics in the Bay State," *Civil War History* 28 (Fall 1982): 241–43; Oscar E. Olin, *Akron & Its Environs* (Chicago, 1917), 115; C. D. Galbreath, "Antislavery Movement in Columbiana County," *Ohio Archaeological and Historical Society Publications* (1921): 392; George D. Hunt, *History of Salem and the Immediate Vicinity, Columbiana County, Ohio* (Salem, Ohio, 1898), 48–56, 132, 147–48, 223–30, 239.

31. See letter, "William West (Liberty Party) and Equal Suffrage," *National Anti-Slavery Standard*, March 22, 1849.

32. See William Elder, *Periscopics; or, Current Subjects Extemporaneously Treated* (New York, 1854), v–vi. William Elder ran the *Liberty Herald* in 1847 and wrote for the Free-Soil campaign paper *The Republic* in 1848. He was trained as a physician, studied law, and ran as local Free-Soil candidate in Pennsylvania. He assisted the careers of Paulina Wright Davis, Elizabeth Blackwell, and Ann Preston in their efforts as health lecturers or female physicians. He served on the Central Committee for the national women's rights convention held in Worcester in 1850. See *Worcester WRC 1850*, 18; "William Elder," in *Dictionary of American Biography*, 20 vols. (New York: Scribner's, 1928–36), 6:68. Also see Elizabeth A. Thompson, "Elizabeth Blackwell," in James, James, and Boyer, *Notable American Women*, 1:161–63. For Elder's public endorsement of Paulina Wright Davis's lectures, see *Water-Cure Journal*, June 1, 1846, 11. For Ann Preston's connection to Elder through her close friend Hannah Darlington, see Ann Preston to Hannah Darlington, January 9, 1851, Hannah Darlington Letters, Chester County Historical Society, West Chester, Pa. For Elder's nomination as a candidate for the Liberty Party and National Reformers, see *Pennsylvania Freeman*, September 10, 1846.

33. Geary, *Balanced in the Wind*, 48, 73.

34. In 1849 the Liberty League debated the resolution that endorsed "suffrage to all persons (of mature age) without regard to sex, colour, or character." The measure lost, 22 to 13. Gerrit Smith, who served as chairman of the Committee of Resolutions, had supported the resolution. By the time of the next Liberty League convention held in Syracuse, New York, in July, the same resolution was passed "unanimously." See *National Anti-Slavery Standard*, February 15, March 1, July 19, 1849.

35. Sanford Levinson discusses the American creed, and Werner Sollors covers the tension between chosen identities based on consent and imposed identities based on descent. While Sollors and Levinson use marriage as an example of a chosen identity, this does not have the same meaning for women as compared with men. The conditions viewed as inherited or imposed can range from those of class, race, religion, and sex, because they are based on birth, custom, or physical inheritance. Levinson does not address the implication of sex on theories of descent. See Samuel Levinson, *Constitutional Faith* (Princeton: Princeton University Press, 1988), 94–95. Also see Werner Sollors, *Beyond Ethnicity: Consent and Descent in American Culture* (New York: Oxford University Press, 1986).

36. Desley Deacon and Jean Baker stress the symbolic importance of the vote for cementing party loyalties. Voting became a "hollowed ceremony" and ritual during the period between 1828 and 1840. See Desley Deacon, "Politicizing Gender," *Genders*, no. 6 (Fall 1989): 5; Jean H. Baker, *Affairs of Party: The Political Culture of Northern Democrats in the Mid-Nineteenth Century* (Ithaca: Cornell University Press, 1983), 268–69.

37. Lydia Maria Child, "Home and Politics," *Union Magazine*, August 1848, 63–68.

38. Two scholars make this point about Jefferson: Joan R. Gunderson, "Independence, Citizenship, and the American Revolution," *Signs: Journal of Women in Culture and Society* 13 (Autumn 1987): 64, and Mary Loeffelholz, who quotes Gunderson in "Posing the Woman Citizen: The Contradictions of Stanton's Feminism," *Genders*, no. 7 (March 1990): 90. This argument reappears in the deliberations of the Virginia constitutional convention in 1829–30, the home state of Jefferson. See *Proceedings and Debates of the Virginia State Convention, of 1829–1830* (Richmond, Va., 1830), 638.

39. Disunionism had several meanings for abolitionists. For some it was a moral and political strategy for calling the state back to its original principle of freedom and liberty, and for others it was a radical act of dissent and revolution that required completely reconstituting a new social compact. For an example of how disunion could encompass reformers who desired complete rejection of the federal Constitution as well as those who did not support complete disunion but advocated agitation on the subject, see "Call for a National Convention," [Disunion Convention] (1857), Slavery in the United States Collection, Manuscript Collections, American Antiquarian Society, Worcester, Mass.

40. See petition from the Business Committee of the Anti-Slavery Society of Eastern Pennsylvania, New Jersey, and Delaware, drafted by Lucretia Mott and six other officers who supported women's rights. It specifically described the federal Constitution as violating divine law, making war on human rights, and being grossly inconsistent with republican principles, and thus slavery and freedom could not coexist in "one body politic." See "Ninth Annual Meeting of the Anti-slavery Society of Eastern Pennsylvania, New Jersey and Delaware," in the *Pennsylvania Freeman*, August 13, 1846.

41. See Mott's "Discourse on Woman" (1849), in Dana Greene, ed., *Lucretia Mott: Her Complete Speeches and Sermons* (New York: Edwin Mellen Press, 1980), 156.

42. See his remarks made at the Anti-Slavery Meeting in Cazenovia, New York, in 1847, in *National Anti-Slavery Bugle*, March 25, 1847. At this convention "women's rights" was discussed and debated, particularly the difference between the Liberty Party's new pro-woman suffrage position and the Garrisonians defense of "human rights." John Hathaway attended the first national woman's rights convention in Worcester in 1850, where he was chosen as president pro tem and later elected as one of the secretaries. See *Worcester WRC 1850*, 3, 5.

43. See Michael Grossberg, *Governing the Hearth: Law and the Family in Nineteenth-Century America* (Chapel Hill: University of North Carolina Press, 1985), 106.

44. See Neil H. Cogan, "'Standing' before the Constitution: Membership in the Community," *Law and History Review* 7 (Spring 1989): 5–9.

45. Gunderson, "Independence, Citizenship, and the American Revolution," 63–64.

46. See Michael Walzer, "Citizenship," in *Political Innovation and Conceptual Change*, ed. Terence Ball, James Farr, and Russell L. Hanson (Cambridge: Cambridge University Press, 1989), 214–16.

47. Linda Kerber, "'May all our Citizens be Soldiers, and all our Soldiers Citizens': The Ambiguities of Female Citizenship in the New Nation," in *Arms at Rest: Peacemaking and Peacekeeping in American History*, ed. Joan R. Challinor and Robert L. Beisner (Westport, Conn.: Greenwood Press, 1987), 3.

48. Levinson, *Constitutional Faith*, 93–95.

49. Gunderson, "Independence, Citizenship, and the American Revolution," 65–66. For the decision, see *Kempe's Lessee v. Kennedy et al.*, U.S. Supreme Court Reports 5 (Cranch) 70, 71–72 (1809). Significantly, the idea of single women having the vote was endorsed by St. George Tucker, one of the first Americans to publish a commentary on *Blackstone's Commentaries* in 1803. Tucker himself did not write the note advocating taxation and representation for single women; it was drafted by Edward Christian, an Englishman. See Richard H. Chused, "Married Women's

Property Law, 1800–1850," *Georgetown Law Journal* 71 (1983): 1388. Also see Elizabeth Kelley Bauer, *Commentaries on the Constitution, 1790–1860* (New York: Russell and Russell, 1965), 21, 260.

50. "Letter from R. M. M. Sanford," *Salem WRC 1850*, 34.

51. See Elisha P. Hurlbut, *Essays on Human Rights, and Their Political Guaranties* (New York, 1848), 109–12, 116, 122–23.

52. Peterson, *Portable Jefferson*, 555.

53. Walzer stresses how the ancient citizenship placed great importance on service, which applied to political discussion, participation in juries and councils, military service, and common worship. See Walzer, "Citizenship," 214. Also see definition of "conscribere" in *The Compact Edition of the Oxford English Dictionary*, 2 vols. (Oxford: Oxford University Press, 1971), 1:848.

54. "Suffrage—France and America," *United States Magazine and Democratic Review*, August 1851, 1.

55. The property requirement for black men was instituted in 1821 after the first revision of the state constitution, and it added the stipulation of three years of residence. At the 1846 constitutional convention, efforts to secure equal suffrage for black men were voted down, and the 1821 provision for a property and residency requirement remained unchanged. See Charles Z. Lincoln, *The Constitutional History of New York*, 5 vols. (Rochester, N.Y.: Lawyers Co-operative Pub. Co., 1906), 2:122–23.

56. See "Black Suffrage," *National Anti-Slavery Standard*, October 15, 1846. This article was reprinted from the *Albany Evening Journal*, where it was titled "The Elective Franchise," and covered the debate on extending equal suffrage to black men during the 1846 constitutional convention.

57. Senex [Anson Bingham], "Equality of Rights to Woman," *Lily*, December 1851, 92. Bingham is identified as Senex in Elizabeth Cady Stanton, Susan B. Anthony, and Matilda Joslyn Gage, eds., *History of Woman Suffrage*, 6 vols. (New York, 1881; reprint, New York: Arno Press, 1985), 1:688. Gordon and Holland also confirm his authorship and pseudonym as Senex, relying on Susan B. Anthony's diary and copybook of 1854, which includes the note "'Senex' of 'The Lily'—was Anson Bingham—of Nassau-Rensaeler C.N.Y." He practiced as a lawyer in Nassau after moving from Connecticut at an early age, and in 1856 he moved to Albany, New York, working in the law firm as a partner with his brother-in-law, Hugh W. McClennan, and the Honorable Andrew J. Colvin. He also served as a member of the assembly in 1859 and 1860. See Patricia G. Holland and Ann D. Gordon, eds., *The Papers of Elizabeth Cady Stanton and Susan B. Anthony* (Wilmington, Del., 1991, microfilm), reel 7, frame 879; William D. Murphy, *Biographical Sketches of the Officers and Members of the Legislature of the State of New York in 1861* (New York, 1861), 158–59.

58. This omission from Bingham's article is telling because a comparison between single women and black men was made during the 1846 constitutional convention. The issue was raised by a delegate who opposed equal suffrage for black men and women. But he pointed out that single women were "two to one in number to the negroes, and of infinitely greater intelligence." See Lincoln, *Constitutional History of New York*, 2:119.

59. This issue of manhood appeared in the remarks of Mr. Kennedy during the 1846 New York state constitutional convention. He used "manhood" to distinguish the entitlement to vote as based on property qualification for black male voters, and political rights emanating from being male. This theme of manhood was later applied to granting black men limited equality or certain minimum rights, which emerged in the famous Lincoln-Douglas debates of 1858. Later the theme of limited rights would expand to include the vote. See *Debates and Proceedings of the New-York State Convention, for the Revision of the Constitution* (Albany, N.Y., 1846), 783; also see Earl M. Maltz, "Fourteenth Amendment Concepts in the Antebellum Era," *American Journal of Legal History* 32 (1988): 307.

60. As an example of conservative arguments later adopted by proslavery forces, Maltz uses the argument made at the Massachusetts convention; see Maltz, "Fourteenth Amendment Concepts," 309–10. This theme, however, reappeared at the 1829–30 Virginia constitutional convention and was used by antisuffrage factions during the Dorr War. While most states removed property qualifications for the vote by the 1840s, this issue had not been resolved in Rhode Island, and it persisted in the larger constitutional theme of having a "vested stake" in society. Taxpayers and militiamen could be viewed as having a vested interest in the government. States that denied black men the right also refused to allow them to join the state militia. See *Proceedings and Debates of the Virginia State Convention*, 84; William M. Wiecek, "Popular Sovereignty in the Dorr War: Conservative Counterblast," *Rhode Island History* 32 (May 1973): 38.

61. Thomas Hobbes's *Leviathan* is quoted in Judith Richards, Lotte Mulligan, and John K. Graham, " 'Property' and 'People': Political Usages of Locke and Some Contemporaries," *Journal of the History of Ideas* 42 (January–March 1982): 34.

62. Hurlbut, *Essays on Human Rights*, 112, 115.

63. According to Levinson and Sollors, "descent" refers to "hereditary qualities, liabilities, and entitlements." My point here is that suffrage qualifications, and the political rhetoric defending the exclusion of women, free blacks, and other groups, did not adhere to the idea of the consenting community. On the contrary, the key criteria were "hereditary qualities" such as race and sex, two attributes imposed by "nature" and not freely chosen as part of one's identity. See Levinson, *Constitutional Faith*, 105.

64. *Syracuse WRC 1852*, 58.

65. *Compact Edition of the Oxford English Dictionary*, 1:421.

66. James H. Kettner, *The Development of American Citizenship, 1608–1870* (Chapel Hill: University of North Carolina Press, 1978), 287–88.

67. *Seneca Falls WRC 1848*, 3, 7.

68. For a brief discussion of Burke and the "Age of Rights," see Richard Dagger, "Rights," in Ball, Farr, and Hanson, *Political Innovation and Conceptual Change*, 301–2.

69. *Seneca Falls WRC 1848*, 7.

70. Charles Shively, ed., introduction to *The Collected Works of Lysander Spooner*, 6 vols. (Weston, Mass.: M & S Press, 1971), 4:10. As Wiecek has argued, the theme of national citizenship emerged earlier in the defense of the 1833 Prudence Crandall case but was not endorsed by a prominent court until 1844 in New York. See William M. Wiecek, *The Sources of Antislavery Constitutionalism in America, 1760–1848* (Ithaca: Cornell University Press, 1977), 164, 166–67.

71. Lysander Spooner, "The Unconstitutionality of Slavery," in Shively, *Collected Works of Lysander Spooner*, 4:36–37. Spooner believed that the Declaration of Independence was the constitution until 1782, when the Articles of Confederation were ratified, and thus argued that the declaration was a "substantive and operative component of the Constitution." Furthermore, he contended that the "Declaration overrode all inferior laws, including statutory enactments, court decisions, and inconsistent provisions in the federal and state constitutions." See Wiecek, *Sources of Antislavery Constitutionalism*, 264–65.

72. *Seneca Falls WRC 1848*, 4. It is important to note that Spooner quoted the same passage from Blackstone in "The Unconstitutionality of Slavery." See Wiecek, *Sources of Antislavery Constitutionalism*, 259.

73. Shively, *Collected Works of Lysander Spooner*, 8.

74. *Seneca Falls WRC 1848*, 6.

75. Hurlbut, *Essays on Human Rights*, 15, 26, 31.

76. Cogan, " 'Standing' before the Constitution," 5–9.

77. Spooner wrote, "The constitution is a contract; a written contract, consisting of a certain number of precise words, to which, and to which only, all the parties to it have, in theory, agreed.

Manifestly neither this contract, nor the meaning of its words, can be changed, without the consent of all the parties to it. Nor can it be changed on a representation, to be made by any number of them less than the whole, that they intended anything different from what they have said. To change it, on the presentation of a part, without the consent of the rest, would be a breach of contract to all the rest." See Spooner, "Unconstitutionality of Slavery," 123.

78. As Edward Mansfield argued, all contracts must be mutually binding, "for no contract is binding without the consent of both parties to it." Fraud could make a contract void, and Mansfield argued that fraud implied "the substitution of one person for another." See Edward D. Mansfield, *The Legal Rights, Liabilities, and Duties of Women; with an Introductory History of their Legal Condition in the Hebrew, Roman and Feudal Civil Systems* (Salem, Ohio, 1845), 236–38.

79. *Seneca Falls WRC 1848*, 7.

80. Hurlbut made the same argument, that the "moment we admit the principle that one natural right must necessarily be surrendered under government as the price of protection to another, we open the door to fraud and force." See A Phrenologist [Elisha Hurlbut], "On Rights and Government," *United States Magazine and Democratic Review*, November 1841, 475; Hurlbut, *Essays on Human Rights*, 15, 26, 31.

81. Shively, *Collected Works of Lysander Spooner*, 4:7; Wiecek, *Sources of Antislavery Constitutionalism*, 218.

82. *Seneca Falls WRC 1848*, 5.

83. For a reference to Bascom's newspaper and his election to the 1846 constitutional convention, see Gilbert Wilcoxen, "The Legal Profession," in *Papers Read Before the Seneca Falls Historical Society for the Year 1908: Proceedings of the Sixtieth Anniversary of the Woman's Rights Convention held in Seneca Falls in July, 1848* (Seneca Falls, N.Y., 1908), 15; Harrison Chamberlain, "The Seneca Falls Press," in *Papers Read Before the Seneca Falls Historical Society for the Year 1905* (Seneca Falls, N.Y., 1905), 2–3.

84. During the constitutional convention Bascom did offer an amendment for reforming the marriage contract, arguing that it should not be treated any differently than other contracts. Here he shared Spooner's concern for defending the right of contract. See Peggy Rabkin, "The Origins of Law Reform: The Social Significance of the Nineteenth Century Codification Movement and Its Contribution to the Passage of the Early Married Women's Property Acts," *Buffalo Law Review* 29 (Spring 1980): 736. Also see Wellman, "Women's Rights, Republicanism, and Revolutionary Rhetoric," 375; Elisabeth Griffiths, *In Her Own Right: The Life of Elizabeth Cady Stanton* (New York: Oxford University Press, 1984), 43. Bascom and his wife, Elizabeth, were active in the temperance movement in Seneca Falls, and several women who attended the Seneca Falls women's rights convention in July organized the Ladies Temperance Society of Seneca Falls in September 1848. See "Ladies Temperance Society of Seneca Falls," *Lily*, January 1, 1849, 1; Louise Noun, "Amelia Bloomer: A Biography," pt. 1, "The Lily of Seneca Falls," *Annals of Iowa* 47 (Winter 1985): 582–84.

85. Hurlbut, *Essays on Human Rights*, 135.

86. One of the resolutions referred to the "sacred right to the elective franchise," and the Declaration of Sentiments used the phrase "inalienable right to the elective franchise." See *Seneca Falls WRC 1848*, 4, 6.

87. Ibid., 4.

88. Wellman notes that twenty-three of the eighty-three signers of the Declaration of Sentiments at the Seneca Falls convention were associated with this wing of the Friends, and that Thomas McClintock had been a minister of the Junius Monthly Meeting and a clerk of the Genesee Yearly Meeting from 1839 to 1843; his wife, Mary Ann, had been an assistant clerk of the Women's Yearly Meeting. See Judith Wellman, "The Mystery of the Seneca Falls Women's

Rights Convention: Who Came and Why?" (personal paper in possession of author) and "The Seneca Falls Women's Rights Convention: A Study of Social Networks," *Journal of Women's History* 3 (Spring 1991): 14, 27; also see A. Day Bradley, "Progressive Friends in Michigan and New York," *Quaker History* 52 (Autumn 1963): 97.

89. Mott refers to McClintock as the author of the "Basis" in one of her letters. See Anna Davis Hallowell, ed., *James and Lucretia Mott: Life and Letters* (Boston: Houghton Mifflin, 1884), 308. For references to the McClintocks' speeches given at the Seneca Falls convention, see *Seneca Falls WRC 1848*, 5, 9.

90. "Basis of Religious Association" (1848), in *Proceedings of the Yearly Meeting of Congregational Friends, held at Waterloo, N.Y., on the 1st, 2d and 3d of the 6th Month, 1851.* (Auburn, N.Y., 1851), 20.

91. See *Proceedings of the Yearly Meeting of Congregational Friends, held at Waterloo, N.Y., on the 5th, 6th and 7th of the 6th Month, 1853.* (Auburn, N.Y., 1853), 7–8.

92. This phrase appeared in the call to the national convention held in Worcester, and although the call was unsigned, Davis was without question the author. It not only is similar in style to her other writings, but she was recognized as the prime mover of the convention. In her report for the anniversary celebration of the national conventions in 1870, which was quoted in the *History of Woman Suffrage*, she wrote that after the initial meeting for discussing the convention, the "work soon devolved on one person." That person was Paulina Wright Davis. For a contemporary reference to Davis as the prime mover, see Harriet Farley to Caroline H. Dall, September 18, 1850, Caroline H. Dall Papers, 1811–1917, Massachusetts Historical Society, Boston, Mass. Also see *Worcester WRC 1850*, 5; Paulina Wright Davis, *A History of the National Woman's Rights Movement, for Twenty years, with the Proceedings of the Decade Meeting held at Apollo Hall, October 20, 1870, from 1850 to 1870, with an Appendix Containing the History of the Movement during the Winter of 1871, in the National Capital* (New York, 1871), 13; Stanton, Anthony, and Gage, *History of Woman Suffrage*, 1:216.

93. Paulina W. Davis, "Address," in *Worcester WRC 1850*, 7. Davis also wrote a more extensive historical analysis of class and caste, "Despotism and Democracy" (n.d.), Paulina Kellogg Wright Davis Papers, 1813–1876, Vassar College Library, Poughkeepsie, N.Y. Some of the arguments used in her "Address" for the convention are similar to "Despotism and Democracy."

94. Maltz, "Fourteenth Amendment Concepts," 317, 326.

95. Davis, "Address," 8.

96. 59 Mass. (5 Cush.) 206 (1849); also see Maltz, "Fourteenth Amendment Concepts," 325.

97. The importance of caste is borne out by the Roberts case, when Charles Sumner, arguing for the plaintiff, devoted a large portion of his argument to defining "caste." See "Argument of Charles Sumner, Esq., Against the Constitutionality of Separate Colored Schools," *Emancipator and Republican*, December 20, 1849.

98. Grossberg identifies this pattern in nineteenth-century family law; see Grossberg, *Governing the Hearth*, 290.

99. Maltz identifies the "pure vested rights" theory, and he refers to the New York decision striking down the Married Woman's Property Act in 1849 but does not see this as vested rights theory. However, the decision fits within this framework, since the judge was protecting the citizen from "arbitrary legislation." See Maltz, "Fourteenth Amendment Concepts," 317, 308. For the case, see *White v. White*, 5 Barb. (N.Y.), 474, 484 (1849).

100. See the address read to the women's rights convention at Worcester by Mrs. Abby H. Price of Hopedale, Mass., in *Worcester WRC 1850*, 32, 34.

101. See Stanton's letter to the convention, in *Worcester WRC 1850*, 51.

102. *Rochester WRC 1848*, 11.

103. *Worcester WRC 1850*, 14.

104. Ibid., 5, 18–19; also see "Paulina Wright Davis" and "Elizabeth Blackwell," in James, James, and Boyer, *Notable American Women*, 1:444, 161–65.

105. *Worcester WRC 1850*, 18.

106. Mott's relationship to Nathaniel and Eliza Barney is demonstrated through their correspondence, as recorded in Hallowell, *James and Lucretia Mott*. Also see Margaret Hope Bacon, *Valiant Friend: The Life of Lucretia Mott* (New York: Walker, 1980); Walter M. Merrill and Louis Ruchames, eds., *The Letters of William Lloyd Garrison*, 8 vols. (Cambridge: Belknap Press of Harvard University Press, 1971–75), 3:272. For a reference to Sarah Earle's relation to Mott, and John Milton Earle's political career, see Edwin B. Bronner, *Thomas Earle as a Reformer* (Philadelphia, 1948), 18–19, 24. Sarah Earle was on the executive committee of the Worcester County Anti-Slavery Society, South Division, from 1841 until her death in 1859. She also organized the Worcester Female Anti-Slavery Sewing Circle and helped coordinate the Worcester Anti-Slavery Fair Committee beginning in 1848, and she helped found the Worcester City Anti-Slavery Society in 1853, which held the first meeting in her home. See Worcester County Anti-Slavery Society, South Division Record Book, 1840–1865, and Earle Family Papers, both in the Worcester Historical Society Manuscript Collection, Worcester, Mass. For an account of the school board dispute in Nantucket and Barney's and Earle's involvement, see Barbara Linebaugh, *The African School and the Integration of the Nantucket Public Schools, 1825–1847* (Boston: Boston University, 1978), 17, 23, 29, 39, 41, 56.

107. See extracts of Hunt's address on the medical education of women, in *Worcester WRC 1850*, 46–47.

108. Harriot K. Hunt, *Glances and Glimpses; or, Fifty Years Social, Including Twenty Years of Professional Life* (Boston: John P. Jewett, 1856), 218, 264, 266, 293–94, 299–300. Also see "Harriot K. Hunt," in James, James, and Boyer, *Notable American Women*, 2:235–37.

109. Maltz, "Fourteenth Amendment Concepts," 322–23.

110. See Amringe, "Woman's Rights in Church and State," 40, 42.

111. *Worcester WRC 1851*, 11.

112. See resolutions from the business committee (whose members included E. Oakes Smith, Lucy Stone, Paulina W. Davis, Harriot K. Hunt, Gerrit Smith, Jane Elizabeth Jones, Sarah L. Miller, James Mott, Ernestine Rose, Elizabeth W. Phillips, Pliny Sexton, and Benjamin Jones), which read, "*Resolved*, That it is the right of every woman holding property, and as a citizen of the Republic, to resist taxation, till such time she is fully recognized at the Ballot Box." Also see address of E. O. Smith, letter sent from Elizabeth Cady Stanton, and comments by Clarina H. I. Nichols. See *Syracuse WRC 1852*, 13, 15, 19, 30.

113. *Worcester WRC 1850*, 28.

114. See "Address by Ann Preston," in *West Chester WRC 1852*, 27.

115. Child, "Home and Politics," 64–65, 68.

116. See *Worcester WRC 1850*, 40.

117. "Women's Rights Convention," *Daily Evening Travellor* (Boston), September 19 and 21, in Miscellaneous Clippings, 1849–1860, Caroline H. Dall Papers.

Chapter 3

1. Charles Giles, *The Convention of Drunkards: A Satirical Essay on Intemperance* (New York, 1840), 1, 11, 17, 46, 63, esp. 20–21.

2. For a discussion of greatness, self-mastery, and speech as the crucial ingredients to civility,

see Hannah Arendt, *The Human Condition* (Chicago: University of Chicago Press, 1958), 19, 26–27, 30–32, 36–37. Also see Wendy Brown, *Manhood and Politics: A Feminist Reading in Political Theory* (Totowa, N.J.: Rowan and Littlefield, 1988), 24–25, 82–83.

3. Giles, *Convention of Drunkards*, 32, 34. Frances Wright (a Scottish writer and reformer) lectured to large audiences in American cities as early as 1828. Her name became an epithet for public women who behaved as men. She was jeered at and condemned as a "female monster." See Celia Morris Eckhardt, *Fanny Wright: Rebel in America* (Cambridge: Harvard University Press, 1984), 1, 3.

4. For classical allusions to a woman's body as a "net," "prison," or "tomb," see Wendy Brown, *Manhood and Politics*, 55. For an example of the nineteenth-century medical theory that placed a woman's womb at the center of her existence, see John Wiltbank, M.D., *Peculiarities of the Female: A Lecture Introductory to the Course on Obstetrics in the Medical Department of Pennsylvania College, for the Session of 1845-46* (Philadelphia, 1845), 14. Also see Susan E. Cayleff, *Wash and Be Healed: The Water-Cure Movement and Women's Health* (Philadelphia: Temple University Press, 1887), 11; Carroll Smith-Rosenberg, "Puberty to Menopause: The Cycle of Femininity in Nineteenth Century America," in *Clio's Consciousness Raised: New Perspectives in the History of Women*, ed. Mary Hartman and Lois W. Banner (New York: Harper and Row, 1974), 24.

5. *New York Herald*, September 14, 1852.

6. Nineteenth-century scientists developed a perverse fascination with the similarities between the reproductive functions of animals and women, which led them to conclude that women were less capable than men of transcending their brutish nature. Indeed, as Thomas Laqueur writes, medical science made the case that "women would behave like brutes were it not for the thin veneer of civilization." See Thomas Laqueur, "Orgasm, Generation, and the Politics of Reproductive Biology," *Representations* 14 (Spring 1986): 27–31.

7. Jürgen Habermas, *The Structural Transformation of the Public Sphere: An Inquiry into a Category of Bourgeois Society*, trans. Thomas Burger (Cambridge: MIT Press, 1991), 37, 55–56, 85, 109–12.

8. Desley Deacon, "Politicizing Gender," *Genders*, no. 6 (Fall 1989): 6.

9. Habermas, *Structural Transformation of the Public Sphere*, 28, 43, 48–51, 56, 109–11.

10. Ibid., 129–32.

11. "Political Non-Existence of Women" (extracts from Miss Martineau's "Society in America"), *Lily*, November 1850, 81.

12. See Andrew Burstein, *The Inner Jefferson: Portrait of a Grieving Optimist* (Charlottesville: University Press of Virginia, 1995), 113.

13. Publicity and politics were combined to create an image of the polls as places filled with "rowdies" (allusion to street thugs or rioters) and Congress as a domain for "coarse and indecent language." See quote from the *New York Herald* in 1850 in Deacon, "Politicizing Gender," 7. The term "loose woman" referred to women who moved too freely with their bodies and spoke too openly by expressing their opinions. The term "loose" had links to prostitutes who propositioned men with sexually suggestive speech and moved their bodies more freely to display their wares and attract male customers. For a discussion of "loose women" and its contrast to the socially sanctioned behavior of women, see Sandra Lee Bartky, "Foucault, Femininity, and the Modernization of Patriarchal Power," in *Feminism and Foucault: Reflections on Resistance*, ed. Irene Diamond and Lee Quinby (Boston: Northeastern University Press, 1988), 66–67. The theme of "disconnected women" applied to women jailed for debt, which usually referred to widows and deserted women. This practice continued into the 1840s, although reform efforts began in the 1820s. See Richard H. Chused, "Married Women's Property Law, 1800-1850," *Georgetown Law Journal* 71 (1983): 1400, 1407.

14. Several historians have noted that prostitutes were seen as "disorderly women," a term that

implied their ability to bring sexual disorder into public places. See Marcia Carlisle, "Disorderly City, Disorderly Women: Prostitution in Antebellum Philadelphia," *Pennsylvania Magazine of History and Biography* 110 (October 1986): 549–68; Carroll Smith-Rosenberg, "Beauty, the Beast, and the Militant Woman: A Case Study in Sex Roles and Social Stress in Jacksonian America," *American Quarterly* 23 (October 1971): 562–84; Barbara Meil Hobson, *Uneasy Virtue: The Politics of Prostitution and the American Reform Tradition* (Chicago: University of Chicago Press, 1990).

15. See Lynda Lange, "Rousseau: Women and the General Will," in *The Sexism of Social and Political Theory: Women and Reproduction from Plato to Nietzsche*, ed. Lorenne M. G. Clark and Lynda Lange (Toronto: University of Toronto Press, 1979), 43–49.

16. See Habermas, *Structural Transformation of the Public Sphere*, 31. Also see Patricia M. Spacks, "The Talent of Ready Utterance: Eighteenth-Century Female Gossip," in *Women and Society in the Eighteenth Century*, ed. Ian P. H. Duffy (Bethlehem, Pa.: Lawrence Henry Gipson Institute, 1983), 1.

17. For a discussion of Angelina Grimké and the burning of Pennsylvania Hall, see Jean Fagan Yellin, *Women and Sisters: The Antislavery Feminists in American Culture* (New Haven: Yale University Press, 1989), 44–46, 48–49. Also see Ira V. Brown, "Racism and Sexism: The Case of Pennsylvania Hall," *Phylon* 37 (1976): 126–36; *History of Pennsylvania Hall, which was Destroyed by a Mob, on the 17th of May, 1838* (Philadelphia, 1838).

18. See a reprinting of the negative report from the *Sunday Times* of Philadelphia in the *National Anti-Slavery Standard*, November 4, 1854.

19. Sarah M. Grimké, *Letters on the Equality of the Sexes, and the Condition of Woman. Addressed to Mary S. Parker, President of the Boston Female Anti-Slavery Society* (Boston, 1838), 20. The same argument of "self-defense" against women demanding equality reappeared in the press in response to women's rights conventions; see *New York Times*, August 2. 1852.

20. See account of antislavery anniversary in New York City in a letter reprinted from the *Globe* in the *National Anti-Slavery Standard*, May 16, 1850.

21. Ibid.

22. See "Male Impersonation," *National Anti-Slavery Bugle*, April 28, 1853. Also see article in the *Lily* that doubts a report in a New York newspaper that a woman tried to vote "in male attire." For activists this stratagem, if based on a true story, hardly presented a solution (based on common sense) for securing women's political rights. See "Crossdressing at the Polls," *Lily*, December 1, 1852, 102.

23. For an excerpt from Jane Swisshelm's article, see "Women's Dresses," *Water-Cure Journal*, February 1850, 58. For an argument that women's dress should be a matter of "beauty, economy, comfort, or convenience," see R. B. Gleason, ibid., February 1851, 31; also see R. B. Gleason, "Women's Dresses," ibid., April 1851, 81, and Mary G. Nichols, "The New Costume," ibid., August 1851, 30.

24. "Mrs. Kemble and Her New Costume," *Lily*, December 1, 1849, 94. In September 1849 "Mrs. Butler's Pantaloons" appeared in the *Home Journal*, which criticized Fanny Kemble (married name Butler) for her masculine costume. See Faye E. Dudden, *Women in the American Theatre: Actresses and Audiences, 1790–1870* (New Haven: Yale University Press (1994), 53, 203.

25. Most previous studies identify 1850 and 1851 as the beginning of the "new costume" campaign, because they missed the influence of the Kemble controversy. See Louise Noun, "Amelia Bloomer: A Biography," pt. 1, "The Lily of Seneca Falls," *Annals of Iowa* 47 (Winter 1985): 595–97; Robert E. Riegel, "Women's Clothes and Women's Rights," *American Quarterly* 15 (Fall 1963): 391–92; Sylvia D. Hoffert, *When Hens Crow: The Woman's Rights Movement in Antebellum America* (Bloomington: Indiana University Press, 1995), 23.

26. E.C.S. [Elizabeth Cady Stanton], "Our Costume," *Lily*, April 1851, 31.

27. Ibid.; also see Senex [Anson Bingham], "Equality of Right to Woman," *Lily*, October 1851, 76.

28. M. S. Gove Nichols, "A Lecture on Woman's Dresses," *Water-Cure Journal*, August 1851, 35.

29. See Lange, "Rousseau," 46.

30. See Jay Fliegelman, "Familial Politics, Seduction, and the Novel: The Anxious Agenda of an American Literary Culture," in *The American Revolution: Its Character and Limits*, ed. Jack P. Greene (New York: New York University Press, 1987), 350. For Rousseau's celebration of the enclosed garden, see Tony Tanner, "Julie and 'La Maison Paternelle': Another Look at Rousseau's *La Nouvelle Héloise*," in *The Family in Political Thought*, ed. Jean Bethke Elshtain (Amherst: University of Massachusetts Press, 1982), 115.

31. Transcendentalists believed that "nature was the school of life" and that there should be a direct correspondence between things in nature and human representations of nature. See Catherine L. Albanese, *Corresponding Motion: Transcendental Religion and the New America* (Philadelphia: Temple University Press, 1977), 6–7, 16.

32. See "Bloomer Costume Meeting at Hopedale," *Practical Christian*, July 19, 1851.

33. Albanese found this pattern in her study on the early republican Masonic lodges, which presented the view that the members discovered a more perfect "representation of the world" when entering the lodge. See Catherine L. Albanese, "Whither the Sons (and Daughters)? Republican Nature and the Quest for the Ideal," in Jack P. Greene, *American Revolution*, 370.

34. One writer captured this paradox, asking, "Does a woman sin less against propriety when she bares her arms and bosom to the gaze, than when she shows a neatly dressed foot and ankle?" See "Woman's Dress," *Water-Cure Journal*, October 1851, 87.

35. "Dress—To Readers and Writers," reply to communication published in the *Dollar Newspaper* from a person in East Marlborough, Chester Co., Pa., reprinted in the *Water-Cure Journal*, May 1852, 115.

36. Identified as reprinted from the *Art of Living*, see "The Lowell Bloomer Institute," *Lily*, December 15, 1851. Other reformers made similar observations about the rule of "Dame Fashion" and the "enthralling" nature of women's dress. See Gleason, "Women's Dresses," 81; Nichols, "New Costume," 30.

37. See E.C.S., "Our Costume," 31.

38. Helene E. Roberts, "The Exquisite Slave: The Role of Clothes in the Making of the Victorian Woman," *Signs: Journal of Women in Culture and Society* 2 (Spring 1977): 557, 562.

39. E.C.S., "Our Costume," 31.

40. Elizabeth Cady Stanton, "Our Young Girls," *Lily*, March 1, 1853, 9.

41. For a discussion of nature and the sublime, see Albanese, "Whither the Sons (and Daughters)?," 373. Also see Genevieve Lloyd, "Selfhood, War, and Masculinity," in *Feminist Challenges: Social and Political Theory*, ed. Carole Pateman and Elizabeth Gross (Boston: Northeastern University Press, 1987), 66–69. For a reference to John Adams's suggestion to use a mountain labeled "Virtue" as part of the official seal of the new nation, see Samuel Levinson, *Constitutional Faith* (Princeton: Princeton University Press, 1988), 117.

42. See Karen Halttunen, *Confidence Men and Painted Women: A Study of Middle-Class Culture in America, 1830–1870* (New Haven: Yale University Press, 1982).

43. For the concealment of labor through the pastoral narrative, Raymond Williams quotes Alexander Pope, who wrote, "We must therefore use some illusion to render a Pastoral delightful; and this consists in exposing the best side of a shepherd's life, and in concealing its miseries." See Raymond Williams, *The Country and the City* (New York: Oxford University Press, 1973), 19; also see Jeanne Boydston, *Home and Work: Housework, Wages, and the Ideology of Labor in the Early Republic* (New York: Oxford University Press, 1990), 147.

44. Helena Michie best captures the contrast between vanity and the devaluation of female labor when she describes a *Punch* cartoon "The Haunted Lady of 'The Ghost' in the Looking-Glass," published in 1863. Here a young lady is looking at herself in the mirror in her new gown, and she sees the dead figure of the woman who presumably made the dress gazing back at her. The women look alike, and as Michie writes, "The dead seamstress is merely the young lady 'undressed' of her finery and her class position." See Helena Michie, *The Flesh Made Word: Female Figures and Women's Bodies* (New York: Oxford University Press, 1987), 56. For the connection between reproduction and the curse of pain, see Mary Poovey, *Uneven Developments: The Ideological Work of Gender in Mid-Victorian England* (Chicago: University of Chicago Press, 1988), esp. chap. 2, "Scenes of an Indelicate Character: The Medical Treatment of Victorian Women," 24–50.

45. Stanton, "Our Young Girls," 9.

46. Nichols, "Lecture on Woman's Dresses," 35.

47. "Letter from Harriet Torrey," *Lily*, March 1, 1853, 11.

48. "Bloomer Costume Meeting at Hopedale."

49. For a discussion of political caricature, see Gary Bunker, "Antebellum Caricature and Woman's Sphere," *Journal of Women's History* 3 (Winter 1992): 6–43. Also see Hoffert, *When Hen's Crow*, 24, 101, and see diagrams accompanying Nichols, "Lecture on Woman's Dresses," 35.

50. Reprinted from the *Arkansas Intelligencer*, see "Mrs. Bloomer at the Woman's Convention," *Water-Cure Journal*, February 1852, 44.

51. Martha C. Wright to Lucretia Mott, March 8, 1854, Garrison Family Papers, Sophia Smith Collection, Smith College, Northhampton, Mass. "Shanghai" was probably a slang term for Oriental woman, which identified feminists with the Orient through their Turkish pants.

52. Noun, "Amelia Bloomer," 599.

53. Not only the popular press but even some publications that favored women's rights treated the Bloomer costume as another fashion. In 1857 the *Woman's Advocate* of Philadelphia wrote, "But our Bloomer Sisters insist on the entire adoption of their fashion—for it is a fashion, as much as long skirts and hoops." See Bertha Monica Stearns, "Philadelphia Magazines for Ladies, 1830–1860," *Pennsylvania Magazine of History and Biography* 64 (July 1945): 218. Also see Riegel, "Women's Clothes and Women's Rights," 393.

54. See reprinted account from the *Tribune* in the *Water-Cure Journal*, March 1853, 70.

55. Martha C. Wright to Lucretia Mott, March 8, 1854, Garrison Family Papers.

56. See "Mrs. Stanton's Reminiscences," in *History of Woman Suffrage*, 6 vols., ed. Elizabeth Cady Stanton, Susan B. Anthony, and Matilda Joslyn Gage (New York, 1881; reprint, New York: Arno Press, 1985), 1:837, 841. See also "A Letter from Mrs. Stanton to Gerrit Smith," broadside (1855), Scrapbook 1, Douglass Library Collection, Rutgers University, New Brunswick, N.J., which was used as part of the Papers of Elizabeth Cady Stanton and Susan B. Anthony, and "Extract of a Letter from H. M. Weber," in *Worcester WRC 1850*, 77. For a comparison between the Bloomer dress and the Weber outfit, see Mary B. Williams, "The Bloomer and Weber Dresses. A Glance at their Respective Merits and Advantages," *Water-Cure Journal*, August 1851, 33.

57. It is clear that Smith's "revealing" dress posed a problem for advocates such as Anthony who believed that the Bloomer outfit represented greater modesty and republican simplicity. In the *New York Herald*, Smith was described as a woman "who displays a magnificent bust and a dignified person"; see *New York Herald*, September 10, 1852. Anthony's position reflected the struggle over the meaning of "modesty" between defenders of fashion and the advocates of the reform dress. See Ida Husted Harper, *The Life and Work of Susan B. Anthony*, 2 vols. (Indianapolis: Hollenbeck Press, 1898), 1:72; Martha C. Wright to Lucretia Mott, January 29, 1856, Garrison Family Papers.

58. For the definition of the "reading public" as the public use of reason through writing and publishing, see John Christian Laursen, "The Subversive Kant: The Vocabulary of 'Public' and

'Publicity," *Political Theory* 14 (November 1986): 584–85; also see Habermas, *Structural Transformation of the Public Sphere*, 28–29, 36–37, 42–43. For an emphasis on the anonymous nature of the literary public sphere in eighteenth-century America, see Michael Warner, *The Letters of the Republic: Publication and the Public Sphere in Eighteenth-Century America* (Cambridge: Harvard University Press, 1990), x, xiii.

59. Horace Greeley, "The Sphere of Woman," *Union Magazine*, June 1848, 270.

60. Habermas stresses the importance of "self-understanding" as crucial to publicity, for he claims the "public held a mirror to itself" and essentially "read and debated about itself." See Habermas, *Structural Transformation of the Public Sphere*, 43.

61. Greeley, "Sphere of Woman," 271. For accounts of Fuller's life and writings, see Bell Gale Chevigny, *The Woman and the Myth: Margaret Fuller's Life and Writings* (Old Westbury, N.Y.: Feminist Press, 1976); Paula Blanchard, *Margaret Fuller: From Transcendentalism to Revolution* (Reading, Mass.: Addison-Wesley, 1987); Joel Myerson, ed., *Critical Essays on Margaret Fuller* (Boston: G. K. Hall, 1980).

62. For an insightful examination of Fuller and her relationship to the world of letters, see Cheryl Fish, "'Unconnected Intelligence': Darting (Dial)logues in Margaret Fuller's Letters and Early Criticism" (personal paper in possession of author).

63. Perry Miller, ed., *The American Transcendentalists: Their Prose and Poetry* (Garden City, N.Y.: Doubleday Anchor, 1957).

64. See letter from Margaret Fuller to Sophia Ripley (1839) about the conversation group, in Mary Kelley, ed., *The Portable Margaret Fuller* (New York: Penguin, 1994), 494–95; Charles Capper, "Margaret Fuller as Cultural Reformer: The Conversations in Boston," *American Quarterly* 39 (Winter 1987): 514–15. Caroline Dall published an account of her participation in Fuller's conversations; see Caroline H. Dall, *Margaret and Her Friends or Ten Conversations with Margaret Fuller upon the Mythology of the Greeks and Its Expression in Art* (Boston, 1895). Stanton also established her own "conversational" in Seneca Falls.

65. Kelley, *Portable Margaret Fuller*, 499.

66. Greeley, "Sphere of Woman," 273.

67. "Our Public Men. Edward Everett," *Brother Jonathan*, July 29, 1843, 376, 378. Neal was a friend of Paulina Wright Davis, and he sent a letter to the Syracuse women's rights convention in 1852. See *Syracuse WRC 1852*, 24–28. Also see letters and "Biography of John Neal, 1793–1876," with a note that seems to be written by Davis that praises him for being "one of the first and foremost champions of women's rights," in Paulina Kellogg Wright Davis Papers, 1813–1876, Vassar College Library, Poughkeepsie, N.Y.

68. "American Women," *United States Magazine and Democratic Review*, August 1839, 136, 138–39.

69. Ibid., 129–30.

70. Ibid., 140–41.

71. For an excellent review of this literature, see Anne M. Boylan, "Women and Politics in the Era before Seneca Falls," *Journal of the Early Republic* 10 (Fall 1990): 370, 372.

72. Ibid., 365, 367, 373. Also see Mary P. Ryan, "A Women's Awakening: Evangelical Religion and the Families of Utica, New York, 1800–1840," *American Quarterly* 30 (Winter 1978): 618, 622–23.

73. Constitution of the Philadelphia Female Anti-Slavery Society; minutes of the Philadelphia Female Anti-Slavery Society, December 14, 1833; and reprinted in their annual reports. See, for example, Philadelphia Female Anti-Slavery Society, *23rd Annual Report* (Philadelphia, 1857), 19.

74. For Worcester Anti-Slavery Cent-a-Week Society, formed by Sarah Earle in her house, see James Mooney, "Antislavery in Worcester County, Massachusetts: A Case Study" (Ph.D. diss., Clark University, 1971), 43. For a reference to the school for black children, see Ira V. Brown,

"Cradle of Feminism: The Philadelphia Female Anti-Slavery Society, 1833–1840," *Pennsylvania Magazine of History and Biography* 102 (April 1978): 149–50. Lucretia Mott was also involved in the Association for the Relief and Employment of Poor Women, a benevolence association, and it is clear that antislavery activists were concerned with the poverty of "colored women" in Philadelphia. See *Pennsylvania Freeman*, January 8, June 25, 1846. The Tatnuck Ladies Sewing Circle, of which Abby Kelley Foster was a member, formed the Tatnuck Female Benevolent Society in May 1847, which aided the sick and provided clothing for their families. See Records of Tatnuck Ladies Sewing Circle, Worcester, Mass., Collection, American Antiquarian Society, Worcester, Mass. ·

75. For the best discussion of the antislavery fairs, see Deborah Bingham Van Broekhoven, "Spheres and Webs: The Organization of the Antislavery Fairs, 1830–1860" (personal paper in possession of author), 5, 14–16, 18–20. For evidence of the connection of women's later support of women's rights and sewing circles, see "Constitution of the Anti-Slavery Sewing Circle," drafted by J. Elizabeth Jones, *Anti-Slavery Bugle*, January 22, 1847. For the organization of regular "sewing meetings" by the Philadelphia Female Anti-Slavery Society, see Minute Book Records of Philadelphia Female Anti-Slavery Society, June 13, 1835, Pennsylvania Historical Society, Philadelphia, Pa.

76. Annual Report for 1836, in Minute Book Records of Philadelphia Female Anti-Slavery Society, January 12, 1837.

77. Philadelphia Female Anti-Slavery Society, *15th Annual Report* (Philadelphia, 1849), 7.

78. The same sense of moral economy and scarcity of funds affected the production of the *Liberty Bell*, which was published by the Boston Female Anti-Slavery Society. In comparison with other gift books, it was far less ornate in design and decoration. See Ralph Thompson, *American Literary Annuals and Gift Books, 1825–1865* (New York: H. W. Wilson, 1936), 85.

79. Ira V. Brown, "Cradle of Feminism," 148–49, 152–53. Mary Grew, who wrote the annual reports for the Philadelphia Female Anti-Slavery Society and played a major role in organizing the Philadelphia fairs, also served as coeditor of the *Pennsylvania Freeman* during the 1840s. Grew later supported women's rights.

80. For accounts of phonography, see "Universal Language and Phonography," *Pennsylvania Freeman*, April 2, 1846; this essay emphasizes how "there will be an exhibition of a class of colored persons, (adults) who have learned to read Phonography in a few weeks." In Ohio, lessons on phonography were given in Salem; see "Phonography," *Anti-Slavery Bugle*, November 5, 1847.

81. For a discussion of the abolitionist emblem, see Yellin, *Women and Sisters*, 3–5, 14–15.

82. Joel Bernard, "Authority, Autonomy, and Radical Commitment: Stephen and Abby Kelley Foster," *Proceedings of the American Antiquarian Society* 90 (October 1980): 349–50, 358–59, 375.

83. Margaret Hope Bacon, *I Speak for My Slave Sister: The Life of Abby Kelley Foster* (New York: Thomas Crowell, 1974), 45.

84. Jane Hanna Pease, "The Freshness of Fanaticism: Abby Kelley Foster: An Essay in Reform" (Ph.D. diss., University of Rochester, 1969; facsimile by University Microfilms, Ann Arbor, 1972), 31.

85. *Worcester WRC 1851*, 102; Bernard, "Authority, Autonomy, and Radical Commitment," 373, 383–84.

86. See Dana Greene, ed., introduction to *Lucretia Mott: Her Complete Speeches and Sermons* (New York: Edwin Mellen Press, 1980), 2.

87. Bernard, "Authority, Autonomy, and Radical Commitment," 363.

88. Kelley continued to use this style at the women's rights conventions, for at the 1851 gathering she is recorded as saying, "I hope, however, that you do not feel that I speak to you in anger. Oh, no; it is in the hope of inducing you to be willing to assume more responsibilities, to be more willing to have a sleepless night occasionally, and days of toil and trouble." See *Worcester WRC 1851*, 102.

89. Martha C. Wright to Lucretia Mott, February 2, 1852, Garrison Family Papers.

90. Ibid.

91. Kathryn Sklar discusses the importance of the Quaker background of these women as well their rather prominent and wealthy family connections. See Kathryn Kish Sklar, "'Women Who Speak for an Entire Nation': American and British Women Compared at the World Anti-Slavery Convention, London, 1840," in *The Abolitionist Sisterhood: Women's Political Culture in Antebellum America*, ed. Jean Fagan Yellin and John C. Van Horne (Ithaca: Cornell University Press, 1994), 316.

92. Stanton, Anthony, and Gage, *History of Woman Suffrage*, 1:54.

93. Anna Davis Hallowell, ed., *James and Lucretia Mott: Life and Letters* (Boston: Houghton Mifflin, 1884), 112–14, 124.

94. Sklar, "'Women Who Speak for an Entire Nation,'" 307.

95. Frederick B. Tolles, ed. "Slavery and 'The Woman Question': Lucretia Mott's Diary of Her Visit to Great Britain to Attend the World's Anti-Slavery Convention of 1840." *Journal of the Friends Historical Society Supplement*, no. 23 (1952): 9.

96. Hallowell, *James and Lucretia Mott*, 124–25.

97. Ibid., 150.

98. *Memorial of Sarah Pugh: A Tribute of Respect from Her Cousins* (Philadelphia, 1888), 26.

99. Hallowell, *James and Lucretia Mott*, 162.

100. Sklar, "'Women Who Speak for an Entire Nation,'" 311–12, 320–21.

101. Sklar argues that the petition campaign in England "reinforced their respect for government." See ibid., 330.

102. For the use of deferential language in female antislavery petitions, see Deborah Bingham Van Broekhoven, "'Let Your Name Be Enrolled': Method and Ideology in Women's Petitioning" (personal paper in possession of author), 4.

103. See John Quincy Adams, *Speech of John Quincy Adams, of Massachusetts, Upon the Right of the People to Petition; on the Freedom of Speech and Debates in the House of Representatives of the United States; on Resolutions of Seven State Legislatures, and the Petitions of More Than One Hundred Thousand Petitioners, relating to the Annexation of Texas* (Washington, D.C., 1838; reprint, New York: Arno Press, 1969), 64–74; also see his account of his "defense of the rights and fair fame of women," in *Memoirs of John Quincy Adams, Comprising Portions of His Diary from 1795–1848*, 10 vols., ed. Charles Francis Adams (Freeport, N.Y.: Books for Libraries, 1969), 10:36–37.

104. John Quincy Adams, *Speech*, 63.

105. When Adams spoke at a picnic in his honor organized by female petitioners from Quincy, Massachusetts, he clearly divided antislavery petitioning from other political concerns (banks, currency exchange, subtreasuries, and internal improvements), which he argued "profoundly agitate the men of the country." As for women, he claimed, "Women, so far from intermeddling with them, could scarcely be prevailed upon to bestow a thought upon them. . . . But, for objects of kindness, of benevolence, of compassion, women, so far from being debarred by any rule of delicacy from exercising the right of petition or remonstrance, are, by the law of their nature, fitted above all others for that exercise." See Samuel Flagg Bemis, *John Quincy Adams and the Union* (New York: Knopf, 1956), 373.

106. John Quincy Adams, *Speech*, 81.

107. John Quincy Adams, *The Social Compact, Exemplified in the Constitution of the Commonwealth of Massachusetts; with Remarks on the Theories of Divine Right of Hobbes and of Filmer, and the Counter Theories of Sidney, Locke, Montesquieu, and Rousseau, Concerning the Origin of Government: A Lecture, Delivered Before the Franklin Lyceum, at Providence, R.I., November 25, 1842* (Providence, R.I.: Knowles and Vose, 1842), 12–13, 18–19.

108. Ibid., 12–13, 17.

109. William Ellery Channing, "The Union," in *The Works of William E. Channing, D.D.*, 2 vols. (Boston, 1849), 1:338–43, 353. Originally published as *Correspondence between John Quincy Adams, Esquire, President of the United States, and several citizens of Massachusetts, concerning the Charge of a Design to dissolve the Union alleged to have existed in that State* (Boston, 1829).

110. "Letter Writing; in Its Effects on National Character," *Ladies Magazine and Literary Gazette*, June 1831, 244.

111. Keith Melder, *The Beginnings of Sisterhood: The American Women's Rights Movement, 1800–1850* (New York: Schocken, 1977), 74.

112. "The Right of Women to Vote," *Anti-Slavery Bugle*, November 23, 1850. For the eighteenth-century antecedents of sympathy as a nation-building strategy, see Andrew Burstein, *Sentiment Democracy: The Evolution of America's Romantic Self-Image* (forthcoming).

113. See argument by George W. Owens of Georgia in 1836, in Henry H. Simms, *Emotion at High Tide: Abolition as a Controversial Factor, 1830–1845* (Richmond, Va.: William Byrd Press, 1960), 105.

114. Arendt, *Human Condition*, 52; also see Wendy Brown, *Manhood and Politics*, 60–63.

115. Yellin, *Women and Sisters*, 44–45.

116. See "A Woman Politician," *Lily*, December 1852, 100.

117. Senex [Anson Bingham], "The Democratic Review on Woman's Rights—No. 10," *Lily*, March 15, 1853, 16.

118. See "Defense of Dr. Hollick Lectures (medical knowledge for the common people)," "Notice from 300 Ladies on Hollick's Lectures," and "Freedom of Speech and Dr. Hollick's Lecture," *Pennsylvania Freeman*, March 12, 19, 1846. Frederick Hollick was a New York physician and one of the most popular writers and lecturers on sexuality and contraception. See Wilson Yates, "Birth Control Literature and the Medical Profession in Nineteenth Century America," *Journal of the History of Medicine* (January 1976): 43, 46–48.

119. "Peace, Woman, and Elihu Burritt" and "Peace Meeting and the Women of Philadelphia," *Pennsylvania Freeman*, June 4, June 25, 1846.

120. Paulina Wright Davis began giving lectures on anatomy and physiology in Philadelphia in 1847, which explains the connection between the Hollick protest and feminist reformers in the city. See "Paulina S. Wright Lectures in Philadelphia," notice for "A Public Meeting of Women," "Anti–Capital Punishment Meeting," and report from the "Committee of Correspondence appointed from the public meeting of women to promote the abolition of capital punishment," *Pennsylvania Freeman*, January 7, 21, April 8, 1847.

121. Stanton, Anthony, and Gage, *History of Woman Suffrage*, 1:69.

122. See letter from Stanton where she regrets her "foolish comment" in regard to the president of the convention in Rochester. See Elizabeth Cady Stanton to Amy Kirby Post, September 24, 1848, Papers of Elizabeth Cady Stanton and Susan B. Anthony, Rutgers University, New Brunswick, N.J. Also see Nancy Hewitt, "Amy Kirby Post," *University of Rochester Library Bulletin* 37 (1984): 11–12.

123. A "public meeting for women" on the "Woman Question" was held in Philadelphia in 1849. Mott and Lucy Stone participated, and the meeting was conducted "without the aid of 'gentlemen officers.'" See *Pennsylvania Freeman*, May 10, 1849.

124. See a review of Dana's speech, "Woman's Rights," *Lily*, April 1851, 28.

125. See Mott's "Discourse on Woman," in *Salem WRC 1850*, 44.

126. "Address by Abby Price," *Worcester WRC 1850*, 20.

127. Wilson sent letters to the Salem women's rights convention and the Worcester national convention. She explained her theory of cosovereignty in the Salem letter and referred to women's equal status at creation in her letter to the Worcester convention. See *Salem WRC 1850*, 31; *Worcester WRC 1850*, 72–73. In two letters, one addressed to Stanton, the other to Stanton

and Elizabeth McClintock, Lucretia Mott discussed Wilson's new book and the author. She explained that Wilson was the daughter of a Scotch Presbyterian minister and that the book was "orthodox" because the "arguments are mainly drawn from scriptural authority." Mott noted that the book would be of use and that she had seen "a few pages of the proofs which are good." Mott also mentioned that Wilson's book was "a work of ten years research & hard labor." See Lucretia Mott to Elizabeth Cady Stanton and Elizabeth McClintock, November 27, 1849, in *The Papers of Elizabeth Cady Stanton and Susan B. Anthony*, ed. Patricia G. Holland and Ann D. Gordon (Wilmington, Del., 1991, microfilm), reel 6, frames 936–47, 979–89.

128. For Wilson's use of the scriptural phrase "It is not good for man to be alone," see *Salem WRC 1850*, 31. For Price's argument, see A.H.P., "Woman's Right to Suffrage," *Practical Christian*, January 15, 1853.

129. See "On Creation," *Anti-Slavery Bugle*, July 22, 1848.

130. See "What Is Truth?" (written in reaction to 1st Acts and Resolutions passed at the first session of the 29th Congress of the United States, and 2nd Sections adopted at the New-York Constitutional Convention), *United States Magazine and Democratic Review*, October 1846, 271.

131. Cyrus Eaton, *Woman: An Address Delivered to the Ladies' Sewing Circle, Warren, Maine, at their Anniversary Meeting, February 9, 1854.* (Hallowell, Maine, 1854), 8–9.

132. A.H.P. [Abby H. Price], "National Woman's Rights Convention," *Practical Christian*, September 25, 1852.

133. Habermas, *Structural Transformation of the Public Sphere*, 110.

134. Greeley, "Sphere of Woman," 273.

135. "Political Non-Existence of Women," 82.

Chapter 4

1. See two published letters, Elizabeth Wilson McClintock and Elizabeth Cady Stanton, "Woman's Rights," *National Reformer*, September 21, 1848, which was a Rochester and Auburn paper, and Elizabeth Cady Stanton and Elizabeth W. McClintock, "To the Editors," *Seneca County Courier*, n.d., Elizabeth Cady Stanton Papers, Manuscript Division, Library of Congress, Washington, D.C. Originally, I read these letters at the Papers of Elizabeth Cady Stanton and Susan B. Anthony, University of Massachusetts, Amherst, Mass. Both are available on microfilm; see Patricia G. Holland and Ann D. Gordon, eds., *The Papers of Elizabeth Cady Stanton and Susan B. Anthony* (Wilmington, Del., 1991, microfilm), reel 6, frames 773, 779–81.

2. See *Rochester WRC 1848*, 11.

3. Carol Weisbrod, "Family, Church, and State," in *Legal History Program: Working Papers*, ser. 1 (Madison, Wis.: Institute for Legal Studies, 1986), 3.

4. Joseph Story, *Commentaries on the Constitution of the United States; with a preliminary review of the constitutional history of the colonies and states, before the adoption of the Constitution*, 3 vols. (Boston, 1833), 3:729.

5. James Kent believed that attacking religion threatened "the essential interests of civil society," and founders such as George Washington and James Madison considered religion the moral foundation of the state. For the reference to Kent, see Daniel R. Ernst, "Church-State Issues and the Law: 1607–1870," in *Church and State in America, a Bibliographical Guide: The Colonial and Early National Periods*, ed. John F. Wilson (New York: Greenwood Press, 1986), 338. For an astute discussion of the role of "constitutional faith" in the vision of the founders, see Samuel Levinson, *Constitutional Faith* (Princeton: Princeton University Press, 1988), 9–14.

6. *Sprecht v. Commonwealth*, 8 Pa. 312 (1848). For a brief overview of *Sprecht v. Commonwealth*

(1848), see J. William Frost, *A Perfect Freedom: Religious Liberty in Pennsylvania* (University Park: Pennsylvania State University Press, 1993), 139.

7. A full report of the convention was reprinted as *Proceedings of the Anti-Sabbath Convention, held in the Melodeon, March 23 and 24, 1848* (Boston, 1848).

8. This was the opinion of Judge Coulter from *Sprecht v. Commonwealth*, reprinted in "Sabbath Laws in Pennsylvania," *United States Magazine and Democratic Review*, November 1848, 443.

9. See J. William Frost, "Pennsylvania Institutes Religious Liberty, 1682–1860," *Pennsylvania Magazine of History and Biography* 112 (July 1988): 346.

10. See letter reprinted from the (Episcopal) *Christian Witness and Church Advocate*, in *Proceedings of the Anti-Sabbath Convention*, 151.

11. See Justin Edwards, *The Sabbath Manual; including "The Sabbath a Family Institution"* (New York, n.d.), 71. His *Permanent Sabbath Documents* (n.p.) appeared in 1844, and document number one is the same as the first tract in *Sabbath Manual*. Justin Edwards (1787–1853) served as secretary of the American and Foreign Sabbath Union. See *First Annual Report of the American and Foreign Sabbath Union* (Boston, 1844), 9.

12. See Thomas L. Haskell, "The Curious Persistence of Rights Talk in the 'Age of Interpretation,'" *Journal of American History* 74 (December 1987): 995.

13. Edwards, *Sabbath Manual*, 18.

14. See Catherine Zuckert, "Not by Preaching: Tocqueville on the Role of Religion in American Democracy," *Review of Politics* 43 (April 1981): 264–65.

15. Tocqueville wrote, "Thus, in the United States, the inexorable opinion of the public carefully circumscribes woman within her narrow circle of domestic interests and duties, and forbids her to step beyond it." See Richard D. Heffner, ed., *Democracy in America* (New York: New American Library, 1956), 236.

16. Elizabeth Wilson, *A Scriptural View of Woman's Rights and Duties, in all the Important Relations of Life* (Philadelphia, 1849).

17. For a brief summary of the career of Justin Edwards, see *Dictionary of American Biography*, 20 vols. (New York: Scribner's, 1928–36), 6:40.

18. David Paul Nord argues persuasively for the importance of the American Tract Society as the key organization for aggressively mobilizing the "sanctified press" through "systematic management." See his "Systematic Benevolence: Religious Publishing and the Marketplace in Early Nineteenth-Century America," in *Communication and Change in American Religious History*, ed. Leonard I. Sweet (Grand Rapids, Mich.: Eerdmans, 1993), 241, 243–48, 252.

19. See Philip Schaff, *The Anglo-American Sabbath: Read before the National Sabbath Convention, Saratoga, August 11, 1863* (New York: American Tract Society, 1863), 62. Edwards also stressed the vital importance of the Sabbath on character formation. He wrote, "Man is a *moral* as well as an intellectual being. His excellence, his usefulness, and his happiness depend chiefly on his *character*. To the right formation and proper culture of this the Sabbath is *essential*." See Edwards, *Sabbath Manual*, 52–53.

20. See Philip Schaff, "Church and State in the United States or the American Idea of Religious Liberty and its Practical Effects," *Papers of the American Historical Association* 2, no. 4 (1888): 53. He used a similar phrase in his tract when he wrote, "Our separation of church and state rests on mutual respect and friendship, and is by no means a separation of the nation from Christianity." See Schaff, *Anglo-American Sabbath*, 31. Also see Richard R. John, "Taking Sabbatarianism Seriously: The Postal System, the Sabbath, and the Transformation of American Political Culture," *Journal of the Early Republic* 10 (Winter 1990): 517–67. For his entire study on the postal system, see Richard R. John, *Spreading the News: The American Postal System from Franklin to Morse* (Cambridge: Harvard University Press, 1995).

21. Schaff, *Anglo-American Sabbath*, 62; *The American Colporteur System* (New York, 1845), 8–9.

22. See R. Lawrence Moore, *Selling God: American Religion in the Marketplace of Culture* (New York: Oxford University Press, 1994), 76; also see Edwards, *Sabbath Manual*, 81, 87, 94.

23. See Stephen Botein, "Religious Dimensions of the Early American State," in *Beyond Confederation: Origins of the Constitution and American National Identity*, ed. Richard Beeman, Stephen Botein, and Edward C. Carter II (Chapel Hill: University of North Carolina Press, 1987), 319–20.

24. The enduring popularity of Washington's Farewell Address is evidenced by its reprinting in *The American Keepsake, or Book for Every American* (Boston, 1845), 44–45.

25. L. H. Butterfield, ed., *Letters of Benjamin Rush*, 2 vols. (Princeton: Princeton University Press, 1951), 1:461–67.

26. See *The Political Duties of Christians. A Report, Adopted at Spring Meeting of the South Middlesex Conference of Churches, April 18, 1848* (Boston, 1848), 8.

27. Ibid., 30.

28. In one classic statement that appeared in 1784, just months before Immanuel Kant wrote "What Is Enlightenment?," Wilhelm Werkhrlin, in his periodical, *Das grave Ungeheur*, defined moral supervision as one of the key functions of publicity: "What must it have been like in the times before printing presses existed! Tyrants had no bridles, the people no refuge. Vice could grow impudent, without becoming red with shame. Virtue knew no means of sharing its suffering, or gaining the sympathy of society. The laws had no critics, morals had no supervisor, reason was monopolized. Providence spoke: let the human race become free! And 'publicity' appeared." See John Christian Laursen, "The Subversive Kant: The Vocabulary of 'Public' and 'Publicity,'" *Political Theory* 14 (November 1986): 594–95.

29. See Melvin Yazawa, "Creating a Republican Citizenry," in *The American Revolution: Its Character and Limits*, ed. Jack P. Greene (New York: New York University Press, 1987), 293–96.

30. See Richard D. Brown, *Knowledge Is Power: The Diffusion of Information in Early America, 1700–1865.* (New York: Oxford University Press, 1986).

31. For a discussion of Milton's notion of civil liberty, see Francis Barker, *The Tremulous Private Body: Essays on Subjection* (London: Methuen, 1984), 46–47.

32. For the popularity of this perspective, see a quotation taken from the *New York Recorder* and repeated in the *Home Missionary* in 1846, which stated that the "progress of the Gospel, and hence its triumphs have been more those of opinions, than of swords. . . . The triumph of Christianity is the triumph of popular liberty, and the school teacher, the tract distributor and the home missionary will do more for liberty than troops of vaunting politicians." See Rush Welter, *The Mind of America, 1820–1860* (Ithaca: Cornell University Press, 1975), 263.

33. Jean-Jacques Rousseau argued that only "right opinions" ensured that the public voice would speak the truth. See J. A. W. Gunn, "Public Opinion," in *Political Innovation and Conceptual Change*, ed. Terence Ball, James Farr, and Russell L. Hanson (Cambridge: Cambridge University Press, 1989), 252.

34. See Yazawa, "Creating a Republican Citizenry," 299. Nina Baym makes the point that Emma Willard, in her 1819 *Plan for Improving Female Education*, called for "discipline for its own sake, in the sense of developing rules and regulations for the purpose of providing training in obedience." See Baym, "Women and the Republic: Emma Willard's Rhetoric of History," in *Feminism and American Literary History* (New Brunswick: Rutgers University Press, 1992), 128.

35. Organized in 1828, the General Union for the Promotion of the Christian Sabbath enlisted the support of ministers from various benevolent societies, such as the American Tract Society,

the American Bible Society, and the American Sunday-School Union. See John, "Taking Sabbatarianism Seriously," 22.

36. Ibid., 23. Catharine Beecher openly endorsed that the "duties of subordination" on the part of women served the "general good" and "public benefit." She wrote, "There must be the magistrate and the subject, one of whom is the superior, and other the inferior. There must be relations of husband and wife, parent and child, teacher and pupil, employer and employed, each involving the relative duties of subordination. The superior, in certain particulars, is to direct, and the inferior is to yield obedience." See selection from *A Treatise on Domestic Economy* (1841), in *The American Intellectual Tradition*, 2 vols., ed. David A. Hollinger and Charles Capper (New York: Oxford University Press, 1993), 1:245.

37. See the abridged version of *An Essay on the Education of Female Teachers* (New York, 1835), in *The Educated Woman in America: Selected Writings of Catharine Beecher, Margaret Fuller, and M. Carey Thomas*, ed. Barbara M. Cross (New York: Teachers College Press, 1965), 68–72, 74.

38. Jay Fliegelman demonstrates the emergence of this view of human character in the aftermath of the American Revolution. He offers a compelling example through his contrast of the two most important literary texts of the 1790s, Benjamin Franklin's *Autobiography* and Charles Brockden Brown's *Wieland or the Transformation*—its "dark side." In *Wieland* Brown captures the devastating consequences of Lockean epistemology, portraying a world where appearance and reality cannot be fixed and language tyrannizes over things, in a fashion that is beyond human and moral control. In contrast, Franklin's *Autobiography*, although following the same theory, suggests that through the "successful manipulation of appearances," individuals can be "masters" rather than the "victims of language." See Fliegelman, "Familial Politics, Seduction, and the Novel: The Anxious Agenda of an American Literary Culture," in Jack P. Greene, *American Revolution*, 347.

39. See J. Bronowski and Bruce Mazlish, *The Western Intellectual Tradition* (New York: Harper Torchbooks, 1960), 202–3.

40. This is a quote by Washington Irving taken from Anne Norton, *Alternative Americas: A Reading of Antebellum Political Culture* (Chicago: University of Chicago Press, 1986), 19.

41. For a discussion of Noah Webster's view toward creating a national language and his advocacy of the plain style, see Michael P. Kramer, *Imagining Language in America: From the Revolution to the Civil War* (Princeton: Princeton University Press, 1992), 55. Also see Richard M. Rollins, *The Long Journey of Noah Webster* (Philadelphia: University of Pennsylvania Press, 1980), 63–64, 117. For Webster's reference to making language simple and plain, which he believed contributed to the cause of Christianity, see his 1839 address *Observations on Language, and on the Errors of the Classbooks*, quoted in Philip Gura, *The Wisdom of Words: Language, Theology, and Literature in the New England Renaissance* (Middletown, Conn.: Wesleyan University Press, 1981), 15.

42. Giambattista Vico used the phrase "common mental dictionary" when examining the relationship between language and *sensus communis*. Vico viewed common sense as the sense of the community that was both religious and bounded by shared meanings. For a discussion of this point, see John D. Schaeffer, "The Use and Misuse of Giambattista Vico: Rhetoric, Orality, and Theories of Discourse," in *The New Historicism*, ed. H. Aram Vesser (London: Routledge, 1989), 89–101.

43. Mark Noll makes the argument that John Witherspoon decided to meet the infidels on their "own ground, and to show them from reason itself, the fallacy of their principles." He also notes how Elias Boudinot turned to common sense and identifies this as a common practice among orthodox Protestants. See Noll, "The Evangelical Enlightenment and the Task of Theological Education," in Sweet, *Communication and Change in American Religious History*, 281–83. Also see "Elias Boudinot," in *Biographical Directory of the United States Executive Branch, 1774–1989*, ed. Robert Sobel (New York: Greenwood Press, 1990), 35.

44. Kramer, *Imagining Language in America*, 45.

45. See James H. Moorhead, "The Millennium and the Media," in Sweet, *Communication and Change in American Religious History*, 228.

46. Webster approvingly quoted Johann David Michaelis's *A Dissertation on the Influence of Opinions on Language and of Language on Opinions*. See Kramer, *Imagining Language in America*, 58.

47. See Lyman Beecher, *The Bible A Code of Law. A Sermon, Delivered in Park Street Church, Boston, September 3, 1817, at the Ordination of Mr. Sereno Edwards Dwight, as the Pastor of that Church; and of Messrs. Elisha P. Swift, Allen Graves, John Nichols, Levi Parsons, & Daniel Buttrick, as Missionaries to the Heathen* (Andover, Mass., 1827), 38.

48. For a religious tract that used this definition of "common sense," see Samuel Marsh, *"Hard Questions" Answered: In Two Parts* (Montpelier, Vt., 1849), 6.

49. For the reference to the Bible as a "store-house of facts," see Noll, "Evangelical Enlightenment and the Task of Theological Education," 287. For the reference to "erroneous opinions," see Lyman Beecher, *Bible A Code of Law*, 36.

50. William Ellery Channing, "Remarks on Associations" (1829), in *The Works of William E. Channing, D.D.*, 2 vols. (Boston, 1849), 1:283–84, 290–91, 296, 307.

51. See reprints of the decisions rendered for *People v. Ruggles* (1811) and *Updegraph v. Commonwealth* (1822), both blasphemy cases, and the Sabbath case of *Lindenmuller v. the People* (1861), which also asserted that "Christianity is part of the common law," all included as documents in Schaff, "Church and State in the United States," 139, 141, 145, 148–50.

52. In regard to biblical interpretation, Lyman Beecher argued that "to the common people, the obvious, is the only meaning of terms." See his 1823 sermon "The Faith Once Delivered to the Saints," in *The American Evangelicals, 1800–1900*, ed. William G. McLoughlin (New York: Harper Torchbooks, 1968), 75. For the quotation, see Catharine Beecher and Harriet Beecher Stowe, *An Essay on Slavery and Abolitionism, with Reference to the Duty of American Females* (Philadelphia, 1837; reprint, Freeport, N.Y.: Books for Libraries Press, 1970), 40.

53. See Thomas Herttell, *The Demurrer: Proofs of Error in the Decision of the Supreme Court of the State of New-York, Requiring Faith in Particular Religious Doctrines as a Legal Qualification of Witnesses; Thence Establishing by Law a Religious Test, and a Religious Creed*. (New York, 1828), 127.

54. Thomas Herttell, *Remarks Comprising in Substance Judge Herttell's Argument in the House of Assembly of the State of New-York, in the Session of 1837, in Support of the Bill to Restore Married Women "The Right of Property," as Guarantied by the Constitution of the State* (New York, 1839), 40.

55. See Thomas Herttell, *The People's Rights Re-Claimed; Being an Exposition of the Unconstitutionality of the Law of the State of New York Compelling the Observation of a Religious Sabbath Day; and Erroneously entitled "An Act for the Suppression of Immorality," Passed March 13, 1813*. (New York, 1826), 14.

56. Most nineteenth-century decisions were generally in agreement that the Sabbath was a civil institution entitled to protection. At least twenty-six cases from all regions of the country confirmed this precedent throughout the nineteenth century. See Richard C. Wylie, *Sabbath Laws in the United States* (Pittsburgh: National Reform Association, 1905), 209.

57. For the argument that even a "large minority" must submit to the "conscience of the mass," see *Report Relative to the Observation of the Sabbath, made to the House of Representatives* (Harrisburg, 1850), 3–4.

58. See "Sabbath Laws in Pennsylvania," 438–39.

59. Unitarians began to raise the issue of "Free churches" (no pew fees) following disestablishment as early as 1835. Yet it was mainly the younger ministers who put the principle into practice, while other societies used voluntary subscriptions, taxes assessed to those who rented pews, and pew rentals to support their churches. See Richard Eddy Sykes, "Massachusetts Uni-

tarianism and Social Change: A Religious and Social System in Transition, 1780–1870" (Ph.D. diss., University of Minnesota, 1966), 190–91, 196.

60. See A. Gregory Schneider, "From Democratization to Domestication: The Transitional Orality of the American Methodist Circuit Rider," in Sweet, *Communication and Change in American Religious History*, 145–49.

61. See Mary Maples Dunn, "Latest Light on Women of Light," in *Witnesses for Change: Quaker Women over Three Centuries*, ed. Elisabeth Potts Brown and Susan Mosher Stuard (New Brunswick: Rutgers University Press, 1989), 74.

62. See Mott's sermon given in a Unitarian church, "Righteousness Gives Respect to Its Possessor" (1843), in *Lucretia Mott: Her Complete Speeches and Sermons*, ed. Dana Greene (New York: Edwin Mellen Press, 1980), 43–44.

63. Child uses the phrase "surface of things," and this same quote is repeated by Elizabeth Wilson in her study of religion. See Lydia Maria Child, *Letters from New York* (1843), in *Provisions: A Reader from Nineteenth-Century American Women*, ed. Judith Fetterley (Bloomington: Indiana University Press, 1985), 196; Wilson, *Scriptural View of Woman's Rights and Duties*, 352.

64. Sarah Grimké, "Letter from Sarah M. Grimké to her friend Gerrit Smith," *Lily*, October 1856, 131.

65. See "Discourse on Woman" (1849), in Dana Greene, *Lucretia Mott*, 154–55.

66. See James Porter, *Three Lectures Delivered in the First Methodist Episcopal Church, Lynn, Mass., Dec., 1843, on Come-out-ism* (Lynn, Mass., 1844), 17.

67. Edwards, *Sabbath Manual*, 94.

68. William Ellery Channing, "Remarks on Associations," 288–89.

69. See "Remarks by Charles C. Burleigh," in *Proceedings of the Anti-Sabbath Convention*, 20, 102.

70. Mott most likely referred in this comment to Hugh Blair, the author of *Lectures on Rhetoric and Belles-Lettres*, which first appeared in 1783 and had become the most popular textbook on rhetoric by the mid-nineteenth century. See Lucretia Mott, "Abuses and Uses of the Bible" (1849), in Dana Greene, *Lucretia Mott*, 130. For a discussion of Blair, see Lillian O'Connor, *Pioneer Women Orators: Rhetoric in the Antebellum Reform Movement* (New York: Columbia University Press, 1954), 110.

71. "Remarks of Parker Pillsbury," in *Proceedings of the Anti-Sabbath Convention*, 83–84.

72. See "Remarks of C. C. Burleigh," in ibid., 21.

73. For references to "demure piety" and the problem of adherence to "outward authority," see "Remarks of Lucretia Mott," in ibid., 95–96. While Mott rebuked consecration or "inherent holiness" of the day, Stephen Foster attacked as "absurd" the notion that "holiness" was an attribute of time. William Lloyd Garrison used the phrase "holiness of time" in his remarks as well. See "Remarks of S. S. Foster," and "Remarks of Mr. Garrison," in ibid., 80, 25.

74. See "Remarks of Theodore Parker," in ibid., 46.

75. See "Remarks of Elizur Wright," in ibid., 115.

76. For references to "cloaks of religions," see "Remarks of Elizur Wright"; for the almost burlesque use of the figure of holy hats and sanctified coats, see "Remarks of Henry C. Wright"; for the allusion to the Chinese custom of putting wooden shoes on the feet of female children, see "Remarks of C. C. Burleigh," all in ibid., 115–16, 92–93, 71–72.

77. Wilson, *A Scriptural View of Woman's Rights and Duties*, 204–7.

78. See excerpt from 1891 decision in the U.S. Circuit Court of Western District of Tennessee, in Wylie, *Sabbath Laws in the United States*, 210.

79. Taken from the fourth resolution presented at the anti-Sabbath meeting. See *Proceedings of the Anti-Sabbath Convention*, 11.

80. Ibid., 8, 11, 20.

81. See *Seneca Falls WRC 1848*, 4.

82. "Sabbath Laws in Pennsylvania," 443.

83. *Worcester WRC 1851*, 51.

84. Wilson, *Scriptural View of Woman's Rights and Duties*, 146.

85. See "Have We A Despotism Among Us?," *Una*, January 1854, 207.

86. Wilson, *Scriptural View of Woman's Rights and Duties*, 94, 309.

87. Beecher and Stowe, *Essay on Slavery and Abolitionism*, 98–103, 108, 120–21.

88. See "Remarks of Lucretia Mott," *Proceedings of the Anti-Sabbath Convention*, 97; "Discourse of Woman," in Dana Greene, *Lucretia Mott*, 147.

89. See Elwyn A. Smith, *Religious Liberty in the United States: The Development of Church-State Thought since the Revolutionary Era* (Philadelphia: Fortress Press, 1972), 74–75, 77, 86–88.

90. Mary Ann Johnson served as president of the West Chester women's rights convention and supported the Progressive Friends. She was married to Oliver Johnson, author of *Expositions of Sentiments*, the major treatise of the Pennsylvania Progressive Friends. See *West Chester WRC 1852*, 10; *Proceedings of the Pennsylvania Yearly Meeting of Progressive Friends, 1853*, 7; *Minutes*, Pennsylvania Yearly Meeting of Progressive Friends (n.p., 1857), 9.

91. See Judith Wellman, "The Seneca Falls Women's Rights Convention: A Study of Social Networks," *Journal of Women's History* 3 (Spring 1991): 24–27; A. Day Bradley, "Progressive Friends in Michigan and New York," *Quaker History* 52 (Autumn 1963): 97.

92. See "The Trial of Rhoda Bement: Transcript from the Session of the First Presbyterian Church of Seneca Falls," and Jan M. Saltzgaber, "For the Salvation of the World! Revivalism and Reform in Seneca Falls, New York," in *Revivalism, Social Conscience, and Community in the Burned-over District: The Trial of Rhoda Bement*, ed. Glenn C. Altschuler and Jan M. Saltzgaber (Ithaca: Cornell University Press, 1983), 35, 50, 62, 76, 87–88, 90–96, 99, 102.

93. "Trial of Rhoda Bement," 96, 99, 140; also see *Seneca Falls 1848*, 3.

94. For the Hicksite's federated system and the critique by the Congregational Friends found in the "Basis of Association," see Albert J. Wahl, "Congregational or Progressive Friends in the Pre-Civil-War Reform Movement" (Ed. D. diss., Temple University, 1951), 23, 328.

95. See Lucretia Mott to Richard D. and Hannah Webb, March 23, 1846, in Anna Davis Hallowell, ed., *James and Lucretia Mott: Life and Letters* (Boston: Houghton Mifflin, 1884), 275.

96. Ruling elders were considered the "representatives of the people, chosen by them, for the purpose of exercising government and discipline, in conjunction with ministers and pastors." See *Constitution of the Presbyterian Church in the United States* (1842), 450.

97. See "Review of John Keep, 'Congregationalism and Church Action,'" *Emancipator and Republican*, May 28, 1845. For a recent argument by Daniel Walker Howe, who agrees that "the evangelical movement in the antebellum United States was in many respects the functional equivalent of an established church," see Daniel Walker Howe, "The Evangelical Movement and the Political Culture of the Second Party System," *Journal of American History* 77 (March 1991): 1222.

98. For Smith quotation, see Ralph Volney Harlow, "Gerrit Smith and the Free Church Movement," *New York History* 43 (July 1937): 279. For "respective circles of theology," see article reprinted from the *Chronotype* titled "Individual Freedom," *Pennsylvania Freeman*, May 21, 1846. For the sectarian as "exclusive and intolerant," see "An Earnest and Affective Address," in *Proceedings of the Yearly Meeting of Congregational Friends, held at Waterloo, N.Y., from the 4th to the 6th of the Sixth month, inclusive, 1849* (Auburn, N.Y., 1849), 23. See letter sent to the Methodist Episcopal Church of Deerfield from Almira Betts, "Renunciation of Sect," *Anti-Slavery Bugle*, December 22, 1849. For "evangelical empire," see Howe, "Evangelical Movement," 1223.

99. See Lucretia Mott to Nathaniel Barney, March 19, 1853, in Hallowell, *James and Lucretia Mott*, 348.

100. For references to creeds as "a yoke on posterity" and "blind obedience," see "Address to the Public," in *Proceedings of the Ohio Yearly Meeting of Progressive Friends, held in Salem, from the 5th to the 7th of Ninth Month, inclusive, 1852* (Salem, Ohio, 1852), 14.

101. See "Withdrawal of Jane Trescott," *Anti-Slavery Bugle*, December 15, 1849. For her connection to the Ohio Progressive Friends and the Salem women's rights convention, see *Anti-Slavery Bugle*, March 17, 1848, and October 8, 1853.

102. Dissenters borrowed the language of "comeouterism" from William Penn and Romantic poetics. Seventeenth-century Quakers had criticized the "dead letter of the law" and advanced the notion of spontaneous inspiration and testimony as the "living spirit." Similarly, a dominant theme of Romantic poetics was to convey the idea that religion must shed the husks of formal creeds to rediscover the truth. Both types of metaphors can be found in the language of antebellum dissenters. See [Oliver Johnson], *Expositions of Sentiments, Adopted by the Pennsylvania Yearly Meeting of Progressive Friends* (n.p., [1853]); "Address to the Public," in *Proceedings of the Ohio Yearly Meeting of Progressive Friends*, 13–14; Massachusetts women's rights supporter Valentine Nicholson's "Comeouterism," *Pennsylvania Freeman*, May 15, 1846. Also see Melvin B. Endy Jr., "Theology in a Religiously Plural World: Some Contributions of William Penn," *Pennsylvania Magazine of History and Biography* 105 (October 1981): 460–61; Richard Bauman, *Let Your Words Be Few: Symbolism of Speaking and Silence among Seventeenth-Century Quakers* (Cambridge: Cambridge University Press, 1983); Richard Bauman, "Speaking in the Light: The Role of the Quaker Minister," in *Explorations in the Ethnography of Speaking*, ed. Richard Bauman and Joel Sherzer (Cambridge: Cambridge University Press, 1974); Stephen Prickett, *Words and the Word: Language, Poetics, and Biblical Interpretation* (Cambridge: Cambridge University Press, 1986), 138–48, 201–4.

103. See A.H.P. [Abby H. Price], "Woman," *Practical Christian*, October 23, 1852.

104. Dissenters used a variety of synonyms, such as "fetters," "shackles," and "trammels." Price's use of the word "blaze" captured what Hannah Arendt described as public disclosure. Disclosure conveys immediacy and transcendence ("shining brightness once called glory"), in which the performance exhausts the full meaning in the "blaze," so that the performance cannot be repeated or preserved. The truth defies written codification, what Oliver Johnson called the "ossification" of creeds. See [Johnson], *Expositions of Sentiments*, 35; Hannah Arendt, *The Human Condition* (Chicago: University of Chicago Press, 1958), 65.

105. For a description of Hopedale granting women an equal voice in political and religious affairs, see Price's speech in *Worcester WRC 1850*, 31.

106. See "The Hopedale Community" (1855), 5, available in the Miscellaneous Pamphlet Collection, American Antiquarian Society, Worcester, Mass.

107. For information on Price, see Adin Ballou, *History of the Hopedale Community, from its Inception to its Virtual Submergence in the Hopedale Parish* (Lowell, Mass., 1897), 186–88, and *History of the Town of Milford, Worcester County, Massachusetts, from its First Settlement to 1881*, 2 vols. (Lowell, Mass., 1897), 2:979. For Price's role in the Practical Christian ministry, see *Practical Christian*, December 6, 1851, January 3, March 29, 1852, January 1, July 2, 1853. For her role in the Worcester convention, see *Worcester WRC 1851*, 31–35.

108. For a letter from Paulina Wright Davis to James T. Fisher, one of the founders of the Boston Religious Union of Associationists, see James T. Fisher Papers, 1790–1865, Massachusetts Historical Society, Boston. Also see Paulina Wright Davis's name listed under "Associationists from other places" in the Records of the Religious Union of Associationists, of Boston, also at the Massachusetts Historical Society. For a more general discussion of the Religious Union of Associationists and William Henry Channing's role as minister, see Charles Crowe, "Christian Socialism and the First Church of Humanity," *Church History* 35 (March 1966): 93–106.

109. For Parker's and Higginson's ties to the Progressive Friends, see Parker's letters to Joseph

Dugdale, one of the founders of the Pennsylvania Progressive Friends, in Joseph Dugdale Papers, Friends Historical Library, Swarthmore College, Swarthmore, Pa. Also see letters of support sent from Higginson, Gerrit Smith, and the Hopedale Association to the first meeting of the Pennsylvania Progressive Friends, in *Proceedings of the Pennsylvania Yearly Meeting of Progressive Friends, 1853, Old Kennett Meeting House, Chester County, Pennsylvania, 22nd of May (fifth month), 1853* (n.p., n.d.).

110. For a reference to a free church as a "people-church," see William Henry Channing's sermon in the *Ordination Service of Thomas Wentworth Higginson, with Charge by James Freeman Clarke* (Boston, 1847), in the Miscellaneous Pamphlet Collection. For Smith, Parker, Channing, and Higginson as supporters of free churches, see Harlow, "Gerrit Smith and the Free Church Movement," 276; William R. Hutchinson, *The Transcendentalist Ministers: Church Reform in the New England Renaissance* (New Haven: Yale University Press, 1959), 173–74, 179–80; James Mooney, "Antislavery in Worcester County, Massachusetts: A Case Study" (Ph.D., Clark University, 1971), 191; and see Worcester Free Church, Subscription List for the Establishment of a "New Religious Society," in Worcester, Mass., Collection, Miscellaneous Records, American Antiquarian Society.

111. For Smith's definition of *ecclesia*, see *Gerrit Smith on Sectarianism or Abstract of the Argument in the Public Discussion of the Question: "Are the Christians of a Given Community the Church of such a Community?" made by Gerrit Smith in Hamilton, N.Y., April 12–14, 1847*, in *Gerrit Smith Papers, 1775–1924*, part of the Special Collections in the George Arents Research Library, Syracuse University, Syracuse, N.Y. (Glen Rock, N.J.: Microfilming Corporation of America, 1974), reel 73.

112. For the democratic imperative of the Congregational and Progressive Friends, see article reprinted from the *New York Tribune*, "Dissenting Friends at Waterloo," *National Anti-Slavery Standard*, June 21, 1849. Also see Thomas McClintock to William Logan Fisher, July 20, 1849, in Logan-Fisher-Fox Collection, Pennsylvania Historical Society, Philadelphia; William Logan Fisher, *Progressive Friends. An Account of the Fourth Annual Meeting of the Progressive Friends, with some Observations on their Principles and Prospects* (Philadelphia, 1856), 18, 20–22. For how Ohio Congregational Friends used the language of George Fox and his definition of a society as "two or three assembled together" (taken from the New Testament), see "Epistle," in *Minutes of the Proceedings of the Annual Meeting of the Friends, Composed of Persons from Parts of Ohio and Indiana, held at Green Plain, Clark County, Ohio, who have adopted the Congregational Order* (Springfield, Ohio, 1848), 7. For Fox's definition of *ecclesia*, see Emerson W. Shideler, "The Concept of the Church in Seventeenth-Century Quakerism," *Bulletin of Friends Historical Association* 45 (Autumn 1956): 70.

113. Wilson, *Scriptural View of Woman's Rights and Duties*, 182, 240; also see Frost, *Perfect Freedom*, 119.

114. For a reference to ministers being "vested" in their carefully crafted "pulpit eloquence," see "On Preaching," *United States Magazine and Democratic Review*, July 1845, 45. Wilson, *Scriptural View of Woman's Rights and Duties*, 184. Also see Desley Deacon, "Politicizing Gender," *Genders*, no. 6 (Fall 1986): 7; Gary Bunker, "Antebellum Caricature and Woman's Sphere," *Journal of Women's History* 3 (Winter 1992): 6–43. The motif of the "battle for the pants" came from the Protestant Reformation in Germany; see Keith Moxey, "The Battle of the Sexes and the World Turned upside Down," in *That Gentle Strength: Historical Perspectives on Women in Christianity*, ed. Lynda L. Coon, Katherine J. Haldane, and Elisabeth W. Sommer (Charlottesville: University Press of Virginia, 1990), 136, 139.

115. For women as public spectacles, see Joan B. Landes, *Women and the Public Sphere in the Age of the French Revolution* (Ithaca: Cornell University Press, 1988), 71–75. For the use of "disorderly conduct" as a term of derision, often applied to prostitutes, see Carroll Smith-Rosenberg,

"Beauty, the Beast, and the Militant Woman: A Case Study in Sex Roles and Social Stress in Jacksonian America," *American Quarterly* 23 (October 1971): 567.

116. See *New York City WRC 1853*, 85.

117. "Editor's Table," *Harper's New Monthly Magazine*, November 1853, 838–41.

118. Ibid., 841. Mott covered over 2,800 miles in 69 days, visiting 71 meetings in New England, New York, Ohio, Indiana, and Pennsylvania, in a speaking tour in 1847. See "Lucretia and James Mott Journey," *National Anti-Slavery Standard*, November 25, 1847. For the range of her lecture topics, see "Lucretia Mott at Mt. Pleasant," *Anti-Slavery Bugle*, October 1, 1847. Also see Margaret Hope Bacon, *Valiant Friend: The Life of Lucretia Mott* (New York: Walker, 1980), 102, 106, 144–50, 157–58; "Women's Rights Convention," *National Anti-Slavery Standard*, August 10, 1848.

119. For the description of Mott as a matron, see article reprinted from the *Nantucket Inquirer*, "Lucretia Mott and Public Speaking," *National Anti-Slavery Standard*, July 22, 1847. For Furness's remarks, see "Unitarian Convention in Philadelphia," *National Anti-Slavery Standard*, November 5, 1846. For White's remarks "nearly verbatim," see Lucretia Mott to Nathaniel and Eliza Barney, November 8, 1839, in Hallowell, *James and Lucretia Mott*, 206–7; Bacon, *Valiant Friend*, 83–84, 101–2, 106, 115.

120. In 1847 Mott was criticized by Friends for not "preaching but lecturing" because she did not use the "singing tone." See "Convention in Salem," *Anti-Slavery Bugle*, September 10, 1847; also see Bacon, *Valiant Friend*, 122. For her discussion of Blanco White and "conscientious reason," see Lucretia Mott to James Pierce, March 15, 1849, in Hallowell, *James and Lucretia Mott*, 317–19.

121. For how Hobbes's theory—*veritas non actuoritas facit legem* (truth, not authority, makes law)—applied to public disclosure, see Jürgen Habermas, *The Structural Transformation of the Public Sphere: An Inquiry into a Category of Bourgeois Society*, trans. Thomas Burger (Cambridge: MIT Press, 1991), 53. Mott's saying became the motto of the Pennsylvania Progressive Friends. See Albert Wahl, "The Progressive Friends of Longwood," *Bulletin of Friends Historical Association* 42 (Spring 1953): 27; also see article reprinted from the *New York Times*, "Lucretia Mott in New York," *National Anti-Slavery Standard*, November 17, 1855.

122. M.L.S., "Woman's Rights," *Practical Christian*, January 31, 1852.

123. See Price's address in *Syracuse WRC 1852*, 53–54.

124. William Ellery Channing and Theodore Parker used the analogy of the cloak or "drab coat and surplice" to describe the insignia of the clerical caste. See "Another quote by Channing 'The True Minister,'" *Anti-Slavery Bugle*, March 16, 1850; Theodore Parker, "Conscience," *Spiritual Philosopher*, December 7, 1850. For the revived use of the term "priestcraft," see "Basis of Association," in Wahl, "Congregational or Progressive Friends in the Pre-Civil-War Reform Movement," 330.

125. See "To Speak Out the Truth," October 20, 1846, in Dana Greene, *Lucretia Mott*, 56; Wilson, *Scriptural View of Woman's Rights and Duties*, 242–43, 248; *Rochester WRC 1848*, 9.

126. See John F. Watson to William Logan Fisher, June 11, 1856, in the Logan-Fisher-Fox Collection, and unsigned letter published in the *National Anti-Slavery Standard*, October 25, 1849. For Price's comment, see *Worcester WRC 1850*, 23.

127. See two articles by "C." both titled "Women-Woman," in the *Anti-Slavery Bugle*, November 10, December 8, 1849. Brown gave the most complete account of events in her speech at the women's rights convention held in Cleveland in 1853. See *Cleveland WRC 1853*, 117, 119, 121–22; also see Elizabeth Cady Stanton, Susan B. Anthony, and Matilda Joslyn Gage, eds., *History of Woman Suffrage*, 6 vols. (New York, 1881; reprint, New York: Arno Press, 1985), 1:506. The Whole World Temperance Convention was held September 1–2; the World Temperance Convention, September 4–6th; and the women's rights convention was on the 6th.

128. Brown had attended Oberlin College for her theological training, and she was ordained on September 15, 1853. See "Ordination of Antoinette Brown," *National Anti-Slavery Standard*, September 24, 1853. For her connection to Gerrit Smith, see Antoinette Brown to Gerrit Smith, December 26, 1851, in *Gerrit Smith Papers*, reel 3. Also see account of her ordination in Elizabeth Cazden, *Antoinette Brown Blackwell: A Biography* (Old Westbury, N.Y.: Feminist Press, 1983), 74–84. For the article with excerpts from most of the major newspapers, see "Hostile Accounts of the Whole World Temperance convention in New York Newspapers," *National Anti-Slavery Standard*, September 17, 1853, and Brown's remarks in *New York City WRC 1853*, 41–42.

129. At the constitutional convention one opponent of women's rights argued that the covenantal model of headship provided both a legal and a religious foundation for male representation. The most articulate defender of women's rights countered with the claim that Christian democracy protected against such tyranny, for the true basis of democratic representation was the universal right of conscience. See *Official Report of the Debates and Proceedings, in the State Convention, assembled May 4th, 1853, to Revise and Amend the Constitution of the Commonwealth of Massachusetts*, 2 vols. (Boston, 1853), 2:252–53, 260–64.

130. For Brown's remarks, see *Worcester WRC 1851*, 95.

Chapter 5

1. G. W. Knapp, "Democracy Versus Man-Ocracy," *Lily*, August 1, 1854, 107.

2. Ibid.

3. See Christopher Hill, "Covenant Theology and the Concept of 'A Public Person,'" in *Essays in Honour of C. B. Macpherson: Power, Possessions, and Freedom*, ed. Alkis Kontos (Toronto: University of Toronto Press, 1979), 8.

4. "Political Non-Existence of Women" (extracts from Miss Martineau's "Society in America"), *Lily*, November 1850, 81.

5. See Wendy Brown, *Manhood and Politics: A Feminist Reading in Political Theory* (Totowa, N.J.: Rowan and Littlefield, 1988), 82–84, 118–19; Genevieve Lloyd, "Selfhood, War, and Masculinity," in *Feminist Challenges: Social and Political Theory*, ed. Carole Pateman and Elizabeth Gross (Boston: Northeastern University Press, 1987), 66.

6. The phrase "weaker vessel" has been attributed to Tyndale's translation of the New Testament into English in 1526 and was later highlighted in the King James version of the Bible. It appears in St. Paul's epistle to the Ephesians, where he urges wives to be in subjection to their husbands and refers to wives as "the weaker vessel." It also became a part of Protestant marriage service and theories of physiology, which stressed woman's carnality, her dangerous potential for lust, temptation, and the sins of the flesh. See F. F. Bruce, *History of the Bible in English* (New York: Oxford University Press, 1981), 31. Also see George H. Tavard, *Woman in Christian Tradition* (Notre Dame: University of Notre Dame Press, 1973), 172–74.

7. Rousseau equated prostitution with civic vice, claiming that prostitutes or "fallen women" could never defend the state. Machiavelli captured the powerful theme of female subversion in the character of Fortuna, the seductive, powerful force of effeminacy that lured men away from their political ambition. For the theme of fallen women and the dangerous female subversive in republican discourse, see Jean Bethke Elshtain, *Women and War* (New York: Harvester Press, 1987), 58–59, 62–63, 70. In addition, women pose a danger because they are both complicitous and resistant to the cause of war; the two extreme archetypes are the Spartan mother (who sends her sons willingly to die for the state) versus Antigone (whose mourning ritual challenges the authority of the state).

8. For a reference to women being placed "under the primal curse," see speech by Paulina Wright Davis, in *Syracuse WRC 1852*, 58. For Antoinette Brown's interpretation of the curse as "blessing," see ibid., 67.

9. See Jean-Jacques Rousseau, "The Social Contract or Principles of Political Right," in *Social Contract: Essays by Locke, Hume and, Rousseau*, with introduction by Sir Ernest Barker (London: Oxford University Press, 1960), 257. For Lucy Stone's comment, see *Worcester WRC 1851*, 29. For Mott's use of "cypher," see her "Discourse on Woman" (1849), in *Salem WRC 1850*, 17, 48. Also see *Salem WRC 1850*, 56, for Jane Elizabeth Jones's use of the term "cypher" at the same convention.

10. This argument was used in the political contest over extending voter rights to men without property in the famous Dorr War in 1842. See William M. Wiecek, "Popular Sovereignty in the Dorr War: Conservative Counterblast," *Rhode Island History* 32 (May 1973): 40.

11. Harriet Beecher Stowe, *Uncle Tom's Cabin* (1851–52; reprint, New York: Bantam Books, 1981), 116, 327–28, 334.

12. Jean Fagan Yellin defines the "tragic mulatto" as a "slave woman of mixed race who wants to conform to patriarchal definitions of true womanhood but is prevented from doing so by white patriarchy." See Jean Fagan Yellin, *Women and Sisters: The Antislavery Feminists in American Culture* (New Haven: Yale University Press, 1989), 53.

13. In one account of a slave auction, the writer described how the auctioneer "torn asunder the dress which covered her bosom and exposed to the libertine gaze around him a bust in beauty and purity never surpassed by a painter or sculptor." See "Sale of a White Girl," *Emancipator and Republican*, June 21, 1849.

14. Stowe, *Uncle Tom's Cabin*, 327–34; for the problem of slave women, sexuality, and public display, see Deborah Gray White, *Ar'n't I a Woman? Female Slaves in the Plantation South* (New York: Norton, 1985), 32–38.

15. See "Declaration of Sentiments," in *Seneca Falls WRC 1848*, 6.

16. Rousseau, "Social Contract," 246–48, 252–53.

17. Earl M. Maltz, "Fourteenth Amendment Concepts in the Antebellum Era," *American Journal of Legal History* 32 (1988): 321.

18. See "Speech by Paulina W. Davis," in *Worcester WRC 1850*. This notion of forfeiture or ransom was derived from Grotius, which Rousseau addressed and critiqued in "Social Contract," 248.

19. Walker is quoted several times during the Salem convention, and his reference to women's status as the "exact definition of political slavery" appeared in their Memorial. See *Salem WRC 1850*, 24.

20. "Letter from Elizabeth Cady Stanton," in *Syracuse WRC 1852*, 31.

21. Melton A. McLaurin, *Celia, a Slave* (New York: Avon Books, 1991).

22. See *George v. State*, 37 Miss. 316 (1859), 317, 319, 320, as cited in Peter W. Bardaglio, *Reconstructing the Household: Families, Sex, and the Law in the Nineteenth-Century South* (Chapel Hill: University of North Carolina Press, 1995), 68.

23. Ibid., 48.

24. Victoria E. Bynum, *Unruly Women: The Politics of Social and Sexual Control in the Old South* (Chapel Hill: University of North Carolina Press, 1992), 70–71.

25. William Goodell, *Views of American Constitutional Law, in its Bearing upon American Slavery* (Utica, N.Y., 1844), 40, 47–48.

26. Ibid., 75.

27. See William M. Wiecek, *The Sources of Antislavery Constitutionalism in America, 1760–1848* (Ithaca: Cornell University Press, 1977), 155.

28. See Paul Finkelman, "*Prigg v. Pennsylvania* and Northern State Courts: Anti-Slavery Use of a Proslavery Decision," *Civil War History* 25 (March 1979): 5–35.

29. Wiecek, *Sources of Antislavery Constitutionalism*, 156–57, 159.

30. Maltz, "Fourteenth Amendment Concepts," 326–27.

31. Goodell, *Views of American Constitutional Law*, 35–36, 40.

32. Finkelman, "*Prigg v. Pennsylvania* and the Northern Courts," 6–7, 11.

33. Barbara Meil Hobson, *Uneasy Virtue: The Politics of Prostitution and the American Reform Tradition* (Chicago: University of Chicago Press, 1990), 69.

34. Goodell, *Views of American Constitutional Law*, 35–36, 40.

35. *Lily*, August 1856, 105–6.

36. "Woman's Rights in Rhode Island," *Lily*, September 1, 1856, 128.

37. Edward D. Mansfield, *The Legal Rights, Liabilities, and Duties of Women; with an Introductory History of their Legal Condition in the Hebrew, Roman and Feudal Civil Systems* (Salem, Ohio, 1845), 307.

38. James H. Kettner, *The Development of American Citizenship, 1608–1870* (Chapel Hill: University of North Carolina Press, 1978); Linda K. Kerber, *Women of the Republic: Intellect and Ideology in Revolutionary America* (Chapel Hill: University of North Carolina Press, 1980).

39. Kettner notes that in 1848 Judge Hiram Warner of the Georgia Supreme Court ruled that free blacks should be considered "our wards." See Kettner, *Development of American Citizenship*, 320. Also see my discussion of citizenship and single women in Chapter 2, and for an example of the idea of women's political guardianship, see the arguments for and against woman suffrage in *Official Report of the Debates and Proceedings, in the State Convention, assembled May 4th, 1853, to Revise and Amend the Constitution of the Commonwealth of Massachusetts*, 2 vols. (Boston, 1853), 2:251, 262.

40. Kettner, *Development of American Citizenship*, 322.

41. In a response to an article that claimed that blacks were not entitled to "all the privileges of citizens," the author asserted that this was "not true," because in "Massachusetts, if not in most of the free states, a *colored woman* is entitled by law, to every 'privilege and immunity' which a *white woman* is entitled to. The law makes no distinction whatever between them." See "Passports," *Emancipator and Republican*, September 6, 1849.

42. Richard H. Sewell, *Ballots for Freedom: Antislavery Politics in the United States, 1837–1860* (New York: Oxford University Press, 1976), 180–81.

43. Kettner, *Development of American Citizenship*, 322; Maltz, "Fourteenth Amendment Concepts," 346.

44. Goodell, *Views of American Constitutional Law*, 60.

45. Mansfield, *Legal Rights, Liabilities, and Duties of Women*, 130.

46. Elisha P. Hurlbut, *Essays on Human Rights, and Their Political Guaranties* (New York, 1848), 162.

47. Mansfield, *Legal Rights, Liabilities, and Duties of Women*, 272–73.

48. *Pennsylvania Freeman*, February 18, 1847.

49. See Dana Greene, ed., *Lucretia Mott: Her Complete Speeches and Sermons* (New York: Edwin Mellen Press, 1980), 73–74; also see the original account of her speech in the *National Anti-Slavery Standard*, May 18, 1848.

50. Dana Greene, *Lucretia Mott*, 74.

51. E.C., "Appeal to Women," *Anti-Slavery Bugle*, January 14, 1848.

52. See "Memorial," "Letter from Mercy Holmes," and "Letter from Elizabeth Wilson," in *Salem WRC 1850*, 25, 30, 32.

53. See *New York City WRC 1856*, 75, and *Worcester WRC 1851*, 37.

54. In August 1836 Lydia Maria Child learned that the slave had been brought to Massachusetts by a woman from New Orleans. At first the members of the Boston Female Anti-Slavery Society sent a delegation of women to ask for the child's freedom. When the owner refused to com-

ply, the society, according to Child, "petitioned for a writ of habeas corpus; the judge granted the petition; and the man who held little Med in custody was brought up for trial." See Milton Meltzer and Patricia G. Holland, eds., *Lydia Maria Child, Selected Letters, 1817–1880* (Amherst: University of Massachusetts Press, 1982), 52–53. Wiecek notes that the 1837 Massachusetts Personal Liberty Act restored the writ of *homine replegiando* (right of jury trial) and that it was based on the ruling of the Med case of 1836. See Wiecek, *Sources of Antislavery Constitutionalism*, 96–97.

55. See "Constitution of the Anti-Slavery Society," as the one adopted by the Leicester, Mass., society in 1840. A copy of the pamphlet can be found in the American Antiquarian Society, Worcester, Mass. For the date of the Leicester society, see C. Van D. Chenoweth, *History of the Second Congregational Church and Society in Leicester, Massachusetts* (Worcester, Mass., 1908), 132.

56. William Goodell, in his chapter "Slaves cannot constitute Families," quoted John Woolman, who wrote that slaveholders "often part men from their wives by selling them far asunder." The word "asunder" had a particular meaning because it was taken from Matthew 19:6, in which Jesus forbade divorce: "Wherefore they are no more twain, but one flesh. What therefore God hath joined together, let no man put asunder." The word was often used in divorce cases as well. See Goodell, *The American Slave Code in Theory and Practice: Distinctive Features Shown by Its Statutes, Judicial Decisions, and Illustrative Facts* (New York, 1853), 144. For a reference to this biblical passage and its relationship to divorce law, see Mansfield, *Legal Rights, Liabilities, and Duties of Women*, 247.

57. *Commonwealth v. Aves*, 18 Pick. (Mass.) 194 (1836).

58. William Jay quoted an 1835 address of the Presbyterian Synod of Kentucky that recounted how "brothers and sisters, parents and children, husbands and wives, are torn asunder" by the slave trade. "*There is not a village or road* that does not behold the sad procession of *manacled* outcasts, whose mournful countenances tell that they are exiled by force from all that their heart's hold dear." In a later account Samuel May Jr. described the fugitive slave as "an outcast, wretched man—escaping from those who have cruelly entreated him all his days, who have defrauded and plundered him, beaten and bruised his wife and children before his eyes continually, and then sold that wife and those children, out of his sight forever, to other demons in human shape— flies to us and implores protection from those who are about to seize and carry him back to renewed sufferings." See William Jay, "A View of the Action of the General Government in Behalf of Slavery" (1839), in *Miscellaneous Writings on Slavery* (Boston, 1853), 259; Samuel May Jr., "Christianity a Crime," *Liberty Bell* (Boston, 1854), 240–41.

59. Goodell, *Views of American Constitutional Law*, 87.

60. Ibid., 68–69.

61. Ibid.

62. Betsey Mix Cowles, later the president of the women's rights convention held in Salem, Ohio, in 1850, distributed a circular that employed this phrase in the opening line. For a copy of the circular, see *Anti-Slavery Bugle*, June 18, 1847. The "Constitution of the Anti-Slavery Sewing Circle," drafted by J. Elizabeth Jones, another women's rights advocate, used a similar phrase: "We have a system in our midst which rob mothers of their children, should not mothers labor for its overthrow?" See *Anti-Slavery Bugle*, January 22, 1847.

63. See "Ruling in Fugitive Slave Case in Philadelphia," *National Anti-Slavery Standard*, March 10, 1851.

64. *Worcester WRC 1851*, 27, 39–40, 72.

65. Civis, "Woman's Rights and Woman's Wrongs According to the Law: No. 5," *Lily*, September 15, 1854, 135.

66. See address by Lucy Stone, in *Syracuse WRC 1852*, 20.

67. Lucy Lichen noted that women, like slaves, despite the appearance of being made in "God's image, breathing the breath of life, endowed with organs of speech, and human hand, and im-

mortal soul," still had no "*personal* existence." See "Letter to Mrs. Bloomer," *Lily*, August 15, 1854, 119. Another feminist, Lydia Jenkins, offered the same assessment, concluding that life had to offer more than simply being "*allowed to stay* in the world," and liberty also had to extend beyond what "my master sees fit in the wisdom of his councils to allow me." See *Syracuse WRC 1852*, 11.

68. For an account of a case in Rhode Island where a husband attempted to use recaption against his wife but the courts found him guilty of assault, see "Woman's Rights in Rhode Island," 128.

69. Civis, "Woman's Rights and Woman's Wrongs According to the Law: No. 5," 135.

70. See remarks by B. Rush Plumly, who referred both to oppression through "constant vigilance" and to the husband as the "keeper of her conscience," in *West Chester WRC 1852*, 32–34.

71. Stone told the following tale:

In Massachusetts, a few months ago, we were speaking of the law which gives the husband the custody of his wife's person when a man said to me—"In that house there is a wife who, for three years, has not set her foot out of doors. Every time her husband goes out, he nails down the windows, locks the door, and puts the key in his pocket. That woman," said my informant, "has not yet reached the mid-day of existence, yet her hair is gray and her face is full of wrinkles; and because the law gives that man the right of custody, and she cannot show any bruises, and has no friend to take up her cause, she lives on in that helpless and bitter wrong."

See *New York City WRC 1853*, 51.

72. See comments by Abby Kelley Foster, in *Cleveland WRC 1853*, 106–7.

73. E.C.S. [Elizabeth Cady Stanton], "Progress of Woman's Cause," *Lily*, July 15, 1854, 100.

74. "The Cincinnati Slave Case," *Lily*, March 1, 1856, 40.

75. In one account the newspaper correspondent claimed that after appeals to the "sympathy" of the master, because of the presence of the mother, the master responded that he would sell Emily Russell to a "Southern gentleman" for a lower price rather than allow her to go north. Not only did she have more "market value" as a sexual commodity exchanged among southern men, but her mother had no claim to her daughter, even though it was her mother "whom God had given her" and who had "endowed" her "with no ordinary qualities of person and mind." See "The Abominations of the Slave Trade. A White Woman for sale. Awful Depravity of the Human Heart. A Monster in Human Form," *Emancipator and Republican*, February 26, 1850.

76. For an example of this "tragic" theme, see "Liberty or Death," *Emancipator and Republican*, June 14, 1848. Here the author compared the suicide of a Roman slave family to that of an American slave family. Death is portrayed as the only "escape." As a result, the mother kills her child, the husband kills the wife, and then the husband attempts "to complete the sacrifice by cutting his own throat."

77. Abby Price described one of the universal qualities of female slavery as reducing women to an "appendage" of men; see *Worcester WRC 1851*, 19.

78. *Cleveland WRC 1853*, 43.

79. See *New York City WRC 1853*, 58.

80. See reprint of article "To My Old Master," originally published in the *North Star*, titled "Fred Douglass and Corresponding Equality," *National Anti-Slavery Standard*, September 14, 1848.

81. See *Worcester WRC 1851*, 37.

82. "Letter from Jane Swisshelm to the AS Convention of Young Men and Women of Ohio," *National Anti-Slavery Standard*, October 18, 1849.

83. *Cleveland WRC 1853*, 77.

84. Susanna Rowson, *Charlotte Temple*, ed. with an introduction by Cathy N. Davidson (New

York: Oxford University Press, 1988); Patricia L. Parker, *Susanna Haswell Rowson* (Boston: Twayne, 1986); also see Rose's comments in *Cleveland WRC 1853*, 78.

85. Rowson, *Charlotte Temple*, 53–56.

86. For a discussion of the English common-law model of seduction, see Anna K. Clark, "Rape or Seduction? A Controversy over Sexual Violence in the Nineteenth Century," in *The Sexual Dynamics of History: Men's Power, Women's Resistance*, ed. London Feminist History Group (London: Pluto Press, 1993), 14. In the colonial period a sexual double standard also defined the prosecution and punishment of men and women in bastardy and fornication cases. See Cornelia Hughes Dayton, "Unequal in Transgression: The Double Standard in Bastardy/Fornication in Eighteenth-Century New England," *Critical Matrix* 1 (1985): 1–36; also see Dayton, *Women before the Bar: Gender, Law, and Society in Connecticut, 1639–1789* (Chapel Hill: University of North Carolina Press, 1995).

87. Hurlbut, *Essays on Human Rights*, 132.

88. Hendrik Hartog, "Lawyering, Husbands' Rights, and 'the Unwritten Law' in Nineteenth-Century America," *Journal of American History* 84 (June 1997): 67–96.

89. See Meltzer and Holland, *Lydia Maria Child*, 82.

90. See Walt Whitman, "A Dialogue," *United States Magazine and Democratic Review*, November 1845, 360–64; Lydia Maria Child, *Letters from New York* (1843), in *Provisions: A Reader from Nineteenth-Century American Women*, ed. Judith Fetterley (Bloomington: Indiana University Press, 1985), 188–89; William S. Osborne, *Lydia Maria Child* (Boston: Twayne, 1980), 98.

91. David Brion Davis, "The Movement to Abolish Capital Punishment in America, 1787–1861," *American Historical Review* 63 (October 1957): 38, 40; Philip English Mackey, *Hanging in the Balance: The Anti-Capital Punishment Movement in New York State, 1776–1861* (New York: Garland, 1982), 127, 135, 142–44, 156–57; Louis P. Masur, *Rites of Execution: Capital Punishment and the Transformation of American Culture, 1776–1865* (New York: Oxford University Press, 1989), 117–24, 141–59.

92. George B. Cheever, *Punishment by Death: Its Authority and Expediency* (New York, 1849), 135, 162, 220, 272–75. This book also includes a copy of Cheever's 1843 speech "Argument in Reply to J. L. O'Sullivan, Esq., During the Debate in the Broadway Tabernacle in 1843." Cheever paraphrased Genesis 4:14 in reference to Cain in his debate with O'Sullivan. Cheever's book was praised by religious and secular reviewers; see Mackey, *Hanging in the Balance*, 156–57.

93. Cheever, *Punishment by Death*, 222.

94. See *The Impropriety of Capital Punishment; or, The Report of a Committee on Dr. Cuyler's Sermon entitled "The Law of God with Respect to Murder"* (Philadelphia, 1842), 21–22. Also see public handbill, *Philadelphia Committee on Capital Punishment* (1845). This pamphlet and handbill are available at the Philadelphia Library Company, Philadelphia, Pa. The arguments presented here are similar to those in O'Sullivan's sixty-eight page *Report in Favor of the Abolition of the Punishment of Death* (New York, 1841), which, as Mackey notes, became the handbook for reformers in other states, such as Pennsylvania and Massachusetts, and even a southern reviewer praised its content. See Mackey, *Hanging in the Balance*, 141–43.

95. Child, *Letters from New York*, in Fetterley, *Provisions*, 193.

96. Child discussed the "Burton" (which probably is a reference to the Beauchamp case) in her letter on the Colt execution; see *Letters from New York*, in Fetterley, *Provisions*, 193–94. For her story "Elizabeth Wilson," see Lydia Maria Child, *Fact and Fiction: A Collection of Stories* (New York, 1849), 126–49, esp. 146–47. For her reference to the legal system as a "gallows-game," see another letter published on February 17, 1842, also in *Letters from New York*, in Fetterley, *Provisions*, 181. For information on Elizabeth Wilson and her confession narrative, see Daniel A. Cohen, *Pillars of Salt, Monuments of Grace: New England Crime Literature and the Origins of American Popular Culture, 1674–1860* (New York: Oxford University Press, 1993), 147–49;

Daniel E. Williams, *Pillars of Salt: An Anthology of Early American Crime Narrative* (Madison, Wis.: Madison House, 1993), 271–81.

97. See Lydia Maria Child, "The Juryman: A Sketch," *Emancipator and Republican*, January 12, 1850.

98. Marybeth Hamilton Arnold, "'The Life of a Citizen in the Hands of a Woman': Sexual Assault in New York City, 1790 to 1820," in *Passion and Power: Sexuality in History*, ed. Kathy Peiss and Christina Simmons, with Robert A. Padgug (Philadelphia: Temple University Press, 1989), 35–56.

99. Michael Grossberg, *Governing the Hearth: Law and the Family in Nineteenth-Century America* (Chapel Hill: University of North Carolina Press, 1985), 42, 44.

100. Robert Griswold, "Adultery and Divorce in Victorian America, 1800–1900," *Legal History Program: Working Papers*, ser. 1 (Madison: Institute for Legal Studies, 1986), 31.

101. See Andie Tucher, *Froth and Scum: Truth, Beauty, Goodness, and the Ax Murder in America's First Mass Medium* (Chapel Hill: University of North Carolina Press, 1994), 100, 105–6. Also see John D. Lawson, ed., *American State Trials*, 2 vols. (St. Louis: F. H. Thomas Law, 1914), 1:474; "Trial of John C. Colt for the Murder of Samuel Adams," *Sun-Extra* (N.Y.), January 31, 1842.

102. See John Locke, *Two Treatises of Government*, ed. Peter Laslett (Cambridge: Cambridge University Press, 1963), 389.

103. Cover quotes Blackstone:

The punishment of treason in general is very solemn and terrible. 1. That the offender be drawn to the gallows, and not be carried or walk; though usually (by connivance, at length ripened by human into law) a sledge or hurdle is allowed, to preserve the offender from the extreme torment of being dragged on the ground or pavement. 2. That he be hanged by the neck, and then cut down alive. 3. That his entrails be taken out, and burned, while yet he is alive. 4. That his head be cut off. 5. That his body be divided into four parts. 6. That his head and quarters be at the king's disposal.

See Robert M. Cover, "Violence and the Word," *Yale Law Journal* 95 (1986): 1606.

104. See Douglas Sturm, "Corporations, Constitutions, and Covenants: On Forms of Human Relation and the Problem of Legitimacy," *Journal of the American Academy of Religion* 41 (September 1973): 350–51. Shirley Samuels highlights that adultery and religious infidelity were intertwined as the two major dangers of infidelity during the early republic. See Samuels, "Infidelity and Contagion: The Rhetoric of the Revolution," *Early American Literature* 22 (Fall 1987): 183–84.

105. Civis, "Woman's Rights and Woman's Wrongs According to the Law, No. 4," *Lily*, September 1, 1854, 126. The idea that adultery was an act of treason by the wife against the husband persisted into the nineteenth century. It was "treason" against the marriage bond. See Theodore D. Woolsey, *Divorce and Divorce Legislation, especially in the United States*, 2nd ed. (New York: Scribner's, 1882), 259. One writer compared adultery to a crime against the social compact, for adultery was equated with polygamy, a crime against all men. See Charles Caverno, *Treatise on Divorce* (Madison, Wis., 1889).

106. For a discussion of *petit treason* and its impact on women's civil standing during the early republic, see Linda K. Kerber, "The Paradox of Women's Citizenship in the Early Republic: The Case of *Martin v. Massachusetts*, 1805," *American Historical Review* 97 (April 1992): 352. In his study of criminal sentencing in New York, Boston, and Philadelphia, William Kuntz discovered that adultery invoked a double standard for women, with women serving more time for the crime. See William Francis Kuntz II, *Criminal Sentencing in Three Nineteenth-Century Cities: Social History of Punishment in New York, Boston, and Philadelphia, 1830–1880* (New York: Garland, 1988), 400.

107. *O'Bryan v. O'Bryan*, 13 Missouri Reports 20 (1850).

108. See [Lucretia Chapman], *Trial of Lucretia Chapman; otherwise called Lucretia Espos y Mina, who was jointly indicted with Lino Amalia Espos y Mina, for the murder of William Chapman, Esq. late of Andalusia, County of Bucks, Pennsylvania: in the Court of Oyer and Terminer, held at Doylestown, for Bucks, December term, 1831, continued to February term, 1832* (Philadelphia, 1832), 100–111, 182, 192; Karen Halttunen, "'Domestic Differences': Competing Narratives of Womanhood in the Murder Trial of Lucretia Chapman," in *The Culture of Sentiment: Race, Gender, and Sentimentality in Nineteenth-Century America*, ed. Shirley Samuels (New York: Oxford University Press, 1992), 46–47.

109. *New York City WRC 1856*, 71–72.

110. Margaret Fuller, *Woman in the Nineteenth Century* (New York, 1845; reprint, Columbia: University of South Carolina Press, 1980), 134–35.

111. Hobson, *Uneasy Virtue*, 74.

112. Lydia Maria Child, "Amelia Norman," *New York Daily Tribune*, February 8, 1844.

113. Timothy Walker, "Case of Amelia Norman: Ought Seduction to be Punished as a Crime," *Western Law Journal*, February 1844, 276–77. For an account of Mercer's case, see *The Trial of Singleton Mercer, for the Murder of M. Hutchinson Memberton, at Camden, N.J., on Friday, 10th February, 1843* (New York, 1843).

114. Timothy Walker, "Case of Amelia Norman," 277.

115. W. David Lewis, *From Newgate to Dannemora: The Rise of the Penitentiary in New York, 1796–1848* (Ithaca: Cornell University Press, 1965), 224. In her biography of Isaac Hopper, Child described how Abby H. Gibbons, his daughter, was "as vigilant and active in behalf of women discharged from prison, as her father was in behalf of men." At that time Child lived with Isaac Hopper, and she wrote a lengthy letter for the newspapers in support of the Prison Association (before the formation of the Female Department) in December 1844. See Lydia Maria Child, *Isaac T. Hopper: A True Life* (Boston, 1845), 411; Child, *Letters from New York*, 2nd ed. (New York, 1853), 258–72. Also see "Abigail Hopper Gibbons," in *Notable American Women, 1607–1950: A Biographical Dictionary*, 3 vols., ed. Edward T. James, Janet Wilson James, and Paul S. Boyer (Cambridge: Belknap Press of Harvard University Press, 1971), 2:28; Meltzer and Holland, *Lydia Maria Child*, 265.

116. A notice and brief description of the purpose of this meeting appeared in *Pennsylvania Freeman*, January 21, 1847.

117. An account of the meeting and its connection to the antislavery meeting appeared in the *National Anti-Slavery Standard*, February 18, 1847. On March 24 the Committee of Correspondence reported that they had distributed 800 petitions and circulars throughout the state, and a copy of the report printed by the public meeting was given to every member of the legislature. In this report they noted that 11,777 signatures appeared on the petitions. See *Pennsylvania Freeman*, April 8, 1847. In an article reprinted from the *New York Daily Tribune* on legislative reforms in Pennsylvania, it was reported that "the Ladies of the State seem to be taking the lead" in collecting petitions against capital punishment. See *Pennsylvania Freeman*, February 18, 1847. It was fitting that capital punishment reform had a gender dimension within the context of politics in Pennsylvania. In 1841 an attempt to abolish capital punishment for females was defeated, which probably generated an awareness of the sexual double standard in the law. See Albert Post, "Early Efforts to Abolish Capital Punishment in Pennsylvania," *Pennsylvania Magazine of History and Biography* 68 (January 1944): 45.

118. For an account of the organization of the Rosine Society, see Emilie S. Troth and Mrs. Edward D. Lorimer, "Mira Sharpless Townsend, 1798–1859," in *Notable Women of Pennsylvania*, ed. Gertrude Bosler Biddle and Sarah Dickinson Lowrie (Philadelphia, 1942), 129–30.

Townsend's own account appeared in the introduction of *Report and Realities from a Sketch-Book of a Manager of the Rosine Society* (Philadelphia, 1855), 7.

119. For a similar view of women's lack of sympathy, see L.A.M. [Lydia Mack], "Women Never Forgive an Erring Woman," *Una*, September 1854, 325.

120. For the reform theories advocated by Townsend and other supporters of the society, see *The Annual Report of the Managers of the Rosine Association, May, 1847* (Philadelphia, 1847), 1–10; *Constitution and Report of the Managers of the Rosine Association, with a List of the Annual Subscribers and Contributors* (Philadelphia, 1848), 8–9, 12–13; *The Annual Report of the Managers of the Rosine Association, May, 1849* (Philadelphia, 1849), 4–5.

121. *Syracuse WRC 1852*, 41.

122. *Cleveland WRC 1853*, 101.

123. *Syracuse WRC 1852*, 40.

124. "Men's Justice Unfair to Women," *Una*, September 15, 1855, 136.

125. See L.A.M., "Women Never Forgive an Erring Woman," 325.

126. *Salem WRC 1850*, 38.

127. Ibid.

128. Ibid., 57.

129. "Just and Equal Rights of Women," *Lily*, July 15, 1855, 95.

130. *Salem WRC 1850*, 57.

131. *Akron WRC 1851*, 13.

132. See "Justice to Woman: Address of the Women's Rights Convention, to the Legislature," *Una*, April 1854, 250.

133. The theme of necessity emerged in the call for the anti–capital punishment meeting of women in 1847; see "Anti–Capital Punishment Meeting," *Pennsylvania Freeman*, January 21, 1847. For the quote by Madame de Staël, see "Anti–Capital Punishment Meeting," ibid., February 4, 1847. Lydia Maria Child used the same quote in her letter against corporal punishment; see *Letters from New York* (1853), 264. The same quote was used by Lucy Stone at the Seventh National Woman's Rights Convention; see *New York City WRC 1856*, 44.

134. See his remarks made during the 1851 Worcester women's rights convention, in *Worcester WRC 1851*, 57.

135. Jane Swisshelm, *Half a Century*, 2nd ed. (Chicago: Janson, McClurg, 1880), 92–94; also see "Jane Gray Swisshelm: Abolitionist, Feminist, Journalist, 1815–1884," in *Great Women of the Press*, ed. Medelon Golden Schilpp and Sharon M. Murphy (Carbondale: Southern Illinois Press, 1983), 76–77.

136. Peter Walker, *Moral Choices: Memory, Desire, and Imagination in Nineteenth-Century American Abolition* (Baton Rouge: Louisiana State University Press, 1978), 128–29.

137. Thomas R. Hietala, *Manifest Design: Anxious Aggrandizement in Late Jacksonian America* (Ithaca: Cornell University Press, 1985), 121.

138. Swisshelm, *Half a Century*, 93–96.

139. Such views of Mexican women gained circulation during the war, and "internal enemies posed a constant concern for advocates of expansion." See Reginald Horsman, *Race and Manifest Destiny: The Origins of American Racial Anglo-Saxonism* (Cambridge: Harvard University Press, 1981), 233–35, 243–44; also see Hietala, *Manifest Design*, 213.

140. Jane Swisshelm, "Masculine Qualifications for the Rights of Citizenship," *Lily*, January 1851, 4. Swisshelm made a similar argument in one of her letters published after the declaration of the war with Mexico. This piece first appeared in the *Spirit of Liberty* and then was reprinted under the title "Political Suffrage" in the *National Anti-Slavery Standard*, June 18, 1846.

141. The biblical metaphor of "one flesh" was a common phrase used by southern and northern

politicians. The Whig Alexander H. Stephens of Georgia, for example, employed it to describe Texans as Anglo-Saxons: "They are from us and of us; bone of our bone, and flesh of our flesh." The issue of keeping the United States as a homogeneous population of "common interests, desires, and feelings" also emerged as a central issue of the Mexican War. See Horsman, *Race and Manifest Destiny*, 218, 240–42.

142. Swisshelm used the term "proxy" in both her articles on suffrage and citizenship. She not only pursued her own legal case for retaining control of her inherited property, but she was an active supporter of married women's property reform. See Swisshelm, *Half a Century*, 101–5. For a discussion of the "one-flesh doctrine" and its use in the 1846 New York state constitutional convention, see Norma Basch, *In the Eyes of the Law: Women, Marriage, and Property in Nineteenth-Century New York* (Ithaca: Cornell University Press, 1982), 19, 147, 152.

143. Horsman, *Race and Manifest Destiny*, 238, 242–43.

144. Swisshelm, "Masculine Qualifications." Horsman has noted that the wording "white male citizens" was used to specify suffrage qualifications during the 1849 California state constitutional convention. This phrase not only excluded blacks, but Mexicans with Indian blood who previously held the right to vote. See Horsman, *Race and Manifest Destiny*, 278.

145. *Akron WRC 1851*, 4–5.

146. Arendt identifies the classical notion of the household as a place ruled by force and violence, and that subordinate members, such as slaves and women, were viewed as "tamed animals." See Hannah Arendt, *The Human Condition* (Chicago: University of Chicago Press, 1958), 27, 84.

147. Rousseau, "Social Contract," 244–45.

148. *Akron WRC 1851*, 5.

149. *Worcester WRC 1850*, 8.

150. See Eric Sundquist, *Home as Found: Authority and Genealogy in Nineteenth-Century American Literature* (Baltimore: Johns Hopkins University Press, 1979), 1; Jane Tompkins, *Sensational Designs: The Cultural Work of American Fiction, 1790–1860* (New York: Oxford University Press, 1986), esp. chap. 4, "No Apologies for the Iroquois: A New Way to Read the Leatherstocking Novels," 95, 102–11, 117–19.

151. See John P. McWilliams Jr., *The American Epic: Transforming a Genre, 1770–1860* (Cambridge: Cambridge University Press, 1989), 137–41, 158–62.

152. See discussion of barbarous tribes in Timothy Walker, "The Legal Condition of Woman," *Western Law Journal*, January 1849, 316–17; Roy Harvey Pearce, *The Savages of America*, rev. ed. (Baltimore: Johns Hopkins University Press, 1965), 82–91.

153. Frederick Grimké, *Considerations Upon the Nature and Tendency of Free Institutions* (Cincinnati, 1848), 229–331.

154. Richard Slotkin appropriately uses this quote of Tocqueville as an opening epigraph to his book *Gunfighter Nation: The Myth of the Frontier in Twentieth-Century America* (New York: Atheneum, 1992).

155. Hietala, *Manifest Design*, 22–23, 51. The phrase "mighty march" is from a speech by Sam Houston, "Valedictory to the Texas Congress, December 9, 1844," in *The Writings of Sam Houston*, ed. Amelia W. Williams and Eugene C. Barker, 8 vols. (Austin: University of Texas Press, 1938–43), 4:403.

156. Walker argued that Texas could serve as a "safety-valve" that would siphon off the free black population from the United States; this would eventually result in their migration out of the United States and into Central and South America. His argument had appeal not only for southern Democrats who supported expansion but for northerners who feared mass migrations of free blacks into the northern states. For a copy of his letter and a discussion of its impact on the Texas question, see Frederick Merk, *Fruits of Propaganda in the Tyler Administration* (Cambridge:

Harvard University Press, 1971), 98–100, 114–15, 221–52; also see Hietala, *Manifest Design*, 14, 31, 33.

157. "White Slavery," *United States Magazine and Democratic Review*, September 1842, 261, 270.

158. In 1831, for example, Stephen Simpson of the Philadelphia Working Men's Party compared factory laborers to a "serf class," which suggested how notions of feudalism contributed to antebellum views of white slavery. See David Roediger, *The Wages of Whiteness: Race and the Making of the Working Class* (London: Verso, 1991), 70.

159. "Annexation," *United States Magazine and Democratic Review*, July 1845, 7; "Legislative Embodiment of Public Opinion," ibid., August 1846, 86.

160. Rhode Island suffered from both malapportionment and disfranchisement because the state refused to abandon the freehold qualification. It is estimated that in the entire state almost 60 percent of all adult white males were excluded from the ballot, whereas in Providence—the center of labor activism—possibly 94 percent of the adult male population had no recourse to the vote. Another aristocratic feature of the system in Rhode Island was that a freeholder's son could vote without meeting the property qualification. The Dorr supporters clearly challenged the suffrage restrictions on the grounds of aristocratic privilege, white slavery, and the right of dissent and revolution, as detailed in the most complete contemporary history of the movement by a Dorr supporter, Francis Harriet (Whipple) Greene McDougall, *Might and Right: A History of the Dorr Rebellion* (Providence, R.I., 1844), 15–16, 43–45. For a good summary of these issues, also see Wiecek, "Popular Sovereignty in the Dorr War," 37.

161. Wendy Brown, *Manhood and Politics*, 38–42.

162. For images of working women, see Helena Michie, *The Flesh Made Word: Female Figures and Women's Bodies* (New York: Oxford University Press, 1987), 51–56. Lowell mill women addressed the issue of women being transformed into the "*white slave of the North*" and the image of the female drudge; see *The Lowell Offering: Writings by New England Mill Women, 1840–1845*, ed. Benita Eisler (New York: Harper Torchbooks, 1977), 75–82, 203–8.

163. See Sandra L. Myres, *Westering Women and the Frontier Experience, 1800–1915* (Albuquerque: University of New Mexico Press, 1982), 5; Julie Roy Jeffrey, *Frontier Women: The Trans-Mississippi West, 1840–1880* (New York: Hill and Wang, 1979), 46, 55, 76.

164. Myres, *Westering Women*, 75, 80–81.

165. Houston, "To Santa Anna, Executive Department, City of Houston," March 21, 1842, in Walker and Barker, *Writings of Sam Houston*, 2:253; "To Captain Charles Elliot," May 13, 1843, in ibid., 3:386; "Speech on the Boundary of Texas," in ibid., 5:29, 32, 33–34.

166. Houston, "Houston's Inaugural Address," October 22, 1836, 1:449–50; "To Santa Anna," 2:514–15, 523–24; "To Captain Charles Elliot," 3:386; "To William S. Murphy," May 6, 1844, 4:323; "Valedictory," 4:404; and "Speech on the Boundary of Texas," 5:31, 33–35, all in ibid.

167. For an astute rebuttal of the argument that war is the "highest trial of right," see "Time and Right Against War," *Emancipator and Republican*, June 14, 1849.

168. William Jay, *A Review of the Causes and Consequences of the Mexican War*, 2nd ed. (Boston, 1849), 245, 247–48.

169. The phrase "might makes right" was used in the Dorr trial. See George M. Dennison, *The Dorr War: Republicanism on Trial, 1831–1861* (Lexington: University Press of Kentucky, 1976), 175, 178, 180, 183.

170. See "Anti-War Meeting in Kennett Square," *Pennsylvania Freeman*, July 2, 1846.

171. Jay, *Review of the Causes and Consequences of the Mexican War*, 249–53. A prowar mob disrupted a large public meeting organized by Samuel J. May. See "Anti-War Meeting at Syracuse, NY" *National Anti-Slavery Standard*, July 2, 1846; also see John Schroeder, *Mr. Polk's War: American Opposition and Dissent, 1846–48* (Madison: University of Wisconsin Press, 1973), 100.

172. Jay, *Review of the Causes and Consequences of the Mexican War*, 164–66, 248–49. It was common for critics to equate war with "wild violence" and "manifest barbarism, down-right fist, foot, tooth, and nail." See "Time and Right Against War," *Emancipator and Republican*, July 14, 1849.

173. In both the Syracuse and Kennett Square meetings the participants raised the issue of conquest, while the Pennsylvania reformers strongly opposed the war on the grounds of "blind obedience" in the name of patriotism. Other resolutions called for opposition to this war by all "moral and peaceable means," and at the Syracuse meeting reformers called for "the laboring classes to decline from volunteering," because this would leave the "military and political" demagogues" without a "vocation" as well as free "soldiers of the poor" from the "heavy burden of war." See "Anti-War Meeting at Syracuse, NY"; "Anti-War Meeting in Kennett Square." For calls for circulating and signing antiwar pledges in Salem, Ohio, and Worcester, Mass., see *Anti-Slavery Bugle*, July 10, 1846, and *Practical Christian*, October 3, 1846. For a brief summary of the tactics used by protesters, see Clayton Sumner Ellsworth, "The American Churches and the Mexican War," *American Historical Review* 45 (January 1940): 316–17.

174. For a summary of the meeting and a copy of the letter drafted by the women of Philadelphia, see *Pennsylvania Freeman*, June 25, 1846. Elihu Burritt's letter and "the friendly address of the undersigned women, inhabitants of the City of Exeter, in England, to the Women of the City of Philadelphia, and of the United States generally," appeared in ibid., June 4, 1846.

175. For a request to "the Women of the United States" to join the petition campaign against the Mexican War, see *Pennsylvania Freeman*, September 23, 1847. At the antiwar meeting held in Kennett Square on June 13, 1847, several women's rights advocates—Grace Ann Lewis, Sydney Pierce, and Ann Preston—served on the committee to prepare and publish the address protesting the war. See ibid., July 2, 1846. In Ohio a peace convention was held in Randolph on September 14 and 15, 1847, and several women's rights supporters signed the call for the meeting. The list included Elizabeth Stedman, K. G. Thomas and Rebecca Thomas, Joseph Dugdale, Eliza Holmes, Cordelia Smalley, Sophonia Smalley, and Louisa Ladd. All of these women signed the call for the Salem women's rights convention, and the men either attended the meeting following the women's convention or they supported the women's movement in print or at future conventions. See "Call for Peace Convention in Randolph," *Anti-Slavery Bugle*, September 17, 1847.

176. Jay, *Review of the Causes and Consequences of the Mexican War*, 106.

177. *Pennsylvania Freeman*, September 3, 1846. Jay makes the same argument for the extension of slavery in his chapter "Motive for Acquiring Territory—The Wilmot Proviso." Here he quoted several southern newspapers, including a statement from the *Charlestown Courier*: "Every battle fought in Mexico, and every dollar spent there, but insures the acquisition of territory which must widen the field of southern enterprise and power for the future." See Jay, *Review of the Causes and Consequences of the Mexican War*, 182. This argument was not new but was the consistent refrain used by most antislavery and Liberty Party supporters when protesting the annexation of Texas. See Arthur Harry Rice, "Henry B. Stanton as a Political Abolitionist" (Ed.D. diss., Columbia University, 1968), 253–55, 258–61, 267–68; also see Merk, *Fruits of Propaganda*, 96.

178. *United States Magazine and Democratic Review*, November 1847, 381–82, 388–90.

179. Houston, "Speech on the Boundary of Texas" (1848), 5:36.

180. Josiah Nott advanced this theory in his 1844 treatise *Two Lectures on the Natural History of the Caucasian and Negro Races*. Nott was one of the most popular advocates of ethnology, a field of natural science that gained increasing acceptance among scientists and politicians during the antebellum period. In his discussion of the law of hybrids, Nott argued that when the "white man is crossed upon the Negresse or Indian woman," then "in the offspring the brain is enlarged, the facial angle increased, and the intellect improved in a marked degree." He also asserted that when hybrids are bred together, they "have a tendency to run out, and change back to one of the

parent stocks." For his views on this subject, see *The Ideology of Slavery: Proslavery Thought in the Antebellum South, 1830–1860*, ed. Drew Gilpin Faust (Baton Rouge: Louisiana State University Press, 1981), 230–31.

181. See *The Compact Edition of the Oxford English Dictionary*, 2 vols. (Oxford: Oxford University Press, 1971), 1:142.

182. Titled "They Wait for Us," this poem was originally published in Boston in 1846. See Horsman, *Race and Manifest Destiny*, 230, 233. Houston also wrote a poem in 1837 in which he described "Anglo-Saxon chivalry" as embodied by one "Who guards the weak that are oppressed." See "To Anna Raguet," in Walker and Barker, *Writings of Sam Houston*, 2:31.

183. Josiah Nott used the metaphor of the seed to demonstrate his belief that white men carried, planted, and infused the "principle of action" into the march of civilization: "But what does the history of the Caucasian show in all climes and in all times—strike off the fetters of bad government, and he takes up the march of civilization and presses onward—the principle of action within him is like the life in an acorn—take an acorn which has laid in a box for a thousand years and plant it in congenial soil, it sprouts at once and grows into the majestic oak." See Faust, *Ideology of Slavery*, 234–35.

184. Webster wrote a detailed account of her trial and prison experience; see Delia Webster, *Kentucky Jurisprudence. A History of the Trial of Miss Delia A. Webster. At Lexington, Kentucky, Dec. 17–21, 1844, Before the Hon. Richard Buckner. On a Charge of Aiding Slaves to Escape from that Commonwealth—with Miscellaneous Remarks, including her Views on American Slavery. Written by Herself* (Vergennes, Vt., 1845).

185. For a review of the legal proceedings, see "Case of Delia Webster," *Emancipator and Republican*, January 27, 1845.

186. After Webster's pardon, Governor Owsley explained that his decision was based on the following: "The moral effect of the conviction had already been secured by the confinement she had already undergone; and it was believed the generous people of Kentucky could take no pleasure in her further suffering in prison." But the odd twist in the case came when Webster claimed that she planned to convince northerners of "the illegality, the folly, and the injustice" of abolitionists "intermeddling" with the question of slavery. Thus, Webster was expected to become an emissary for proslavery in the North, which clearly added an unusual condition to the terms of her pardon and release. See "Delia Webster," *Emancipator and Republican*, March 12, 1845.

187. Jane Swisshelm, "Chivalry," *Emancipator and Republican*, February 26, 1845.

188. See "Mrs. Rose," *Anti-Slavery Bugle*, October 22, 1853.

189. See a description of her playlet in Linda L. Geary, *Balanced in the Wind: A Biography of Betsey Mix Cowles* (Lewisburg, Pa.: Bucknell University Press, 1989), 62–63.

190. *Salem WRC 1850*, 17.

191. *Akron WRC 1851*, 39.

192. *Salem WRC 1850*, 54. Women could just as easily be blinded by glory and gallantry, as William H. Burleigh argued in his antiwar article "Woman on the War-field." He criticized the Yankee women of Newburyport for their public demonstrations of approval "of murder and rapine" in their celebrations of Colonel Cushing. He contrasted this false celebration of honor and courage with the Mexican women who risked their lives aiding fallen soldiers on the battlefield. Here women faced death and danger and displayed both compassion and courage. See *Emancipator and Republican*, April 28, 1847.

193. *Akron WRC 1851*, 28–29; for reference to "flowers of chivalry," see Swisshelm, "Chivalry."

194. *Worcester WRC 1850*, 41.

195. *Syracuse WRC 1852*, 26.

196. See Jay, "Patriotism," in *Review of the Causes and Consequences of the Mexican War*, 281.

197. Geary, *Balanced in the Wind*, 63.

198. For a reference to man assuming the role of the "*chevalier*, and who would upon the first note of alarm rush to our aid," see "Letter from Mrs. C. M. Steele," in *Akron WRC 1851*, 39.

199. See Senex [Anson Bingham], "Chivalry vs. Women's Enfranchisement No. 1," *Lily*, February 1, 1855, 21.

200. Senex [Anson Bingham], "Chivalry vs. Woman's Enfranchisement No. Two," *Lily*, April 11, 1855, and "Chivalry vs. Woman's Enfranchisement No. Three," ibid., July 1, 1855.

201. "Chivalry vs. Woman's Enfranchisement No. Two," 53.

202. "Woman's Rights Convention at Massillon," *Anti-Slavery Bugle*, June 5, 1852.

203. Senex [Anson Bingham], "The Democratic Review on Woman's Rights—No. 6," *Lily*, September 1852, 76.

204. Mott's comment appeared in her "Discourse on Woman" (1849), which was sent and published as part of the Salem women's rights convention proceedings. Jones made her reference in her "Address on Woman's Rights and Wrongs," which was given at the Salem convention. See *Salem WRC 1850*, 42, 56.

205. *New York City WRC 1853*, 66–67.

206. *Cleveland WRC 1853*, 14.

207. Ibid., 56.

208. In her letter to the Akron convention in 1851, Stanton wrote, "Better, far, suffer occasional insults, or die outright, than live the life of a coward, or never move without a protector." See *Worcester WRC 1850*, 52, and *Akron WRC 1851*, 34.

209. For the reference to the rejection of bloodletting as a mark of honor, see *Worcester WRC 1851*, 108. For the allusion to man's "boundless capacity," see resolutions from the same convention, ibid., 18. For the argument that man is just as much out of his sphere for engaging in the practices of conquest, for "God did not create either of them to be the murderers and marauders of their kind," see B. Rush Plumly's speech in *West Chester WRC 1852*, 32.

210. *Worcester WRC 1851*, 37; for "padlocks are on our lips," see *Salem WRC 1850*, 27.

211. *Akron WRC 1851*, 41.

212. See *Congressional Globe*, 33rd Cong., 2nd sess., 91–92, and appendix, 378.

213. *Reports on the Laws of New England, Presented to the New England Meeting, Convened at the Meionaon, Sept. 19 and 20, 1855* (Boston, 1855), 1–2, 4; also see "Marriage of Lucy Stone Under Protest," *Una*, June 1855, 87.

214. David H. Bennett, *The Party of Fear: From Nativist Movements to the New Right in American History* (Chapel Hill: University of North Carolina Press, 1988), 118, 123.

215. *Congressional Globe*, 33rd Cong., 2nd sess., appendix, 31, 83. Augustus Rhodes Sollers was elected as a Whig to the 27th Congress (March 4, 1841–March 3, 1843), served as a delegate to the state constitutional convention in 1851, and was reelected to the 33rd Congress (March 1853–March 3, 1855). See *Biographical Directory of the United States Congress, 1774–1989* (Washington, D.C.: Government Printing Office, 1989), 1846. Maryland had a foreign-born population of 11 percent by 1850, and the state had the highest population of fugitive and manumitted slaves in the United States. In 1855 the Know-Nothings won four of six congressional seats, and in 1856 Maryland was the only state to go for Millard Fillmore, the Know-Nothing presidential candidate, granting him the only electoral votes he won during the national election. See Bennett, *Party of Fear*, 141, 150.

216. *Congressional Globe*, 33rd Cong., 2nd sess., appendix, 83.

217. See Hietala, *Manifest Design*, 156–62; Horsman, *Race and Manifest Destiny*, 276–83. The remarks of Millard Fillmore in 1852 in his annual presidential message demonstrate a similar racial concern in regard to the acquisition of Cuba: "Were this Island comparatively destitute of inhabitants, or occupied by a kindred race, I should regard it, if voluntarily ceded by Spain,

as a most desirable acquisition. But, under existing circumstances, I should look upon its incorporation into our Union as a very hazardous measure. It would bring into the Confederacy a population of a different national stock, speaking a different language, and not likely to harmonize with other members" (from the *Congressional Globe*, 32nd Cong., 2nd sess., appendix, 1). Know-Nothing politicians in Baltimore fit this pattern of adapting the patriotism of the Mexican War and extending this sense of mission and conquest to keeping America for Americans. See Jean H. Baker, *Ambivalent Americans: The Know-Nothing Party in Maryland* (Baltimore: Johns Hopkins University Press, 1977), 32.

218. *Congressional Globe*, 33rd Cong., 2nd sess., 168; Dale T. Knobel, *"America for the Americans": The Nativist Movement in the United States* (New York: Twayne, 1996), 142; Bennett, *Party of Fear*, 144–45; Horsman, *Race and Manifest Destiny*, 276–78. Not surprisingly, in 1855 a strong critique of the Know-Nothings was published in the *Una*, noting, "The man that can find reason and the disposition to manacle a Catholic or a foreigner, will never help to break the bonds of the negro or a woman; and if he could, he would not be fit for service, nor could we willingly accept his aid." See "Know Nothings," *Una*, June 1855, 89.

219. *Congressional Globe*, 33rd Cong., 2nd sess., appendix, 171.

220. Knobel, *"America for the Americans,"* 138.

221. See the comments of Maryland congressman Henry Winter Davis: "Foreigners who have grown up under despotic governments must learn the habits of republicanism. A boy of fifteen of American birth carries more of inherent and living republic in his breast than any man born in a foreign country can." See *Congressional Globe*, 34th Cong., 1st sess., 1855–56, 25, 730. The issue, then, was whether the young boy inherited this faith (almost genetically from his father) in American values, or whether he acquired this lesson by living in a free country and not having "grown up under despotic governments."

222. At the height of their power Know-Nothings never held more than 30 percent of the seats in the House. But the debate over the Adams bill, which was intended to require a twenty-one-year residency for citizenship, reinforced the distinction between residency and voting rights as the mark of full citizenship. Know-Nothing representatives such as Sollers also worked to exclude all foreign-born from the army and navy, which gained few supporters, and this furthered the distinction between white males as citizens (manhood measured by the citizen-soldier) and resident aliens (even the larger category of all foreign-born) and women—who were already excluded from the military. See Jean H. Baker, *Ambivalent Americans*, 44–45.

223. See Linda K. Kerber, "A Constitutional Right to be Treated Like American Ladies: Women and the Obligations of Citizenship," in *U.S. History as Women's History: New Feminist Essays*, ed. Linda K. Kerber, Alice Kessler-Harris, and Kathryn Kish Sklar (Chapel Hill: University of North Carolina Press, 1995), 27–28. Also see Candice Lewis Bredbenner, *A Nationality of Her Own: Women, Marriage, and the Law of Citizenship* (Berkeley: University of California Press, 1998), 16–17, 20–22.

224. See "The Cincinnati Slave Case," *Lily*, March 1, 1856, 40, and "In the Matter of Jane, a Woman of Color, on Habeas Corpus," *Western Law Journal*, February, 1848, 202–6. Chief Justice William Wilson ruled that "by bringing Jane" to Illinois and "domiciling" here there, her master lost claim to her. Domiciling was the act of establishing residence, which was crucial to the decision in this case. For a discussion of this case, see Paul Finkelman, "Slavery, the 'More Perfect Union,' and the Prairie State," *Illinois History* 70 (Winter 1987): 256.

225. See "Slavery—Case of Pierre," *Western Law Journal*, April 1849, 334–35.

226. Finkelman, "*Prigg v. Pennsylvania* and the Northern Courts," 6–7, 12. In this case the right of Morgan's child contributed to the debate over birthright citizenship. Her child had been born in Pennsylvania as a free resident but had been seized and made a slave through the right of descent.

227. *Hair v. Hair*, 10 Rich (S.C.) 175–76 (1858).

228. Kerber, "Paradox of Women's Citizenship in the Early Republic," 352.

229. "The State of Indiana v. Eliza Hubbard," *Western Law Journal*, February 1844, 210–13.

230. *New York City WRC 1859*, 13–16.

231. Ibid., 16.

232. Frances Dana Gage, "Woman's Warfare," *Genius of the West*, August 1854, 34.

233. Ibid., 33.

Chapter 6

1. Thomas Herttell, *Remarks Comprising in Substance Judge Herttell's Argument in the House of Assembly of the State of New-York, in the Session of 1837, in Support of the Bill to Restore to Married Women "The Right of Property," as Guarantied by the Constitution of the State* (New York, 1839), 10.

2. See Astell, "Reflections Upon Marriage" (1706), in *The First English Feminist: Reflections on Marriage and Other Writings by Mary Astell*, ed. and with an introduction by Bridget Hill (New York: St. Martin's Press, 1986), 71–132; Ruth Perry, "Mary Astell and the Feminist Critique of Possessive Individualism," *Eighteenth-Century Studies* 23 (1990): 444–557.

3. See "A Vindication of the Rights of Woman (1792)," in *A Mary Wollstonecraft Reader*, ed. and with an introduction and notes by Barbara H. Solomon and Paula S. Berggren (New York: New American Library, 1983), 287.

4. See Abigail Adams to John Adams, March 31, 1776, in *Adams Family Correspondence*, ed. L. H. Butterfield, Wendell D. Garrett, and Marjorie E. Sprague, 4 vols. (Cambridge: Belknap Press of Harvard University Press, 1963), 1:370.

5. William Thompson, *Appeal of One Half of the Human Race, Women, Against the Pretensions of the Other Half, Men, to Retain them in Political, and Thence in Civil and Domestic Slavery* (n.p., 1825; repr., London: Virago Press, 1983), 55.

6. Sarah M. Grimké, *Letters on the Equality of the Sexes, and the Condition of Woman. Addressed to Mary S. Parker, President of the Boston Female Anti-Slavery Society* (Boston, 1838), 75.

7. Herttell described women as "piece[s] of property," vassals (landless tenants), slaves, servants, and workers dispossessed of their right to their labor and subsistence. Thompson had made a similar argument, stressing women's economic subjugation and that women are "domestic, civil, and political slave[s]." Wollstonecraft and Astell referred to women as "abject slaves," "born slaves," and "Man's upper-servant." See Herttell, *Remarks*, 42, 55, 67, 78, 80; William Thompson, *Appeal of One Half of the Human Race*, 54–55, 56, 58, 61, 67; Wollstonecraft, in Solomon and Berggren, *Mary Wollstonecraft Reader*, 291, 322; Astell, in Hill, *First English Feminist*, 76, 131.

8. Timothy Walker observed that the "universal panegyric" of dower was that it offered married women true protection: "In the worst shipwreck of his property, dower would be the widow's plank of safety, unless her own hand cast it away." But its defects were clear to Walker because it only applied to real estate, and he noted that "the cases are too frequent in which husbands, taking advantage of the yielding and confiding disposition of their wives, on the pretext of converting land into money, to be employed in trade, have procured them to join in the sale and thus seal their own ruin." Here again it was the "hand" of the wife that sealed her fate. In addition, as Marylynn Salmon has discovered, the trend after the American Revolution was to deny women traditional dower rights in all cases involving creditors and to encourage wives to take cash instead of real property. The early republican economy was geared toward the protection of creditors over widows and promoted the selling of land, which worked against the interests of wives for protecting their real property rights. See Timothy Walker, "The Legal Condition of

Woman," *Western Law Journal*, January 1849, 156, and Marylynn Salmon, "'Life, Liberty, and Dower': The Legal Status of Women after the American Revolution," in *Women, War, and Revolution*, ed. Carol R. Berkin and Clara M. Lovett (New York: Holmes and Meier, 1980), 92–93, 95.

9. See Joseph Warren, "Husband's Right to Wife's Services," *Harvard Law Review* 38 (February 1925): 421–23, 426–28, 433. Also see Harold C. Havighurst, "Services in the Home: A Study of Contract Concepts in Domestic Relations," *Yale Law Journal* 41 (1932): 390. For a discussion of the postbellum period, see Amy Dru Stanley, "Conjugal Bonds and Wage Labor: Rights of Contract in the Age of 'Emancipation,'" *Journal of American History* 75 (September 1988): 477, 482.

10. For the feudal notion that the relationship between husband and wife was defined as a "property relationship between political superiors and inferiors," see Peggy Rabkin, "The Origins of Law Reform: The Social Significance of the Nineteenth Century Codification Movement and Its Contribution to the Passage of the Early Married Women's Property Acts," *Buffalo Law Review* 29 (Spring 1980): 689. For the importance of coverture in the common law as a means for ensuring lawful heirs, see Norma Basch, *In the Eyes of the Law: Women, Marriage, and Property in Nineteenth-Century New York* (Ithaca: Cornell University Press, 1982), 49–50. For the issue of allegiance and fidelity and the control of the wife's body, see Timothy Walker, "Legal Condition of Woman," 321, 344. For the persistence of the traditional and customary belief that husbands had a right to own everything in their homes, including their wife's body (and a corresponding right to take away that right by dispossessing the wife and killing her, see Christine Stansell, *City of Women: Sex and Class in New York, 1789–1860* (Urbana: University of Illinois Press, 1987), 29; Merril D. Smith, *Breaking the Bonds: Marital Discord in Pennsylvania, 1730–1830* (New York: New York University Press, 1991), 86.

11. Herttell was not the first to use the analogy of "hands." Astell emphasized how "men have the power in their Hands," and Thompson used the image of the "same hands which relaxed the chains can again impose them with double rivets" to explain the male love of "despotism." See Astell, "Reflections Upon Marriage," 129; William Thompson, *Appeal of One Half of the Human Race*, 168.

12. See Claude Lévi-Strauss, *Structural Anthropology*, trans. Claire Jacobson and Brooke Grundfest Schoepf (New York: Basic Books, 1963), 61; also see Gayle Rubin, "The Traffic in Women: Notes on the 'Political Economy' of Sex," in *Towards an Anthropology of Women*, ed. Rayna R. Reiter (New York: Monthly Review Press, 1975), 171–75. For a more recent discussion of the exchange of women, see Linda J. Nicholson, *Gender and History: The Limits of Social Theory in the Age of the Family* (New York: Columbia University Press, 1986), 96–100; Gerda Lerner, *The Creation of Patriarchy* (New York: Oxford University Press, 1986), 46–47, 212–14.

13. Henry Folsom Page, *A View of the Law Relative to the Subject of Divorce in Ohio, Indiana, and Michigan* (Columbus, Ohio, 1850), 116, 137, 225–27. Wives were expected to "reclaim" their erring husbands, either by reforming their sins, such as drunkenness, or forgiving their sexual indiscretions. The law even created a category of condonation, in which the erring party was forgiven by the aggrieved party. Also see Theodore D. Woolsey, *Divorce and Divorce Legislation, especially in the United States*, 2nd ed. (New York: Scribner's, 1882), 259.

14. As Arendt explains, John Locke drew a distinction between working hands and a laboring body. Like the ancient Greeks, he identified those who worked with their bodies as slaves, tame animals, and women. See Hannah Arendt, *The Human Condition* (Chicago: University of Chicago Press, 1958), 80. The same distinction between manual labor and labor elevated through its mental content continued into the nineteenth-century vocabulary and understanding of work; see Jonathan A. Glickstein, *Concepts of Free Labor in Antebellum America* (New Haven: Yale University Press, 1991), 35, 40.

15. H. T. Tuckman, "A Chapter on Hands," *Union Magazine*, June 1848, 266.

16. For the argument that the home became a haven, see Christopher Lasch, *Haven in a Heart-*

less World: The Family Besieged (New York: Basic Books, 1977). For the connection between domesticity and the home as a "sanctuary," see Nancy F. Cott, *The Bonds of Womanhood: "Woman's Sphere" in New England, 1780–1835* (New Haven: Yale University Press, 1977), 64–70. One of the problems with this kind of analysis is that scholars see domesticity as a "positive good" that enhances women's status. Scholars promoting this thesis generally ignore marriage law and power relations in the family. For examples of this approach that celebrates domesticity or "domestic feminism," see Daniel Scott Smith, "Family Limitation, Sexual Control, and Domestic Feminism in Victorian America," in *A Heritage of Her Own: Toward a New Social History of American Women*, ed. Nancy F. Cott and Elizabeth H. Pleck (New York: Simon and Schuster, 1979), 231, 233–36; Carl Degler, *At Odds: Women and the Family in America from the Revolution to the Present* (New York: Oxford University Press, 1980), 43.

17. "The Widow's Appeal," *Una*, December 1853, 180.

18. Ibid.

19. See Edward D. Mansfield, *The Legal Rights, Liabilities, and Duties of Women; with an Introductory History of their Legal Condition in the Hebrew, Roman and Feudal Civil Systems* (Salem, Ohio, 1845), 236.

20. Amos Dean, *Principles of Medical Jurisprudence: Designed for the Professions of Law and Medicine* (Albany, N.Y., 1850), 496, 500, 523–24. The theory of irresistible impulse had been introduced in the Ohio Supreme Court as early as 1834, but the concept did not gain widespread approval until 1844, when the highly respected jurist Lemuel Shaw of the Massachusetts Supreme Court used the theory as part of his opinion written for *Commonwealth v. Rogers*. See Robert M. Ireland, "Insanity and the Unwritten Law," *American Journal of Legal History* 32 (April 1988): 165–66.

21. "Widow's Appeal."

22. Page, *View of the Law Relative to the Subject of Divorce*, 172–73.

23. Elizabeth Pleck also argues that temperance reformers saw the "very survival of the drunkard's wife" was at stake and that in the early nineteenth century, reformers began to emphasize the connection between wife beating and drinking. See Pleck, *Domestic Tyranny: The Making of American Social Policy against Family Violence from Colonial Times to the Present* (New York: Oxford University Press, 1987), 50.

24. The following is an example of a typical "drunkard's tale," recorded during a Washingtonian meeting held in New York City in 1840:

> He stated that he had been a confirmed drunkard for fifteen years, and that he had been brought to the lowest depths of degradation and misery, insomuch as he wanted to die, and had almost been tempted to put an end to his life. . . . He also stated that his wife, after living and enduring poverty and misery to the greatest extent, would cling to him with affection and love, and did so for years, but at last was compelled to leave him and seek protection among her friends; and that they had been separated for seven years by that foul monster, rum.

See Ian R. Tyrrell, *Sobering Up: From Temperance to Prohibition in Antebellum America, 1800–1840* (Westport, Conn.: Greenwood Press, 1979), 164.

25. Such language was used in an appeal sent from the women of Wisconsin to the state legislature in 1853, in which they stated,

> Not a century has passed away, and our beautiful country groans under a yoke of bondage more galling, a foe more formidable, a tyrant ten thousand times more relentless, a fiend invading the dearest rights of man, the holiest sanctuary of woman, turning the fruitful garden into a desolate waste, spreading misery, devastation, and death, and all their attendant

evils in their train. Was the destruction of the tea in Boston harbor a worthy act? If so, we call upon you to imitate the noble example, to manifest a corresponding zeal in a noble cause, to lend your aid in freeing our State from the curse of intemperance, and our halls of legislature from the influence of rum.

See "Appeal of Woman," *Prisoners' Friend*, December 1853, 172. For a brief discussion of the patriotic allusions used by the Washingtonians, see Tyrrell, *Sobering Up*, 160, 183.

26. The Martha Washingtonian societies in New York City had enrolled 6,000 members by 1842. Other societies formed in Rochester and Seneca Falls, N.Y., Philadelphia, Pa., and Worcester, Mass., all later strongholds of women's rights activism. Virginia Allen organized and ran the *New York Pearl*, which began in 1846, while other women wrote for similar women's temperance publications such as *New York Olive Plant* (1842). In Seneca Falls, Amelia Bloomer began her temperance career writing for the *Water Bucket* in 1842 before she organized her own paper, *Lily*, in 1849. See Tyrrell, *Sobering Up*, 179. Also see Tyrrell, "Women and Temperance in Antebellum America, 1830–1860," *Civil War History* 27 (June 1982): 138; Louise Noun, "Amelia Bloomer: A Biography," pt. 1, "The Lily of Seneca Falls," *Annals of Iowa* 47 (Winter 1985): 582–83.

27. See "Widow's Appeal."

28. Tyrrell, *Sobering Up*, 160, 181.

29. Jed Dannenbaum has argued that the more militant phase of temperance reform came when the Martha Washingtonian societies were replaced by the Daughters of Temperance, which appeared in 1845 and reached its peak membership in 1848 with 30,000 supporters. Between 1853 and 1859 women organized into bands that physically destroyed the liquor stock of local salons. In 1854 when the women of Marion, Illinois, were brought to trial for destroying a saloon, their lawyer, Abraham Lincoln, used the Boston Tea Party as a moral precedent for their action. See Jed Dannenbaum, "The Origins of Temperance Activism and Militancy among American Women," *Journal of Social History* 15 (December 1981): 237, 242–43.

30. See Robert M. Cover, "Violence and the Word," *Yale Law Journal* 95 (1986): 1606–7.

31. The interesting aspect of a blood pact was that it could be based on actual blood relations, or it could constitute a brotherhood through a mutual exchange of blood, the joint sacrificial offering of blood, or the shared experience of the shedding of blood. See Walter Brueggeman, "Of the Same Flesh and Bone (GN 2,23a)," *Catholic Biblical Quarterly* 32 (1970): 535–38.

32. "Ladies Temperance Society of Seneca Falls," *Lily*, January 1, 1849; also see "Woman's Work in the Temperance Cause," ibid., March 1849, 21, and "Temperance and Politics," ibid., September 1849, 69.

33. Sarah Coates-Kinney, "Love's Triumph by Stratagem," *Genius of the West*, August 1854, 35–38.

34. Elisha P. Hurlbut, *Essays on Human Rights, and Their Political Guaranties* (New York, 1848), 15, 26, 31.

35. See "Women's State Temperance Convention," *Anti-Slavery Bugle*, January 29, 1853. Several prominent feminists supported this organization, including M. A. Bronson (second editor of the *Lily* after Amelia Bloomer); Frances D. Gage and Caroline Severance were both members of the Executive Committee, along with other women's rights activists who supported the movement in Ohio, such as Martha Tilden, Josephine Griffing, Sarah Ernst, and R. A. S. Janney. Also see "Women's State Temperance Convention," *Anti-Slavery Bugle*, January 8, 1852. For reference to women having to submit to indignities "no man would bear," see "Woman's Rights," *Lily*, October 1849, 77.

36. See Asa Earl Martin, "The Temperance Movement in Pennsylvania prior to the Civil War," *Pennsylvania Magazine of History and Biography* 49 (1925): 214–15. For the same kind of argument in Massachusetts, see "The License Question," *Emancipator and Republican*, March 10, 1847.

37. References are made to the "poisonous upas (Indonesian Malay poison tree) among us" and the "incendiary who applies his torch to peaceful dwellings," spreading a "fearful conflagration." See "A Temperance Convention of Women of Chester County," held in 1848, in *History of Woman Suffrage*, 6 vols., ed. Elizabeth Cady Stanton, Susan B. Anthony, and Matilda Joslyn Gage (New York, 1881; reprint, New York: Arno Press, 1985), 1:345–47.

38. See "A Heroic Woman," *Lily*, June 1853; Stanton, Anthony, and Gage, *History of Woman Suffrage*, 1:475. This article stressed the use of violence and called the tavern or grocery "worse than a plague."

39. "A Temperance Bill Passed," *Lily*, May 1854, 72; Tyrrell, *Sobering Up*, 164.

40. "Woman's Work in the Temperance Cause."

41. "Widow's Appeal."

42. Dean, *Principles of Medical Jurisprudence*, 521–24. Published in 1843, one year after the autopsy of the drunkard, Poe's poem "The Conqueror Worm" portrayed the horror of death:

> But see, amid the mimic rout
> A crawling shape intrude!
> A blood-red thing that writhes from out
> The scenic solitude!
> It writhes—it writhes!—with mortal pangs
> The mimes become its food,
> And seraphs sob at vermin fangs
> In human gore imbued.
>
> Out—out are the lights—out all!
> And, over each quivering form,
> The curtain, a funeral pall,
> Comes down with the rush of a storm,
> While the angels, all pallid and wan,
> Uprising, unveiling, affirm
> That play is the tragedy, "Man,"
> And its hero the Conqueror Worm.

See *Edgar Allan Poe: Tales and Poetry* (New York: Library of America, 1984), 78–79.

43. Page, *View of the Law Relative to the Subject of Divorce*, 18–27, 66–73; Mansfield, *Legal Rights, Liabilities, and Duties of Women*, 237–38, 240–41, 247, 251, 256.

44. Hurlbut, *Essays on Human Rights*, 157–58.

45. Dean, *Principles of Medical Jurisprudence*, 13–14, 35–36. In addition, in the early nineteenth century, judges, juries, and lawyers had accepted the argument that women who became pregnant could not have been raped and must have consented. Volition was seen as necessary for conception. See James C. Mohr, *Doctors and the Law: Medical Jurisprudence in Nineteenth-Century America* (New York: Oxford University Press, 1993), 31.

46. For a reference to the drunkard as "loathsome corpse" and marriage as "living death," see "Letter from Mary Vaughan," *Lily*, January 1851, 7. Although Robert Louis Stevenson did not write *Dr. Jekyll and Mr. Hyde* until 1886, his gothic vision of the split personality had been prefigured in Edgar Allan Poe's "William Wilson," published in 1839. American antebellum audiences, then, were familiar with this disturbed portrait of the individual divided against himself. See David Punter, *The Literature of Terror: A History of Gothic Fictions from 1765 to the Present Day* (New York: Longman Press, 1980), 202.

47. S.F. [Stanton], "Divorce," *Lily*, April 1850; Mansfield, *Legal Rights, Liabilities, and Duties of Women*, 238.

48. See F. A. Erwin, "Assault and Battery (Wife vs. Husband)," *University Law Review* 3 (February 1897): 67–68.

49. Page, *View of the Law Relative to the Subject of Divorce*, 43.

50. Dean defined rape as "the having unlawful and carnal knowledge of a woman by force and against her will." See Dean, *Principles of Medical Jurisprudence*, 22.

51. Robert L. Griswold, "Sexual Cruelty and the Case for Divorce in Victorian America," *Signs: Journal of Women in Culture and Society* 11 (Spring 1986): 529–30.

52. Dean, *Principles of Medical Jurisprudence*, 22.

53. Page, *View of the Law Relative to the Subject of Divorce*, 99.

54. For a discussion of onanism (not wasting sexual energy in unnatural acts), see Stephen Nissenbaum, *Sex, Deity, and Debility in Jacksonian America: Sylvester Graham and Health Reform* (Westport, Conn.: Greenwood Press, 1980), 29, 32. Also see John S. Haller Jr. and Robin M. Haller, *The Physician and Sexuality in Victorian America* (Urbana: University of Illinois Press, 1974); G. J. Barker-Benfield, *Horrors of the Half-Known Life: Male Attitudes toward Women and Sexuality in Nineteenth-Century America* (New York: Harper and Row, 1976).

55. Thomas Laqueur, "Orgasm, Generation, and the Politics of Reproductive Biology," *Representations* 14 (Spring 1986): 19.

56. See Mary Somerville Jones, *An Historical Geography of the Changing Divorce Law in the United States* (New York: Garland, 1987), 21–22.

57. *Shaw v. Shaw*, 17 Connecticut Reports 190–91 (1845).

58. Ibid., 192–95.

59. *Butler v. Butler*, 1 Parsons (Pa.) 337–38, 339, 344 (1849).

60. "Huldah A. Barber, by her next friend, George Cronkite, v. Hiram Barber," *Western Law Journal*, March 1850, 277–85. The same reasoning appeared in the later case of *Duhme v. Duhme*, in which "extreme cruelty" was defined by either personal violence, the reasonable apprehension of the same, or "a systematic course of ill-treatment affecting the health and endangering the life of the party against whom it is directed." As in the Butler case, the cause was a "systematic course of ill-treatment" or, in the Barber case, the "accumulated wrongs." The theme here is repetition, which reflects a physiological view, in which the human body was affected by an imbalance in physical or emotional stimuli—the repeated sense of aversion, leading to ill health. See *Duhme v. Duhme*, 3 Ohio Decisions 95, 100 (1859).

61. Frances D. Gage, "Letter from Mrs. Gage," *Lily*, April 15, 1855, 57.

62. Page, *View of the Law Relative to the Subject of Divorce*, 44, 136–37.

63. "Huldah A. Barber v. Hiram Barber," 284.

64. In an earlier letter Gage emphasized the "restraining influence" that held the drunkard's wife "by violence and fear" and the "fear of domestic reprisal." See "Letter from Mrs. Gage" and "Letter from F. D. Gage to Mrs. Bloomer," *Lily*, November 1851, 83.

65. William A. Alcott, *The Young Husband, or Duties of Man in the Marriage Relation*, 5th ed. (Boston: George W. Light, 1841), 342.

66. *New York City WRC 1860*, 72.

67. John Wiltbank, M.D., *Peculiarities of the Female: A Lecture Introductory to the Course on Obstetrics in the Medical Department of Pennsylvania College, for the Session of 1845–46* (Philadelphia, 1845), 7. Also see Laqueur, "Orgasm, Generation, and the Politics of Reproductive Biology," 1–41; Carroll Smith-Rosenberg and Charles Rosenberg, "The Female Animal: Medical and Biological View of Woman and Her Role in Nineteenth-Century America," in *Women and Health in America*, ed. Judith Walzer Leavitt (Madison: University of Wisconsin Press, 1984), 13–14. As Emily Martin demonstrates, female reproduction still retains the image of machine, in which birth adheres to involuntary forces, and menstruation and menopause are pathologies, in which

women's physical system breaks down and becomes dysfunctional. See Emily Martin, *The Woman in the Body: A Cultural Analysis of Reproduction* (Boston: Beacon Press, 1987), 46–51, 61–62.

68. Harriot K. Hunt, *Glances and Glimpses; or, Fifty Years Social, Including Twenty Years of Professional Life* (Boston: John P. Jewett, 1856), 157, 394–95, 412. Also see the poem "Light and Truth," *Anti-Slavery Bugle*, May 11, 1850, and Mrs. S. C., "Physical Purity," *Harmony of Truth*, April 1847, 304–5.

69. "Lectures on Physiology," *Anti-Slavery Bugle*, February 1, 1851. Also see W.T.C, "The Study of Physiology," *Genius of the West*, October 1855, 312. This paper was edited by Sarah Coates-Kinney, who was a health lecturer and women's rights activist.

70. This credo, "Know thyself," taken from the biblical verse, appeared as the slogan of the Boston Physiological Institute, which was established in 1838 and included Harriot Hunt, Caroline Dall, and Caroline Severence as members. It also was used in the announcement of the Female Medical College of Philadelphia, which had the support of many women's rights activists and had three feminists, Ann Preston, Martha Mowry, and Almira Fowler, as members of the faculty. See Martha H. Verbrugge, *Able-Bodied Womanhood: Personal Health and Social Change in Nineteenth-Century Boston* (New York: Oxford University Press, 1988), 30, 50–51, 65; "Announcement of Female Medical College of Philadelphia," *Practical Christian*, August 17, 1850.

71. *New York City WRC 1860*, 72. Also see Dean, *Principles of Medical Jurisprudence*, 500–501; Nissenbaum, *Sex, Deity, and Debility in Jacksonian America*, 33, 106.

72. "Woman's Rights," *Lily*, April 1851, 28.

73. See "Letter from Mrs. Wright," *Water-Cure Journal*, June 15, 1846, 29. Also see Regina Markell Morantz, "Nineteenth-Century Health Reform and Women: A Program of Self-Help," in *Medicine without Doctors: Home Health Care in American History*, ed. Guenter B. Risse, Ronald L. Numbers, and Judith Walzer Leavitt (New York: Science History Publications, 1977).

74. See "Mrs. Wright's Lectures to Ladies on Anatomy, Physiology, and Health," *Water-Cure Journal*, June 1, 1846, 11. Jane Elizabeth Jones, Mary Ann Johnson, and Sarah Coates (later Sarah Coates-Kinney) all studied with Quaker physician K. G. Thomas of Salem, Ohio. See "Announcement of Medical Study with K. G. Thomas," *Anti-Slavery Bugle*, July 29, 1849; "Lectures on Anatomy and Physiology," *Anti-Slavery Bugle*, May 4, 1850; "Sarah Coates as Health Lecturer," *Anti-Slavery Bugle*, May 25, 1850. Paulina Wright Davis founded the Providence Physiological Society in 1850, an organization modeled on the Ladies Physiological Society of Boston. Martha Mowry joined the Providence Physiological Society, and she later joined Ann Preston and Almira Fowler as members of the faculty at the Female Medical College of Pennsylvania. See Papers of the Providence Physiological Society, 1850, Providence Historical Society, Providence, R.I.

75. Harriot K. Hunt, *Glances and Glimpses*, 384; account of lectures given by Sarah Coates (later Coates-Kinney), where she described interpreting the "human form divine," in "Female Lectures," *Water-Cure Journal*, February 1851, 49.

76. See T. L. Nichols, M.D., and Mrs. Mary S. Gove Nichols, *Marriage: Its History, Character, and Results; Demonstrating Its Influence as a Civilized Institution, on the Happiness of the Individual in the Progress of the Race*, rev. ed. (Cincinnati, 1854), and her fictionalized autobiography, Mary Gove Nichols, *Mary Lyndon, or Revelations of a Life* (New York, 1855), 130, 135, 198. Also see John B. Blake, "Mary Gove Nichols, Prophetess of Health," in Leavitt, *Women and Health in America*, 359–75.

77. "Huldah A. Barber v. Hiram Barber," 283.

78. Nissenbaum, *Sex, Deity, and Debility in Jacksonian America*, 167–68. Linda Gordon and Ellen Carol DuBois have argued that nineteenth-century feminists called for "voluntary motherhood," or the right for mothers to choose when to have children. They also note that feminists acknowledged women's sexual desire. However, as I have argued, feminists did develop a cri-

tique of "marital rape," which went beyond the issues of sex on demand from husbands. Rape was at the center of the power relations in marriage, and their arguments against submission and tolerable cruelty and for sanctuary and restraint were significant because they exposed the complicated legacy of marriage law. See Linda Gordon and Ellen DuBois, "Seeking Ecstasy on the Battlefield: Danger and Pleasure in Nineteenth-Century Feminist Sexual Thought," in *Sexuality: A Reader*, ed. *Feminist Review* (London: Virago Press, 1987), 86–87, 91–92.

79. See "Every-day Life of Woman," *Lily*, February 1852, 10. This piece was originally published anonymously in *The Ladies Repository*, October 1851, 365–66.

80. Ibid.

81. See another parody of the exploited wife, "A Convention in the Inner Life," *Una*, May 1853, 71, and Frederick Grimké, *Considerations Upon the Nature and Tendency of Free Institutions* (Cincinnati, 1848), 64.

82. For example, Immanuel Kant defined a "personal right of real kind" as the "Right of the possession of an external object as a THING," when referring to a man's right over his wife, children, and domestic servants. See Joan B. Landes, "Hegel's Conception of the Family," in *The Family in Political Thought*, ed. Jean Bethke Elshtain (Amherst: University of Massachusetts Press, 1982), 127.

83. Alexander Hamilton, "Report on the Subject of Manufactures" (1791), in *The Philosophy of Manufactures: Early Debates over Industrialization in the United States*, ed. Michael Brewster Folsom and Steven D. Lubar (Cambridge: MIT Press, 1982), 84.

84. See Glickstein, *Concepts of Free Labor*, 38, 82, 93–112, 130, 184–259.

85. See Elizabeth Kelley Bauer, *Commentaries on the Constitution, 1790–1860* (New York: Russell and Russell, 1965), 166.

86. Norma Basch and Elizabeth Clark, both legal historians, have tended to view women's rights advocates within the tradition of liberal feminism. Hendrik Hartog has suggested that rights discourse may best be seen within the framework of eighteenth-century liberalism. Martha Minow, however, has suggested that property rights may pose a different set of concerns, because property rights express overlapping relations among individuals rather than simply focusing on the liberal concern for autonomy. See Norma Basch, *In the Eyes of the Law*; Elizabeth B. Clark, "Matrimonial Bonds: Slavery and Divorce in Nineteenth Century America," *Law and History Review* 8 (Spring 1990): 25–54; Hendrik Hartog, "The Constitution of Aspiration and 'The Rights That Belong to Us All,'" *Journal of American History* 74 (December 1987): 1017–18; Martha Minow, "An Essay on Rights," *Yale Law Journal* 96 (July 1987): 1860. Unlike Boydston, I argue that antebellum women's rights activists had a sophisticated analysis of housework, and they did not simply focus on wages for wives; see Jeanne Boydston, *Home and Work: Housework, Wages, and the Ideology of Labor in the Early Republic* (New York: Oxford University Press, 1990), ix–x.

87. Paulina Wright Davis, "Pecuniary Independence of Woman," *Una*, December 1853, 184.

88. Sir William Blackstone, *Commentaries on the Laws of England in Four Books*, 2 vols., 2nd ed., ed. Thomas M. Cooley (Chicago: Callagham, 1879), 1:441. Stanton noted how the signing of the marriage contract meant that the wife had no right to "her person, her time, her services," which were "the property of another." See "Justice to Woman: Address of the Women's Rights Convention, to the Legislature," *Una*, April 1854, 249.

89. Christopher L. Tomlins, *Law, Labor, and Ideology in the Early American Republic* (Cambridge: Cambridge University Press, 1993), 9–10, 226, 263–64; also see Donald S. Lutz, "From Covenant to Constitution in American Political Thought," *Covenant, Polity, and Constitutionalism: Publius, the Journal of Federalism* 10 (Fall 1980): 112.

90. Tomlins, *Law, Labor, and Ideology*, 79.

91. Duncan Kennedy, "The Structure of Blackstone's Commentaries," *Buffalo Law Review* 28 (1979): 250, 269, 280, 283.

92. Ibid. Also see Tomlins, *Law, Labor, and Ideology*, 104.

93. Tomlins, *Law, Labor, and Ideology*, 105.

94. Herttell, *Remarks*, 7, 15; Rabkin, "Origins of Law Reform," 729.

95. Timothy Walker, *Introduction to American Law* (Philadelphia, 1837); Rabkin, "Origins of Law Reform," 683, 696.

96. Herttell, *Remarks*, 16.

97. Rowland Berthoff, "Conventional Mentality: Free Blacks, Women, and Business Corporations as Unequal Persons, 1820–1870," *Journal of American History* 76 (December 1989): 765; Earl M. Maltz, "Fourteenth Amendment Concepts in the Antebellum Era," *American Journal of Legal History* 32 (1988): 327.

98. Tomlins, *Law, Labor, and Ideology*, 10, 190.

99. Ibid., 190; Herttell, *Remarks*, 21–23, 80.

100. Charles Sears, "Extract of a Letter from a Member of the North American Phalanx," *Una*, March 1854, 234.

101. "Female Compositors, and the Opposition of Interests," *Una*, October 1853, 152; also "Women's Labor: Excerpts from Professor Bush in the *New Church Repository*," *Una*, December 1853, 180–81; "Memorial and Remonstrance" and "Statement of Facts and Arguments. The Operatives Appeal to the Working Men of Rhode Island," *Una*, August 1853, 115. Also see unsigned letter, *Una*, May 1853, 79.

102. "Equal Political Rights in Massachusetts," *Una*, February 1853, 45.

103. Kennedy, "Structure of Blackstone's Commentaries," 226; also see Carol Weisbrod, *The Boundaries of Utopia* (New York: Pantheon, 1980), 178.

104. Mansfield, *Legal Rights, Liabilities, and Duties of Women*, 285, 288.

105. Christopher L. Tomlins, "Law and Power in the Employment Relationship," in *Labor Law in America: Historical and Critical Essays*, edited by Christopher L. Tomlins and Andrew J. King (Baltimore: Johns Hopkins University Press, 1992), 88.

106. Timothy Walker, "Legal Condition of Woman," 153.

107. Walker suggests this relationship when he writes about debts and contracts between husband and wife: "To illustrate still further the husband's supremacy, I will add a few more particulars. If debts were due the wife before marriage, the husband may collect them, and she cannot. If the husband himself was her debtor before marriage, or if any contracts subsisted between them, the marriage cancels them all. Men have been known to borrow money of single women, and then marry them to pay the debt. Again, if a wife by actual labor has earned money, her husband may collect and spend it, in spite of her remonstrance." See Timothy Walker, "Legal Condition of Woman," 153.

108. Richard H. Chused, "Married Women's Property Law, 1800–1850," *Georgetown Law Journal* 71 (1983): 1398, 1400–1402, 1410–11.

109. Hurlbut, *Essays on Human Rights*, 160, 162, 168–69.

110. *Debates and Proceedings of the New-York State Convention, for the Revision of the Constitution* (Albany, N.Y., 1846), 907–8.

111. Ibid., 812; also see Rabkin, "Origins of Law Reform," 740.

112. "Memorial of Mrs. Caroline Severance of Cleveland," *Una*, June 1854, 276.

113. The argument of comparing marriage to a "domestic corporation" was made at the 1850 Indiana state constitutional convention. Here again the comparison was used to reject a resolution for giving wives separate title to their property. See Berthoff, "Conventional Mentality," 762.

114. Mansfield, *Legal Rights, Liabilities, and Duties of Women*, 236, 267.

115. Ibid., 288.

116. Here I disagree with Norma Basch, who concludes that feminists believed the 1848 statute was "the death-blow to the old Blackstone code for married women in this country." This quo-

tation is taken from *History of Woman Suffrage*, and it does not reflect the views of activists in 1848. More accurately, this opinion reflects Elizabeth Cady Stanton's assessment as a historian of the movement in 1881. See Norma Basch, *In the Eyes of the Law*, 161; also see Stanton, Anthony, and Gage, *History of Woman Suffrage*, 1:64.

117. *Seneca Falls WRC 1848*, 6, 9.

118. *Rochester WRC 1848*, 15.

119. Amelia Bloomer, "Letter to the Woman's Rights Convention, held at Akron, Ohio, May 28, 1851," *Lily*, August 1851, 61.

120. Chused, "Married Women's Property Law," 1398, 1424.

121. *Raybold v. Raybold*, 20 Pa. Supreme Court Reports 311 (1853); Charles W. Dahlinger, "The Dawn of the Woman's Movement: An Account of the Origin and History of the Pennsylvania Married Women's Property Law of 1848," *Western Pennsylvania Magazine* 1 (April 1918): 80–81. Judge Woodward of Pennsylvania argued that the husband was entitled to a wife's "savings and earnings during coverture," a principle that was endorsed in the 1854 Maine case that ruled that the husband was "entitled to the services of the wife. What she earns by personal labor become his and not her property." In this case as well, the precedent laid down was that "the *earnings* of a *feme covert* are the property of her husband." See *Merrill v. Smith*, 37 Maine Reports 394, 396 (1854).

122. Warren, "Husband's Right to Wife's Services," 421–25.

123. *Cropsey v. Sweeney*, 27 Barb. (N.Y.) 315 (1858). The same argument was used in *Raybold v. Raybold*, for Judge Woodward argued that a wife would be entitled to her wages if she was "degraded to the condition of a hireling, which she would be if servants' wages could become her separate property." See *Raybold v. Raybold*, 311.

124. *Cropsey v. Sweeney*, 313, 315. The judge also ruled that the wife's work was "voluntary, and performed without any view to compensation," which was used to distinguish her services from the work performed "*as a servant or laborer.*"

125. Paulina Wright Davis, "Pecuniary Independence of Woman," *Una*, January 1854, 200.

126. "Letter from Harriet Torrey," *Lily*, March 1, 1853, 11. Torrey focused on women's wage labor in agriculture, or what she defined as women "earning money by working in a barn-yard." For an example of the same argument applied to women wage earners in general, see "Women's Rights," *Lily*, April 1851, 28.

127. See Mrs. Jane Frohock, "Getting Men's Wages," *Lily*, June 1, 1854, 77; Senex [Anson Bingham], "The Democratic Review on Woman's Rights—No. 4," *Lily*, July 1852, 60.

128. See *Voice of Industry*, April 16, 1847. This quotation is taken from Teresa Anne Murphy, *Ten Hours' Labor: Religion, Reform, and Gender in Early New England* (Ithaca: Cornell University Press, 1992), 216–17.

129. In an 1853 call to a convention in Rochester, the organizers argued that the movement addressed first and foremost the following "practical" concerns:

1. Why should not Woman's work be paid according to the *quality* of the work done, and not the SEX of the worker?
2. How shall we open for Woman's energies new spheres of well-remunerated industry?
3. Why should not Wives, equally with Husbands, be entitled to their own earnings?

See "The Just and Equal Rights of Woman," *Una*, December 1853, 185.

130. Davis, "Pecuniary Independence of Woman," *Una*, January 1854, 200.

131. Ibid.; Paulina Wright Davis, "The Moral Character of Woman," *Una*, August 1, 1853, 105.

132. "Co-operative Industry," *Una*, August 1853, 123. For a general discussion of a cooperative idea developed by the labor movement in the 1860s, see Daniel T. Rodgers, *The Work Ethic in Industrial America, 1850–1920* (Chicago: University of Chicago Press, 1974), 40–46.

133. Lydia A. Jenkins, "Self-Dependent-Monopoly," *Lily*, October 1852, 83.

134. "Marriage of Lucy Stone Under Protest," *Una*, June 1855, 87.

135. "The Sybil," *Lily*, September 1856, 125.

136. "Marriage of Lucy Stone Under Protest."

137. Elizabeth Cady Stanton, "How to Make Woman Independent," *Una*, September 1855, 139. Also see the discussion of the problems resulting from restricting the right of contract to exclude wives in "Woman's Rights and Woman's Wrongs According to the Law," *Lily*, November 1, 1854, 159.

138. See Stanton, "Justice to Women," April 1854, 250; Glickstein, *Concepts of Free Labor*, 28, 38.

139. See Judith Richards, Lotte Mulligan, and John K. Graham, "'Property' and 'People': Political Usages of Locke and Some Contemporaries," *Journal of the History of Ideas* 42 (January–March 1982): 38–39; Landes, "Hegel's Conception of the Family," 128; and the definitions of "peculiar," "pecuniary," and "personality," in *The Compact Edition of the Oxford English Dictionary*, 2 vols. (Oxford: Oxford University Press, 1971), 2:2110, 2141.

140. "The Moral Character of Woman," *Una*, June 1, 1853, 73.

141. Elizabeth Oakes Smith, "Woman's Petitions," *Una*, January 1855, 5.

142. *Una*, May 1853, 53.

143. For the phrase "uncertain estate," see Elisha Hurlbut, "Rights of Woman," *Lily*, September 1852, 80.

144. See Steven H. Gifis, *Law Dictionary* (Woodbury, N.Y.: Barron's Educational Series, 1975), 73.

145. Mansfield, *Legal Rights, Liabilities, and Duties of Women*, 274–75.

146. Hurlbut, "Rights of Woman," 80.

147. "Is Society Right?," *Lily*, March 1, 1856, 35.

148. "Editor's Notes," *Una*, April 1854, 254.

149. Senex [Anson Bingham], "Report of the Select Committee of the Assembly of New York in Relation to Woman's Rights," *Lily*, April 15, 1854.

150. For the most astute discussion of these issues as derived from John Locke, and their implications for family law and women's property rights, see Lorenne M. G. Clark, "Women and Locke: Who Owns the Apples in the Garden of Eden," in *The Sexism of Social and Political Theory: Women and Reproduction from Plato to Nietzsche*, ed. Lorenne M. G. Clark and Lynda Lange (Toronto: University of Toronto Press, 1979), 27–36.

151. Mansfield, *Legal Rights, Liabilities, and Duties of Women*, 319.

152. See Michael Grossberg, *Governing the Hearth: Law and the Family in Nineteenth-Century America* (Chapel Hill: University of North Carolina Press, 1985), 235–36; Mansfield, *Legal Rights, Liabilities, and Duties of Women*, 345, 348.

153. See Marylynn Salmon, "Republican Sentiment, Economic Change, and the Property Rights of Women in American Law," in *Women in the Age of the American Revolution*, ed. Ronald Hoffman and Peter J. Albert (Charlottesville: University Press of Virginia, 1989), 461–62, 465, 471.

154. Mansfield, *Legal Rights, Liabilities, and Duties of Women*, 319.

155. Salmon, "'Life, Liberty, and Dower,'" 99, and see Grossberg's account of the two Pennsylvania rulings in *Commonwealth v. Addicks* (1813) and *Commonwealth v. Addicks* (1815), in Grossberg, *Governing the Hearth*, 239.

156. See Joan B. Landes, *Women and the Public Sphere in the Age of the French Revolution* (Ithaca: Cornell University Press, 1988), 86.

157. Mansfield, *Legal Rights, Liabilities, and Duties of Women*, 266. Mansfield used the same principle of head of the family to justify the legal custody of children and the custody of the wife as belonging to the husband. He wrote, "The *legal custody* of the children belongs, by law, to the

father as the head of the family," and here he cited Blackstone's commentaries as his authority. Then he also stated, "In one word, in the theory of law, the *custody* of the wife belongs to the husband. She has no such custody over him. This principle is evidently derived from the Scripture rule, that the husband is head of the family." See ibid., 337, 307.

158. See Elizabeth Cady Stanton, "Mrs. E. C. Stanton's Address to the Legislature of New York," *Una*, May 1854, 260.

159. See Mansfield, *Legal Rights, Liabilities, and Duties of Women*, 280, 292–305, and a superb summary of the differences between tenancy by courtesy and dower by a Rochester lawyer, Mr. Hopkins, who spoke at the women's rights convention held in Rochester in 1853. See "Notice," *Una*, January 1854, 202.

160. Bingham used the same allusion to "homeless wanderer" in his description of the widow:

> Then a household ceases to exist. For more desolating than the scythe of death and time, less respectful to the family compact and the family altar, the law dissipates and obliterates all that is left of the living, as though a kind of heathen rite had compelled the sacrifice, in honor and deification of masculine supremacy. It is true, that the widow is not here, as in some heathen countries, immolated upon the funeral pyre of her husband, in comparative importance and her relative insignificance; but after forty days of quarantine in the family mansion, may be expelled, houseless and homeless, to wander up and down upon the face of the earth.

See Senex [Anson Bingham], "The Democratic Review on Woman's Rights—No. 3," *Lily*, June 1852, 52.

161. Norma Basch, *In the Eyes of the Law*, 149.

162. See Elizabeth Blackmar, *Manhattan for Rent, 1785–1850* (Ithaca: Cornell University Press, 1989), 246, 256–57.

163. Elizabeth Blackmar, "The Distress of Property Law: Landlord-Tenant Relations in Antebellum New York," in *The Law in America, 1607–1861*, ed. William Pencak and Wythe W. Holt Jr. (New York: New-York Historical Society, 1989), 219.

164. See "New items," *Spirit of the Age*, July 21, 1849. This paper was edited by reformer and women's rights advocate William Henry Channing. Two of the objectives of the paper were support for land reform and equal rights for women.

165. See an account of a public lecture she gave in Ohio in the *Anti-Slavery Bugle*, November 23, 1850.

166. For an account of the resolutions that advocated women's political, civil, and educational rights, see "Good Resolutions," *Spiritual Philosopher*, November 2, 1850, 111.

167. See Chused, "Married Women's Property Law," 1408.

168. See Civis, "Woman's Rights and Woman's Wrongs According to the Law," *Lily*, February 15, 1854, 28.

169. Two difficulties limited the ability of a wife to collect necessaries for herself or her children. First, the common law tempered this right by claiming that "no 'original, inherent, primogeni[t]al, and uncountermandable power'" existed to "charge the husband for her necessaries." Second, necessaries had to "correspond with the pecuniary circumstances of the husband." Thus, the obligation for necessaries was both a contingent and qualified right rather than an absolute right. Of course, the husband's right to the profits and rents of his wife's property was absolute under the common law.

In contrast the landlord's right to rent was absolute, and the tenant's liability to pay rent was absolute. By the early nineteenth century state legislatures began to protect the necessaries of tenants from the landlord's right of "distress," which allowed landlords to seize the private property of their tenants as a pledge for their unpaid rent. For a discussion of the common-law interpretation of necessaries, see Timothy Walker "Legal Condition of Woman," 348–49. For an example of how American law restricted the liability for necessaries according to the husband's ability to pay, see *Every Woman Her Own Lawyer* (New York, 1858), 181. And for the rights and liabilities of landlords and tenants, also see Blackmar, *Manhattan for Rent*, 219–25, 232.

170. Walker seems to imply that the obligation of parents to provide maintenance, protection, and education for their children was even less subject to legal enforcement. Walker further argued that performance of these parental duties was at most only a matter of "moral obligation." Walker's comment suggests that the courts would evaluate the father's role as a legal guardian only in instances where the child's custody was contested. See Timothy Walker, *Introduction to American Law*, 235.

171. Blackmar, *Manhattan for Rent*, 232, 235.

172. George Henry Evans, the key organizer of the national reform movement, which land reformers organized in 1844, captured these sentiments in an earlier 1841 editorial for his monthly, *The Radical*, when he wrote, "If a man has any right on earth . . . he has the right to land enough to raise a habitation on." See Sean Wilentz, *Chants Democratic: New York and the Rise of the American Working Class, 1788–1850* (New York: Oxford University Press, 1984), 336.

173. Stanton, "Mrs. E. C. Stanton's Address," 260.

174. Mansfield, *Legal Rights, Liabilities, and Duties of Women*, 266.

175. See Drew R. McCoy's summary of the role of family labor in the production of household necessaries, *The Elusive Republic: Political Economy in Jeffersonian America* (New York: Norton, 1982), 64; also see Boydston's discussion of family production and how it affected female labor in the household economy, in Boydston, *Home and Work*, esp. her chapter "The Political Economy of Housework," 120–41.

176. See Sally McMurry, "Progressive Farm Families and their Houses, 1830–1855: A Study in Independent Design," *Agricultural History* 58 (July 1984): 331.

177. See Chamomile [Sarah Coates], "Woman's Wrongs, &c.," *Ohio Cultivator*, August 1, 1851, 239.

178. The meaning of dower according to the common law reflected the tradition in which the husband endowed his newly married bride with a portion of his lands. In English law, dower offered some guarantee for the wife's future maintenance, since she could not be deprived of dower by any deed, devise, or other legal act by her husband. At the same time, dower was a contingent right that required the wife to fulfill her marital duties, since she could be barred of it by elopement or divorce. Nevertheless, dower remained a promise for maintenance and not management. This limitation meant that the wife had the right to use the land, but she could not exploit the land through waste for its proceeds, nor could she sell it for a profitable return. Dower did have other legal and customary meanings. It also implied the goods or money that the husband paid for his wife that was derived from the tradition of the "bride price." And dower was associated with dowry, or the goods and money that the wife contributed to the maintenance of the marriage. Even so, the common-law meaning undermined its connection with dowry—or dower as the wife's marriage portion—which fell under the rubric of civil law. Antebellum feminists sought to recognize the older notion of dowry as a way to emphasize the wife's contribution to maintenance of the family. See Timothy Walker, "Legal Condition of Woman," 349–50; also see *Compact Edition of the Oxford English Dictionary*, 1:793.

179. Timothy Walker, "Legal Condition of Woman," 349–50.

180. It was assumed that wives, as members of the same household, rendered their services gratuitously, without any presumption of payment. Because the husband assumed the role of patron, the wife returned his "bounty" with her gratitude or voluntary or free labor. For the notion of gratuitously rendered labor, see Havighurst, "Services in the Home," 390. In the case

of *Charles Rands and Wife v. Ussiah Kendall*, discussed by Timothy Walker, he made the point that for a wife to be entitled to a dower, her husband must have legally prospered during marriage. This notice reinforced the idea that the dower was a bounty, a surplus, given to the wife, rather than something earned in return for her services or labor. See "Charles Rands and Wife v. Ussiah Kendall," *Western Law Journal*, March 1847, 251. The same premise that the wife performed her labor "voluntarily" also appeared in *Cropsey v. Sweeney*, 315.

181. *West Chester WRC 1852*, 22.

182. *Proceedings of the New Jersey State Constitutional Convention of 1844* (Trenton: New Jersey State House Commission, 1942), 88, 101–2.

183. See a review of Timothy Walker's oration "The Reform Spirit of the Day," which he gave at Harvard University on July 18, 1850, in *National American Review*, October 1850, 515.

184. "Memorial of Mrs. Caroline Severance," 292.

185. Caroline Severance, "Women's Right Advocate, No. 1," *Lily*, January 15, 1853, 1.

186. See Lizzie Linn, "The Disappointed Wife," *Una*, September 1853, 129–31. For the conclusion of the story, see ibid., October 1853, 145–46.

187. See "Love and Money," *Genius of the West*, July 1850, 208–11.

188. "Education of Farmer's Daughters. Letter from Aunt Patience to Helen," *Ohio Cultivator*, February 1, 1850, 46.

189. Ibid.

190. Here I disagree with the conclusion of Marylynn Salmon, who views these changes primarily in a positive light. I believe the laws had a double-edged effect. On one hand, the laws did grant married women control over their separate property and limited powers to convey, contract, and will that property, which was an improvement over the common law. On the other hand, the laws rather intentionally limited the impact of these changes, since wives still inherited less than their husbands (these laws did not establish equal inheritance of community property), and wives did not gain the full benefits of property ownership (custodial rights, suffrage, status as head of household, or rights to their wages). At best the laws responded to some of the pressing economic demands of the time and offered a less than satisfactory and nonegalitarian solution. The laws also gave the typical family only a partial safety net that did not extend to necessaries. In addition, the same laws refused to acknowledge the active contribution of married women to the support of their families. Wives were still not recognized as joint or sole providers of the family unless by default when the family faced a financial crisis. By preserving all of these civil disabilities, the law carefully retained the common-law fiction that treated wives as passive and not active economic agents in the family. See Salmon, "Republican Sentiment," pp. 465–68.

191. Stanton, "Mrs. E. C. Stanton's Address," 260.

192. Civis, "Woman's Rights and Woman's Wrongs According to the Law," *Lily*, November 1, 1854, 159.

193. Walker's quote was included in the "Address to the Women of Ohio," which was prepared by the members of the Salem women's rights convention. See *Salem WRC 1850*, 27.

194. Adeline Swift, "Men and Women of Ohio, Read! Read!! Read!!! Read the Laws which Oppress the Widow and Rob the Fatherless," *Lily*, December 1, 1856, 149.

195. *State of Ohio ex rel. Stephen Ball v. Anna Hand*, 5 Ohio Decisions 239, 243–44 (1848).

196. Grossberg, *Governing the Hearth*, 249.

197. Salmon, "Republican Sentiment," 471.

198. *People ex rel. Barry v. Mercein*, 3 Hill (N.Y.) 400, 412, 415, 420, 422–23 (1842).

199. Frances D. Gage, "Woman's Sphere—What Mrs. Jone's said about it," *Ohio Cultivator*, January 1, 1851, 15.

200. "St. Paul and the Women," *Lily*, August 1, 1854, 108.

201. Chamomile [Sarah Coates], "Woman's Wrongs, &c.," *Ohio Cultivator*, August 1, 1851, 238.

202. Hannah M. Tracy, "Woman's Sphere," *Ohio Cultivator*, April 1, 1851, 110.

203. Stanton, "Mrs. E. C. Stanton's Address," 261.

Chapter 7

1. *New York City WRC 1860*, 4.

2. See James H. Kettner, *The Development of American Citizenship, 1608–1870* (Chapel Hill: University of North Carolina Press, 1978), 334, 343.

3. Ibid., 344–45. Kettner makes the point that in the second clause of the Fourteenth Amendment and in the Fifteenth Amendment the language was "indirect and negative, open to interpretations that left states with wide powers to curtail access to suffrage." See Ellen Carol DuBois, "Taking the Law into Our Own Hands: *Bradwell, Minor*, and Suffrage Militance in the 1870s," in *Visible Women: New Essays on American Activism*, ed. Nancy A. Hewitt and Suzanne Lebsock (Urbana: University of Illinois Press, 1993), 21; Jane J. Mansbridge, *Why We Lost the ERA* (Chicago: University of Chicago Press, 1986).

4. See "Reminiscences by Clarina I. Howard Nichols," in *History of Woman Suffrage*, 6 vols., ed. Elizabeth Cady Stanton, Susan B. Anthony, and Matilda Joslyn Gage (New York, 1881; reprint, New York: Arno Press, 1985), 1:185–92; Joseph G. Gambone, ed., "The Forgotten Feminist of Kansas: The Papers of Clarina I. H. Nichols, 1854–1885," *Kansas Historical Quarterly* 39–40 (Spring 1973–Winter 1974); Wilda M. Smith, "A Half Century of Struggle: Gaining Woman Suffrage in Kansas," *Kansas History* 4 (Summer 1981): 74–91. Also see James Rawley, *Race and Politics: "Bleeding Kansas" and the Coming of the Civil War* (Philadelphia: Lippincott, 1969).

5. Nichols, in Stanton, Anthony, and Gage, eds., *History of Woman Suffrage*, 1:193–94; Rawley, *Race and Politics*.

6. Nichols, in Stanton, Anthony, and Gage, eds., *History of Woman Suffrage*, 1:193.

7. See Catherine A. MacKinnon, "Feminism, Marxism, Method, and the State: Toward a Feminist Jurisprudence [1983]," in *Feminist Legal Theory: Readings in Law and Gender*, ed. Katharine T. Bartlett and Rosanne Kennedy (Boulder: Westview Press, 1991), 194–95.

8. Catherine A. MacKinnon, "Legal Perspectives on Sexual Difference," in *Theoretical Perspectives on Sexual Difference*, ed. Deborah L. Rhode (New Haven: Yale University Press, 1990), 217, 221.

9. See my discussion of the Roberts case in Chapter 2; also see 59 Mass. (5 Cush.) 206 (1849), and Earl M. Maltz, "Fourteenth Amendment Concepts in the Antebellum Era," *American Journal of Legal History* 32 (1988): 325.

10. MacKinnon, "Legal Perspectives on Sexual Difference," 214; Catherine Belsey, "Constructing the Subject: Deconstructing the Text," in *Feminisms: An Anthology of Literary Theory and Criticism*, ed. Robyn R. Warhol and Diane Price Herndl (New Brunswick: Rutgers University Press, 1991), 594. Belsey draws her critical perspective from Louis Althusser, which has influenced those scholars interested in discourse theory. See my "The Personal Is Political: Gender, Feminism, and the Politics of Discourse Theory," *American Quarterly* 44 (September 1992): 449–58. See Louis Althusser, "Ideology and Ideological State Apparatuses (Notes toward an Investigation)," in *Lenin and Philosophy and Other Essays*, trans. Ben Brewster (New York: Monthly Review Press, 1971), 142–45, 164–65, 168–73.

11. See Michel Foucault, *Discipline and Punish: The Birth of the Prison*, trans. Alan Sheridan (New York: Vintage, 1979), 222; Foucault, *The History of Sexuality: An Introduction*, trans. Robert Hurley (New York: Random House, 1980), 154; Foucault, "Truth and Power," in *The*

Foucault Reader, ed. Paul Rabinow (New York: Pantheon, 1984), 54–55. Also see Jana Sawicki, *Disciplining Foucault: Feminism, Power, and the Body* (New York: Routledge, 1995), 25; Sandra Lee Bartky, "Foucault, Femininity, and the Modernization of Patriarchal Power," in *Feminism and Foucault: Reflections on Resistance*, ed. Irene Diamond and Lee Quinby (Boston: Northeastern University Press, 1988), 74–75; Judith Butler, "Variations on Sex and Gender: Beauvoir, Wittig, and Foucault," in *Feminism as Critique: On the Politics of Gender*, ed. and with an introduction by Seyla Benhabib and Drucilla Cornell (Minneapolis: University of Minnesota Press, 1987), 138. For an example of how Foucault appropriates religious concepts to explain disciplinary power (although he does not acknowledge the importance of the influence), see his definition of disciplinary power as "pastorship," in "Politics and Reason," in *Michel Foucault: Politics, Philosophy, and Culture: Interviews and Other Writings, 1977–1984*, ed. and with an introduction by Lawrence D. Kritzman, trans. Alan Sheridan and others (New York: Routledge, 1988), 60.

12. Hendrik Hartog, "The Constitution of Aspiration and 'The Rights That Belong to Us All,'" *Journal of American History* 74 (December 1987): 1014.

13. Clifford Geertz, *The Interpretation of Cultures: Selected Essays by Clifford Geertz* (New York: Basic Books, 1973), 112.

14. For the Enlightenment notion of reason and sight, see Ernst Cassirer's chapter "Psychology and Epistemology," in *The Philosophy of the Enlightenment*, trans. Fritz C. A. Koellin and James P. Pettegrove (Boston: Beacon Press, 1951), 93–133. For language and speech and its connection to democracy, see Steven H. Shiffrin, *The First Amendment, Democracy, and Romance* (Princeton: Princeton University Press, 1990). For the connection between labor, hands, and the body, see Jonathan A. Glickstein, *Concepts of Free Labor in Antebellum America* (New Haven: Yale University Press, 1991), 3–11, 23–52.

15. See my discussion of eyes and jury service in Chapter 5; for speech and public standing and the negative portrayals of women's public displays, see Chapters 2 and 4; for hands and women's lack of economic value, see Chapter 6.

16. See Nel Noddings, *Women and Evil* (Berkeley: University of California Press, 1989), 34–38, and see Chapter 5 for the tripartite caste division between good and bad women on one hand, and men as separate and distinct from both castes.

17. For the importance of masculinity and the sublime experience of war, see Genevieve Lloyd, "Selfhood, War, and Masculinity," in *Feminist Challenges: Social and Political Theory*, ed. Carole Pateman and Elizabeth Gross (Boston: Northeastern University Press, 1987), 63–76. For the connection between religious covenants and national identity, see Samuel Levinson, *Constitutional Faith* (Princeton: Princeton University Press, 1988), 11; also see Ernest Tuveson, *Redeemer Nation: The Idea of America's Millennial Role* (Chicago: University of Chicago Press, 1968). For the use of the "one flesh" trope in the Mexican war, see Chapter 5.

18. See Hannah Arendt, *The Human Condition* (Chicago: University of Chicago Press, 1958), 48–51, 57; "Women's Rights Convention," *Daily Evening Travellor*, in Caroline H. Dall Papers, 1811–1917, Massachusetts Historical Society, Boston, Mass.; *New York City WRC 1860*, 24, 39.

19. For quotation by Brown, see *Worcester WRC 1851*, 95. For fallen women as political outcasts, see Chapter 5, and for Stanton's reference to women as monsters, see *New York City WRC 1860*, 38.

20. *New York City WRC 1860*, 44.

21. For Mott's quotation, see her "Discourse on Woman" (1849), in *Salem WRC 1850*, 147. For Mary Ann Johnson, see *West Chester WRC 1852*, 10.

22. Loeffelholz makes the point that Stanton's speech does not resolve the contradiction between real women and the idealized female statue; see Mary Loeffelholz, "Posing the Woman Citizen: The Contradictions of Stanton's Feminism," *Genders*, no. 7 (March 1990): 92–97. Yet I suggest, in addition, Stanton tried to emphasize the problem of perception and the imagi-

nary nature of constructing citizenship and, ultimately, its unnatural embodiment. For Stanton civic embodiment organizes past and current practices, and it is not fixed; it is a process of "becoming" a citizen. For the theoretical implications of this assumption, see Butler, "Variations on Sex and Gender," 131.

23. *New York City WRC 1860*, 65–67.

24. Ibid., 66–71.

25. Ibid., 73–79.

26. Ibid., 75.

27. Ibid., 78–80.

28. Ibid., 81–82.

29. Ibid., 82–84.

30. Ibid., 85–87, 89–90.

31. See DuBois, "Taking the Law into Our Own Hands," 21–22. Although DuBois sees the postbellum movement as a radical departure from the antebellum period, I see the roots of this strategy in the earlier campaign.

32. See *Bradwell v. Illinois* 83 U.S. (16 Wall.) 130 (1873), 132, 141–42. For the importance of the Bradwell case, see Joan Hoff, *Law, Gender, and Injustice: A Legal History of U.S. Women* (New York: New York University Press, 1991), 164–70, and for its place as setting the precedent for sex-based discrimination, see Kenneth Davidson, Ruth B. Ginsburg, and Herma H. Kay, eds., *Sex-Based Discrimination: Texts, Cases, and Materials* (St. Paul: West, 1974), 3–10.

33. For the entire text of Carpenter's remarks, see "Argument of Hon. Matt. H. Carpenter, Jan. 18, 1872, upon the Application of Myra Bradwell to be Admitted to the Bar," in *Chicago Legal News*, January 20, 1872, 108–9, esp. 108. For the similar views of James Wilson, see Jan Lewis, "'Of Every Age Sex and Condition': The Representation of Women in the Constitution," *Journal of the Early Republic* 15 (Fall 1995): 363, 365, esp. 370–72, 374–75, 379–81.

34. See "Argument of Hon. Matt. H. Carpenter," 108, and *Bradwell v. Illinois*, 141–42.

Bibliography

Primary Sources

Manuscripts

American Antiquarian Society, Worcester, Mass.
  Broadside Collection
  Chase Family Papers
  Lucy Chase Papers
  Edward Earle Papers
  Stephen and Abby Kelley Foster Papers
  Thomas Wentworth Higginson Papers
  Miscellaneous Pamphlet Collection
  Miscellaneous Records Collection
  Northampton Association of Education and Industry Records
  Slavery in the United States Collection
  U.S. Manuscript Census, Worcester, with Index, 1850
  Worcester, Mass., Collection
Boston Public Library, Boston, Mass.
  Antislavery Collection
Chester County Historical Society, West Chester, Pa.
  Chester County Census Records
  Hannah Darlington Letters
  Ann Preston Letters
Friends Historical Society, Swarthmore College, Swarthmore, Pa.
  Joseph Dugdale Papers
  Kennett [Friends] Monthly Meeting Records

Mott Manuscripts, 1834–1896
Painter Collection
Massachusetts Historical Society, Boston
Caroline H. Dall Papers, 1811–1917
James T. Fisher Papers, 1790–1865
Records of the Religious Union of Associationists
Pennsylvania Historical Society, Philadelphia
Autograph Collection of Simon Gratz
Ferdinand J. Dreer Autograph Collection
Female Medical College of Pennsylvania Records
Logan-Fisher-Fox Collection
Philadelphia Female Anti-Slavery Society Records
Rosine Association Records
Philadelphia Library Company, Philadelphia, Pa.
"The Death Penalty. Town Meeting" (1844)
Rhode Island Historical Society, Providence, R.I.
Papers of the Providence Physiological Society
Arthur and Elizabeth Schlesinger Library on the History of Women in America, Radcliffe
College, Cambridge, Mass.
Blackwell Family Papers
Abby Kelley Foster Papers
Sophia Smith Collection, Smith College, Northampton, Mass.
Martha Coffin Wright Correspondence, in Garrison Family Papers
Vassar College Special Collections, Poughkeepsie, N.Y.
Paulina Kellogg Wright Davis Papers, 1813–1876
Worcester Historical Society, Worcester, Mass.
Earle Family Papers
Abby Kelley Foster Papers
Reverend Samuel B. May Papers
Worcester Anti-Slavery Sewing Circle Records
Worcester County Anti-Slavery Society, South Division Records

Newspapers and Periodicals

American Vegetarian and Health Journal, 1852–53
Anti-Slavery Bugle, 1845–55
Brother Jonathan, 1842–43
Chicago Legal News, 1872
Emancipator and Republican, 1845–50
Genius of the West, 1854–55
Harper's New Monthly Magazine, 1850–73
Herald of Truth, 1847–49
Ladies Magazine and Literary Gazette, 1831
Ladies' National Magazine, 1848
Ladies Repository, 1850–51
Lily, 1849–56
Massachusetts Spy, 1848–50
National Anti-Slavery Standard, 1846–56
National Reformer, 1848

New England Farmer, 1850
New York Herald, 1850–60
New York Times, 1852–60
New York Tribune, 1844–60
North American Review, 1825–52
Ohio Cultivator, 1849–55
Pennsylvania Farm Journal, 1853–55
Pennsylvania Freeman, 1846–53
Practical Christian, 1845–53
Prisoner's Friend, 1853–54
Spirit of the Age, 1849–50
Spiritual Philosopher, 1850–51
Una, 1853–56
Union Magazine, 1848–50
United States Magazine and Democratic Review, 1841–52
Water-Cure Journal, 1845–53
Western Law Journal, 1840–54
Woman's Journal, 1870

Government Documents

Congressional Globe, 1835–56

Legal Cases

CONNECTICUT
Shaw v. Shaw, 17 Connecticut Reports 194 (1845).

IOWA
Inskeep v. Inskeep, 5 Iowa Reports 208 (1857).

MAINE
Merrill v. Smith, 37 Maine Reports 394 (1854).

MASSACHUSETTS
Commonwealth v. Aves, 18 Pick. (Mass.) 194 (1836).
Commonwealth v. John Cook, 12 Metcalf (Mass.) 93 (1846).
Roberts v. City of Boston, 59 Mass. (5 Cush.) 198 (1849).

MISSOURI
O'Bryan v. O'Bryan, 13 Missouri Reports 17 (1850).

NEW YORK
Cropsey v. Sweeney, 27 Barb. (N.Y.) 310 (1858).
Holmes v. Holmes, 4 Barb. (N.Y.) 295 (1848).
Lindenmuller v. the People, 33 Barb. (N.Y.) 560 (1861).
People ex rel. Barry v. Mercein, 3 Hill (N.Y.) 399 (1842).
People v. Colt, 3 Hill (N.Y.) 432 (1842).
People v. Ruggles, 8 Johns R. (N.Y.) 290 (1811).
White v. White, 5 Barb. (N.Y.) 474 (1849).

NORTH CAROLINA
Coble v. Coble, 55 North Carolina Reports 395 (1856).

OHIO
Duhme v. Duhme, 3 Ohio Decisions 95 (1859).
State of Ohio ex rel. Stephen Ball v. Anna Hand, 5 Ohio Decisions 238 (1848).

PENNSYLVANIA
Butler v. Butler, 1 Parsons (Pa.) 337 (1849).
Matchin v. Matchin, Pa. 332 (1847).
Raybold v. Raybold, 20 Pa. 308 (1853).
Sprecht v. Commonwealth, 8 Pa. 312 (1848).
Updegraph v. Commonwealth, 11 Pa. 398 (1822).

SOUTH CAROLINA
Hair v. Hair, 10 Rich. (S.C.) 163 (1858).

U.S. SUPREME COURT
Bradwell v. Illinois, 83 U.S. (16 Wall.) 130 (1873).
Kempe's Lessee v. Kennedy et al., U.S. Supreme Court Reports 5 (Cranch) 70 (1809).
Prigg v. Pennsylvania, 16 Peters (U.S.) 539 (1842).

Autobiographies, Letters, Memoirs, and Papers

Adams, Charles Francis, ed. *Memoirs of John Quincy Adams, Comprising Portions of His Diary from 1795–1848*. 10 vols. Freeport, N.Y.: Books for Libraries, 1969.
———. *The Works of John Adams*. 10 vols. Boston, 1851.
Barnes, Gilbert H., and Dwight L. Dumond, eds. *Letters of Theodore Dwight Weld, Angelina Grimké, and Sarah Grimké, 1822–1844*. 2 vols. Published for the American Historical Association. New York: Appleton-Century, 1934. Reprint, Gloucester, Mass.: Peter Smith, 1965.
Butterfield, L. H., ed. *Letters of Benjamin Rush*. 2 vols. Princeton: Princeton University Press, 1951.
Butterfield, L. H., Wendell D. Garrett, and Marjorie E. Sprague, eds. *Adams Family Correspondence*. Vol. 1. Cambridge: Belknap Press of Harvard University Press, 1963.
Colman, Lucy N. *Reminiscences of Lucy N. Colman*. Buffalo: H. L. Green, 1891.
Edgar Allan Poe: Tales and Poetry. New York: Library of America, 1984.
Elizabeth Buffum Chase, 1806–1899: Her Life and Its Environment. Boston, 1914.
Ford, Lewis. *The Variety Book, Containing Life Sketches and Reminiscences*. Boston: George E. Crosby, 1892.
Gambone, Joseph G., ed. "The Forgotten Feminist of Kansas: The Papers of Clarina I. H. Nichols, 1854–1885." *Kansas Historical Quarterly* 39–40 (Spring 1973–Winter 1974), in eight installments.
Gerrit Smith Papers, 1775–1924. Part of the Special Collections in the George Arents Research Library, Syracuse University, Syracuse, N.Y. Glen Rock, N.J.: Microfilming Corporation of America, 1974.
Hallowell, Anna Davis, ed. *James and Lucretia Mott: Life and Letters*. Boston: Houghton Mifflin, 1884.
Higginson, Mary Thacher, ed. *Letters and Journal of Thomas Wentworth Higginson, 1846–1906*. Boston: Houghton Mifflin, 1921. Reprint, New York: Da Capo, 1969.

Holland, Patricia G., and Ann D. Gordon, eds. *The Papers of Elizabeth Cady Stanton and Susan B. Anthony*. Wilmington, Del., 1991, microfilm.

Hunt, Harriot K. *Glances and Glimpses; or, Fifty Years Social, Including Twenty Years of Professional Life*. Boston: John P. Jewett, 1856.

Lasser, Carol, and Marlene Merrill, eds. *Friends and Sisters: Letters between Lucy Stone and Antoinette Brown Blackwell, 1846–93*. Urbana: University of Illinois Press, 1987.

———. *Soul Mates: The Oberlin Correspondence of Lucy Stone and Antoinette Brown, 1846–1850*. Oberlin: Oberlin College Press, 1983.

Meltzer, Milton, and Patricia G. Holland, eds. *Lydia Maria Child, Selected Letters, 1817–1800*. Amherst: University of Massachusetts Press, 1982.

Memorial of Sarah Pugh: A Tribute of Respect from Her Cousins. Philadelphia, 1888.

Merrill, Walter M., and Louis Ruchames, eds. *The Letters of William Lloyd Garrison*. 8 vols. Cambridge: Belknap Press of Harvard University Press, 1971–75.

Shively, Charles, ed. *The Collected Works of Lysander Spooner*. 6 vols. Weston, Mass.: M & S Press, 1971.

Stanton, Elizabeth Cady. *Eighty Years and More: Reminiscences, 1815–1897*. New York: T. Fisher Unwin, 1898. Reprint, New York: Schocken, 1971.

Tolles, Frederick B., ed. "Slavery and 'The Woman Question': Lucretia Mott's Diary of Her Visit to Great Britain to Attend the World's Anti-Slavery Convention of 1840." *Journal of the Friends Historical Society Supplement*, no. 23 (1952).

Walker, Amelia W., and Eugene C. Barker, eds. *The Writings of Sam Houston, 1813–1863*. 8 vols. Austin: University of Texas Press, 1938.

Wheeler, Leslie, ed. *Loving Warriors: Selected Letters of Lucy Stone and Henry B. Blackwell, 1853 to 1893*. New York: Dial, 1981.

Wyman, Mary Alice, ed. *Selections from the Autobiography of Elizabeth Oakes Smith*. Lewiston, Maine: Lewiston Journal, 1924.

Articles, Books, Essays, and Pamphlets

Adams, John Quincy. *The Social Compact, Exemplified in the Constitution of the Commonwealth of Massachusetts; with Remarks on the Theories of Divine Right of Hobbes and of Filmer, and the Counter Theories of Sidney, Locke, Montesquieu, and Rousseau, Concerning the Origin of Government: A Lecture, Delivered Before the Franklin Lyceum, at Providence, R.I., November 25, 1842*. Providence, R.I.: Knowles and Vose, 1842.

———. *Speech of John Quincy Adams, of Massachusetts, Upon the Right of the People to Petition; on the Freedom of Speech and Debates in the House of Representatives of the United States; on Resolutions of Seven State Legislatures, and the Petitions of More Than One Hundred Thousand Petitioners, relating to the Annexation of Texas*. Washington, D.C., 1838. Reprint, New York: Arno Press, 1969.

Alcott, William A. *The Young Husband, or Duties of Man in the Marriage Relation*. 5th ed. Boston: George W. Light, 1841. Reprint, New York: Arno and the New York Times, 1972.

The American Colporteur System. New York, 1845.

The American Keepsake, or Book for Every American. Boston, 1845.

Ballou, Adin. *The Bible: In its fundamental principles absolutely DIVINE. In its Explicative Ideas and Language Properly HUMAN*. Practical Christian Tracts, no. 3. Hopedale, Mass.: Hopedale Press, 1849.

Beecher, Catharine, and Harriet Beecher Stowe. *The American Woman's Home, or Principles of Domestic Science*. New York, 1869.

———. *An Essay on Slavery and Abolitionism, with Reference to the Duty of American Females.* Philadelphia, 1837. Reprint, Freeport, N.Y.: Books for Libraries Press, 1970.

Beecher, Lyman. *The Bible A Code of Law. A Sermon, Delivered in Park Street Church, Boston, September 3, 1817, at the Ordination of Mr. Sereno Edwards Dwight, as the Pastor of that Church; and of Messrs. Elisha P. Swift, Allen Graves, John Nichols, Levi Parson, & Daniel Buttrick, as Missionaries to the Heathen.* Andover, Mass., 1827.

Blackstone, Sir William. *Commentaries on the Laws of England in Four Books.* 2 vols. 2nd ed. Edited by Thomas M. Cooley. Chicago: Callagham, 1879.

Bowles, Ada C. "Women in the Ministry." In *Woman's Work in America*, edited by Annie Nathan Meyer, 206–17. New York: Henry Holt, 1891.

Caverno, Charles. *Treatise on Divorce.* Madison, Wis., 1889.

Channing, William Ellery. *The Works of William E. Channing, D.D.* 2 vols. Boston, 1849.

Channing, William Henry. *The Christian Church and Social Reform. A Discourse Delivered Before the Religious Union of Associationists.* Boston, 1848.

———. *The Ordination Service of Thomas Wentworth Higginson, with Charge by James Freeman Clarke.* Boston, 1847.

———. Review of *The History of Woman Suffrage*, by Elizabeth Cady Stanton, Susan B. Anthony, and Matilda Joslyn Gage, eds. *London Inquirer*, November 5, 1881. Reprint, New York: National Woman's Suffrage Association, 1882.

[Chapman, Lucretia.] *Trial of Lucretia Chapman; otherwise called Lucretia Espos y Mina, who was jointly indicted with Lino Amalia Espos y Mina, for the murder of William Chapman, Esq. late of Andalusia, County of Bucks, Pennsylvania: in the Court of Oyer and Terminer, held at Doylestown, for Bucks, December term, 1831, continued to February term, 1832.* Philadelphia, 1832.

Cheever George B. *Punishment by Death: Its Authority and Expediency.* New York, 1849.

Child, Lydia Maria. *Isaac T. Hopper: A True Life.* Boston, 1845.

———. *Letters from New York.* 2nd ed. New York, 1853.

———. *Memoirs of Madame de Staël, and Madame Roland.* Auburn, Maine, 1861.

Christianity Opposed to the "Death Penalty." Addressed to the Editors and Readers of the Providence Journal, and to all Professed Ministers of the Gospel, who Pleade Divine Authority for the Shedding of Human Blood. Providence, R.I., 1852.

Clemmer, Mary. "Lucretia Mott." In *Our Famous Women: An Authorized Record of the Lives and Deeds of Distinguished American Women of Our Times*, 463–97. Hartford: A. D. Worthington, 1884.

Dall, Caroline H. *The College, the Market, and the Court.* Boston, 1867. Reprint, Concord, N.H.: Rumford Press, 1914.

———. *Margaret and her Friends or Ten Conversations with Margaret Fuller upon the Mythology of the Greeks and Its Expression in Art.* Boston, 1895.

Davis, Paulina Wright. *A History of the National Woman's Rights Movement, for Twenty years, with the Proceedings of the Decade Meeting held at Apollo Hall, October 20, 1870, from 1850 to 1870, with an Appendix Containing the History of the Movement during the Winter of 1871, in the National Capital.* New York, 1871.

Dean, Amos. *Principles of Medical Jurisprudence: Designed for the Professions of Law and Medicine.* Albany, N.Y., 1850.

Dix, Dorothea L. *Remarks on Prisons and Prison Discipline in the United States.* Boston, 1845.

Eaton, Cyrus. *Woman: An Address Delivered to the Ladies' Sewing Circle, Warren, Maine, at their Anniversary Meeting, February 9, 1854.* Hallowell, Maine, 1854.

Edwards, Justin. *Permanent Sabbath Documents.* N.p., 1844.

———. *The Sabbath Manual; including "The Sabbath a Family Institution."* New York, n.d.

Elder, William. *Periscopics; or, Current Subjects Extemporaneously Treated.* New York, 1854.

First Annual Report of the American and Foreign Sabbath Union. Boston, 1844.

Fisher, William Logan. *The Light of Truth in the Mind of Man, the only Rule of Faith and Practice. With Some Observations upon the Formality and Idolatry of Religious Sects.* Philadelphia: Atkinson and Alexander, 1824.

———. *A Memorial for the Repeal of All Sunday Laws. To the Senate and House of Representatives of the State of Pennsylvania in General Assembly Met.* Wakefield, Pa., 1850.

———. *Observations on Mental Phenomena, as Connected with the Philosophy of Divine Revelation.* Philadelphia: Merrihew and Thompson, 1851.

———. *Progressive Friends. An Account of the Fourth Annual Meeting of the Progressive Friends, with some Observations on their Principles and Prospects.* Philadelphia, 1856.

———. *Unconstitutionality of the Sabbath Laws.* N.p., n.d.

Fisher, William Logan, and Edward M. Davis. *The Sunday Question. Sabbath of the Jews. Sunda of the Constintine. To the General Assembly of the Commonwealth of Pennsylvania.* Philadelphia, 1855.

Forman, J. G. *The Christian Martyrs; or, the Conditions of Obedience to the Civil Government: A Discourse by J. G. Forman, Minister of the Second Congregational Church in Nantucket.* Boston, 1851.

———. *The Fugitive Slave Law. A Discourse Delivered in the Congregational Church in West Bridge, Mass., on Sunday, November 17th, 1850. By J. G. Forman, Minister of the Congregation.* Boston, 1850.

Fowler, L. N. *Marriage: Its History and Ceremonies; with a Phrenological and Physiological Exposition. Of the Functions and Qualifications for Happy Marriages.* 22nd ed. New York, 1856.

Fuller, Margaret. *Women in the Nineteenth Century.* New York, 1845. Reprint, Columbia: University of South Carolina Press, 1980.

Furness, William H. *Communion with the Unseen. Discourse, Delivered in the First Congregational Unitarian Church, Sunday, Oct. 1, 1843, By William H. Furness, Pastor.* Philadelphia, 1843.

Fussell, Edwin, M.D. *Valedictory Address to the Graduating Class of the Female Medical College, of Pennsylvania, for the Session 1856–57.* Philadelphia, 1857.

Giles, Charles. *The Convention of Drunkards: A Satirical Essay on Intemperance.* New York, 1840.

Goodell, William. *The American Slave Code in Theory and Practice: Distinctive Features Shown by Its Statutes, Judicial Decisions, and Illustrative Facts.* New York, 1853.

———. *The Rights and the Wrongs of Rhode Island.* Whitesboro, N.Y., 1842.

———. *Views of American Constitutional Law, in its Bearing upon American Slavery.* Utica, N.Y., 1844.

Grimké, Angelina. *An Appeal to the Women of the Nominally Free States, issued by an Anti-Slavery Convention of American Women. Held by Adjournments from the 9th to the 12th of May, 1837.* 2nd ed. Boston: Isaac Knapp, 1838.

Grimké, Frederick. *Considerations Upon the Nature and Tendency of Free Institutions.* Cincinnati, 1848.

Grimké, Sarah M. *Letters on the Equality of the Sexes, and the Condition of Woman. Addressed to Mary S. Parker, President of the Boston Female Anti-Slavery Society.* Boston, 1838.

Hamilton, Alexander. "Report on the Subject of Manufactures." In *The Philosophy of Manufactures: Early Debates over Industrialization in the United States,* edited by Michael Brewster Folsom and Steven D. Lubar, 81–93. Cambridge: MIT Press, 1982.

Harper, Ida Husted. *The Life and Work of Susan B. Anthony.* 2 vols. Indianapolis: Hollenbeck Press, 1898.

Herttell, Thomas. *The Demurrer: Proofs of Error in the Decision of the Supreme Court of the State of New-York, Requiring Faith in Particular Religious Doctrines as a Legal Qualifications of Witnesses; Thence Establishing by Law a Religious Test, and a Religious Creed.* New York, 1828.

————. *The People's Rights Re-claimed; Being an Exposition of the Unconstitutionality of the Law of the State of New York Compelling the Observation of a Religious Sabbath Day; and Erroneously entitled "An Act for the Suppressing of Immorality," Passed March 13th, 1813.* New York, 1826.

————. *Remarks Comprising in Substance Judge Herttell's Argument in the House of Assembly of the State of New-York, in the Session of 1837, in Support of the Bill to Restore to Married Women "The Right of Property," as Guarantied by the Constitution of the State.* New York, 1839.

History of Pennsylvania Hall, which was Destroyed by a Mob, on the 17th of May, 1838. Philadelphia, 1838.

Hurlbut, Elisha P. *Essays on Human Rights, and Their Political Guaranties.* New York, 1848.

The Impropriety of Capital Punishment; or, the Report of a Committee on Dr. Cuyler's Sermon entitled "The Law of God with Respect to Murder." Philadelphia, 1842.

Jameson, John Alexander. *The Constitutional Convention: Its History, Powers, and Modes of Proceeding.* New York, 1867.

Jay, William. *Miscellaneous Writings on Slavery.* Boston, 1853.

————. *A Review of the Causes and Consequences of the Mexican War.* 2nd ed. Boston, 1849.

[Johnson, Oliver.] *Expositions of Sentiments, Adopted by the Pennsylvania Yearly Meeting of Progressive Friends.* N.p., [1853].

————. *William Lloyd Garrison and His Times.* Boston, 1880.

Lawson, John D. *American State Trials.* 2 vols. St. Louis: F. H. Thomas Law, 1914.

The Liberty Bell. By the Friends of Freedom. Boston: Massachusetts Anti-Slavery Fair, 1841, 1843, 1844, 1846.

The Liberty Bell. By the Friends of Freedom. Boston: National Anti-Slavery Bazaar, 1848, 1849, 1851, 1852, 1853, 1854.

Locke, John. *Two Treatises of Government.* Edited by Peter Laslett. Cambridge: Cambridge University Press, 1963.

McDougall, Francis Harriet (Whipple) Greene. *Might and Right: A History of the Dorr Rebellion.* Providence, R.I., 1844.

Mansfield, Edward D. *The Legal Rights, Liabilities, and Duties of Women; with an Introductory History of their Legal Condition in the Hebrew, Roman and Feudal Civil Systems.* Salem, Ohio, 1845.

Marsh, Samuel. *"Hard Questions" Answered: In Two Parts.* Montpelier, Vt., 1849.

Marshall, Clara. *The Woman's Medical College of Philadelphia. An Historical Outline.* Philadelphia, 1897.

May, Samuel J. *Letters to Andrew T. Judson, Esq. and others in Canterbury, Remonstrating with them on their unjust and unjustifiable procedure relative to Miss Crandall and Her School for Colored Females.* Brooklyn, N.Y., 1833.

————. *The Rights and Condition of Women; A Sermon Preached in Syracuse, Nov., 1845, By Samuel J. May.* N.p., n.d.

A Memorial for the Repeal of All Sunday Laws. To the Senate and House of Representatives of the State of Pennsylvania in General Assembly Met. Wakefield, Pa., 1850.

Miller, John G. *The Great Convention. Description of the Convention of the People of Ohio, held at Columbus on 21st and 22nd February 1840.* Columbus, Ohio, 1840.

Nichols, Mary Gove. *Mary Lyndon, or Revelations of a Life.* New York, 1855.

Nichols, T. L., M.D., and Mrs. Mary S. Gove Nichols. *Marriage: Its History, Character, and Results; Demonstrating Its Influence as a Civilized Institution, on the Happiness of the Individual in the Progress of the Race.* Rev. ed. Cincinnati, 1854.

Norton, A. B. *The Great Revolution of 1840. Reminiscences of the Log Cabin and Hard Cider Campaign.* Mount Vernon, Ohio, 1888.

Page, Henry Folsom. *A View of the Law Relative to the Subject of Divorce in Ohio, Indiana, and Michigan*. Columbus, Ohio, 1850.

Parker, Theodore. *A Sermon on the Public Function of Woman, Preached at the Music Hall, March 27, 1853*. Boston, 1853.

Philadelphia Committee on Capital Punishment. N.p., 1845.

Phillips, Wendell, Theodore Parker, Mrs. Mill (of England), T. W. Higginson, and Mrs. C. I. J. Nichols. *Woman's Rights Tracts*. Boston: Robert F. Wallcut, 1854.

The Political Duties of Christians. A Report, Adopted at Spring Meeting of the South Middlesex Conference of Churches, April 18, 1848. Boston, 1848.

Porter, James. *Three Lectures Delivered in the First Methodist Episcopal Church, Lynn, Mass., Dec., 1843, on Come-out-ism*. Lynn, Mass. 1844.

The Practical Christian Republic. Hopedale, Mass.: Hopedale Press, [1854?].

Report of the Trial of Thomas Wilson Dorr, for Treason; including the Testimony at Length, Arguments of Counsel — the Charge of the Chief Justice — The Motions and Arguments on the Questions of a New Trial and in Arrest of Judgment: Together with the Sentence of the Court, and the Speech of Mr. Dorr Before Sentence. Providence, R.I., 1844.

Report Relative to the Observation of the Sabbath, made to the House of Representatives. Harrisburg, 1850.

Rogers, Nathaniel P. "Free Speech." In *Liberty Chimes*, 13–19. Providence, R.I., 1845.

Rose, Mrs. Ernestine L. *An Address on Woman's Rights, Delivered before the People's Sunday Meeting, in Cochituate Hall, on Sunday Afternoon, Oct. 19th, 1851*. Boston, 1851.

———. *Defense of Atheism: Being a Lecture, Delivered in Mercantile Hall, Boston, April 10, 1861, By Ernestine L. Rose*. N.p., n.d.

Rousseau, Jean-Jacques. "The Social Contract or Principles of Political Right." In *Social Contract: Essays by Locke, Hume, and Rousseau*, with introduction by Sir Ernest Barker. London: Oxford University Press, 1960.

Rowson, Susanna. *Charlotte Temple*. Edited with an introduction by Cathy N. Davidson. New York: Oxford University Press, 1988.

Schaff, Philip. *The Anglo-American Sabbath: Read before the National Sabbath Convention, Saratoga, August 11, 1863*. New York: American Tract Society, 1863.

———. "Church and State in the United States or the American Idea of Religious Liberty and its Practical Effects." *Papers of the American Historical Association* 2, no. 4 (1888).

[Spear, John Murray.] *John M. Spear's Labors for the Destitute Prisoner*. N.p., n.d.

———. *Labors for the Prisoner*. Boston, 1848.

———. *Labors for the Prisoner*. N.p., 1849, 1850.

Stanton, Elizabeth Cady. "The Woman's Rights Movement and Its Champions in the United States." In *Eminent Women of the Age; Being Narratives of the Lives and Deeds of the Most Prominent Women of the Present Generation*, 362–404. Hartford, 1869.

Stanton, Elizabeth Cady, Susan B. Anthony, and Matilda Joslyn Gage, eds. *History of Woman Suffrage*. 2 vols. New York, 1881. Reprint, New York: Arno Press, 1985.

Story, Joseph. *Commentaries on the Constitution of the United States; with a preliminary review of the constitutional history of the colonies and states, before the adoption of the Constitution*. Boston, 1833.

Stowe, Harriet Beecher. *Uncle Tom's Cabin*. 1851–52. Reprint, New York: Bantam Books, 1989.

Swisshelm, Jane. *Half a Century*. 2nd ed. Chicago: Janson, McClurg, 1880.

Thompson, William. *Appeal of One Half of the Human Race, Women, Against the Pretensions of the Other Half, Men, to Retain them in Political, and Thence in Civil and Domestic Slavery*. N.p., 1825. Reprint, London: Virago Press, 1983.

Thorpe, Frances N. *The Federal and State Constitutions, Colonial Charters, and Other Organic Law.* Washington, D.C., 1909.

Tilton, Theodore. "Elizabeth Cady Stanton." In *Eminent Women of the Age: Being the Narratives of the Lives and Deeds of the Most Prominent Women of the Present Generation.* Hartford, 1869.

"Trial of John C. Colt for the Murder of Samuel Adams." *Sun-Extra* (N.Y.), January 31, 1842.

The Trial of Singleton Mercer, for the Murder of M. Hutchinson Meberton, at Camden, N.J., on Friday, 10th February, 1843. New York, 1843.

Walker, Timothy. *Introduction to American Law.* Philadelphia, 1837.

Webster, Delia. *Kentucky Jurisprudence. A History of the Trial of Miss Delia A. Webster. At Lexington, Kentucky, Dec. 17–21, 1844, Before the Hon. Richard Buckner. On a Charge of Aiding Slaves to Escape from that Commonwealth—with Miscellaneous Remarks, including her View on American Slavery. Written by Herself.* Vergennes, Vt., 1845.

Wilson, Elizabeth. *A Scriptural View of Woman's Rights and Duties, in all the Important Relations of Life.* Philadelphia, 1849.

Wiltbank, John, M.D. *Peculiarities of the Female: A Lecture Introductory to the Course on Obstetrics in the Medical Department of Pennsylvania College, for the Session of 1845–46.* Philadelphia, 1845.

Woolsey, Theodore D. *Divorce and Divorce Legislation, especially in the United States.* 2nd ed. New York: Scribner's, 1882.

Wright, Henry C. *Marriage and Parentage; or, The Reproduction Element in Man, as a Means to his Elevation and Happiness.* Boston, 1854.

Wylie, Richard C. *Sabbath Laws in the United States.* Pittsburgh: National Reform Association, 1905.

Printed Reports

ANTI-SLAVERY SOCIETIES

Annual Report Presented to the Massachusetts Anti-Slavery Society by its Board of Managers. 1st–21st: Jan. 1833–Jan. 1853. Reprint, Westport, Conn.: Negro Universities Press, 1970.

Philadelphia Female Anti-Slavery Society. *13th Annual Report.* Philadelphia, 1847.

————. *14th Annual Report.* Philadelphia, 1848.

————. *15th Annual Report.* Philadelphia, 1849.

————. *16th Annual Report.* Philadelphia, 1850.

————. *17th Annual Report.* Philadelphia, 1851.

————. *18th Annual Report.* Philadelphia, 1852.

————. *19th Annual Report.* Philadelphia, 1853.

————. *20th Annual Report.* Philadelphia, 1854.

————. *21st Annual Report.* Philadelphia, 1855.

————. *22nd Annual Report.* Philadelphia, 1856.

————. *23rd Annual Report.* Philadelphia, 1857.

————. *Report of the 24th and 25th Years.* Philadelphia, 1859.

————. *26th Annual Report.* Philadelphia, 1860.

FEMALE MEDICAL COLLEGE OF PENNSYLVANIA

First Annual Announcement and Catalogue of the Female Medical College of Pennsylvania. Philadelphia, 1850.

Second Annual Announcement and Catalogue of the Female Medical College of Pennsylvania. Philadelphia, 1851.

Fourth Annual Announcement of the Female Medical College of Pennsylvania. Philadelphia, 1853.

ROSINE ASSOCIATION

The Annual Report of the Managers of the Rosine Association, May, 1847. Philadelphia, 1847.

The Annual Report of the Managers of the Rosine Association, May, 1849. Philadelphia, 1849.

Annual Report of the Managers of the Rosine Association. Philadelphia, 1850, 1851, 1852.

Annual Report of the Managers of the Rosine Association, no. 320 North Eighth Street. April 5th, 1860. Philadelphia, 1860.

Constitution and Report of the Managers of the Rosine Association, with a List of the Annual Subscribers and Contributors. Philadelphia, 1848.

Report of the Managers of the Rosine Association, no. 204 North Eighth Street. October 25th, 1855. Incorporated April 11th, 1848. Philadelphia, 1855.

Report of the Managers of the Rosine Association, no. 204 North Eighth Street. April 2nd, 1857. Incorporated April 11th, 1848. Philadelphia, 1857.

Report of the Managers of the Rosine Association, no. 320 North Eighth Street. April 1st, 1858. Incorporated April 11th, 1848. Philadelphia, 1858.

Report of the Managers of the Rosine Association, no. 320 North Eighth Street. April 7th, 1859. Incorporated April 11th, 1848. Philadelphia, 1859.

Semi-Annual Report of the Managers of the Rosine Association. Philadelphia, 1848.

[Townsend, Mira.] *Reports and Realities from the Sketch-Book of a Manager of the Rosine Association. December, 1855.* Philadelphia, 1855.

WORCESTER FEMALE EMPLOYMENT SOCIETY

Records of the Worcester Female Employment Society. Worcester, Mass., 1857.

Report of the Worcester Female Employment Society, Presented by the Executive Board at the Second Annual Meeting, October 12, 1857. Worcester, Mass., 1857.

Report of the Worcester Female Employment Society, Presented by the Executive Board, at the Third Annual Meeting, October 11, 1858. Worcester, Mass., 1858.

WORCESTER MINISTRY-AT-LARGE

[Burton, Warren.] *Report of the Ministry at Large in the City of Worcester, for one Year, ending April 14, 1850. By Warren Burton.* Worcester, Mass., 1850.

Second Annual Report of the Ministry at Large in the City of Worcester. For the Year Ending May 31st, 1851. Worcester, Mass., 1851.

Third Annual Report of the Ministry at Large in the City of Worcester. For the Year ending May 31st, 1852. Worcester, Mass., 1852.

Printed Proceedings of Conventions

ANTI-SABBATH AND TEMPERANCE CONVENTIONS

Massachusetts Anti-Liquor Law: with an Analysis and Exposition. Also the Proceedings of the State Temperance Convention, held at Worcester, June 23d and 24th, Embracing Resolutions and Letters, the Address to the Citizens of Massachusetts, and forms of Complaint and Warrant. Boston, 1852.

Proceedings of the Anti-Sabbath Convention, held in the Melodeon, March 23 and 24, 1848. Boston, 1848.

ANTI-SLAVERY CONVENTION OF WOMEN

Proceedings of the Anti-slavery Convention of American Women, held in New York, May 9th, 10th, 11th, 12th, 1837. New York, 1837.

Proceedings of the Anti-slavery Convention of American Women, held in Philadelphia, May 15th, 16th, 17th, and 18th, 1838. Philadelphia, 1838.

Proceedings of the Third Anti-slavery Convention of American Women, held in Philadelphia, May 1st, 2nd, 3rd, 1839. Philadelphia, 1839.

Report of a Delegate to the Anti-Slavery Convention of American Women. Boston, 1838.

CONGREGATIONAL AND PROGRESSIVE FRIENDS

New York

Proceedings of the Yearly Meeting of Congregational Friends, held at Waterloo, N.Y., from the 4th to the 6th of the Sixth month, inclusive, 1849. Auburn, N.Y., 1849.

Proceedings of the Yearly Meeting of Congregational Friends, held at Waterloo, N.Y., on the 1st, 2d and 3rd of the 6th Month, 1851. Auburn, N.Y., 1851.

Proceedings of the Yearly Meeting of Congregational Friends, held at Waterloo, N.Y., from the 6th to the 8th of the 6th Month, 1852. Auburn, N.Y., 1852.

Proceedings of the Yearly Meeting of Congregational Friends, held at Waterloo, N.Y., on the 5th, 6th and 7th of the 6th Month, 1853. Auburn, N.Y., 1853.

Ohio

Minutes of the Proceedings of the Annual Meeting of the Friends, Composed of Persons from Parts of Ohio and Indiana, held at Green Plain, Clark County, Ohio, who have adopted the Congregational Order. Springfield, Ohio, 1848.

Proceedings of the Ohio Yearly Meeting of Progressive Friends, held in Salem, from the 5th to the 7th of Ninth Month, inclusive, 1852. Salem, Ohio, 1852.

Pennsylvania

Minutes. Pennsylvania Yearly Meeting of Progressive Friends. N.p., 1856, 1857, 1858.

Proceedings of the Pennsylvania Yearly Meeting of Progressive Friends, 1853, Old Kennett Meeting House, Chester County, Pennsylvania, 22nd of May (fifth month), 1853. N.p., n.d.

STATE CONSTITUTIONAL CONVENTIONS

The Constitutional Debates of 1847. Edited by Arthur Charles Cole. Vol. 2. Springfield, Ill., 1919.

Debates and Proceedings of the New-York State Convention, for the Revision of the Constitution. Albany, N.Y., 1846.

The Debates of the Constitutional Convention; of the State of Iowa, Assembled at Iowa City, Monday, January 19, 1857. 2 vols. Davenport, Iowa, 1857.

Official Report of the Debates and Proceedings, in the State Convention, assembled May 4th, 1853, to Revise and Amend the Constitution of the Commonwealth of Massachusetts. 2 vols. Boston, 1853.

Proceedings and Debates, Embracing the Secretary's Journal, of the Kansas Constitutional Convention, Convened at Wyandot, July 5, 1859, Under the Act of the Territorial Legislature Entitled "An Act Providing for the Formation of a State Government for the State of Kansas." Approved February 11, 1859. Wyandot, Kans., 1859.

Proceedings and Debates of the Virginia State Convention, of 1829–1830. Richmond, Va., 1830.

Proceedings of the New Jersey State Constitutional Convention of 1844. Trenton: New Jersey State House Commission, 1942.

Report of the Debates and Proceedings of the Convention for the Revision of the Constitution of the State of Ohio, 1850–51. Columbus, Ohio, 1851.

Report of the Proceedings and Debates in the Convention to Revise the Constitution of the State of Michigan. 1850. Lansing, Mich., 1850.

Women's Rights Conventions: Reports and Proceedings

MASSACHUSETTS

The Proceedings of the Woman's Rights Convention, held at Worcester, October 23d & 24th, 1850. Boston, 1851.

Report of the Second General Convention of the Friends of Woman's Rights, Wednesday, October 15th, 1851. Boston, 1852.

Report of the Woman's Rights Meeting, at Mercantile Hall, May 27, 1859. Boston, 1859.

Reports on the Laws of New England, Presented to the New England Meeting, Convened at the Meionaon, Sept. 19 and 20, 1855. Boston, 1855.

NEW YORK

Proceedings of the Ninth National Woman's Rights Convention held in New York City, Thursday May 12, 1859, with a Phonographic Report of the Speech of Wendell Phillips, by J. M. W. Yerrinton. Rochester, N.Y., 1859.

Proceedings of the Seventh National Woman's Rights Convention, held in New York City, at the Broadway Tabernacle, on Tuesday and Wednesday, Nov. 25th and 26th, 1856. New York, 1856.

Proceedings of the Tenth National Woman's Rights Convention, Held at the Cooper Institute, New York City, May 10th and 11th, 1860. Boston, 1860.

The Proceedings of the Woman's Rights Convention, held at Syracuse, September 8th, 9th & 10th, 1852. Syracuse, N.Y., 1852.

Proceedings of the Woman's Rights Convention, held at the Broadway Tabernacle, in the City of New York, on Tuesday and Wednesday, Sept. 6th and 7th, 1853. New York, 1853.

Proceedings of the Woman's Rights Convention, held at the Unitarian Church, Rochester, N.Y., August 2, 1848, to Consider the Rights of Woman, Politically, Religiously and Industrially. New York, 1870. Reprinted in *Woman's Rights Conventions: Seneca Falls and Rochester, 1848.* New York: Arno Press, 1969.

Report of the Woman's Rights Convention, held at Seneca Falls, N.Y., July 19th & 20th, 1848. Rochester, N.Y., 1848. Reprinted in *Woman's Rights Conventions, Seneca Falls and Rochester, 1848.* New York: Arno Press, 1969.

OHIO

Proceedings of the National Woman's Rights Convention, Held at Cleveland, Ohio, on Wednesday, Thursday, and Friday, October 5th, 6th, and 7th, 1853. Cleveland, Ohio, 1854.

The Proceedings of the Woman's Rights Convention, Held at Akron, Ohio, May 28 and 29, 1851. Cincinnati, 1851.

The Salem, Ohio, 1850 Women's Rights Convention Proceedings. Compiled and edited by Robert W. Audretsch. Salem, Ohio: Salem Public Library, 1976.

PENNSYLVANIA

The Proceedings of the Woman's Rights Convention held at West Chester, PA., June 2d and 3d, 1852. Philadelphia, 1852.

Local Histories and Genealogies

Ballou, Adin. *History of the Hopedale Community, from its Inception to its Virtual Submergence in the Hopedale Parish.* Lowell, Mass., 1897.

————. *History of the Town of Milford, Worcester County, Massachusetts, from its First Settlement to 1881.* 2 vols. Lowell, Mass., 1897.

Becker, John. *A History of the Village of Waterloo, New York, and Thesaurus of Related Facts.* Waterloo, N.Y., 1929.

Bierce, L. V. *Historical Reminiscences of Summit County, Ohio.* Akron, Ohio, 1854.

Bronner, Edwin B. *Thomas Earle as a Reformer.* Philadelphia, 1948.

Chamberlain, Harrison. "The Seneca Falls Press." In *Papers Read Before the Seneca Falls Historical Society for the Year 1905.* Seneca Falls, N.Y., 1905.

Chenoweth, C. Van D. *History of the Second Congregational Church and Society in Leicester, Massachusetts.* Worcester, Mass., 1908.

Cope, Gilbert. *Genealogy of the Darlington Family.* West Chester, Pa., 1900.

Cope, Gilbert, and Henry B. Ashmead. *Genealogical and Personal Memoirs of Chester and Delaware County, Pennsylvania.* 2 vols. New York, 1904.

Cowing, Mrs. Philo, and Rev. S. F. Frazier. "Early Church of Junius." In *100th Anniversary of the Town of Junius: Historical Papers Read before the Seneca Falls Historical Society.* Seneca Falls, N.Y., 1903.

Cowles, Calvin. *Genealogy of the Cowles Family in America.* New Haven, 1929.

Earle, Pliny. *Ralph Earle and Descendants.* Worcester, Mass.: Charles Hamilton, 1888.

Fuller, A. O. "Early Annals of the Austinburg Church." *Papers of the Ohio Church Society* 10 (1899): 63–79.

Futhey, J. Smith, and Gilbert Cope. *History of Chester County.* Philadelphia: Louis H. Everts, 1881.

Hale, Edward Everett. *Worcester in 1850.* Worcester, Mass., 1850.

Hinchman, Lydia S. *Early Settlers of Nantucket.* Philadelphia: Ferris and Leach, 1901.

Hinshaw, William W. *Encyclopedia of American Quaker Genealogy.* 2 vols. Ann Arbor: Edwards Brothers, 1938.

Hunt, George D. *History of Salem and the Immediate Vicinity, Columbiana County, Ohio.* Salem, Ohio, 1898.

Lincoln, Charles H. "The Antecedents of the Worcester Society of Friends." *Worcester Historical Society Publications* 1 (April 1928): 24–39.

Murphy, William D. *Biographical Sketches of the Officers and Members of the Legislature of the State of New York in 1861.* New York, 1861.

Nutt, Charles. *History of Worcester and Its People.* 4 vols. New York, 1919.

Olin, Oscar E. *Akron & Its Environs.* Chicago, 1917.

Perrin, William Henry. *History of Summit County, with an Outline Sketch of Ohio.* Philadelphia, 1881.

Smith, Theodore Clarke. *The Liberty and Free Soil Parties in the Northeast.* New York: Russell and Russell, 1897. Reprint, New York: Arno Press, 1969.

West Chester Directory. West Chester, Pa., 1857.

Wilcoxen, Gilbert. "The Legal Profession." In *Papers Read Before the Seneca Falls Historical Society for the Year 1908: Proceedings of the Sixtieth Anniversary of the Woman's Rights Convention held in Seneca Falls in July, 1848,* 15–16. Seneca Falls, N.Y., 1908.

The Worcester Almanac, Directory, and Business Advertiser, for 1850, including City Ordinances. Worcester, Mass., 1850.

The Worcester Almanac, Directory, and Business Advertiser, for 1851. Worcester, Mass., 1851.

Secondary Sources

Books

Aichele, George, Jr. *The Limits of Story*. Philadelphia: Fortress Press, 1985.

Albanese, Catherine L. *Corresponding Motion: Transcendental Religion and the New America*. Philadelphia: Temple University Press, 1977.

Altschuler, Glenn C., and Jan M. Saltzgaber. *Revivalism, Social Conscience, and Community in the Burned-over District: The Trial of Rhoda Bement*. Ithaca: Cornell University Press, 1983.

Arendt, Hannah. *The Human Condition*. Chicago: University of Chicago Press, 1958.

Armstrong, Judith. *The Novel of Adultery*. London: Macmillan, 1976.

Armstrong, Nancy. *Desire and Domestic Fiction: A Political History of the Novel*. New York: Oxford University Press, 1987.

Bacon, Margaret Hope. *I Speak for My Slave Sister: The Life of Abby Kelley Foster*. New York: Thomas Crowell, 1974.

———. *Valiant Friend: The Life of Lucretia Mott*. New York: Walker, 1980.

Bailey, Derrick Sherrin. *Sexual Relations in Christian Thought*. New York: Harper and Brothers, 1959.

Baker, Jean H. *Affairs of Party: The Political Culture of Northern Democrats in the Mid-Nineteenth Century*. Ithaca: Cornell University Press, 1983.

Baker, Paula. *The Moral Frameworks of Public Life: Gender, Politics, and the State in Rural New York, 1870–1930*. New York: Oxford University Press, 1991.

Bardaglio, Peter W. *Reconstructing the Household: Families, Sex, and the Law in the Nineteenth-Century South*. Chapel Hill: University of North Carolina Press, 1995.

Barker, Francis. *The Tremulous Private Body: Essays on Subjection*. London: Methuen, 1984.

Barker-Benfield, G. J. *The Culture of Sensibility: Sex and Eighteenth-Century Britain*. Chicago: University of Chicago Press, 1992.

———. *Horrors of the Half-Known Life: Male Attitudes toward Women and Sexuality in Nineteenth-Century America*. New York: Harper and Row, 1976.

Basch, Norma. *In the Eyes of the Law: Women, Marriage, and Property in Nineteenth-Century New York*. Ithaca: Cornell University Press, 1982.

Bauer, Elizabeth Kelley. *Commentaries on the Constitution, 1790–1860*. New York: Russell and Russell, 1965.

Bauman, Richard. *Let Your Words Be Few: Symbolism of Speaking and Silence among Seventeenth-Century Quakers*. Cambridge: Cambridge University Press, 1983.

Baym, Nina. *American Women Writers and the Work of History, 1790–1860*. New Brunswick: Rutgers University Press, 1995.

———. *Feminism and American Literary History*. New Brunswick: Rutgers University Press, 1992.

Belsey, Catherine. *Critical Practical*. London: Methuen, 1980.

Bemis, Samuel Flagg. *John Quincy Adams and the Union*. New York: Knopf, 1956.

Bennett, David H. *The Party of Fear: From Nativist Movements to the New Right in American History*. Chapel Hill: University of North Carolina Press, 1988.

Blackmar, Elizabeth. *Manhattan for Rent, 1785–1850*. Ithaca: Cornell University Press, 1989.

Blanchard, Paula. *Margaret Fuller: From Transcendentalism to Revolution*. Reading, Mass.: Addison-Wesley, 1987.

Boydston, Jeanne. *Home and Work: Housework, Wages, and the Ideology of Labor in the Early Republic*. New York: Oxford University Press, 1990.

Brandt, Nat. *The Congressman Who Got Away with Murder*. Syracuse, N.Y.: Syracuse University Press, 1991.

Braude, Ann. *Radical Spirits: Spiritualism and Women's Rights in Nineteenth-Century America*. Boston: Beacon Press, 1989.

Bredbenner, Candice Lewis. *A Nationality of Her Own: Women, Marriage, and the Law of Citizenship*. Berkeley: University of California Press, 1998.

Brinton, Howard H. *The Religious Philosophy of Quakerism: The Beliefs of Fox, Barclay, and Penn Based on the Gospel of John*. Wallingford, Pa.: Pendle Hill, 1973.

Brock, William R. *Parties and Political Conscience: American Dilemmas, 1840–1850*. Milwood, N.Y.: KTO Press, 1979.

Bronowski, J., and Bruce Mazlish. *The Western Intellectual Tradition*. New York: Harper Torchbooks, 1960.

Brown, Richard D. *Knowledge Is Power: The Diffusion of Information in Early America, 1700–1865*. New York: Oxford University Press, 1989.

Brown, Wendy. *Manhood and Politics: A Feminist Reading in Political Theory*. Totowa, N.J.: Rowan and Littlefield, 1988.

Bruce, F. F. *History of the Bible in English*. 3rd ed. New York: Oxford University Press, 1978.

Buhle, Mari Jo, and Paul Buhle, eds. *The Concise History of Woman Suffrage: Selections from the Classic Work of Stanton, Anthony, Gage, and Harper*. Urbana: University of Illinois Press, 1978.

Burstein, Andrew. *The Inner Jefferson: Portrait of a Grieving Optimist*. Charlottesville: University Press of Virginia, 1995.

Bynum, Victoria E. *Unruly Women: The Politics of Social and Sexual Control in the Old South*. Chapel Hill: University of North Carolina Press, 1992.

Cassirer, Ernst. *The Philosophy of the Enlightenment*. Translated by Fritz C. A. Koellin and James P. Pettegrove. Boston: Beacon Press, 1951.

Catterall, Helen T. *Judicial Cases Concerning American Slavery and the Negro*. 5 vols. Washington, D.C.: Carnegie Institute, 1931.

Cayleff, Susan E. *Wash and Be Healed: The Water-Cure Movement and Women's Health*. Philadelphia: Temple University Press, 1987.

Cazden, Elizabeth. *Antoinette Brown Blackwell: A Biography*. Old Westbury, N.Y.: Feminist Press, 1983.

Chambers-Schiller, Lee Virginia. *Liberty, a Better Husband: Single Women in America, the Generations of 1780–1840*. New Haven: Yale University Press, 1984.

Chevigny, Bell Gale. *The Woman and the Myth: Margaret Fuller's Life and Writings*. Old Westbury, N.Y.: Feminist Press, 1976.

Cohen, Daniel A. *Pillars of Salt, Monuments of Grace: New England Crime Literature and the Origins of American Popular Culture, 1674–1860*. New York: Oxford University Press, 1993.

The Compact Edition of the Oxford English Dictionary. 2 vols. Oxford: Oxford University Press, 1971.

Conrad, Susan Phinney. *Perish the Thought: Intellectual Women in Romantic America, 1830–1860*. New York: Oxford University Press, 1976. Reprint, Secaucus, N.J.: Citadel Press, 1978.

Cook, Charles M. *The American Codification Movement: The Study of Antebellum Legal Reform*. Westport, Conn.: Greenwood Press, 1981.

Cott, Nancy F. *The Bonds of Womanhood: "Woman's Sphere" in New England, 1780–1835*. New Haven: Yale University Press, 1977.

Cromwell, Otelia. *Lucretia Mott*. Cambridge: Harvard University Press, 1958.

Cross, Barbara M., ed. *The Educated Woman in America: Selected Writings of Catharine Beecher, Margaret Fuller, and M. Carey Thomas*. New York: Teachers College Press, 1965.

Cross, Whitney R. *The Burned-over District: The Social and Intellectual History of Enthusiastic Religion in Western New York, 1800–1850*. Ithaca: Cornell University Press, 1950.

Davidson, Kenneth M., Ruth B. Ginsburg, and Herma H. Kay, eds. *Sex-Based Discrimination: Texts, Cases, and Materials*. St. Paul: West, 1974.

Davis, David Brion. *The Slave Power Conspiracy and the Paranoid Style*. Baton Rouge: Louisiana State University Press, 1969.

Davis, Susan G. *Parades and Power: Street Theatre in Nineteenth-Century Philadelphia*. Philadelphia: University of Pennsylvania Press, 1986.

Dayton, Cornelia Hughes. *Women before the Bar: Gender, Law, and Society in Connecticut, 1639–1789*. Chapel Hill: University of North Carolina Press, 1995.

Degler, Carl. *At Odds: Women and the Family in America from the Revolution to the Present*. New York: Oxford University Press, 1980.

Dennison, George M. *The Dorr War: Republicanism on Trial, 1831–1861*. Lexington: University Press of Kentucky, 1976.

Dictionary of American Biography. 20 vols. New York: Scribner's, 1928–36.

Douglas, Ann. *The Feminization of American Culture*. New York: Knopf, 1976.

DuBois, Ellen Carol. *Feminism and Suffrage: The Emergence of an Independent Women's Movement in America, 1848–1869*. Ithaca: Cornell University Press, 1978.

Dudden, Faye E. *Women in the American Theatre: Actresses and Audiences, 1790–1870*. New Haven: Yale University Press, 1994.

Dunn, John. *The Political Thought of John Locke: An Historical Account of the Argument of the "Two Treatises of Government."* Cambridge: Cambridge University Press, 1969.

Eckhardt, Celia Morris. *Fanny Wright: Rebel in America*. Cambridge: Harvard University Press, 1984.

Eisler, Benita, ed. *The Lowell Offering: Writings by New England Mill Women, 1840–1845*. New York: Harper Torchbooks, 1977.

Elshtain, Jean Bethke. *Women and War*. New York: Harvester Press, 1987.

Faust, Drew Gilpin, ed. *The Ideology of Slavery: Proslavery Thought in the Antebellum South, 1830–1860*. Baton Rouge: Louisiana State University Press, 1981.

Fetterley, Judith, ed. *Provisions: A Reader from Nineteenth-Century American Women*. Bloomington: Indiana University Press, 1985.

Fiorenza, Elizabeth Schussler. *In Memory of Her: A Feminist Theological Reconstruction of Christian Origins*. New York: Crossroad, 1983.

Flexner, Eleanor. *Century of Struggle: The Woman's Rights Movement in the United States*. Cambridge: Harvard University Press, 1959. Rev. ed., 1975.

Fliegelman, Jay. *Prodigals and Pilgrims: The American Revolution against Patriarchal Authority, 1750–1800*. Cambridge: Cambridge University Press, 1982.

Foner, Eric. *Free Soil, Free Labor, and Free Men: The Ideology of the Republican Party before the Civil War*. New York: Oxford University Press, 1970.

Foucault, Michel. *The Archaeology of Knowledge and the Discourse on Language*. Translated by A. M. Sheridan Smith. New York: Pantheon, 1972.

———. *Discipline and Punish: The Birth of the Prison*. Translated by Alan Sheridan. New York: Vintage, 1979.

———. *The Foucault Reader*. Edited by Paul Rabinow. New York: Pantheon, 1984.

———. *The History of Sexuality: An Introduction*. Translated by Robert Hurley. New York: Random House, 1980.

———. *Michel Foucault: Politics, Philosophy, and Culture: Interviews and Other Writings, 1977–1984*. Edited and with an introduction by Lawrence D. Kritzman. Translated by Alan Sheridan and others. New York: Routledge, 1988.

BIBLIOGRAPHY

Freedman, Estelle B. *Their Sisters' Keepers: Women's Prison Reform in America, 1830–1930*. Ann Arbor: University of Michigan Press, 1981.

Friedman, Lawrence J. *Gregarious Saints: Self and Community in American Abolitionism, 1830–1870*. New York: Cambridge University Press, 1982.

Frost, J. William. *A Perfect Freedom: Religious Liberty in Pennsylvania*. University Park: Pennsylvania State University Press, 1993.

Geary, Linda L. *Balanced in the Wind: A Biography of Betsey Mix Cowles*. Lewisburg, Pa.: Bucknell University Press, 1989.

Geertz, Clifford. *The Interpretation of Cultures: Selected Essays by Clifford Geertz*. New York: Basic Books, 1973.

Geffen, Elizabeth M. *Philadelphia Unitarianism, 1796–1861*. Philadelphia: University of Pennsylvania Press, 1961.

Gettleman, Marvin E. *The Dorr Rebellion: A Study in American Radicalism, 1833–1849*. New York: Random House, 1973.

Gifis, Steven H. *Law Dictionary*. Woodbury, N.Y.: Barron's Educational Series, 1975.

Ginzberg, Lori D. *Women and the Work of Benevolence: Morality, Politics, and Class in Nineteenth-Century United States*. New Haven: Yale University Press, 1990.

Glenn, Myra C. *Campaigns against Corporal Punishment: Prisoners, Sailors, Women, and Children in Antebellum America*. Albany: State University of New York, 1984.

Glickstein, Jonathan A. *Concepts of Free Labor in Antebellum America*. New Haven: Yale University Press, 1991.

Greene, Dana, ed. *Lucretia Mott: Her Complete Speeches and Sermons*. New York: Edwin Mellen Press, 1980.

Griffiths, Elisabeth. *In Her Own Right: The Life of Elizabeth Cady Stanton*. New York: Oxford University Press, 1984.

Grimsted, David. *Melodrama Unveiled: American Theater and Culture, 1800–1850*. Chicago: University of Chicago Press, 1968.

Grossberg, Michael. *Governing the Hearth: Law and the Family in Nineteenth-Century America*. Chapel Hill: University of North Carolina Press, 1985.

Gura, Phillip. *The Wisdom of Words: Language, Theology, and Literature in the New England Renaissance*. Middletown, Conn.: Wesleyan University Press, 1981.

Habermas, Jürgen. *The Structural Transformation of the Public Sphere: An Inquiry into a Category of Bourgeois Society*. Translated by Thomas Burger. Cambridge: MIT Press, 1991.

Haller, John S., Jr., and Robin M. Haller. *The Physician and Sexuality in Victorian America*. Urbana: University of Illinois Press, 1974.

Halttunen, Karen. *Confidence Men and Painted Women: A Study of Middle-Class Culture in America, 1830–1870*. New Haven: Yale University Press, 1982.

Hansen, Debra Gold. *Strained Sisterhood: Gender and Class in the Boston Female Anti-Slavery Society*. Amherst: University of Massachusetts Press, 1993.

Hatch, Nathan O. *The Democratization of American Christianity*. New Haven: Yale University Press, 1989.

Heffner, Richard D., ed. *Democracy in America*. New York: New American Library, 1956.

Hersh, Blanche Glassman. *The Slavery of Sex: Feminist-Abolitionists in America*. Urbana: University of Illinois Press, 1978.

Hewitt, Nancy A. *Women's Activism and Social Change: Rochester, New York, 1822–1872*. Ithaca: Cornell University Press, 1984.

Hietala, Thomas R. *Manifest Design: Anxious Aggrandizement in Late Jacksonian America*. Ithaca: Cornell University Press, 1985.

Hill, Bridget, ed. *The First English Feminist: Reflections upon Marriage and Other Writings by Mary Astell*. New York: St. Martin's Press, 1986.

Hindus, Michael Stephen. *Prison and Plantation: Crime, Justice, and Authority in Massachusetts and South Carolina, 1767–1878*. Chapel Hill: University of North Carolina Press, 1980.

Hobson, Barbara Meil. *Uneasy Virtue: The Politics of Prostitution and the American Reform Tradition*. Chicago: University of Chicago Press, 1990.

Hodgson, Peter C., and Robert H. King, eds. *Christian Theology: An Introduction to Its Traditions and Tasks*. 2nd rev. ed. Philadelphia: Fortress Press, 1985.

Hoff, Joan. *Law, Gender, and Injustice: A Legal History of U.S. Women*. New York: New York University Press, 1991.

Hoffert, Sylvia D. *When Hens Crow: The Woman's Rights Movement in Antebellum America*. Bloomington: Indiana University Press, 1995.

Hollinger, David A., and Charles Capper, eds. *The American Intellectual Tradition*. 2 vols. New York: Oxford University Press, 1993.

Horsman, Reginald. *Race and Manifest Destiny: The Origins of American Racial Anglo-Saxonism*. Cambridge: Harvard University Press, 1981.

Howe, Daniel Walker. *The Unitarian Conscience: Harvard Moral Philosophy, 1805–1861*. Cambridge: Harvard University Press, 1970.

Hunt, Alan. *Explorations in Law and Society: Toward a Constitutive Theory of the Law*. New York: Routledge, 1993.

Hutchinson, William R. *The Transcendentalist Ministers: Church Reform in the New England Renaissance*. New Haven: Yale University Press, 1959.

Ingle, H. Larry. *Quakers in Conflict: The Hicksite Reformation*. Knoxville: University of Tennessee Press, 1986.

James, Edward T., Janet Wilson James, and Paul S. Boyer, eds. *Notable American Women, 1607–1950: A Biographical Dictionary*. 3 vols. Cambridge: Belknap Press of Harvard University Press, 1971.

Jameson, Fredric. *The Political Unconscious: Narrative as a Socially Symbolic Act*. Ithaca: Cornell University Press, 1981.

Jeffrey, Julie Roy. *Frontier Women: The Trans-Mississippi West, 1840–1880*. New York: Hill and Wang, 1979.

Jensen, Joan M. *Loosening the Bonds: Mid-Atlantic Farm Women, 1750–1850*. New Haven: Yale University Press, 1986.

John, Richard R. *Spreading the News: The American Postal System from Franklin to Morse*. Cambridge: Harvard University Press, 1995.

Jones, Kathleen B. *Compassionate Authority: Democracy and the Representation of Women*. New York: Routledge, 1993.

Jones, Mary Somerville. *An Historical Geography of the Changing Divorce Law in the United States*. New York: Garland, 1987.

Kelley, Mary, ed. *The Portable Margaret Fuller*. New York: Penguin, 1994.

Kerber, Linda K. *Women of the Republic: Intellect and Ideology in Revolutionary America*. Chapel Hill: University of North Carolina Press, 1980.

Kett, Joseph F. *The Formation of the American Medical Profession: The Role of Institutions, 1780–1860*. New Haven: Yale University Press, 1968.

Kettner, James H. *The Development of American Citizenship, 1608–1870*. Chapel Hill: University of North Carolina Press, 1978.

Knobel, Dale T. *"America for the Americans": The Nativist Movement in the United States*. New York: Twayne, 1996.

Kramer, Michael P. *Imagining Language in America: From the Revolution to the Civil War*. Princeton: Princeton University Press, 1992.

Kuntz, William Francis, II. *Criminal Sentencing in Three Nineteenth-Century Cities: Social History of Punishment in New York, Boston, and Philadelphia, 1830–1880*. New York: Garland, 1988.

Landes, Joan B. *Women and the Public Sphere in the Age of the French Revolution*. Ithaca: Cornell University Press, 1988.

Lasch, Christopher. *Haven in a Heartless World: The Family Besieged*. New York: Basic Books, 1977.

Lebsock, Suzanne. *The Free Women of Petersburg: Status and Culture in a Southern Town, 1784–1860*. New York: Norton, 1984.

Lerner, Gerda. *The Creation of Patriarchy*. New York: Oxford University Press, 1986.

———. *The Grimké Sisters from South Carolina: Pioneers for Woman's Rights and Abolition*. New York: Schocken, 1967.

———. *The Majority Finds Its Past: Placing Women in History*. New York: Oxford University Press, 1979.

Levinson, Samuel. *Constitutional Faith*. Princeton: Princeton University Press, 1988.

Lévi-Strauss, Claude. *Structural Anthropology*. Translated by Claire Jacobson and Brooke Grundfest Schoepf. New York: Basic Books, 1963.

Lewis, W. David. *From Newgate to Dannemora: The Rise of the Penitentiary in New York, 1796–1848*. Ithaca: Cornell University Press, 1965.

Lincoln, Charles Z. *The Constitutional History of New York*. 5 vols. Rochester, N.Y.: Lawyers Co-operative Pub. Co., 1906.

Linebaugh, Barbara. *The African School and the Integration of Nantucket Public Schools, 1825–1847*. Boston: Boston University, 1978.

Loeb, Isidor. *The Legal Property Relations of Married Parties: A Study in Comparative Legislation*. New York: Columbia University Press, 1900.

McCoy, Drew R. *The Elusive Republic: Political Economy in Jeffersonian America*. New York: Norton, 1982.

Mackey, Philip English. *Hanging in the Balance: The Anti–Capital Punishment Movement in New York State, 1776–1861*. New York: Garland, 1982.

———. *Voices against Death: American Opposition to Capital Punishment, 1787–1975*. New York: B. Franklin, 1976.

McKivigan, John R. *The War against Proslavery Religion: Abolitionism and the Northern Churches, 1830–1865*. Ithaca: Cornell University Press, 1984.

McLaurin, Melton A. *Celia, a Slave*. New York: Avon Books, 1991.

McLoughlin, William G., ed. *The American Evangelicals, 1800–1900*. New York: Harper Torchbooks, 1968.

Macpherson, C. B. *The Political Theory of Possessive Individualism: Hobbes to Locke*. Oxford: Oxford University Press, 1962.

McWilliams, John P., Jr. *The American Epic: Transforming a Genre, 1770–1860*. Cambridge: Cambridge University Press, 1989.

Maier, Pauline. *American Scripture: Making the Declaration of Independence*. New York: Knopf, 1997.

Mansbridge, Jane J. *Why We Lost the ERA*. Chicago: University of Chicago Press, 1986.

Martin, Emily. *The Woman in the Body: A Cultural Analysis of Reproduction*. Boston: Beacon Press, 1987.

Masur, Louis P. *Rites of Execution: Capital Punishment and the Transformation of American Culture, 1776–1865*. New York: Oxford University Press, 1989.

Matthews, Jean V. *Toward a New Society: American Thought and Culture, 1800–1830*. Boston: Twayne, 1991.

Melder, Keith E. *The Beginnings of Sisterhood: The American Women's Rights Movement, 1800–1850*. New York: Schocken, 1977.

Merk, Frederick. *Fruits of Propaganda in the Tyler Administration*. Cambridge: Harvard University Press, 1971.

Michie, Helena. *The Flesh Made Word: Female Figures and Women's Bodies*. New York: Oxford University Press, 1987.

Miller, Perry, ed. *The American Transcendentalists: Their Prose and Poetry*. Garden City, N.Y.: Doubleday Anchor, 1957.

Mohr, James C. *Doctors and the Law: Medical Jurisprudence in Nineteenth-Century America*. New York: Oxford University Press, 1993.

Moi, Toril. *Sexual/Textual Politics: Feminist Literary Theory*. London: Methuen, 1985.

Moore, R. Lawrence. *Selling God: American Religion in the Marketplace of Culture*. New York: Oxford University Press, 1994.

Morantz, Regina Markell. *Sympathy and Science: Women Physicians in American Medicine*. New York: Oxford University Press, 1985.

Mullan, John. *Sentiment and Sociability: The Language of Feeling in Eighteenth-Century Britain*. Chicago: University of Chicago Press, 1988.

Murphy, Teresa Anne. *Ten Hours' Labor: Religion, Reform, and Gender in Early New England*. Ithaca: Cornell University Press, 1992.

Myerson, Joel, ed. *Critical Essays on Margaret Fuller*. Boston: G. K. Hall, 1980.

Myres, Sandra L. *Westering Women and the Frontier Experience, 1800–1915*. Albuquerque: University of New Mexico Press, 1982.

Nicholson, Linda J. *Gender and History: The Limits of Social Theory in the Age of the Family*. New York: Columbia University Press, 1986.

Nissenbaum, Stephen. *Sex, Deity, and Debility in Jacksonian America: Sylvester Graham and Health Reform*. Westport, Conn.: Greenwood Press, 1980.

Noddings, Nel. *Women and Evil*. Berkeley: University of California Press, 1989.

Norton, Anne. *Alternative Americas: A Reading of Antebellum Political Culture*. Chicago: University of Chicago Press, 1986.

O'Connor, Lillian. *Pioneer Women Orators: Rhetoric in the Antebellum Reform Movement*. New York: Columbia University Press, 1954.

Osborne, William S. *Lydia Maria Child*. Boston: Twayne, 1980.

Pateman, Carole. *The Sexual Contract*. Stanford: Stanford University Press, 1988.

Pearce, Roy Harvey. *The Savages of America*. Rev. ed. Baltimore: Johns Hopkins University Press, 1965.

Perry, Lewis. *Radical Abolitionism: Anarchy and the Government of God in Antislavery Thought*. Ithaca: Cornell University Press, 1973.

Peterson, Merrill D., ed. *The Portable Thomas Jefferson*. New York: Penguin, 1977.

Pleck, Elizabeth. *Domestic Tyranny: The Making of American Social Policy against Family Violence from Colonial Times to the Present*. New York: Oxford University Press, 1987.

Pole, J. R. *The Pursuit of Equality in American History*. Berkeley: University of California Press, 1978.

Poovey, Mary. *Uneven Developments: The Ideological Work of Gender in Mid-Victorian England*. Chicago: University of Chicago Press, 1988.

Prickett, Stephen. *Words and the Word: Language, Poetics, and Biblical Interpretation*. Cambridge: Cambridge University Press, 1986.

Punter, David. *The Literature of Terror: A History of Gothic Fictions from 1765 to the Present Day*. New York: Longman Press, 1980.

Rabkin, Peggy A. *Fathers to Daughters: The Legal Foundations of Female Emancipation*. Westport, Conn.: Greenwood Press, 1980.

Rawley, James. *Race and Politics: "Bleeding Kansas" and the Coming of the Civil War*. Philadelphia: Lippincott, 1969.

Rodgers, Daniel T. *The Work Ethic in Industrial America, 1850–1920*. Chicago: University of Chicago Press, 1974.

Roediger, David. *The Wages of Whiteness: Race and the Making of the Working Class*. London: Verso, 1991.

Rollins, Richard M. *The Long Journey of Noah Webster*. Philadelphia: University of Pennsylvania Press, 1980.

Rose, Anne C. *Transcendentalism as a Social Movement, 1830–1850*. New Haven: Yale University Press, 1981.

Ryan, Mary P. *Women in Public: Between Banners and Ballots, 1825–1880*. Baltimore: Johns Hopkins University Press, 1990.

Salmon, Marylynn. *Women and the Law of Property in Early America*. Chapel Hill: University of North Carolina Press, 1986.

Sawicki, Jana. *Disciplining Foucault: Feminism, Power, and the Body*. New York: Routledge, 1991.

Schroeder, John. *Mr. Polk's War: American Opposition and Dissent, 1846–48*. Madison: University of Wisconsin Press, 1973.

Scott, Anne F., and Andrew M. Scott. *One Half the People: The Fight for Woman Suffrage*. Philadelphia: Lippincott, 1975.

Scott, Joan Wallach. *Gender and the Politics of History*. New York: Columbia University Press, 1988.

Sewell, Richard H. *Ballots for Freedom: Antislavery Politics in the United States, 1837–1860*. New York: Oxford University Press, 1976.

Shiffrin, Steven H. *The First Amendment, Democracy, and Romance*. Princeton: Princeton University Press, 1990.

Simms, Henry H. *Emotion at High Tide: Abolition as a Controversial Factor, 1830–1845*. Richmond, Va.: William Byrd Press, 1960.

Sklar, Kathryn Kish. *Catharine Beecher: A Study in American Domesticity*. New Haven: Yale University Press, 1973. Reprint, New York: Norton, 1976.

Slotkin, Richard. *Gunfighter Nation: The Myth of the Frontier in Twentieth-Century America*. New York: Atheneum, 1992.

Smith, Elwyn A. *Religious Liberty in the United States: The Development of Church-State Thought since the Revolutionary Era*. Philadelphia: Fortress Press, 1972.

Smith, Merril D. *Breaking the Bonds: Marital Discord in Pennsylvania, 1730–1830*. New York: New York University Press, 1991.

Smith-Rosenberg, Carroll. *Disorderly Conduct: Visions of Gender in Victorian America*. New York: Oxford University Press, 1986.

Sobel, Robert, ed. *Biographical Directory of the United States Executive Branch, 1774–1989*. New York: Greenwood Press, 1990.

Sollors, Werner. *Beyond Ethnicity: Consent and Descent in American Culture*. New York: Oxford University Press, 1986.

Solomon, Barbara H., and Paula S. Berggren, eds. *A Mary Wollstonecraft Reader*. New York: New American Library, 1983.

Stansell, Christine. *City of Women: Sex and Class in New York, 1789–1860*. Urbana: University of Illinois Press, 1987.

Sterling, Dorothy, ed. *We Are Your Sisters: Black Women in the Nineteenth Century*. New York: Norton, 1984.

Stewart, James B. *Joshua R. Giddings and Tactics of Radical Politics*. Cleveland, Ohio: Press of Case Western Reserve University, 1970.

————. *Wendell Phillips: Liberty's Hero*. Baton Rouge: Louisiana State University Press, 1986.

Sundquist, Eric. *Home as Found: Authority and Genealogy in Nineteenth-Century American Literature*. Baltimore: Johns Hopkins University Press, 1979.

Tavard, George H. *Woman in Christian Tradition*. Notre Dame: University of Notre Dame Press, 1973.

Thompson, Ralph. *American Literary Annuals and Gift Books, 1825-1865*. New York: H. W. Wilson, 1936.

Tomlins, Christopher L. *Law, Labor, and Ideology in the Early American Republic*. Cambridge: Cambridge University Press, 1993.

Tompkins, Jane. *Sensational Designs: The Cultural Work of American Fiction, 1790-1860*. New York: Oxford University Press, 1986.

Tucher, Andie. *Froth and Scum: Truth, Beauty, Goodness, and the Ax Murder in America's First Mass Medium*. Chapel Hill: University of North Carolina Press, 1994.

Tuveson, Ernest. *Redeemer Nation: The Idea of America's Millennial Role*. Chicago: University of Chicago Press, 1968.

Tyrrell, Ian R. *Sobering Up: From Temperance to Prohibition in Antebellum America, 1800-1860*. Westport, Conn.: Greenwood Press, 1979.

Verbrugge, Martha H. *Able-Bodied Womanhood: Personal Health and Social Change in Nineteenth-Century Boston*. New York: Oxford University Press, 1988.

Walker, Peter. *Moral Choices: Memory, Desire, and Imagination in Nineteenth-Century American Abolition*. Baton Rouge: Louisiana State University Press, 1978.

Warbasse, Elizabeth Bowles. *The Changing Legal Rights of Married Women, 1800-1861*. New York: Garland, 1987.

Warner, Michael. *The Letters of the Republic: Publication and the Public Sphere in Eighteenth-Century America*. Cambridge: Harvard University Press, 1990.

Weisbrod, Carol. *The Boundaries of Utopia*. New York: Pantheon, 1980.

Welter, Rush. *The Mind of America, 1820-1860*. New York: Cornell University Press, 1975.

White, Deborah Gray. *Ar'n't I a Woman? Female Slaves in the Plantation South*. New York: Norton, 1985.

Wiecek, William M. *The Sources of Antislavery Constitutionalism in America, 1760-1848*. Ithaca: Cornell University Press, 1977.

Wilentz, Sean. *Chants Democratic: New York and the Rise of the American Working Class, 1788-1850*. New York: Oxford University Press, 1984.

Williams, Daniel. *Pillars of Salt: An Anthology of Early American Crime Narrative*. Madison, Wis.: Madison House, 1993.

Williams, Raymond. *The Country and the City*. New York: Oxford University Press, 1973.

Wortman, Marlene Stein, ed. *Women in American Law*. Vol. 1. New York: Holmes and Meier, 1985.

Yellin, Jean Fagan. *Women and Sisters: The Antislavery Feminists in American Culture*. New Haven: Yale University Press, 1989.

Articles and Essays

Adams, James T. "Disfranchisement of Negroes in New England." *American Historical Review* 30 (April 1925): 543-47.

Albanese, Catherine L. "Physic and Metaphysic in Nineteenth-Century America: Medical Sectarians and Religious Healing." *Church History* 55 (December 1986): 489–502.

———. "Whither the Sons (and Daughters)? Republican Nature and the Quest for the Ideal." In *The American Revolution: Its Character and Limits*, edited by Jack P. Greene, 362–87. New York: New York University Press, 1987.

Althusser, Louis. "Ideology and Ideological State Apparatuses (Notes toward an Investigation)." In *Lenin and Philosophy and Other Essays*, translated by Ben Brewster, 127–86. New York: Monthly Review Press, 1971.

Armao, Agnes Orsatti. "Devout Legalists: Protestant Reliance on Law in Early Nineteenth-Century America." *American Studies* 26 (Fall 1985): 61–74.

Arnold, Marybeth Hamilton. " 'The Life of a Citizen in the Hands of a Woman': Sexual Assault in New York City, 1790 to 1820." In *Passion and Power: Sexuality in History*, edited by Kathy Peiss and Christina Simmons, with Robert A. Padgug, 35–56. Philadelphia: Temple University Press, 1989.

Baker, Paula. "The Domestication of Politics: Women and American Political Society, 1780–1920." In *Women, the State, and Welfare*, edited by Linda Gordon, 55–91. Madison: University of Wisconsin Press, 1990. Reprinted from *American Historical Review* 89 (June 1984): 620–47.

Bartky, Sandra Lee. "Foucault, Femininity, and the Modernization of Patriarchal Power." In *Feminism and Foucault: Reflections on Resistance*, edited by Irene Diamond and Lee Quinby, 61–86. Boston: Northeastern University Press, 1988.

Basch, Francoise. "Women's Rights and the Wrongs of Marriage in Mid-Nineteenth-Century America." *History Workshop: A Journal of Socialist and Feminist Ideas* 22 (Autumn 1986): 18–40.

Basch, Norma. "The Emerging Legal History of Women in the United States: Property, Divorce, and the Constitution." *Signs: Journal of Women in Culture and Society* 12 (Autumn 1986): 97–117.

———. "Equity vs. Equality: Emerging Concepts of Women's Political Status in the Age of Jackson." *Journal of the Early Republic* 3 (Fall 1983): 297–318.

———. "From the Bonds of Empire to the Bonds of Matrimony." In *Devising Liberty: Preserving and Creating Freedom in the New American Republic*, edited by David Thomas Konig, 217–42. Stanford: Stanford University Press, 1995.

Bauman, Richard. "Speaking in the Light: The Role of the Quaker Minister." In *Explorations in the Ethnography of Speaking*, edited by Richard Bauman and Joel Sherzer, 144–60. Cambridge: Cambridge University Press, 1974.

Belsey, Catherine. "Constructing the Subject: Deconstructing the Text." In *Feminisms: An Anthology of Literary Theory and Criticism*, edited by Robyn R. Warhol and Diane Price Herndl, 593–609. New Brunswick: Rutgers University Press, 1991.

Benson, Susan Porter. "Business Heads and Sympathizing Hearts: The Women of the Providence Employment Society, 1837–1858." *Journal of Social History* 12 (Winter 1978): 302–12.

Bernard, Joel. "Authority, Autonomy, and Radical Commitment: Stephen and Abby Kelley Foster." *Proceedings of the American Antiquarian Society* 90 (October 1980): 347–86.

Berthoff, Rowland. "Conventional Mentality: Free Blacks, Women, and Business Corporations as Unequal Persons, 1820–1870." *Journal of American History* 76 (December 1989): 753–84.

Blackmar, Elizabeth. "The Distress of Property Law: Landlord-Tenant Relations in Antebellum New York." In *The Law in America, 1607–1861*, edited by William Pencak and Wythe W. Holt Jr., 210–37. New York: New-York Historical Society, 1989.

Blake, John B. "Mary Gove Nichols, Prophetess of Health." In *Women and Health in America*, edited by Judith Walzer Leavitt, 359–75. Madison: University of Wisconsin Press, 1984.

———. "Women and Medicine in Ante-Bellum America." *Bulletin of the History of Medicine* 39 (March–April 1965): 99–123.

Blauvelt, Martha Tomhave. "Women and Revivalism." In *Women and Religion in America*, vol. 1, *The Nineteenth Century*, edited by Rosemary Radford Reuther and Rosemary Skinner Keller, 1–45. San Francisco: Harper and Row, 1981.

Bloch, Ruth H. "The Gendered Meanings of Virtue in Revolutionary America." *Signs: Journal of Women in Culture and Society* 13 (Autumn 1987): 37–58.

Botein, Stephen. "Religious Dimensions of the Early American State." In *Beyond Confederation: Origins of the Constitution and American National Identity*, edited by Richard Beeman, Stephen Botein, and Edward C. Carter II, 315–30. Chapel Hill: University of North Carolina Press, 1987.

Bower, Robert K. "Joseph A. Dugdale: A Friend of Truth." *Palimpsest* 56 (November–December 1975): 170–83.

Boylan, Anne M. "Women and Politics in the Era before Seneca Falls." *Journal of the Early Republic* 10 (Fall 1990): 363–82.

———. "Women in Groups: An Analysis of Women's Benevolent Organizations in New York and Boston, 1797–1840." *Journal of American History* 71 (1984): 497–523.

Bradley, A. Day. "Progressive Friends in Michigan and New York." *Quaker History* 52 (Autumn 1963): 95–103.

Brereton, Virginia Lieson, and Christa Ressmeyer Klein. "American Women in Ministry: A History of Protestant Beginning Points." In *Women in American Religion*, edited by Janet Wilson James, 171–90. Philadelphia: University of Pennsylvania Press, 1980.

Brown, Ira V. " 'Am I Not a Woman and a Sister?' The Anti-Slavery Conventions of American Women, 1837–1839." *Pennsylvania History* 50 (January 1983): 1–19.

———. "Cradle of Feminism: The Philadelphia Female Anti-Slavery Society, 1833–1840." *Pennsylvania Magazine of History and Biography* 102 (April 1978): 143–66.

———. "Racism and Sexism: The Case of Pennsylvania Hall." *Phylon* 37 (1976): 126–36.

Brueggeman, Walter. "Of the Same Flesh and Bone (GN 2,23a)." *Catholic Biblical Quarterly* 32 (1970): 532–42.

Bunker, Gary. "Antebellum Caricature and Woman's Sphere." *Journal of Women's History* 3 (Winter 1992): 6–43.

Butler, Judith. "Variations on Sex and Gender: Beauvoir, Wittig, and Foucault." In *Feminism as Critique: On the Politics of Gender*, edited and with an introduction by Seyla Benhabib and Drucilla Cornell, 128–42. Minneapolis: University of Minnesota Press, 1987.

Calvo, Janis. "Quaker Women Ministers in Nineteenth-Century America." *Quaker History* 63 (Autumn 1974): 75–93.

Capper, Charles. "Margaret Fuller as Cultural Reformer: The Conversations in Boston." *American Quarterly* 39 (Winter 1987): 509–28.

Carlisle, Marcia. "Disorderly City, Disorderly Women: Prostitution in Antebellum Philadelphia." *Pennsylvania Magazine of History and Biography* 110 (October 1986): 549–68.

Chused, Richard H. "Married Women's Property Law, 1800–1850." *Georgetown Law Journal* 71 (1983): 1359–1425.

Clark, Anna K. "Rape or Seduction? A Controversy over Sexual Violence in the Nineteenth Century." In *The Sexual Dynamics of History: Men's Power, Women's Resistance*, edited by the London Feminist History Group, 13–27. London: Pluto Press, 1983.

Clark, Elizabeth B. "Matrimonial Bonds: Slavery and Divorce in Nineteenth Century America." *Law and History Review* 8 (Spring 1990): 25–54.

———. "Religion, Rights, and Difference in the Early Women's Rights Movement." *Wisconsin Women's Law Review* 3 (1987): 29–57.

Clark, Lorenne M. G. "Women and Locke: Who Owns the Apples in the Garden of Eden?" In *The Sexism of Social and Political Theory: Women and Reproduction from Plato to Nietzsche*, edited by Lorenne M. G. Clark and Lynda Lange, 17–40. Toronto: University of Toronto Press, 1979.

Cogan, Neil H. " 'Standing' before the Constitution: Membership in the Community." *Law and History Review* 7 (Spring 1989): 1–21.

Cover, Robert M. "Violence and the Word." *Yale Law Journal* 95 (1986): 1601–29.

Crowe, Charles. "Christian Socialism and the First Church of Humanity." *Church History* 35 (March 1966): 93–106.

———. "Utopian Socialism in Rhode Island, 1845–1850." *Rhode Island History* 18 (January 1959): 20–26.

Dagger, Richard. "Rights." In *Political Innovation and Conceptual Change*, edited by Terence Ball, James Farr, and Russell L. Hanson, 292–308. Cambridge: Cambridge University Press, 1989.

Dahlinger, Charles W. "The Dawn of the Woman's Movement: An Account of the Origin and History of the Pennsylvania Married Woman's Property Law of 1848." *Western Pennsylvania Historical Magazine* 1 (April 1918): 68–84.

Dannenbaum, Jed. "The Origins of Temperance Activism and Militancy among American Women." *Journal of Social History* 15 (December 1981): 235–52.

Davis, David Brion. "The Movement to Abolish Capital Punishment in America, 1787–1861." *American Historical Review* 63 (October 1957): 23–46.

———. "Slavery and Sin: The Cultural Background." In *The Antislavery Vanguard: New Essays on Abolitionists*, edited by Martin Duberman, 3–31. Princeton: Princeton University Press, 1965.

Dayton, Cornelia Hughes. "Unequal in Transgression: The Double Standard in Bastardy/Fornication in Eighteenth-Century New England." *Critical Matrix* 1 (1985): 1–36.

Deacon, Desley. "Politicizing Gender." *Genders*, no. 6 (Fall 1989): 1–19.

Delp, Robert W. "American Spiritualism and Social Reform, 1847–1900." *Northwest Ohio Quarterly* 44 (Fall 1972): 85–99.

De Man, Paul. "The Epistemology of Metaphor." *Critical Inquiry* 5 (Autumn 1978): 13–30.

DuBois, Ellen Carol. "Taking the Law into Our Own Hands: *Bradwell, Minor*, and Suffrage Militance in the 1870s." In *Visible Women: New Essays on American Activism*, edited by Nancy A. Hewitt and Suzanne Lebsock, 19–40. Urbana: University of Illinois Press, 1993.

DuBois, Ellen, and Mari Jo Buhle, Temma Kaplan, Gerda Lerner, and Carroll Smith-Rosenberg. "Politics and Culture in Women's History: A Symposium." *Feminist Studies* 6 (Spring 1980): 26–64.

Dunn, Mary Maples. "Latest Light on Women of Light." In *Witnesses for Change: Quaker Women over Three Centuries*, edited by Elisabeth Potts Brown and Susan Mosher Stuard, 71–89. New Brunswick: Rutgers University Press, 1989.

Ellsworth, Clayton Sumner. "The American Churches and the Mexican War." *American Historical Review* 45 (January 1940): 301–26.

Endy, Melvin B., Jr. "Theology in a Religiously Plural World: Some Contributions of William Penn." *Pennsylvania Magazine of History and Biography* 105 (October 1981): 453–66.

Ernst, Daniel R. "Church-State Issues and the Law: 1607–1870." In *Church and State in America, a Biographical Guide: The Colonial and Early National Periods*, edited by John F. Wilson, 331–64. New York: Greenwood Press, 1986.

Erwin, F. A. "Assault and Battery (Wife vs. Husband)." *University Law Review* 3 (February 1897): 67–74.

Estrich, Susan. "Rape." In *Feminist Jurisprudence*, edited by Patricia Smith, 158–87. New York: Oxford University Press, 1993.

Fellman, Michael. "Theodore Parker and the Abolitionist Role in the 1850s." *Journal of American History* 61 (December 1974): 666–84.

Ferguson, Robert A. "Ideology and the Framing of the Constitution." *Early American Literature* 22 (Fall 1987): 157–65.

Finkelman, Paul. "*Prigg v. Pennsylvania* and Northern State Courts: Anti-Slavery Use of a Proslavery Decision." *Civil War History* 25 (March 1979): 5–35.

———. "Slavery, the 'More Perfect Union,' and the Prairie State." *Illinois History* 70 (Winter 1987): 248–69.

Fliegelman, Jay. "Familial Politics, Seduction, and the Novel: The Anxious Agenda of an American Literary Culture." In *The American Revolution: Its Character and Limits*, edited by Jack P. Greene, 331–54. New York: New York University Press, 1987.

Friedman, Lawrence J. "The Gerrit Smith Circle: Abolitionism in the Burned-over District." *Civil War History* 26 (March 1980): 18–38.

———. "Racism and Sexism in Ante-bellum America: The Prudence Crandall Episode Reconsidered." *Societas* 4 (1974): 211–27.

Frost, J. William. "Pennsylvania Institutes Religious Liberty, 1682–1860." *Pennsylvania Magazine of History and Biography* 112 (July 1988): 323–47.

Gagel, Diane VanSkiver. "Ohio Women Unite: The Salem Convention of 1850." In *Women in Ohio History*, edited by Marta Whitlock, 4–8. Columbus: Ohio Historical Society, 1976.

Galbreath, C. D. "Antislavery Movement in Columbiana County." *Ohio Archaeological and Historical Society Publications* (1921): 355–95.

Gittleman, Edwin. "Jefferson's 'Slave Narrative': The Declaration of Independence as a Literary Text." *Early American Literature* 8 (Winter 1974): 239–56.

Gordon, Linda, and Ellen DuBois. "Seeking Ecstasy on the Battlefield: Danger and Pleasure in Nineteenth-Century Feminist Sexual Thought." In *Sexuality: A Reader*, edited by *Feminist Review*, 82–97. London: Virago Press, 1987.

Griswold, Robert L. "Adultery and Divorce in Victorian America, 1800–1900." In *Legal History Program: Working Papers*, ser. 1. (Madison, Wis.: Institute for Legal Studies, 1986), 1–50.

———. "The Evolution of the Doctrine of Mental Cruelty in Victorian American Divorce, 1790–1900." *Journal of Social History* 20 (Fall 1986): 127–48.

———. "Sexual Cruelty and the Case for Divorce in Victorian America." *Signs: Journal of Women in Culture and Society* 11 (Spring 1986): 529–41.

Guarneri, Carl J. "The Associationists: Forging a Christian Socialism in Antebellum America." *Church History* 52 (March 1983): 36–49.

Gundersen, Joan R. "Independence, Citizenship, and the American Revolution." *Signs: Journal of Women in Culture and Society* 13 (Autumn 1987): 59–77.

Gunn, J. A. W. "Public Opinion." In *Political Innovation and Conceptual Change*, edited by Terence Ball, James Farr, and Russell L. Hanson, 247–65. Cambridge: Cambridge University Press, 1989.

Halttunen, Karen. "'Domestic Differences': Competing Narratives of Womanhood in the Murder Trial of Lucretia Chapman." In *The Culture of Sentiment: Race, Gender, and Sentimentality in Nineteenth-Century America*, edited by Shirley Samuels, 39–57. New York: Oxford University Press, 1992.

Harlow, Ralph Volney. "Gerrit Smith and the Free Church Movement." *New York History* 43 (July 1937): 269–87.

Hartog, Hendrik. "The Constitution and 'The Rights That Belong to Us All.'" *Journal of American History* 74 (December 1987): 1013–34.

———. "Lawyering, Husbands' Rights, and 'the Unwritten Law' in Nineteenth-Century America." *Journal of American History* 84 (June 1997): 67–96.

———. "Mrs. Packard on Dependency." *Yale Journal of Law and the Humanities* 1 (December 1988): 79–103.

Haskell, Thomas L. "The Curious Persistence of Rights Talk in the 'Age of Interpretation.'" *Journal of American History* 74 (December 1987): 984–1012.

Havighurst, Harold C. "Services in the Home: A Study of Contract Concepts in Domestic Relations." *Yale Law Journal* 41 (1932): 386–406.

Hewitt, Nancy A. "Amy Kirby Post." *University of Rochester Library Bulletin* 37 (1984): 5–22.

———. "Feminist Friends: Agrarian Quakers and the Emergence of Woman's Rights in America." *Feminist Studies* 12 (Spring 1986): 27–49.

———. "The Fragmentation of Friends: The Consequences for Quaker Women in Antebellum America." In *Witnesses for Change: Quaker Women over Three Centuries*, edited by Elisabeth Potts Brown and Susan Mosher Stuard, 93–119. New Brunswick: Rutgers University Press, 1989.

———. "Yankee Evangelicals and Agrarian Quakers: Gender, Religion, and Class in the Formation of a Feminist Consciousness in Nineteenth-Century Rochester, New York." *Radical History Review* 28–30 (1984): 327–42.

Hill, Christopher. "Covenant Theology and the Concept of 'A Public Person.'" In *Essays in Honour of C. B. Macpherson: Power, Possessions, and Freedom*, edited by Alkis Kontos, 3–22. Toronto: University of Toronto Press, 1979.

Hoffer, Peter Charles. "The Declaration of Independence as a Bill in Equity." In *The Law in America, 1607–1861*, edited by William Pencak and Wythe W. Holt Jr., 186–209. New York: New-York Historical Society, 1989.

Howe, Daniel Walker. "The Evangelical Movement and the Political Culture of the Second Party System." *Journal of American History* 77 (March 1991): 1216–39.

———. "Religion and Politics in Antebellum America." In *Religion and American Politics: From the Colonial Period to the 1980s*, edited by Mark A. Noll, 121–45. New York: Oxford University Press, 1990.

Hutcheson, Maud Macdonald. "Mercy Otis Warren, 1728–1814." *William and Mary Quarterly* 10 (July 1953): 379–402.

Ireland, Robert M. "Insanity and the Unwritten Law." *American Journal of Legal History* 32 (April 1988): 157–72.

Isenberg, Nancy "The Personal Is Political: Gender, Feminism, and the Politics of Discourse Theory." *American Quarterly* 44 (September 1992): 449–58.

———. "Second Thoughts on Gender and Women's History." *American Studies* 36 (Spring 1995): 93–104.

John, Richard R. "Taking Sabbatarianism Seriously: The Postal System, the Sabbath, and the Transformation of American Political Culture." *Journal of the Early Republic* 10 (Winter 1990): 517–67.

Johnson, James T. "The Covenant Idea and the Puritan View of Marriage." *Journal of the History of Ideas* 32 (January–March 1971): 107–18.

Johnson, Reinhard O. "The Liberty Party in Massachusetts, 1840–1848: Antislavery Third Party Politics in the Bay State." *Civil War History* 28 (Fall 1982): 237–65.

Jones, Kathleen B. "On Authority: Or, Why Women Are Not Entitled to Speak." In *Feminism and Foucault: Reflections on Resistance*, edited by Irene Diamond and Lee Quinby, 119–33. Boston: Northeastern University Press, 1988.

Jordan, Cynthia S. "'Old Words' in 'New Circumstances': Language and Leadership in Post-Revolutionary America." *American Quarterly* 40 (December 1988): 491–513.

Kaye, Francis W. "The Ladies' Department of the Ohio Cultivator, 1845–1855: A Feminist Forum." *Agricultural History* 50 (April 1976): 414–23.

Kennedy, Duncan. "The Structure of Blackstone's Commentaries." *Buffalo Law Review* 28 (1979): 205–382.

Kerber, Linda K. "A Constitutional Right to Be Treated Like American Ladies: Women and the Obligations of Citizenship." In *U.S. History as Women's History: New Feminist Essays*, edited by Linda K. Kerber, Alice Kessler-Harris, and Kathryn Kish Sklar, 1–35. Chapel Hill: University of North Carolina Press, 1995.

———. " 'I Have Don . . . much to Carrey on the Warr': Women and the Shaping of Republican Ideology after the American Revolution." In *Women and Politics in the Age of Revolution*, edited by Harriet B. Applewhite and Darline G. Levy, 227–57. Ann Arbor: University of Michigan Press, 1990.

———. " 'May all our Citizens be Soldiers, and all our Soldiers Citizens': The Ambiguities of Female Citizenship in the New Nation." In *Arms at Rest: Peacemaking and Peacekeeping in American History*, edited by Joan R. Challinor and Robert L. Beisner, 1–21. Westport, Conn.: Greenwood Press, 1987.

———. "The Paradox of Women's Citizenship in the Early Republic: The Case of *Martin vs. Massachusetts*, 1805." *American Historical Review* 97 (April 1992): 349–78.

———. "The Republican Ideology of the Revolutionary Generation." *American Quarterly* 37 (Fall 1985): 474–95.

———. "Separate Spheres, Female Worlds, Woman's Place: The Rhetoric of Women's History." *Journal of American History* 75 (June 1988): 9–39.

Kirkpatrick, Frank G. "From Shackles to Liberation: Religion, the Grimké Sisters, and Dissent." In *Women, Religion, and Social Change*, edited by Yvonne Yazbeck Haddad and Ellison Banks Findley, 433–55. Albany: State University of New York Press, 1985.

Klinghoffer, Judith Apter, and Lois Elkis. " 'The Petticoat Electors': Women's Suffrage in New Jersey, 1776–1807." *Journal of the Early Republic* 12 (Summer 1992): 159–94.

Landes, Joan B. "Hegel's Conception of the Family." In *The Family in Political Thought*, edited by Jean Bethke Elshtain, 125–44. Amherst: University of Massachusetts Press, 1982.

Lange, Lynda. "Rousseau: Women and the General Will." In *The Sexism of Social and Political Theory: Women and Reproduction from Plato to Nietzsche*, edited by Lorenne M. G. Clark and Lynda Lange, 41–52. Toronto: University of Toronto Press, 1979.

Laqueur, Thomas. "Orgasm, Generation, and the Politics of Reproductive Biology." *Representations* 14 (Spring 1986): 1–41.

Laursen, John Christian. "The Subversive Kant: The Vocabulary of 'Public' and 'Publicity.' " *Political Theory* 14 (November 1986): 584–603.

Lecompte, Janet. "The Independent Women of Hispanic New Mexico." *Western Historical Quarterly* 22 (January 1981): 17–35.

Lewis, Jan. " 'Of Every Age Sex and Condition': The Representation of Women in the Constitution." *Journal of the Early Republic* 15 (Fall 1995): 359–87.

———. "The Republican Wife: Virtue and Seduction in the Early Republic." *William and Mary Quarterly* 44 (October 1987): 689–721.

Lloyd, Genevieve. "Selfhood, War, and Masculinity." In *Feminist Challenges: Social and Political Theory*, edited by Carole Pateman and Elizabeth Gross, 63–76. Boston: Northeastern University Press, 1987.

Loeffelholz, Mary. "Posing the Woman Citizen: The Contradictions of Stanton's Feminism." *Genders*, no. 7 (March 1990): 87–98.

Lutz, Donald S. "From Covenant to Constitution in American Political Thought." *Covenant, Polity, and Constitutionalism: Publius, the Journal of Federalism* 10 (Fall 1980): 101–33.

Mackey, Philip English. "'The Result May Be Glorious': Anti-Gallows Movement in Rhode Island, 1838–1852." *Rhode Island History* 33 (February 1974): 19–31.

MacKinnon, Catherine A. "Feminism, Marxism, Method, and the State: Toward a Feminist Jurisprudence [1983]." In *Feminist Legal Theory: Readings in Law and Gender*, edited by Katharine T. Bartlett and Rosanne Kennedy, 181–200. Boulder: Westview Press, 1991.

———. "Legal Perspectives on Sexual Difference." In *Theoretical Perspectives on Sexual Difference*, edited by Deborah L. Rhode, 213–25. New Haven: Yale University Press, 1990.

McKivigan, John R. "The Antislavery 'Comeouter' Sects: A Neglected Dimension of the Abolitionist Movement." *Civil War History* 26 (March 1980): 142–60.

McMurry, Sally. "Progressive Farm Families and their Houses, 1830–1855: A Study in Independent Design." *Agricultural History* 58 (July 1984): 330–46.

Maltz, Earl M. "Fourteenth Amendment Concepts in the Antebellum Era." *American Journal of Legal History* 32 (1988): 305–46.

Martin, Asa Earl. "The Temperance Movement in Pennsylvania prior to the Civil War." *Pennsylvania Magazine of History and Biography* 49 (1925): 195–230.

Martin, Biddy. "Feminism, Criticism, and Foucault." *New German Critique* 27 (Fall 1982): 3–30.

Milkman, Ruth. "Women's History and the Sears Case." *Feminist Studies* 12 (Summer 1986): 375–400.

Minow, Martha. "An Essay on Rights." *Yale Law Journal* 96 (July 1987): 1810–60.

Moorhead, James. "The Millennium and the Media." In *Communication and Change in American Religious History*, edited by Leonard I. Sweet, 216–38. Grand Rapids, Mich.: Eerdmans, 1993.

Morantz, Regina Markell. "Nineteenth-Century Health Reform and Women: A Program of Self-Help." In *Medicine without Doctors: Home Health Care in American History*, edited by Guenter B. Risse, Ronald L. Numbers, and Judith Walzer Leavitt, 73–93. New York: Science History Publications, 1977.

Moxey, Keith. "The Battle of the Sexes and the World upside Down." In *That Gentle Strength: Historical Perspectives on Women in Christianity*, edited by Lynda L. Coon, Katherine J. Haldane, and Elisabeth W. Sommer, 134–48. Charlottesville: University Press of Virginia, 1990.

Mullaney, Marie Marmo. "Feminism, Utopianism, and Domesticity: The Career of Rebecca Buffum Spring, 1811–1911." *New Jersey History* 104 (Fall–Winter 1986): 1–22.

Myerson, Joel. "Mary Gove Nichols' *Mary Lyndon*: A Forgotten Reform Novel." *American Literature* 58 (December 1986): 523–39.

Noll, Mark. "The Evangelical Enlightenment and the Task of Theological Education." In *Communication and Change in American Religious History*, edited by Leonard I. Sweet, 270–300. Grand Rapids, Mich.: Eerdmans, 1993.

Nord, David Paul. "Systematic Benevolence: Religious Publishing and the Marketplace in Early Nineteenth-Century America." In *Communication and Change in American Religious History*, edited by Leonard I. Sweet, 239–69. Grand Rapids, Mich.: Eerdmans, 1993.

Noun, Louise. "Amelia Bloomer: A Biography." Pt. 1, "The Lily of Seneca Falls." *Annals of Iowa* 47 (Winter 1985): 575–617.

Numbers, Ronald L. "Do-It-Yourself the Sectarian Way." In *Medicine without Doctors: Home Health Care in American History*, edited by Guenter B. Risse, Ronald L. Numbers, and Judith Walzer Leavitt, 49–72. New York: Science History Publications, 1977.

Perry, Lewis. "Adin Ballou's Hopedale Community and the Theology of Antislavery." *Church History* 39 (September 1970): 372–89.

———. "'Progress, not Pleasure, is our Aim': The Sexual Advice of an Antebellum Radical." *Journal of Social History* 12 (Spring 1979): 354–66.

Perry, Ruth. "Mary Astell and the Feminist Critique of Possessive Individualism." *Eighteenth-Century Studies* 23 (1990): 444–557.

Pitkin, Hanna Fenichel. "Justice: On Relating Private and Public." *Political Theory* 9 (August 1981): 327–52.

Pocock, J. G. A. "Virtues, Rights, and Manners: A Model for Historians of Political Thought." *Political Theory* 9 (August 1981): 353–68.

Post, Albert. "Early Efforts to Abolish Capital Punishment in Pennsylvania." *Pennsylvania Magazine of History and Biography* 68 (January 1944): 38–53.

Rabkin, Peggy. "The Origins of Law Reform: The Social Significance of the Nineteenth Century Codification Movement and Its Contribution to the Passage of the Early Married Women's Property Acts." *Buffalo Law Review* 29 (Spring 1980): 683–760.

Richards, Judith, Lotte Mulligan, and John K. Graham. " 'Property' and 'People': Political Usages of Locke and Some Contemporaries." *Journal of the History of Ideas* 42 (January–March 1982): 29–51.

Riegel, Robert E. "Changing American Attitudes toward Prostitution." *Journal of the History of Ideas* 29 (July–September 1968): 437–52.

———. "Women's Clothes and Women's Rights." *American Quarterly* 15 (Fall 1963): 390–401.

Roberts, Helene E. "The Exquisite Slave: The Role of Clothes in the Making of the Victorian Woman." *Signs: Journal of Women in Culture and Society* 2 (Spring 1977): 554–79.

Robinson, David. "The Political Odessey of William Henry Channing." *American Quarterly* 34 (Summer 1982): 165–84.

Rousseau, G. S. "Nerves, Spirits, Fibres: Towards an Origins of Sensibility." In *Studies in the Eighteenth Century*, edited by F. R. Brissenden, 73–81. Canberra: Australian National University Press, 1975.

Rowe, G. S. "*Femes Covert* and Criminal Prosecution in Eighteenth-Century Pennsylvania." *American Journal of Legal History* 32 (April 1988): 138–56.

———. "Women's Crime and Criminal Administration in Pennsylvania, 1763–1790." *Pennsylvania Magazine of History and Biography* 109 (July 1985): 335–68.

Rubin, Gayle. "The Traffic in Women: Notes on the 'Political Economy' of Sex." In *Towards an Anthropology of Women*, edited by Rayna R. Reiter, 157–210. New York: Monthly Review Press, 1975.

Ruchames, Louis. "Race, Marriage, and Abolition in Massachusetts." *Journal of Negro History* 40 (July 1955): 25–73.

Ryan, Mary P. "The American Parade: Representations of the Nineteenth-Century Social Order." In *The New Cultural History*, edited by Lynn Hunt, 131–53. Berkeley: University of California Press, 1989.

———. "A Women's Awakening: Evangelical Religion and the Families of Utica, New York, 1800–1840." *American Quarterly* 30 (Winter 1978): 602–23.

Salmon, Marylynn. " 'Life, Liberty, and Dower': The Legal Status of Women after the American Revolution." In *Women, War, and Revolution*, edited by Carol R. Berkin and Clara M. Lovett, 85–106. New York: Holmes and Meier, 1980.

———. "Republican Sentiment, Economic Change, and the Property Rights of Women in American Law." In *Women in the Age of the American Revolution*, edited by Ronald Hoffman and Peter J. Albert, 447–75. Charlottesville: University Press of Virginia, 1989.

Samuels, Shirley. "The Family, the State, and the Novel in the Early Republic." *American Quarterly* 38 (October 1986): 381–95.

———. "Infidelity and Contagion: The Rhetoric of Revolution." *Early American Literature* 22 (Fall 1987): 183–91.

Schaeffer, John D. "The Use and Misuse of Giambattista Vico: Rhetoric, Orality, and Theories of Discourse." In *The New Historicism*, edited by H. Aram Vesser. London: Routledge, 1989.

Schilpp, Medelon Golden, and Sharon M. Murphy, eds. "Jane Gray Swisshelm: Abolitionist, Feminist, Journalist, 1815–1884." In *Great Women of the Press*, 76–77. Carbondale: Southern Illinois Press, 1983.

Schneider, A. Gregory. "From Democratization to Domestication: The Transitional Orality of the American Methodist Circuit Rider." In *Communication and Change in American Religious History*, edited by Leonard I. Sweet, 141–64. Grand Rapids, Mich.: Eerdmans, 1993.

Schofield, Mary Anne. " 'Descending Angels': Salubrious Sluts and Pretty Prostitutes in Haywood's Fiction." In *Fetter'd or Free? British Women, British Novelists, 1670–1815*, edited by Mary Anne Schofield and Cecilia Macheski, 186–200. Athens: Ohio University Press, 1986.

Shanley, Mary Lyndon. "Marriage Contract and Social Contract in Seventeenth Century English Political Thought." *Western Political Quarterly* 32 (March 1979): 79–91.

Shideler, Emerson W. "The Concept of the Church in Seventeenth-Century Quakerism." *Bulletin of Friends Historical Association* 45 (Autumn 1956): 67–81.

Shiels, Richard D. "The Feminization of American Congregationalism, 1730–1835." *American Quarterly* 33 (June 1981): 46–62.

Shilling, D. C. "Woman's Suffrage in the Constitutional Convention of Ohio." *Ohio Archaeological and Historical Society Publications* 25 (1916): 166–74.

Sklar, Katharine Kish. " 'Women Who Speak for an Entire Nation': American and British Women Compared at the World Anti-Slavery Convention, London, 1840." In *The Abolitionist Sisterhood: Women's Political Culture in Antebellum America*, edited by Jean Fagan Yellin and John C. Van Horne, 301–34. Ithaca: Cornell University Press, 1994.

Smith, Daniel Scott. "Family Limitation, Sexual Control, and Domestic Feminism in Victorian America." In *A Heritage of Her Own: Toward a New Social History of American Women*, edited by Nancy F. Cott and Elizabeth H. Pleck, 222–45. New York: Simon and Schuster, 1979.

Smith, Wilda M. "A Half Century of Struggle: Gaining Woman Suffrage in Kansas." *Kansas History* 4 (Summer 1981): 74–91.

Smith-Rosenberg, Carroll. "Beauty, the Beast, and the Militant Woman: A Case Study in Sex Roles and Social Stress in Jacksonian America." *American Quarterly* 23 (October 1971): 562–84.

———. "Domesticating 'Virtue': Coquettes and Revolutionaries in Young America." In *Literature and the Body: Essays on Populations and Persons*, edited by Elaine Scarry, 160–84. Baltimore: Johns Hopkins University Press, 1988.

———. "Puberty to Menopause: The Cycle of Femininity in Nineteenth Century America." In *Clio's Consciousness Raised: New Perspectives on the History of Women*, edited by Mary Hartman and Lois W. Banner, 23–37. New York: Harper and Row, 1974.

Smith-Rosenberg, Carroll, and Charles Rosenberg. "The Female Animal: Medical and Biological View of Woman and Her Role in Nineteenth-Century America." In *Women and Health in America*, edited by Judith Walzer Leavitt, 12–27. Madison: University of Wisconsin Press, 1984.

Spacks, Patricia M. "The Talent of Ready Utterance: Eighteenth-Century Female Gossip." In *Women and Society in the Eighteenth Century*, edited by Ian P. H. Duffy, 1–14. Bethlehem, Pa.: Lawrence Henry Gipson Institute, 1983.

Stanley, Amy Dru. "Conjugal Bonds and Wage Labor: Rights of Contract in the Age of 'Emancipation.' " *Journal of American History* 75 (September 1988): 471–500.

Stearns, Bertha Monica. "Philadelphia Magazines for Ladies, 1830–1860." *Pennsylvania Magazine of History and Biography* 64 (July 1945): 205–19.

Sturm, Douglas. "Corporations, Constitutions, and Covenants: On Forms of Human Relation and the Problem of Legitimacy." *Journal of the American Academy of Religion* 41 (September 1973): 331–53.

Tanner, Tony. "Julie and 'La Maison Paternelle': Another Look at Rousseau's *La Nouvelle Heloise*." In *The Family in Political Thought*, edited by Jean Bethke Elshtain, 96–124. Amherst: University of Massachusetts Press, 1982.

Tomlins, Christopher L. "Law and Power in the Employment Relationship." In *Labor Law in America: Historical and Critical Essays*, edited by Christopher L. Tomlins and Andrew J. King, 71–98. Baltimore: Johns Hopkins University Press, 1992.

Tompkins, Jane. "'Pray, therefore without ceasing': From Tracts to Texts." *Genre* 16 (Winter 1983): 423–36.

Troth, Emilie, and Mrs. Edward D. Lorimer. "Mira Sharpless Townsend, 1798–1859." In *Notable Women of Pennsylvania*, edited by Gertrude Bosler Biddle and Sarah Dickinson Lowrie, 129–30. Philadelphia, 1942.

Tyrrell, Ian R. "Women and Temperance in Antebellum America, 1830–1860." *Civil War History* 28 (June 1982): 128–52.

Van Broekhoven, Deborah Bingham. "'A Determination to Labor . . .': Female Antislavery Activity in Rhode Island." *Rhode Island History* 44 (May 1985): 35–46.

Varon, Elizabeth R. "Tippecanoe and the Ladies, Too: White Women and Party Politics in Antebellum Virginia." *Journal of American History* 82 (September 1995): 494–521.

Vicinus, Martha. "'Helpless and Unfriended': Nineteenth-Century Domestic Melodrama." *New Literary History* 13 (Autumn 1981): 127–43.

Waciega, Lisa Wilson. "A 'Man of Business': The Widow of Means in Southeastern Pennsylvania, 1750–1850." *William and Mary Quarterly* 44 (January 1987): 40–64.

Wahl, Albert J. "The Progressive Friends of Longwood." *Bulletin of Friends Historical Association* 42 (Spring 1953): 13–32.

Walters, Ronald G. "The Erotic South: Civilization and Sexuality in American Abolitionism." *American Quarterly* 25 (May 1973): 177–201.

Walzer, Michael. "Citizenship." In *Political Innovation and Conceptual Change*, edited by Terence Ball, James Farr, and Russell L. Hanson, 211–19. Cambridge: Cambridge University Press, 1989.

Warren, Joseph. "Husband's Right to Wife's Services." *Harvard Law Review* 38 (February 1925): 421–46.

Weisbrod, Carol. "Family, Church, and State." In *Legal History Program: Working Papers*, ser. 1 (Madison, Wis.: Institute for Legal Studies, 1986), 1–12.

Wellman, Judith. "The Seneca Falls Women's Rights Convention: A Study of Social Networks." *Journal of Women's History* 3 (Spring 1991): 9–37.

———. "Women and Radical Reform in Antebellum Upstate New York: A Profile of Grassroots Female Abolitionists." In *Clio Was a Woman: Studies in the History of American Women*, edited by Mabel E. Deutrich and Virginia C. Purdy, 113–27. Ithaca: Cornell University Press, 1980.

———. "Women's Rights, Republicanism, and Revolutionary Rhetoric in Antebellum New York State." *New York History* 69 (July 1988): 353–84.

Welter, Barbara. "The Cult of True Womanhood, 1800–1860." In *Dimity Convictions: The American Woman in the Nineteenth Century*, 21–41. Athens: Ohio State University Press, 1976.

———. "The Feminization of American Religion, 1800–1860." In *Dimity Convictions: The American Woman in the Nineteenth Century*, 83–102. Athens: Ohio University Press, 1976.

Wiecek, William M. "Popular Sovereignty in the Dorr War: Conservative Counterblast." *Rhode Island History* 32 (May 1973): 35–51.

Williams, Joan C. "Deconstructing Gender." *Michigan Law Review* 87 (February 1989): 797–845.

Wilson, Joan Hoff, and Sharon L. Billinger. "Mercy Otis Warren: Playwright, Poet, and Historian of the American Revolution," 161–82. In *Female Scholars: A Tradition of Learned Women before 1800*, edited by J. R. Brink. Montreal: Eden Press, 1980.

Wrobel, Arthur. "Phrenology as Political Science." *Pseudo-Science and Society in Nineteenth-Century America*, edited by Arthur Wrobel, 122–43. Lexington: University Press of Kentucky, 1987.

Wyatt-Brown, Bertram. "Prelude to Abolitionism: Sabbatarian Politics and the Rise of the Second Party System." *Journal of American History* 58 (September 1971): 316–41.

Yacovone, Donald. "Samuel Joseph May, Antebellum Reform, and the Problem of Patricide." *Perspectives in American History*, n.s. 2 (1985): 99–124.

Yates, Wilson. "Birth Control Literature and the Medical Profession in Nineteenth Century America." *Journal of the History of Medicine* (January 1976): 42–54.

Yazawa, Melvin. "Creating a Republican Citizenry." In *The American Revolution: Its Character and Limits*, edited by Jack P. Greene, 282–308. New York: New York University Press, 1987.

Zagarri, Rosemarie. "Morals, Manners, and the Republican Mother." *American Quarterly* 44 (June 1992): 192–215.

Zuckert, Catherine. "Not by Preaching: Tocqueville on the Role of Religion in American Democracy." *Review of Politics* 43 (April 1981): 259–80.

Dissertations, Theses, and Unpublished Papers

Chasan, Joshua S. "Civilizing Worcester: The Creation of Institutional and Civil Order." Ph.D. diss., University of Pittsburgh, 1974.

Clark, Elizabeth Battelle. "The Politics of God and the Woman's Vote: Religion in the American Suffrage Movement, 1848–1895." Ph.D. diss., Princeton University, 1989.

Dayton, Cornelia Hughes. "Sex, Confession, and the Lash: Changing Legal Regimes in New Haven, 1640–1690." Presented at the Colloquium of the Institute of Early American History and Culture, Williamsburg, Va., October 7, 1991.

Fish, Cheryl. " 'Unconnected Intelligence': Darting (Dial)logues in Margaret Fuller's Letters and Early Criticism." Personal paper in possession of author.

Fitzgerald, Maureen. "The Religious Thought of Elizabeth Cady Stanton." Master's thesis, University of Wisconsin, 1985.

Frost, William Jerry. "The Quaker Family in Colonial America: A Social History of the Society of Friends." Ph.D. diss., University of Wisconsin, 1968.

Hewitt, Nancy A. "From Seneca Falls to Suffrage: Recasting the History of American Women's Activism, 1848–1965." Presented to the Center for Advanced Study in Behavioral Sciences, Stanford, January 23, 1997. Personal paper in possession of author.

Kraut, Alan Morton. "The Liberty Men of New York: Political Abolitionism in New York State, 1840–1848." Ph.D. diss., Cornell University, 1975.

McKivigan, John R. "Abolitionism and the Churches, 1830–1865: A Study of Attitudes and Tactics." Ph.D. diss., Ohio State University, 1977.

Mooney, James. "Antislavery in Worcester County, Massachusetts: A Case Study." Ph.D. diss., Clark University, 1971.

Parkinson, George P., Jr. "Antebellum State Constitution-Making: Retention, Circumvention, Revision." Ph.D. diss., University of Wisconsin, 1972.

Pease, Jane Hanna. "The Freshness of Fanaticism: Abby Kelley Foster: An Essay in Reform."

Ph.D. diss., University of Rochester, 1969. Facsimile by University Microfilms, Ann Arbor, 1972.

Perkal, Meyer Leon. "William Goodell: A Life of Reform." Ph.D. diss., City University of New York, 1972.

Rice, Arthur Harry. "Henry B. Stanton as a Political Abolitionist." Ed.D. diss., Columbia University, 1968.

Smith, Hilda. "False Universals of Human Experience." Personal paper in possession of author.

Sykes, Richard Eddy. "Massachusetts Unitarianism and Social Change: A Religious System in Transition, 1780–1870." Ph.D. diss., University of Minnesota, 1966.

Tomlins, Christopher. "Law and Power in the Employment Relation, 1800–1850." Personal paper in possession of author.

Van Broekhoven, Deborah Bingham. "Female Bonding among Abolitionists: A Rhode Island Case Study." Society of the Early American Republic, July 1987.

———. " 'Let Your Name Be Enrolled': Method and Ideology in Women's Petitioning." Personal paper in possession of author.

———. "Spheres and Webs: The Organization of the Antislavery Fairs, 1835–1860." Personal paper in possession of author.

Wahl, Albert John. "The Congregational or Progressive Friends in the Pre-Civil-War Reform Movement." Ed.D. diss., Temple University, 1951.

Wellman, Judith. "The Mystery of the Seneca Falls Women's Rights Convention: Who Came and Why?" Personal paper in possession of author.

———. "Women's Rights, Free Soil, and Quakerism: The Seneca Falls Women's Rights Convention." Paper delivered at the Society for the History of the Early American Republic Conference, July 1981.

Index

Abolitionism. *See* Antislavery movement;
  Antislavery societies
Adams, Abigail, 155–56
Adams, John, 15–16, 23, 41, 51, 155
Adams, John Quincy, 65–67, 229 (n. 105)
Adams, Samuel, 122, 125
Adultery, 125–27, 152, 162, 167, 181, 247
  (n. 106)
Alienation, 39, 137, 177; of rights, 107, 118
Aliens, xii, 24, 28, 34, 147, 149, 150, 152
Amazons, 66–67, 99, 128, 198–99
American Bible Society, 81
American Tract Society, 78, 81
Anthony, Susan B., 4, 53–55, 73
Antiabduction laws, 110, 113
Anti–capital punishment movement, 122–23,
  130, 248 (n. 117)
Anti-Masons, 47
Anti-Sabbath Convention, 76, 85, 87
Anti-Slavery Bugle, 99
Antislavery conventions. *See* Convention of
  American Women Against Slavery; London
  World Anti-Slavery Convention
Antislavery movement, xvii, 5, 59–65, 106,
  109; fairs, 60–61; fear of abolitionists, 137;
  petitioning, 64–68. *See also* Fugitive slave
  laws; Race
Antislavery societies: American, 2, 11, 46,
  61–62, 113; Boston Female, 63, 114; Lynn
  Female, 62; Philadelphia Female, 59–60,
  63, 69; Worcester Cent-A-Week, 60;
  Worcester County, 36

Arendt, Hannah, xvi, 7, 9, 12, 68, 238 (n. 104),
  257 (n. 14)
Arnold, Marybeth Hamilton, 125
Astell, Mary, 155

Ball v. Hand, 187
Barbarism, 135–36, 148, 150, 252 (n. 172)
Barber v. Barber, 164–65, 167
Barney, Eliza, 35–36
Barry v. Mercein, 188
Basch, Norma, xvii
Bascom, Ansel, 31
Beecher, Catharine, 62, 80, 83, 88, 234 (n. 36)
Beecher, Lyman, 80, 82–83, 88, 158–59, 235
  (n. 47)
Belsey, Catherine, 194–95
Bement, Rhoda, 90–92, 94, 96
Benevolent societies, xvii, 59–60, 65
Bingham, Anson, 26, 68, 144–45, 179, 182, 218
  (n. 57), 267 (n. 160)
Black codes. *See* Free blacks: and black codes
Blackstone, William, 7, 30, 32, 156, 169, 174,
  247
Blackwell, Antoinette Brown, 43, 68, 99–101,
  105, 132, 197, 199–201, 241 (n. 128)
Blackwell, Elizabeth, 35
Blackwell, Henry, 118, 147
Blackwell, Marian, 35
Blasphemy laws, 78, 83
Bloomer, Amelia, 48, 53, 160, 174, 259 (n. 26)
Bloomer costume. *See* Dress reform
Bogue, Horace, 91–92

Boudinot, Elias, 81
Boydston, Jeanne, xvii
Bradburn, George, 64
Bradley, Joseph Justice, 202
Bradwell, Myra, 202
Bradwell v. Illinois, 202
Brown, Antoinette. *See* Blackwell, Antoinette Brown
Burke, Edmund, 29, 51
Burleigh, Charles, 85–86, 100, 146
Burritt, Elihu, 140
Bush, Abigail, 70
Businesses, female-controlled, 176
Butler v. Butler, 164

Cain, mark of, 119–20, 122–23, 128, 133
Capacity, legal. *See* Citizenship
Capital (investment or mental), 175, 186, 189–90
Capital punishment, xv, xvii, 69–70, 104, 121–24, 125, 130, 152–53, 248 (n. 117)
Captivity narratives, 135
Carpenter, Matthew, 203
Caste(s), xvi, 8, 28, 84, 89, 105, 112, 115, 132, 143, 145, 175, 197; as barriers between women, 130; clergy as separate, 90, 98; colonized, 36; disabled, xii, 8, 32–37, 171, 176, 192; men as divinely vested, 100, 202–3; and military service, 145; and privilege, 170; sexual, xii, 131; and slave mothers, 115; as tripartite system, 131, 197. *See also* Divestment of rights
Celia, 1855 trial of, 107, 151
Channing, William Ellery, 67, 82–83, 85, 140
Channing, William Henry, 1, 5, 11–12, 57, 94, 182
Chapman, Lucretia, 127, 151
Charlotte Temple, 120
Cheever, George B., 122–23, 127
Child, Lydia Maria, 19, 22–23, 39, 68, 122, 124, 128–33, 243–44 (n. 54), 248 (n. 115)
Chivalry, xv, 19, 141–44, 146, 152, 153
Church politics: and censorship, 78–79, 91–93; and church-state alliance, xiv, 9, 75, 77–78, 87, 101; and clergy and elders as castes, xvii, 90, 98; and creeds, xvii, 89, 90, 93; and discipline of laity, 78–91 passim; and disestablishment, 10, 77–78, 88; disorderly conduct in, 79, 90–91, 96; *ecclesia*

defined, 89–90, 95; evangelical empire in, 78, 89, 93; and "free churches," 89, 91, 94–95, 98–99, 235 (n. 59); heresy and infidelity in, 64, 75–77, 81, 88–89; and incorporation, 95; and moral associations, 82–83; and omission of religion in historiography, xvi–xvii, 10, 207 (n. 7); and preaching and male authority, 90, 95–96, 98; sects or sectarianism in, 90, 93–94; "spiritual fetters" in, 75, 90, 92–94, 100; and women as ministers, 96–99; and women as moral subjects, 77, 87–88. *See also* Dissent: in religious life
Cipher, woman as, xv, 105, 141, 146, 154
Citizenship, xi–xiii, 11, 13, 20–21, 73, 105–6, 191; and aliens, xii, 24, 28–29, 34, 105, 111, 147, 149, 152; and allegiance, 7, 24, 28, 34–36, 73, 150–51; as birthright, xi–xii, xiv, 22–23, 111, 138, 147–49, 153–54, 199, 255 (n. 226); citizen-soldier ideal, xiv–xv, 7, 104, 138, 143, 153; and civil death, xv, 7, 103–5, 107, 111, 113, 115–16, 118, 125; and civil disobedience, 38, 140; through conscripted status, 25; as consent and standing, 21, 23, 29, 34, 38, 132–33; contractual definition of, 38–39, 219–20 (n. 77); coverture and female civil status in, 7, 11, 23–24, 27, 29, 34, 39, 107–8, 111, 114, 202; as defined through bodily metaphors, 11, 104–5, 134, 141, 145, 196–97, 199, 202–4; and Fourteenth Amendment, 20, 192; and legal capacity, xiv, 23–24, 28, 31, 33, 36, 38, 112, 186; masculine marks of, xiv–xv, 13, 27–28, 104–5, 121, 134, 141, 144–45, 193–94, 196–97, 202–4; and military service, xv, 7–8, 25–26, 28, 143–45, 193, 197; national, xvi, 21, 23, 28–32, 35, 37, 197, 219 (n. 71); party man as symbol of, xiv, 22; problem of definition, 112; and property ownership, 7–8, 26–28, 34, 36, 39, 43, 73, 137; and race, 7–8, 64, 105, 111–12, 141, 149, 193; sacralized nature of, 197; and self-mastery and self-reliance, xiv, 8, 41–43, 73, 135–37, 143; and single women, 7, 24–25, 36, 39, 111, 217 (n. 49), 218 (n. 59); and taxation, 7–8, 24–26, 28, 36; and virtue, 23, 131, 104–5; voluntary, 23–24, 111; and the "woman-citizen," 198; women's exclusion from, xii, xv–xvi, 7, 23–24, 28–29, 32–36, 58, 64, 73, 103–5, 193, 203

Civil death. *See* Citizenship: and civil death; Common law: civil death in; Divestment of rights: through civil death

Civil mastery, 10

Civil War, 6, 20, 89, 191, 192

Clark, Elizabeth, xvii

Class, xii, xvi, 8, 23, 26, 52, 58–64, 66, 87, 175; awareness, 44, 61; "class legislation," 33, 37, 170; conflict, 137; distinctions and entitlement, 8, 36–37, 39, 84, 105, 146–47, 171, 197, 202; as "imaginary classification," 58; interests, 43, 46

Clemmer, Mary, 2–3

Coates-Kinney, Sarah (also Sarah Coates), 160, 166, 189, 262 (n. 74)

Coequality, xviii, 11, 13, 71–74, 100, 147, 152, 192, 195–96, 201; and citizenship, xii; and cosovereignty, 11, 71, 77; in the creation story, xviii, 11, 71–72, 195, 203; defined, xviii, 11; gained through representation in churches, xv, 78, 90, 95, 98–101. *See also* Equality

Colt, John, 122, 125

Colt, Samuel, 122, 125

Commentaries on the Laws of England. See Blackstone, William

Common law, xiv–xv, xvii, 6–7; and allegiance/protection equation, 7, 11, 34, 36, 38, 172, 180, 184; and Christianity, 83–84; civil death in, xv, 103–5, 107, 111, 113, 115–16, 118, 125; and codification movement, 168–69; competence defined by, 172, 185; on coverture, 7, 27, 29, 31, 84, 107–8, 111, 114, 155–57, 168–70, 172–74, 176, 182; on dower, 181, 183–84; on high treason, 126; and mob violence, 47–48; on recaption and runaway wives, xv, xvii, 104, 109–11, 113, 116–17; and self-defense, 47–48, 120–21, 128; and single women, 217 (n. 49). *See also* Marriage

Common man, xiv, 16, 21–23, 26, 193, 195, 199; as false universal, 8. *See also* Democracy: and the common man

Common sense, 25, 76–77, 80–83, 195

Commonwealth v. Aves, 114–15

Commonwealth v. Cook, 110

Conscience, liberty of, 38, 77, 85, 87, 90, 93

Consent, xiii–xvi, 18, 21, 23–24, 29, 32, 34, 38–39, 89, 132–33, 152–53, 180; age of, 23, 25; in civil suits, 23; denial of, 33–34; of the

governed, xiii, xv, 18, 21, 26, 28, 30, 33, 134, 142; illusion of, 82–84, 125–26, 195; in marriage, 27, 108, 150–51, 169, 171, 173, 176; in rape, 129, 162; relation to descent, 21, 28, 176

Constitutional amendments: Fifteenth, 20, 192, 202; Fourteenth, 20, 28, 192; Nineteenth, xv–xvi, 30, 192, 207 (n. 5)

Constitutional conventions, xiv, 7–8, 15–18, 21, 26, 31, 43, 87, 90, 100, 112, 171, 173, 182, 184, 192–93, 213 (n. 11), 213–14 (n. 14), 241 (n. 129)

Constitutionalism, xviii, 6–7, 15–18, 30, 39, 90, 170, 192–93; and due process and equal protection, xi–xiii, xvi, 20–21, 31, 33–39, 84, 105, 107–9, 112, 122–24, 131, 170–71, 184–85, 189, 192, 194, 202–3; and freedom of assembly, press and speech, 16, 43, 79–80, 116; and privileges and immunities, 28, 177, 243 (n. 41). *See also* Right(s)

Contagion, metaphor of, 160–61, 260 (n. 37)

Contract, social, 3, 7–8, 21, 34, 125; breaking of, 23, 38; consent in, xiv, 23–24, 31–32, 88, 176; covenantal model of, 122, 126–27, 197; and the creation story, xviii, 9–10, 66–67, 71–72, 194–95; and general will, 83; as legal contract, 31, 38; regarding male power and patronage, 10, 105, 146; and state of nature, 9–11, 44–46, 71, 138, 145, 163. *See also* Adams, John Quincy; Hobbes, Thomas; Locke, John; Mansfield, Edward; Marriage; Rousseau, Jean-Jacques

Contract, wage, xv, 156, 169–72, 175, 177

Convention of American Women Against Slavery (1838), 46

Convention of Drunkards, 41–42

Cooper, James Fenimore, 135

Cover, Robert, 160, 247 (n. 103)

Coverture. *See* Citizenship: coverture and female civil status in; Common law: on coverture; Divestment of rights: through coverture; Marriage: coverture in

Cowles, Betsey Mix, 19–20, 142, 144, 215 (n. 29)

Creation story, xviii, 2, 10–11, 66–67, 71–72, 194–95

Criminal law, theories of, 120–21, 123, 125

Cropsey v. Sweeney, 174

Cuffee, Paul, 144–45

Custody. *See* Marriage: custody and guardianship of children in; Marriage: custody of wives in

Custom, xvii, 32, 77, 82–85, 87, 155, 157, 169–70, 194–95

Cutler, Hannah Tracy, 178, 185, 189

Dall, Caroline, 39, 147, 197, 262 (n. 70)

Dana, Richard Henry, 71

Davis, Paulina Wright, 113; on capital punishment, 69, 129; on courts and juries, 72, 131; on dress and health reform, 35, 54, 230 (n. 120), 262 (n. 74); on household economy, 166, 169, 171, 175–77; on inalienable and sacred rights, 12, 107; and religious views, 94, 238 (n. 108); on woman as enigma, xii, 28; at Worcester convention (1850), 5, 32–33, 35, 135, 221 (n. 92); on writing, 73

Dean, Amos, 161–62

Death penalty. *See* Capital punishment

Declaration of Independence, xi, 4, 12, 17, 29–30, 37, 71, 105, 156, 160, 167

Declaration of Sentiments, 4, 29–32, 35, 37, 107, 174, 191

Deism, 81

Democracy, xiii–xvi, 4, 8–10, 45, 58–59, 65, 73–74, 95, 170, 204; and the common man, xiv, 8, 16, 21–23, 26, 72, 193, 195, 199; dangers to, 47, 104, 136–38, 145, 148–49; embodied in party system, xiv, 18–19, 21–22, 39, 72, 216 (n. 36); gendered construction of, xvi, 13, 28, 74, 105–6, 145–46, 193; Jacksonian, 21, 193; Jeffersonian, 25, 45; and majority rule, 8, 77, 83–84, 195; male body as model of, 104, 141, 196; as "man-ocracy," 103, 106; and patriotism, 139, 143–44, 159; and popular sovereignty, 18, 103; and self-reliance, 143; women's exclusion from, xv–xvi, 36, 39, 103, 193

Democratic Party, 18, 22

Descent. *See* Divestment of rights: through descent

Disorderly women, 45, 52, 72, 90–91, 96–97, 223–24 (nn. 13, 14)

Dissent, xv, 193, 238 (n. 102); as consent, 23; constitutional, 17–18, 90; as counter to alienation, 93; and disparagement of women, 84, 105; as heresy and iconoclasm, 77, 88–89; in marriage, 84, 167, 169; nonvoting, 23; as public disclosure, 93–94, 96; in religious life, xvii, 88–95, 98; and treason, 139, 141

Disunionism, 23, 217 (n. 39)

Divestment of rights, xiii, xv, xvii, 45, 84, 143, 150, 167, 184; through brute force, 104–5, 109, 118, 139, 143, 146; and capacity, 23, 28, 31, 33–36, 186, 189; through civil death, xv, 7, 103–5, 107, 111, 113, 115–16, 118–19; through coverture, 7, 27–29, 84, 168–69, 172, 174; and creation of outcasts, 105, 115, 119, 122, 127, 197, 244 (n. 58); through descent, 21, 28, 33, 115, 176, 180, 219 (n. 63); and disenfranchisement, 7, 25, 31, 35–36, 103, 145, 192–93; owing to legal disabilities, 34, 64, 84, 171–72, 181, 186, 188, 190; and property, 27, 137, 178, 184; as result of marital consent, 27, 34–35; as scapegoat, 122–23, 126–27, 152; and unfit fathers, 185–87

Divorce, 125, 127, 157, 158, 162–63, 165–67, 182, 199–201

Domestic violence, xv, 31, 109–10, 113, 126, 158, 162–67, 199. *See also* Rape

Dorr War, 18, 137, 139, 219 (n. 60), 251 (n. 160)

Douglass, Frederick, 119

Dress reform, 48–55, 57, 68, 224 (n. 25), 226 (nn. 44, 53)

Drudges/drudgery, 105, 137–38, 141, 143–44, 146, 177; the "devoted drudge," 167–68

Drunkards, 157–58; disease pathology of, 161, 166; female, 42; as political model, 41–44

DuBois, Ellen, 4–5

Due process. *See* Constitutionalism; Rights

Duhme v. Duhme, 261 (n. 60)

Dunn, John, 9

Earle, John Milton, 36

Earle, Sarah, 36, 60, 222 (n. 106)

Eaton, Cyrus, 72–73

Education and reform, xvii, 19–20, 35–36, 57–60, 79, 80–81

Edwards, Justin, 76, 78, 85, 232 (nn. 11, 19)

Elder, William, 20, 216 (n. 32)

Emancipation, 171, 173–74, 176–77

Emancipator and Republican, 112, 141

Enlightenment, xvi, 43, 47–48, 50, 52, 55–56, 58, 69, 79–80, 120

Equality, xi–xiii, xvii–xviii, 30, 74, 84, 95, 106,

119, 143, 176, 203; as conditional right, 87; before God, 11, 38, 71; and legal protection, xiii, xvi, 21, 32–37, 39, 84, 109, 119, 122, 133, 154, 170–71, 178, 185, 189, 201; among peers, 11–12, 72, 132–33; undermining family harmony, 34–35, 188. *See also* Coequality

Eve, 122; as coequal with Adam, 71; curse on, 52, 72, 103–5, 120, 133, 242 (n. 8); as enigma, 28; in the Garden of Eden, 66–67; as imperfect Adam, 98; as temptress, 128

Everett, Edward, 57

"Eye for an eye" (biblical dictum), 120, 123–24

Fallen woman, 104, 119–20, 122, 127–28, 130–31, 197

Family politics. *See* Marriage

Female nature. *See* Gender

Feminist theory: challenging the sexual contract (male sexual rights over women's bodies), xviii, 9–11, 66–67, 104–29 passim, 133–90 passim, 199–202; coequality and sacred rights, xviii, 11–12, 31–32, 71–72, 74, 76, 78, 98–101, 160, 202–3; and concept of caste, xii, 32–37, 64, 85, 98, 105, 112, 115, 122, 130–32, 143, 192, 197; and dissent, xv, xvii, 75, 88–90, 92–95, 97; of economic exploitation, 167–78, 183–86, 189–90, 199–201; emerging from a critical public, xiii–xiv, 69–74, 97, 206 (nn. 3, 4); of male representation, xi–xiii, 7–8, 12–13, 21–23, 27, 30–31, 34–35, 37–39, 66, 77, 91–92, 95–97, 99–104, 132–33, 147–49, 202–3; of the masculine marks of citizenship, xiv, 13, 15–21, 23–29, 73, 105–6, 191, 193–99; and the problem of women's disembodiment from (and discipline in) the public sphere, xvi, 11–13, 42–69, 72–74, 79–80, 84–88, 95–97, 99–100, 106

Fidelity. *See* Infidelity; Marriage: and fidelity

Fillmore, Millard, 148

Filmer, Robert, 10

Flexner, Eleanor, 2, 4

Foster, Abby Kelley, 61–63, 91, 117–18, 228 (n. 88)

Foster, Stephen, 61

Foucault, Michel, 195

Fourier, Charles, 170; and Fourierism, 148, 150

Fox, George, 95

Fratricide, 122, 126

Free blacks, 7–8, 109, 111, 132; and black codes, 20, 112, 215 (n. 29); as dangerous class, xii, 8, 137; and legal differences between men and women among, 112, 243 (n. 41); as wards of the state, 111, 243 (n. 39)

Free churches. *See* Church politics: and "free churches"

Freeland, Margaret, 161

Free love, 150, 201

Free-Soil Party, 19–20, 215 (n. 28)

Friends, Society of, 61–64; Congregational, 21, 31–32, 89–91, 94, 98; Hicksite, 89, 91–92, 96; Orthodox, 64, 84; Progressive, 89, 94

Frolock, Jane, 145

Frost, J. William, 95

Fugitive slave laws, xv, xvii, 104–5, 109, 114, 116, 118, 151; recaption through, 104, 109–10, 113, 117. *See also* Antislavery movement; Free blacks; Race

Fuller, Margaret, 56–58, 73, 128

Furness, Henry, 96

Gage, Frances, 134, 136, 153, 164–65, 167, 189, 259 (n. 35)

Gage, Matilda Josyln, 130

Gannett, Deborah, 65

Gardener, Margaret, 118, 150

Garrison, William Lloyd, 63, 76

Geertz, Clifford, 195

Gender: and citizenship, xiv, 13, 23, 26–27, 113–15, 193, 199; and constitutionalism, xviii, 6, 204; in democracy, xiv, xvi, xviii, 13, 28, 58, 204; and female caricatures, 42–43, 46–48, 53, 67, 96, 99–100, 138, 198–99; feminine weakness versus masculine self-mastery, xiv, 46, 51, 53, 103–4, 138, 141, 144–46, 184–85, 196; and oratory, 58, 95–100, 196; in public sphere, xvi, 9–10; and representations of female nature, xvi, 42–43, 48–52, 55, 63–64, 80, 145, 196; reversal of roles, 15, 19, 72–73, 152; and society's fear of women without men, 46–48; women "passing" as men, 47–48, 54, 72, 96, 100, 144, 160. *See also* Masculinity; Sex

Gibbons, Abby H., 129

Giddings, Maria, 132

Giles, Charles, 41–42

Goodell, William, 109–10, 112, 115
Greeley, Horace, 56–57, 99
Grew, Mary, 60, 67
Grimké, Angelina, 11–12, 46, 60–62, 68, 145
Grimké, Frederick, 136, 168
Grimké, Sarah, 46, 60, 85, 156
Griswold, Robert, 125
Grossberg, Michael, 125

Habeas corpus, 115
Habermas, Jürgen, xvi, 9, 43–45, 73
Hair v. Hair, 151
Hamilton, Alexander, 168, 171
Hanson, Debra Gold, xvii
Harrison, William Henry, 18
Hartog, Hendrik, 121, 195
Hartung, Mrs., 152
Hathaway, John C., 23
Health reform, xv, xviii, 35, 52, 69, 156, 166
Henshaw, Caroline, 125
Hero worship, 143–46
Herttell, Thomas, 83–84, 155–56
Hewitt, Nancy, xvii
Higginson, Thomas Wentworth, 94–95
History of Woman Suffrage, 1–2, 6, 63, 70, 208
    (n. 1)
Hobbes, Thomas, 27, 44, 97, 138, 240
    (n. 121)
Hollick, Frederick, 69, 230 (n. 118)
Homicide. *See* Murder
Homine replegiando, 109
Honor. *See* Masculinity: identified with
    honor and virtue
Hopedale community, 35, 94
Hopper, Isaac, 129
Household economy. *See* Marriage
Houston, Sam, 138–40, 143, 145, 149
Hunt, Harriot, 36, 43, 166, 262 (n. 70)
Hunt, Jane, 32
Hurlbut, Elisha, 25, 27, 31, 112, 173, 179, 184

Identity, political: and accountability, 8,
    38, 87–88, 127–28, 130–33; autonomy as a
    precondition of, 8, 23–24, 26, 34, 36, 42,
    112–13, 116–17, 141, 176, 200, 210 (n. 40);
    and bodily nature, 41–43, 48, 52, 68, 72–73,
    97, 112–13, 134, 137–38, 141, 145, 161, 193,
    196–97, 199, 202–4; and civic capacity, xiv,
    23–26, 33, 36, 177; and civic virtue, 23–24,

42–43, 49, 104–5, 121, 131, 203; through
    civility, 41–46, 58–59, 62–64, 73, 85; and
    financial independence, 7–8, 36, 176–77,
    193; and marital status, 7, 10, 24–25, 36, 39,
    111–12; marked by manhood, xiv, 27–28, 42,
    73, 95, 105, 121, 135, 141, 144, 193, 196–97,
    202–4; and national character, 78, 80–81;
    and patriotism, 64, 104, 143–44, 159–60;
    of a public person, xvi, 11–12, 42, 68, 95–97,
    103–4, 195; public speaking and deliberation
    as attributes of, xvi, 11, 15, 19, 24, 41–43,
    57–58, 62–63, 68–70, 72–73, 95–100, 145,
    196; and race, 7–8, 26, 28, 111–12, 115; and
    role of intellect or reason, xii–xiii, 20, 25,
    42–43, 73, 97, 195–96; and self-mastery and
    self-reliance, xiv, 8, 10, 41–43, 49, 51, 71–73,
    136–38, 196, 198, 202; and valor, xv, 104, 135,
    138, 141–45, 193, 197–98; and willingness to
    take risks, 7, 11–13, 22, 34, 51–52, 104, 136,
    139
Ideology, xiii, xv, 6, 9, 13, 68, 71; defined, 195
Incest, 108
Indiana v. Hubbard, 151–52
Indians, 134–35; squaws, 138
Infanticide, 124
Infidelity, 104, 121, 126–27, 129, 162, 197
Inheritance, 178–80
Insanity, 161, 166; as defense, 129

Jackson, Andrew, 8, 44
Jameson, John Alexander, 16
Jay, William, 109, 139
Jefferson, Thomas, 4, 7, 15–18, 22, 25, 34,
    45–46, 55, 182
Jenkins, Lydia, 176
Johnson, Mary Ann, 90, 166, 198
Jones, Jane Elizabeth, 131–32, 166
Jury: of peers, 129; service in, xv, 8, 12, 72,
    124, 196; of women, 132
Juryman, The, 124, 132

Kant, Immanuel, 9, 73, 263 (n. 82)
Kelley, Abby. *See* Foster, Abby Kelley
Kent, James, 6, 169
Kerber, Linda, 8–9
Kettner, James, 28
Key, Frances, 152
Kemble, Fanny, 48, 224 (nn. 24, 25)
Knapp, G. W., 103

Know-Nothing Party, 148–49, 254–55 (nn. 215, 217, 218, 222)

Landes, Joan, 9
Land reform, xviii, 156, 182–83, 185, 187, 190
Lee, Luther, 99
Lewis, Jan, 8
Liability. *See* Criminal law, theories of; Marriage
Liberal individualism, xiii, xvi
Liberty, 143, 165, 167, 184, 198; Christian, 91–92; civil, xiii, 20, 43, 65, 79, 107, 139; consensus and custom as threat to, 77, 82–87; personal, xv, 104, 106, 109, 113, 116, 118–19; religious, xiv, xvii, 75–76, 84, 88–91. *See also* Conscience, liberty of
Liberty laws, personal, 69, 109, 113–14
Liberty League, 19–20
Liberty Party, 19–20, 31, 215 (n. 28)
Lily, 45, 48, 103, 126, 144, 166, 167, 179, 189
Lincoln, Abraham, xi, 160, 259 (n. 29)
Locke, John, 9–10, 44, 80–81
London World Antislavery Convention (1840), 2, 4–6, 63–64

McClintock, Elizabeth, 32, 75, 90, 92
McClintock, Mary Ann, 32, 90
McClintock, Thomas, 31–32, 90, 221 (n. 89)
MacKinnon, Catherine, 194–95
Maltz, Earl, 107
Mania, 165–66; moral, 158, 167
Manifest destiny. *See* Mexican War: and manifest destiny or dominion
Mansfield, Edward, 111–12, 158, 181
Marriage, xv, xviii; and breach-of-promise cases, 125; chastisement in, 107–8; consideration in, 183–85, 187, 189; contractual nature of, 155, 169, 174, 176–78, 184, 199; covenantal model of, 10–11, 126, 160, 181, 199–202; coverture in, 107, 114, 155–57, 168–69, 172–74, 176, 182, 184, 201; custody and guardianship of children in, xv, xviii, 107, 111, 117, 150, 156, 179–83, 186–89; custody of wives in, 111–13, 117–18, 147, 150, 152, 173, 176–77, 266–67 (n. 157); dower in tenancy in, 156, 181, 183–84, 188, 190, 268 (n. 178); and female head of household, 182, 187–89; and fidelity, 11, 156, 159–60, 172, 188–89; fitness as legal category in, 158–59, 186–87;

husband's property rights in, 11, 34, 117, 173, 179–80, 186–87; husband's right to wife's wages in, xviii, 116, 156, 174–75, 187; liability and debts in, xv, 171–72, 176–77, 182–84, 187; necessaries accorded to wife in, 171–73, 183, 188, 267–68 (n. 169); and oaths or vows, 11, 34, 156–57, 172, 176; and one-flesh trope, xviii, 11, 72, 118–19, 134, 140, 161–62, 176, 201, 211 (n. 55); procreation and sexual desire in, 156, 162–63, 166–67, 199; rape in, 162–63, 166–67; and wedding protests, 147, 176; and widows, 157, 159, 161, 179, 181, 183, 185–86; wife's labor value in, xv, 167–69, 174–75, 177, 189; and women's property rights, xv, 31, 34, 58, 84, 107, 111, 116, 155, 168, 172–86 passim, 264–65 (n. 116)
Martineau, Harriet, 45, 74
Masculinity: and civic identity, 8, 13, 27–28, 41–42, 72–73, 104–5, 193, 196–97; deprivation of, 133–38, 193; identified with honor and virtue, xiv–xv, 104–5, 121, 124, 127–28, 135, 142, 152, 160, 197; and military service, xv, 104, 144–45, 194; physical emblems of, 95, 97, 100, 196–97; and race, 28, 136–37, 218 (n. 59)
Mason, George, 17
Matriarchy, 3, 5, 11
Medical jurisprudence, 158, 161–62
Melder, Keith, xvii, 2, 4–5
Merrill v. Smith, 265 (n. 121)
Mexican War: antiwar tactics, 69, 139–40, 252 (n. 173); idea of women as soldiers in, 144; and manifest destiny or dominion, xv, xvii, 105, 133–34, 137, 140, 143, 148, 153, 252 (n. 177); and martial law, 105; and sexual conquest, xv, 105, 133, 140–41, 153; and suffrage, xv, 142–43, 144–45
Miller, Elizabeth Smith, 48, 54
Milton, John, 71, 79
Minor, Frances, 202
Minor, Virginia, 202
Moral reform, xvi, 9–10, 20. *See also* Church politics: and moral associations
Mott, James, 61, 70
Mott, Lucretia, 35, 54, 129, 182; on coequality, 31, 71; on heresy and dissent, 23, 88–90, 92–93, 98, 140, 198, 240 (n. 121); and "origins" of the movement, 2–5, 11, 29, 69–71; as presidential nominee, 19; as public fig-

and segregation, 33, 35–36, 112, 194; and theories of hybrids, 140, 252–53 (n. 180); and the tragic mulatto, 106; and white slavery, 106, 110, 137–38. *See also* Antislavery movement; Free Blacks; Fugitive slave laws; Slavery

Rape, 108, 110, 120–21, 125; and consent, 129, 162; of married women, 162–63, 166–67; and procreation, 162; of slave women, 107–8. *See also* Domestic violence

Raybold v. Raybold, 265 (n. 123)

Religion. *See* Church politics

Religious Union of Associationists, 94

Representation, 6, 20, 65, 109, 191, 201; coequal, xv, 13, 78, 90, 98–101; in a democracy, xiii, 8; and jury service, xv, 8, 12, 72, 132–33, 196; and marital status of women, 7, 36, 111–12; men as proxy for women, xii, 12, 22, 27, 31, 33–36, 60, 91, 99, 103, 112, 131, 134, 147, 149, 202; and petitioners, 65; religious, 3, 77–79, 90, 98–100; through self-representation, xiii, 12, 17, 23, 70; taxation without, 36–37; whole-and-parts theory of, 7–8, 13, 76–77, 99; by women lawyers, 202; women's inability to represent men; 98, 100, 196, 198, 202–3

Republicanism, xiv, xvi, 6–8, 19, 45, 78; and active citizenship, 24–26, 197; and homogeneous electorate, 7–8, 25–26; and right of protection, 6–7, 109; vigilance and restraint within, 79–80; and virtue, 51, 104, 131, 193

Republican Party, 20, 192–93

Retributive justice, 122–24. *See also* Capital punishment; Vengeance, social

Right(s), xiii–xviii, 9, 13, 29, 191, 193–94; abstract, xvi, 29–30, 193–95; of assembly, 16, 70; birthrights, xii, xiv, 111, 115–16, 138, 147, 153–54, 171, 199, 255 (n. 226); bodily nature of, 112–13; of church laity, 89, 91–94; of conscience, 76, 84–85; of contract, 32, 156, 170–71, 176–77, 184; democratization of, 16; of domicile, 116–19, 147–48, 150–51, 153–54; of dominion, 134, 185, 148; dower, 183, 188; due process, xiii, 33–35, 37, 107–9, 112, 123–24, 131, 194; entitlement defined, 21; ethical basis for, 77; imaginary nature of, 195; to means of subsistence, 170, 173, 176–78; minority, 84; natural and inalienable, xii, 4, 10, 12, 18, 26–27, 30–33, 35,

37–38, 71, 105, 107, 138, 156, 160, 165–66, 169–70, 193–94, 202–3; parental, 115–19, 179, 186, 189; pecuniary, 156, 168, 173–74, 177; to petition, 7, 16, 64–67, 140; versus privileges, xii, 7–8, 27, 203; property, 26–27, 29; to protection, xiii, 6–7, 11, 21, 28–31, 33–35, 143, 184, 202; to redress, xiii, xv, 109–10, 115–16, 121, 125, 128, 184, 158; to reform, alter, or abolish the government, 17–18; sacred, 12, 31–32, 37–38, 76, 107; to self-defense, 104, 107, 118, 120–21, 127–28, 132, 151, 153, 156, 160, 166–67; to self-preservation and self-protection, xiii, 37–39, 116, 119, 127, 132, 153, 155, 160, 164, 167, 171, 177; to sue for damages, 36, 161; tenant's, 182–83; vested, 26, 28, 34–35, 179, 197, 221 (n. 95), 239 (n. 115). *See also* Constitutionalism

Roberts v. City of Boston, 33, 194, 221 (n. 97)

Rochester, N.Y., 29. *See also* Women's rights conventions: Rochester

Romanticism, 49, 238 (n. 102)

Rose, Ernestine, 114, 116, 119–22, 127, 142, 146, 200

Rosine Society, 130

Rousseau, Jean-Jacques, 46, 48–50, 105, 107, 163, 181

Rowson, Susanna, 120

Rush, Benjamin, 79

Ryan, Mary, 9

Sabbatarianism, xiv, 75–78, 80, 82, 84–88, 195

Sand, George, 54

Sanford, Rebecca, 24

Sayer, Lydia, 176

Scott, Andrew, 4

Scott, Ann Firor, 4

Sears, Charles, 170

Sedgwick, Elizabeth, 58

Seduction, xv, xvii, 46, 48, 104, 120–22, 125–26, 128–29, 151–52, 158, 196–97

Self-defense. *See* Right(s): to self-defense

Self-mastery. *See* Identity, political: and self-mastery and self-reliance

Severance, Caroline, 173, 185

Sex: abuse, xv, 31, 106, 108, 110, 114, 162–65, 199; and appearance, 86–87; and attraction, 49–50; aversion to, 159, 161–62; and chastity, fidelity, or virtue, 104, 106, 108, 120–21, 125, 127–28, 130–31, 151, 159–61; and cross-dressing, 48, 53–54, 96, 100; and desire, 44–45, 50, 162–63, 167; and difference, xi–xiii, xviii, 10, 12, 54, 71, 73, 86, 96, 144–45, 150, 194–96, 202, 204; and modesty, 46, 48–53, 55, 57, 60–64, 68, 70, 72; and necrophilia, 162; and perceptions of women's bodies, 42–48, 55, 104, 145, 166, 196–97, 199; and promiscuity, 42, 45–47, 53, 55, 65, 72, 73, 223 (n. 13); and reproduction, 42, 52, 162, 166, 199; sexual slavery, 146. *See also* Gender

Shaw, Lemuel, 33–35, 194, 258 (n. 20)

Shaw v. Shaw, 163, 165

Sickles, Daniel, 152

Slavery, 105–9, 113–14, 133, 137–38, 140–41, 150. *See also* Antislavery movement; Fugitive slave laws; Race

Smith, Elizabeth Oakes, 38, 54–55, 73, 177, 226 (n. 57)

Smith, Gerrit, 20, 31, 54–55, 68, 92–95, 99

Solitary pleasures, 162

Sollers, Augustus, 148, 150, 254 (n. 215)

Sovereignty, popular, xiv, 18–19, 21, 109, 137–39, 196–202; expressing a fictive people, 13, 95, 193; in Kansas statehood, 193; and manhood, 194, 201; and one-flesh trope, 134; and right of dominion, 134; and whole-and-parts theory, 7–8, 13. *See also* Coequality

Spooner, Lysander, 30, 32, 219–20 (n. 77)

Sprecht v. Commonwealth, 84

Staël, Madame Anne Louise Germaine de, 56, 69, 133

Stanley, Amy Dru, xvii–xviii

Stanton, Elizabeth Cady: on citizenship and suffrage, 29–31, 33, 35, 38, 191, 197–98; on dress reform and modesty, 48–49, 51–52, 54–55, 63, 70; on marriage and divorce, 107–9, 118, 162, 166, 176, 181, 183, 186, 190, 199, 201; on origins of the women's rights movement, xvi, 1–5, 11–13; on religious liberty, 75, 90, 92; on sexual representation, 131; on women in the military, 146

Stanton, Theodore, 2

State v. Mann, 108

Stebbins, Sumner, 140

Steele, Mrs. C. M., 143

Stewart, Alvin, 109

Stickney, Hannah, 113

Stone, Lucy, 42, 54, 105, 116, 117–18, 130, 146–47, 76, 230 (n. 123)

Story, Joseph, 75–76, 109–10

Stowe, Harriet Beecher, 106

Stowell, Lord (William Scott), 162

Suffrage: arguments at constitutional conventions, 7–8, 17–18, 26; and autonomy, 8, 38; and brute force, xv, 144–45; and capacity, xii, 8, 20, 23–28; and chivalry, 144–45; and consent, 38; and disenfranchisement, xv–xvi, 25–26, 28–31, 35, 44, 58, 149; and Fifteenth Amendment, 20; and Fourteenth Amendment, 20, 192; gender qualifications for, 7–8, 15, 17–18, 19–21, 25–28, 192; Jefferson defines, 7, 22, 25, 34; in Kansas campaign, 192–93; and marital status, 7, 29, 36, 119, 188; and military service, xv, 7–8, 25, 28, 143; and National Woman's Suffrage Association, 202; and New York State Constitutional Convention (1846), 26, 213–14 (n. 14); and Nineteenth Amendment, xv, 30; and Ohio State Constitutional Convention (1850), 17–18, 213–14 (n. 14); and personal liberty, 20, 119; and property ownership, 7, 22, 26–28, 34, 36, 39, 43–45, 137, 184; by proxy, 12, 27, 34, 66, 103, 113, 149, 250 (n. 142); racial qualifications, 7–8, 17–18, 20, 26, 28, 149, 207 (n. 59), 218 (n. 55); as a right of equal representation, xii–xiii, 37; and school elections, 20, 215–16 (n. 30); and single women, 7, 24–26, 36, 217 (n. 49), 218 (n. 58); and state patronage, 105–6, 134, 142–43; and taxation, 7–8, 24–25, 28, 36; universal ("manhood"), 22, 26–28, 105–6, 149; as vested right, 28, 34–36, 38, 197; in women's history, xvi, 1–6, 11–13

Swift, Adeline, 110, 212 (n. 28)

Swisshelm, Jane, 48, 119, 133, 142, 153, 250 (n. 142)

Sympathy. *See* Public sphere: sympathy in

Taney, Roger, 139

Taylor, Zachary, 142

Temperance, xv, xviii, 31, 99–100, 156, 158–60, 167

Texas annexation, 133, 135–36, 140

Thompson, William, 165, 257 (n. 11)

Tilton, Theodore, 4

Tocqueville, Alexis de, 9, 77, 136

Torrey, Harriet, 52
Townsend, Sarah, 130
Transcendentalism, 49, 56, 76, 94
Treason, xv, 73, 115, 122, 127, 141; in Mexican War, 139; *petit*, 126, 151; as political hyperbole, 47; punishment for high treason, 126, 247 (n. 103); and women as political enemies, 104–5, 134, 141–42
Trescott, Jane, 93
Tyler, John, 136
Tyndale, Sarah, 140

Una, 73, 94, 157, 170–71, 178, 185
Uncle Tom's Cabin, 106
United States Magazine and Democratic Review, 26, 58, 66, 72, 137
Unwritten law, 119, 121, 123–24, 127
Updegraph v. Commonwealth, 83
Upshur, Abel, 136–37

Van Armringe, Henry, 19, 36, 39, 143
Van Buren, Martin, 18
Vengeance, social, xv, 123–24, 128, 129. *See also* Capital punishment; Retributive justice
Virtue/*virtù*. *See* Identity, political: and civic virtue
Voting. *See* Suffrage

Walker, Robert, 250 (n. 156)
Walker, Timothy, 107–8, 129, 168, 170, 183–86
Warren, Mercy Otis, 17
Washington, George, 78, 159
Water-Cure Journal, 50
Waterloo, N.Y., 29
Weber, H. M., 54
Webster, Daniel, 19
Webster, Delia, 141, 253 (n. 186)
Webster, Noah, 81, 83
Wellman, Judith, xvii, 3

Wesleyan Methodists, 91, 99
Whig Party, 18–19, 22, 135, 137
White, Blanco, 97
White, George, 96
White slavery. *See* Race: and white slavery
Whitman, Walt, 122
Wilson, Elizabeth (author of *A Scriptural View of Woman's Rights and Duties*), 71, 77, 86–88, 95–96, 98, 114, 147, 230–31 (n. 127)
Wilson, Elizabeth (executed for infanticide), 124
Wiltbank, John, 166
Wollstonecraft, Mary, 155
Woman's sphere, xiii, xviii, 8–9, 44, 206 (n. 4), 255–58 (n. 16); separate, 8–10
Women's rights. *See* Right(s)
Women's rights conventions, xvi, 15–16, 20–21, 191; Akron (1851), 134, 143; Boston (1855), 147; Cleveland (1853), 117–19, 130, 146; New York City (1853), 53, 96, 117; New York City (1859), 152; New York City (1860), xi–xii, 191, 197, 201, 206 (n. 1); Philadelphia (1854), 46; Rochester (1848), 35, 70, 75, 98; Salem (1850), 15, 19–20, 24, 70–71, 114, 131, 142, 212 (n. 4); Seneca Falls (1848), xvi, 1–6, 15, 29, 31, 37, 56, 70, 75–76, 87, 90–91, 96, 174; Syracuse (1852), 28, 38, 54–55, 73, 97, 130; West Chester (1852), 38, 90, 184; Worcester (1850), 5–6, 32–33, 35–37, 70–71, 87, 107, 135, 143; Worcester (1851), 37, 62, 87, 116
Woodbury, Levi, 138
Woodward (Pennsylvania Supreme Court Judge), 174
Wright, Frances (Fanny), 42, 223 (n. 3)
Wright, Martha, 53–54, 62, 191

Zagarri, Rosemarie, 8

GENDER AND AMERICAN CULTURE

Sex and Citizenship in Antebellum America, by Nancy Isenberg (1998)

Yours in Sisterhood: Ms. Magazine and the Promise of Popular Feminism, by Amy Erdman Farrell (1998)

We Mean to Be Counted: White Women and Politics in Antebellum Virginia, by Elizabeth R. Varon (1998)

Women Against the Good War: Conscientious Objection and Gender on the American Home Front, 1941–1947, by Rachel Waltner Goossen (1997)

Toward an Intellectual History of Women: Essays by Linda K. Kerber (1997)

Gender and Jim Crow: Women and the Politics of White Supremacy in North Carolina, 1896–1920, by Glenda Elizabeth Gilmore (1996)

Delinquent Daughters: Protecting and Policing Adolescent Female Sexuality in the United States, 1885–1920, by Mary E. Odem (1995)

U.S. History as Women's History: New Feminist Essays, edited by Linda K. Kerber, Alice Kessler-Harris, and Kathryn Kish Sklar (1995)

Common Sense and a Little Fire: Women and Working-Class Politics in the United States, 1900–1965, by Annelise Orleck (1995)

How Am I to Be Heard?: Letters of Lillian Smith, edited by Margaret Rose Gladney (1993)

Entitled to Power: Farm Women and Technology, 1913–1963, by Katherine Jellison (1993)

Revising Life: Sylvia Plath's Ariel Poems, by Susan R. Van Dyne (1993)

Made From This Earth: American Women and Nature, by Vera Norwood (1993)

Unruly Women: The Politics of Social and Sexual Control in the Old South, by Victoria E. Bynum (1992)

The Work of Self-Representation: Lyric Poetry in Colonial New England, by Ivy Schweitzer (1991)

Labor and Desire: Women's Revolutionary Fiction in Depression America, by Paula Rabinowitz (1991)

Community of Suffering and Struggle: Women, Men, and the Labor Movement in Minneapolis, 1915–1945, by Elizabeth Faue (1991)

All That Hollywood Allows: Re-reading Gender in 1950s Melodrama, by Jackie Byars (1991)

Doing Literary Business: American Women Writers in the Nineteenth Century, by Susan Coultrap-McQuin (1990)

Ladies, Women, and Wenches: Choice and Constraint in Antebellum Charleston and Boston, by Jane H. Pease and William H. Pease (1990)

The Secret Eye: The Journal of Ella Gertrude Clanton Thomas, 1848–1889, edited by Virginia Ingraham Burr, with an introduction by Nell Irvin Painter (1990)

Second Stories: The Politics of Language, Form, and Gender in Early American Fictions, by Cynthia S. Jordan (1989)

Within the Plantation Household: Black and White Women of the Old South, by Elizabeth Fox-Genovese (1988)

The Limits of Sisterhood: The Beecher Sisters on Women's Rights and Woman's Sphere, by Jeanne Boydston, Mary Kelley, and Anne Margolis (1988)